Semitic Languages

Palestine & Syria (general)

THE

LANGUAGE OF PALESTINE

THE
LANGUAGE OF PALESTINE

THE LANGUAGE OF PALESTINE

AND ADJACENT REGIONS

BY

J. COURTENAY JAMES

M.A., B.D.

WITH A FOREWORD BY

SIR ERNEST A. WALLIS BUDGE, Kt., Litt.D.,

KEEPER OF THE EGYPTIAN AND ASSYRIAN ANTIQUITIES IN THE BRITISH MUSEUM

Edinburgh: T. & T. CLARK, 38 George Street

1920

PRINTED BY

MORRISON AND GIBB LIMITED,

FOR

T. & T. CLARK, EDINBURGH.

LONDON : SIMPKIN, MARSHALL, HAMILTON, KENT, AND CO. LIMITED.

NEW YORK : CHARLES SCRIBNER'S SONS.

TO

MY WIFE

AND

SONS AND DAUGHTERS

WHOSE COMPANIONSHIP MAKES

HOME A SANCTUARY

AND

STUDY A DELIGHT

PREFACE

THE following work is the result of many years' study, which has been conducted amid the multitudinous duties of a busy pastorate. I am not aware of any treatment of the subject along quite the same lines. The material on the historical side is considerable, and is becoming more homogeneous with the progress of archaeological research. On the linguistic side the material is also abundant, but less definite and serviceable. The inscriptions, papyri and other literature, supply no connected chain of evidence. So many dialects are found, so many idioms, and so many exceptions to anything like a general rule, that the construction of a complete grammar and syntax is quite impossible. No doubt more will be achieved in this respect when Hittite and other obscure writings have been clearly read and interpreted.

This work is not a history of the ancient races of western Asia, nor a grammar of their languages. But history is introduced to show the causes which led to the rise of one language and the supersession of another, and to indicate the changes in tribal and national fortunes which resulted in dialectic variations. Grammar and syntax, too, are brought under contribution, to illustrate the types of language which successively triumphed in the regions named, and to show, at least in some general principles, how one language differed from another.

Though the period covered corresponds in the main with the millennium preceding the Christian Era, it seemed necessary to give some account of the earlier civilizations, which prepared the way for the linguistic conditions at the beginning of Biblical history. It was also advisable to state the kind of literary influence exerted on Palestine by Babylonia, Persia and Greece, and the linguistic contributions of these great forces to the *lingua franca* of western Asia.

Not only is the language discussed and illustrated, but the script of different regions is also considered and described. An examination of the inscriptions and papyri has not only shown the changes of dialect, but also the development of the written character from the earliest picture-writing to the latest 'square' character. Incidentally the script in which the Old Testament books were written at different periods is suggested, and specimen lines are frequently given from the inscriptions and other literary documents.

The literature referred to in the footnotes does not always support the views here adopted, but it is added for the sake of those who wish to become acquainted with the subject in its manifold phases. Though the literature named is extensive it has not to any appreciable degree coloured the character of this study. I have followed an independent course and arrived at some conclusions not elsewhere to be found. Many of the results, I believe, rest on sufficient proof, others are less certain and must remain for the present as suggestions more or less probable.

This work could have been considerably extended by discussions on the theories of the chief schools on the subjects of which it treats. I have not been indifferent to the researches of others, but deemed it unnecessary to introduce the conclusion of other explorers, either to refute or confirm. Whether the findings herein are in harmony or disagreement with the leading schools of archaeology and Semitic science, is not a question which I am chiefly anxious to discover. The conclusions reached are such as seemed best warranted by the historical, literary and other data.

The present study in many respects is necessarily tentative, and designed to indicate provinces of Semitic literature which have not yet been fully investigated. It is hoped, however, that the lines of exploration here laid down are in the main valid, and lead to some positive and trustworthy results. The work is offered particularly to those who wish to gain some knowledge of the linguistic problems of western Asia, but who have not the opportunity of studying the wider literature in this field. Such students may find this introduction a useful contribution to a great and fascinating subject.

I have to acknowledge the courtesy of the authorities of the British Museum, the officials of the Rylands Library, Manchester, and the managers of other literary institutions, in facilitating reference and research in the original sources, which are frequently mentioned in this work. The references to the literature on the subject will indicate the achievements of German scholars in this field. Unfortunately the war interrupted the progress of excavation by explorers in the East, and also the minute and continuous study of original sources by experts in Europe and America. Doubtless the great historic events in Mesopotamia and Palestine will stir afresh the enthusiasm of scholars in all departments of archaeological science. I am indebted to all who have preceded me in this province, and would fain hope that I may encourage others to pursue these investigations into wider regions, and with more certain results. I am conscious of the manifold deficiencies in this undertaking of recognized difficulty, but trust that it will present to the reader, at least, a general idea of the great forces and factors which resulted in the linguistic phenomena of the land of Canaan from the earliest historical period to the overthrow of Jerusalem by Titus.

I am particularly indebted to Sir Ernest A. Wallis Budge, Kt., for the cordial and ready manner in which he acceded to my request to write a 'Foreword' for this volume. His reference to the 'Cappadocian' tablets is a real addition to the subject, and is full of interest and instruction for the student. I regret that the recent monumental work of this scholar, *By Nile and Tigris*, came into my hands too late to be used in the preparation of this book.

I must express my indebtedness to Dr. J. Rendel Harris, who encouraged me in the preparation of this work and cordially advised its publication. And also to my son, the Rev. N. Courtenay James, M.R.S.L., who greatly assisted in verifying the references to the literature of the subject, and who saved me much time and labour by reading the manuscript, correcting some errors, and by many suggestions respecting the arrangement and sequence of the matter.

Lastly, I should be wanting in gratitude if I did not mention my obligations to the Publishers for their unfailing courtesy and helpful interest in the production of this book. Reference should be made to the care and skill of the Printers, whose work was rendered difficult by the many founts of Eastern (and sometimes new) characters required.

The work is sent forth with the hope that it will stimulate reading and study in this department of Oriental literature.

J. COURTENAY JAMES.

BOURNEMOUTH,
August 1920.

CONTENTS

I

INTRODUCTION

II

EMPIRE AND LANGUAGE

CONTENTS

III

LINGUISTIC GENEALOGY

CONTENTS

IV

SEMITIC CONSTRUCTIONS

V

ARAMAEANS AND HEBREWS

VI

INSCRIPTIONS AND THE OLD TESTAMENT

VII

SEMITIC SCRIPT: EVOLUTION AND TRANSITION

VIII

ARAMAIC

b

CONTENTS

IX

NABATAEAN

X

TARGUMS

EPILOGUE

ABBREVIATIONS

NEARLY all the literature referred to in the notes is adequately described where cited. The names of the Authors and the Titles of the works, in most instances, are given in full. The following brief list, however, may be useful.

Aboth.	*Pirke Aboth* ('Ethics of the Fathers').
Aphr.	Aphraates, *Homilies*, ed. by Wright.
As. Pap.	*Assuan Papyri*, ed. by Sayce and Cowley.
AV.	Authorized Version.
Bab. Meg.	Babylonian Megilla.
Bibl. Aram.	Biblical Aramaic.
CIL	*Corpus Inscriptionum Latinarum.*
CIS	*Corpus Inscriptionum Semiticarum.*
Cl.-Gan. *Étud.*	Clermont-Ganneau, *Études d'archéologie Orientale.*
Eut. *Nab.*	Euting, *Nabatäische Inschriften.*
Eut. *Sin.*	Euting, *Sinaitische Inschriften.*
Herod.	Herodotus.
MT.	Massoretic Text.
Nab.	Nabataean Inscriptions.
Nêrab	Inscriptions found at Nêrab, S.E. of Aleppo.
NT.	New Testament.
OT.	Old Testament.
Oxy. Pap.	*Oxyrhynchus Papyri*, ed. by Grenfell and Hunt.
Pal. Meg.	Palestinian Megilla.
Pesh.	Peshitta (Syriac) Version.
RV.	Revised Version.
Sall. Bell. Cat.	Sallust, *Bellum Catilinarium.*
Sid.	Phoenician Inscriptions found at Sidon.
Syncell.	George Syncellus, *Chronography.*
Tal. Bab.	Babylonian Talmud.
Tal. Pal.	Palestinian Talmud.
Targ. Jer.	Jerusalem Targum.

Targ. Jon.	.	Targum of Jonathan ben Uzziel.
Targ. Jos.	.	Targum of Joseph the Blind.
Targ. Onk.	.	Targum of Onkelos.
Targ. Ps.-Jon.	.	Targum of Pseudo-Jonathan.
Vog.	. .	de Vogüé, *La Syrie Centrale.*
Wadd.	. .	Waddington, *Inscriptions Greques et Latines de la Syrie.*
ZDMG	. .	*Zeitschrift der Deutschen Morgenländischen Gesellschaft.*
Zenj.	. .	Inscriptions found at Zenjirli, N.W. Syria.

FOREWORD

The Rev. J. Courtenay James, M.A., B.D., has asked me to write a 'Foreword' to his work on the *Language of Palestine*. Now although I think a 'Foreword' by myself or any other student of the Semitic languages wholly unnecessary, I gladly seize the opportunity of putting on record my high appreciation of this volume, and of recommending its perusal to all who are interested in the past and present history of the Holy Land. I do this the more willingly because I know of no book in which the Language of Palestine is similarly treated, and because the need for such an introduction to the study of the languages, history and archaeology of western Asia is very great at the present moment. At no time in the history of the world was information concerning Palestine and Syria more eagerly sought for, and the more scholars can supply the greater will be the demand. The main facts concerning the history of the ancient peoples who inhabited western Asia—the Sumerians, and the Babylonian, Assyrian, Arabian and Palestinian Semites—have been well known to Oriental scholars and archaeologists for many years. But the results of their labours are for the most part enshrined in the publications of learned Societies (usually written in a language other than English), and in volumes which on account of their cost and rarity are not easily accessible to the general reader. The minds of men are now focussed upon Palestine, and all are pondering over the past history of that country, and wondering how far future happenings there may be foretold from it. The appearance of this book is therefore most opportune, and its concise and clear diction, and its honest and impartial statements, should render it a peculiarly trustworthy guide to students, and to all who take more than a general interest in the Christian East.

The Rev. J. Courtenay James is no blind follower of any special group of scholars or any 'school' of thought. As far as I can see from the perusal of his book in the final revises, he has read very widely, and has acquired a good working knowledge of several Semitic languages, and has spent many years in collecting facts and data bearing upon his main subject, the 'Language of Palestine.' These facts he has arranged in the order that seems to him correct, and the deductions which he has made from them are entirely his own. In my opinion the author's independence gives his book an enhanced and special value. He has gone to the best sources for information respecting the intricate subjects about which he writes, but he does not hesitate to differ from experts when the facts as he knows them justify him in so doing. His aim has been to give an account of the language, or rather languages, of Palestine and of their relationship to the Semitic dialects of Assyria, Arabia and Babylonia. In carrying out his project he found it necessary to discuss the languages and history of the Sumerians, Accadians (Babylonians), Assyrians, Hebrews, Syrians, both Eastern and Western, Arabs, Egyptians, etc.; but the information which he has collected about these people is only used by him to illustrate his main thesis and to support part of it. Many authorities will be inclined to challenge some of his conclusions, especially on points about which conclusive evidence is not forthcoming, and, as the author admits, the full history of the Semites and their settlements has not been told by him. Thus the tablets that were found near Kara Eyuk just before the beginning of the Great War, and are now generally known as 'Cappadocian,' reveal the existence, already suspected, of a

large Semitic colony with a distinctive dialect in the neighbourhood of Caesarea at the end of the xxivth century B.C.
These tablets are in reality documents belonging to a great
banking house, which flourished there for about one hundred
years, and are inscribed with the texts relating to the extensive Caravan Traffic which existed between Cilicia and the
more northerly portions of Mesopotamia. The language in
which these texts are written is pure Semitic, and has much in
common with the Syriac language as written during the early
centuries of the Christian Era. A very important characteristic of these texts is that they are written with a simpler
syllabary than any other cuneiform document known to us;
the number of signs regularly employed is about one hundred.
It is of interest also to note that the proper names found in
these texts are partly Assyrian and partly Palestinian. The
first to translate any 'Cappadocian' document was Professor
the Rev. A. H. Sayce, D.D., and his work has been continued
by MM. Thureau Dangin and Contenau; the former published
the 'Cappadocian' tablets preserved in the Louvre, and the
latter those that were in his private possession. I am glad
to be able to say that an edition of the 'Cappadocian' tablets
in the British Museum has been undertaken by Mr. Sidney
Smith, B.A., of the Department of Egyptian and Assyrian
Antiquities in the British Museum, and that his work is in
an advanced state.

It is greatly to be hoped that before many new editions
of this book are called for, our information about many
subjects which are now being discussed intensively may
be greatly increased. There is reason to believe that the
Sumerologists will be able to give us definite information
about the origin of the Sumerians and their language, and to
settle the vexed question of the date of their original occupation of Mesopotamia. Little, probably nothing, has yet been
done which will justify us in assuming that the Hittite

problem is near solution, for the inscriptions in Hittite hieroglyphs from Carchemish cannot be deciphered, and very
much has to be done yet by Hrozny and his followers, before
the Hittite texts written in cuneiform will be made to deliver
up their secrets to us. Our greatest hope lies in the excavations which the Trustees of the British Musuem are carrying
on at Carchemish on the Euphrates, where, it is quite probable, a bilingual inscription in Hittite and some known
language may one day be discovered. Such difficulties and
problems as the alleged relationship of the ancient Egyptian
language to the Semitic languages, the relationship of Hittite
to the Aryan languages, and the character of the languages
of Mitani and Philistia, etc., our author treats carefully and
with due reserve; he says enough to indicate the difficulties,
and he refers to the proper authorities. It will be time
enough to emphasize such abstruse matters to the beginners
when definite information about them has been acquired.

I hope that the Publishers will find it convenient to keep
the type for this book in such a form that the necessary
alterations, due to the progress of Palestinian and Mesopotamian archaeology, may be made without delay.

ERNEST WALLIS BUDGE.

BRITISH MUSEUM, 24th August 1920.

THE
LANGUAGE OF PALESTINE

I

INTRODUCTION

HISTORICAL OUTLINE

WE can never know the immense lapse of time required for
the Semitic branch of the human family to develop into so
many nationalities, and to evolve so many clearly marked
languages, as we find at the beginning of the Graeco-Roman
period. The Semites ceased to march with the progress of
civilization, being static rather than dynamic. Yet through
that extraordinary factor—the Jew—they have exercised
tremendous influence on the commercial and religious history
of the world. The Asiatic section of the Aryan race has
contributed comparatively little to the enlightenment and
progress of mankind. The Hindoo is a visionary, and the
Persian is a genuine nomad. The Sumerian kingdoms were
first conquered by the Babylonians, and these in their turn
by the Assyrians. Babylon again rose in power, but only to
be finally overthrown by Persia in the fifth century B.C.
Egypt after a long struggle with many powers became
subject to the Persians in the fourth century B.C. Once more
Egypt rose in strength and threw off the foreign yoke, but
fell at last under the might of Alexander the Great. Under
the Ptolemies Egypt flourished till 31 B.C., when Cleopatra,
the last of the dynasty of the Ptolemies, was defeated at
Actium by Augustus, and Egypt became a province of Rome.
Thus when the curtain of history is lifted we see Egypt and

I

the empires of Western Asia rising into aggressive life and power. Then the Greeks enter upon the scene, with their wonderful intellectual equipment and artistic skill, to play their part in the world's drama. For a moment the two great forces—Persia and Greece—face each other. The first attack is made by the East upon the West, but ultimately intellect triumphs over numbers, and the conquests of Grecian arms bring East and West together under a common government with a common official language. Meanwhile a new power is rising in the West, and irresistibly grows till no nation is left unconquered, and when the curtain falls the Roman Empire is conterminous with the known world.[1]

We turn again to this alluring panorama of ancient empires, rising and falling, surging to and fro as their fortunes ebbed and flowed. The shadowy Sumerian appeared from an unknown source, possibly from the distant east by way of Persia. Settling on the Indian Sea near the estuary of the rivers Euphrates and Tigris, they founded their kingdom, with centres at ' Babel, and Erech, and Accad, and Calneh, in the land of Shinar.'[2] These primitive tribes brought their rude picture-writing with them, which they turned into wedge-shaped impressions on the ready-found plastic clay of their new habitat. From the south the Semites moved out of Arabia, thrusting themselves northward, and forcing the Sumerian settlers to evacuate, they occupied the plains of Mesopotamia and the Euphrates basin. Perhaps possessing no native system of writing, they adopted the Sumerian alphabet, using it, however confusedly, to record their speech. These Semitic clans pressed beyond Babylon and founded

[1] The following literature, general and special, may be named here : Maspero, *L'histoire ancienne des Peuples de l'Orient classique* (Eng. trans. 3 vols.); Meyer, *Geschichte Alterthums* ; Hall, *The Ancient Hist. of the Near East* ; Rogers, *Hist. of Babl. and Assyr.* ; Garstang, *The Land of the Hittites* ; Evans, *Scripta Minoa*, vol. i. ; Hogarth, *Ionia and the East* ; Hawes, *Crete, the Forerunner of Greece* ; Beloch, *Griechische Geschichte* ; Hogarth, *Philip and Alexander* ; Droysen, *Das Hellenismus* ; Modestov, *Introduction a l'Histoire Romaine*.

[2] Gen. 10[10]. If *Sanḫar* in the Tell el-Amarna tablets, and *Sangara* in the Egyptian inscriptions, can be identified with שׁנער, then ' Shinar ' probably = ' Babylonia ' (cf. Meyer, *Ægyptiaca*, 63 f. ; Rogers, *Hist. of Bab. and Ass.* i. 411).

Asshur and Calah and Resen and Nineveh, and established
Assyria between the Persian hills on the east and the Syrian
desert on the south-west. Looking north-west the *Hatti*
(Hittites) regions stretch along the banks of the Euphrates,
and include Carchemish and Kadesh and Pteria (the modern
Boghaz Keui), extending as far as Smyrna.[1] Turning west-
wards there are mighty movements up the Nile valley of a
people whose origin cannot be traced. They cross the
isthmus and come into conflict with Sumerians and Semites
and Hittites, and then for centuries there are fierce incursions into each other's territory, until both Nineveh and
Memphis are fallen in the dust. Branches of Semites emerge
on the Mediterranean coast-lands, touched with a Minoan
civilization, and Phoenicians and Philistines occupy the
regions west of the Jordan, including Tyre and Sidon and
Sarepta and Byblos. From among the commingling tribes
the *Habiri* (Hebrews) appear on the borders of Palestine, and
urge their way under heroic leaders into a foothold among
the Canaanites.[2] These *Habiri* were probably a community
made up of bold clans, which at different times crossed the
Euphrates, and being of kindred origin, spirit and purpose,
resolved upon concerted action in migration and worship.
The history of these people is the most romantic on record;
they have lost everything, except their soul.

[1] It is now practically proved that the Hittite inscriptions cover the
period 1200–800 B.C. These inscriptions and kindred remains have been
found in Cappadocia, Lycaonia, Phrygia and north Syria. At Karabel
an inscription, with a Hittite warrior and a brief script, has been found,
showing that the sphere of Hittite influence included Smyrna. *Vide*
Jensen, *Hittiter und Armenier*, 1898 ; Koldewey, *Die Hettitische Inschrift
gefunden in der Königsburg von Babylon*, 1900.

[2] The best etymology of כְּנַעַן, כְּנַעֲנִי is from כָּנַע, *to be low*, hence 'low-
land,' 'lowlanders' (cf. G. A. Smith, *Hist. Geogr.* 4–5). This explanation
is supported by the use of the opposite term אֱמֹרִי, 'highlanders,'
'mountaineers' (cf. Num. 13³⁰, Jos. 11³). The אֱמֹרִי (Aram. אֱמוֹרָאֵי) are said
to be descendants of כְּנַעַן (Gen. 10¹⁵· ¹⁶). This suggests close relationship of
origin, they probably migrated together, and afterwards divided, at first
making the Jordan a natural division. Both terms apparently are found
on the Amarna tablets—the *Kinaḫna* or *Kinaḫḫi* and the *Mar-tu* or
Amurru. The *Kinaḫḫi* were perhaps the earlier people, occupying the
lowlands of north-west Palestine, and the *Amurru* the later section and
successors, occupying the highlands of north-east and central Palestine.

II

CONQUEST AND LANGUAGE

It is difficult to estimate the effects on language of the conflicts and mixings of Africans, Asiatics and Europeans in the wide districts around the Red Sea, and in southern Asia generally. The dialectical consequences due to Oriental nomadism are very complex, and not easily described. If the country lying between the Euphrates and the Tigris could deliver up all its secrets, we should follow more intelligibly the movements of the primitive Semitic tribes, and realize more definitely the effect of tribal migrations on the idiom and pronunciation of their languages. The wandering tribes were often in conflict, and conquest often meant exile or slavery for the vanquished. A military defeat was sometimes the precursor of a linguistic defeat, inasmuch as the conqueror imposed both his law and his language on the weaker power. Egypt, Phoenicia, Assyria, Persia, Israel, Greece, contributed to the old-world drama, and each passed on something to the stock vocabulary of later times. The presence of foreign words and idioms in the Old Testament Hebrew, in the LXX, and even in the New Testament Greek, is some evidence of the lexical and syntactical processes that went on.

It must not, however, be imagined that a new government under a foreign power is always, or ever immediately, followed by a new or foreign language. The French government of Brittany did not quickly supersede the Celtic language of the province. Wales has long been under English rule, but Welsh is still the common language of the industrial classes throughout the Principality. For a hundred and fifty years India has been in some sense subject to British statesmanship, but all the provinces continue to speak the native tongues. So the imposition of Greek and Roman law and government upon southern Asia and northern Africa did not supplant the native dialects. These remained almost unaffected in the vast districts beyond the direct influence of the great centres of population and of civilization. But the new language,

Greek, became the official and literary speech in the leading cities, particularly at Alexandria. Here as early as the third century B.C. the need was felt for a Greek version of the Old Testament. But the LXX was not intended for the native tribes of northern Africa and of Asia Minor. It was produced by the most learned men of the age, and was intended for a limited, but fairly well educated, section of the community—the Jews, who through travel and commerce had become acquainted with Greek.[1]

III

RACE-CLASSIFICATION

Ethnologists are not yet agreed on any system of race-classification. With this problem we are not concerned. Our survey only directly covers the Semitic area. The Negro, Malay, and N. American Indian scarcely enter into history. The Mongolian has little more than touched the fringe of history, being static rather than dynamic. It is only where the Mongol is brought into contact with Western civilization, as in the case of the Turks and Japanese, that he can find a place in history. It is to the 'Caucasian' that we must turn to find history. The term 'Caucasian' is used rather topically than literally, to denote the source of those peoples who have played momentous parts in the history of the world. Both nations and languages require much time for their development. The law of gradualism is everywhere evident, and act and speech come into the great cosmic process. No doubt linguistic changes may be effected rapidly. 'If there be nothing like literature or society,' says Max Müller, 'to keep changes within limits, two villages, separated for only a few generations, will soon become mutually unintelligible.'

The differences in the physical and mental states of

[1] The best modern work on the LXX is Swete, *Introd. to the OT. in Gk.* (1900); cf. Thackeray, *Gram. of the OT. in Gk. accord. to the Sept.* (1909); Nestle, in Hastings' *Dict. of the Bible, s.v.* 'Septuagint.'

mankind are to be regarded rather as differences of development than of origin. Perhaps there has not been within
historical times a strictly pure race of men. All the families
and groups of mankind have been more or less crossed and
mixed. Hereditary types have prevailed in certain clearly
marked races. But the origin of the type in every case
eludes us. Along with these physical and mental changes
there have been specific linguistic differentiations. But
definite divisions of race and language cannot be stated in all
cases; there are many intermixtures and overlappings. Two
or three things must be remembered: some divisions of race
and language are transmissible and interchangeable; there
are many exceptions to all ethnological and linguistic rules,
indicating, perhaps, in some instances a reversion to a
common type; the crossings of tribes and the mixtures of
languages are so numerous and subtle that the best analytical
scheme can only be approximately correct. The section in
this work on ' Linguistic Genealogy' will confirm the foregoing statements. The present study is restricted almost
entirely to Semitic; the Aryan belongs to another category,
and there is no clear bridge from the one to the other.
Aryan has never grown on a Semitic stock, neither has
Semitic succeeded on Aryan soil.

IV

EVOLUTION OF THOUGHT AND LANGUAGE

The thesis of Schleicher must not be accepted quite
literally, 'that no grammatical categories exist in the consciousness of the speaker which do not find formal expression in sound.' Probably there are many exceptions to this
rule, but from the nature of the proposition the exceptions
are often difficult to demonstrate. It is, however, pretty
safe to affirm that no clear grammatical associations, as such,
exist in the consciousness of a speaker, which are not
embodied in orderly speech. With the Oriental, thought
and language moved more intimately together than in later

times among Western people. The Semite had the power of transporting himself backward or forward with wonderful vividness, thus he could realize the future as either present or past. In this way the mind of the Semite kept company with his thought, and his speech was the immediate projection of his consciousness. For this reason the so-called Tenses in Hebrew, and kindred languages, are really moods; they express not time past or future, but states complete or incomplete.

We have no means of tracing the orderly evolution of the primitive languages of mankind. There are apparent breaks in the course of human speech, which suggest at first sight that new types of language were attained *per saltum.* The direct evidence would lead to the conclusion that there have been violent disruptions, along with progressive developments in the history of the earliest languages of the world. This fact seems to have occupied the minds of the most ancient writers, as the legend of Babel suggests. No doubt if all the historical facts were available it would be possible to explain the causes of the linguistic changes which are found in the most ancient records. It may readily be believed that many racial and linguistic transformations took place rapidly. The frequent migrations of tribes to distant regions, where they would be brought into contact with new forms of speech, and the devastating wars, which often plunged whole tribes into captivity among foreign peoples and tongues, would result in comparatively sudden changes of language, and the production of new dialects. It is instructive to recall in this connexion the comparatively stable character of Arabic, due to 'the tranquil and secluded habits of the Arab tribes,' and the many fluctuations of Hebrew and Aramaic, due to 'the migratory and unsettled life of the early Hebrews' and later Aramaeans.

It is proved that radical differences of language are contingent upon differences of race. Language is a product of mind, and in its turn becomes an index to the thought of a people. In the evolution of races different types of mind are developed, and these find expression in different modes of speech. Thus the difference between one family of language and another is not primarily in vocabulary and grammar, but in a morphological element which is difficult to define and illustrate. Not only do ideas differ, but the manner in which ideas are formed into sentences is a differentiating factor between various races and nations of men. The Semite and the Greek represent two very different races; they do not think in the same manner, and it follows that their linguistic forms will reveal corresponding varieties. The Semite is a poet and word-painter, not a logician and scientist; a free chronicler, not an expert historian. The constitutional and hereditary traits of the Oriental mind inevitably reveal themselves in the common speech and literature of the people. The Greek is philosophic, precise, finished; he seeks to convince, and strives after literary effect. This original difference of mind is quite apparent in the language of the two races. In general it may be said that the Semitic language is psychologically correct; Greek is mechanically exact. 'Knowledge is power,' not only in the material history of nations,[1] but also in the linguistic development of mankind. Language is dependent on thought, and is closely related to religion and morality. Epicurus taught that words were formed originally, not by an arbitrary law, but by a natural process, in harmony with our sensations and ideas. This is true, but not in the materialistic sense of Epicurus, according to whom the soul is but a collection of infinitesimal atoms. Language is not the product of any 'fortuitous concourse of atoms,' but the coherent articulation of a rational spirit. It is true that, other conditions being equal, the nation with the mightiest intellectual genius must be in the ascendant. It is when the ascendant intellect is supported and directed by a pure religious ideal that the onward march is irresistible. A moral decline generally precedes an intellectual decadence, and along with this a deterioration of language.

Temperament has much to do with the character of a

---

[1] *Postea vero quam in Asia Cyrus, in Graecia Lacedaemonii et Athenienses coepere uebis atque nationes subigere, lubidinem dominandi causam belli habere, maxumam gloriam in maxumo imperio putare, tum demum periculo atque negotiis conpertum est in bello plurumum ingenium posse* (Sall. *Bell. Cat.* ii. 2).

people's speech. The Greek was philosophic and his language academic; the Semite was imaginative and his language pictorial. The former was deductive, the latter intuitive. Whatever the mind of the Semite realized was put in the past, though it might be future. Hence the future could be used of the historic past, and the preterite of the prophetic future. This characteristic of language was due largely to native temperamental qualities. When these inherent dispositions were touched and quickened by religion they affected speech in a still more characteristic way. No word is more strikingly Semitic than the pictorial 'Behold!'[1] which is an appeal to the imagination, and which plays a great part in Hebrew religious phraseology. The language of religion does not require nice grammatical distinctions or exact syntactical codes. Hence in the sacred writings of the Jews we do not find 'propositions moulded by interdependence and mutual subordination into complete periods,' but sentences made up of a succession of co-ordinate propositions, a disregard of particles, and inconsequent phrases expressing emotion. The religion of Israel did not perhaps invent or introduce many new words, but it heightened the meaning of some old terms, and used others in novel and unprecedented ways. Nearly all Hebrew literature that has come down to us is religious, or in some way connected with religion. This fact must always be remembered in any study of the language. It is when the writer attains the clearest spiritual insight that we find the highest forms of impressive language. In the history of the Jews this period was reached just before and soon after the Exile. A language that is largely employed with the expression of religious ideas and cults will be narrow and exclusive; when it breaks over its native boundaries, it loses its individuality and primitive character. It gains in breadth and explicitness at

---

[1] Perhaps the original use of הן, הנה was hypothetical (cf. 1 S. 20¹³, Dt. 13¹⁵); it was often a vivid method of expressing some condition (cf. 1 S. 9⁷, 2 S. 18¹¹). The same applies to some Aram. inscrip. (Zenj. *Hadad*, l. 29; *Nêrab*, l. l. 11). The use of הן in Ex. 4¹ illus. the demonstrative-exhortative significance of the particle. Expressions like כי כה אמר יהוה הנני (Is. 66¹²), הנה אלהיכם (Is. 40⁹), are peculiarly Hebraic and belong to the religious nomenclature of Israel.

the cost of originality; there is a simplification of grammar and orthography, but an impoverishment of rugged expression. Metaphorical funds are augmented, but often only to be stereotyped.   Contact with foreign nations lowered the standard of the Jews' sacred language, and a similar widening of influence led to the degeneration of Periclean Greek.[1]

V

THE ART OF WRITING

This is an inherent possession of all people, but only comes into evidence under certain conditions.   The expression of ideas in writing may be graphically represented as follows :

ORIGINAL IDEAS.

PICTOGRAMS :
i.e. ideographic writing.

SYMBOL-GRAMS :
i.e. abbreviated picture-writing.

PHONOGRAMS :
i.e. symbols as sound-values.

SYLLABIC WRITING :
i.e. the sign represents a whole syllable.

ALPHABETIC WRITING :
i.e. the sign represents a single sound.[2]

The development of the art is more or less empirical, but the art itself is intuitive.   In the earliest records of the nations the introduction of writing seemed the result of mere

[1] It is a curious fact that in the case of most languages the farther we go back the purer is their character.   Then if 'languages are the best mirror of the human mind' (Leibnitz), what becomes of our boasted intellectual advancement ?   We reckon as 'liberally educated' those only who have spent the best years of their youth in acquiring a knowledge of Greek and Latin literature ! (Cf. the ref. to Sanskrit in Schopenhauer, *Parerga und Paralipomena*, sect. 307).

[2] Vide *Facsimiles of MSS and Inscrip. of the Palæographical Society* ; Silvestre, *Universal Palœography* ; Thompson, *Greek and Latin Palœography*, 1903.

caprice and chance. But probably some definite experience called forth the slumbering power, and whenever the need arose the faculty was available. Generally it may be said that in the remotest times, before the original people of the earth became migratory, a written language was not required. But when boundaries between one tribal possession and another had to be marked and ratified, and when communication between more or less distant provinces became necessary, a written signary was called into existence. A surprising feature in this connexion, and one seldom noticed, is the facility with which a people can reduce their speech to writing. In modern times we know how negroes and other tribes promptly seize the idea of writing from the civilized settlers, and how rapidly they adapt our alphabet to their language. A very ancient language may, in this way, quickly assume a modern appearance. This may be regarded as a preliminary hint that the script is not always a safe guide to the age of a language. Here, too, it may be pointed out that the absence of writing on tombs and certain stelae, where we might naturally expect to find it, is not to be regarded as proof of the absence of a written language. It is true that most memorial monoliths are found to have some engraving, but doubtless there were many exceptions in ancient times. Even in our day uninscribed monuments have been raised to the memory of notable persons. A study of inscribed stelae would throw much light on language and history.[1]

VI

PRE-HISTORIC SIGNARY

No attempt is here made to trace the origin of the alphabet. Though in this study we go no farther back than

---

[1] Darius set up two columns on the banks of the Bosphorus to mark the extent of his triumphs—one engraved in Assyrian and the other in Greek characters : θηησάμενος δὲ καὶ τὸν Βόσπορον, στήλας ἔστησε δύο ἐπ' αὐτῷ λίθου λευκοῦ, ἐνταμὼν γράμματα, ἐς μὲν τὴν Ἀσσύρια, ἐς δὲ τὴν Ἑλληνικὰ, ἔθνεα πάντα ὅσαπερ ἦγε (Herod. iv. 87).

on papyrus is probably that found at Sakkara,[1] recording events in the time of Assa, the last king of the fifth dynasty, *circa* 3550 B.C. The earliest records extant written in a Canaanitish language are apparently the Tell el-Amarna tablets.[2] These were written by vassal princes in Palestine and Syria to the Egyptian king and his officers, *circa* 1400 B.C., perhaps a little before, or about the time of the Israelitish invasion of Canaan. The Cretan inscriptions discovered at Knossos, written on tablets partly hieroglyphic, but chiefly linear script, belong to the same period as the Tell el-Amarna correspondence. These are, of course, earlier than the Phoenician monuments with which the Aegean abounds.

An interesting point is raised here and will be considered later, how far the Greek writing was indebted to Egypt, to the Aegean, and to Phoenicia. In Crete Phoenicians and Greeks lived side by side, and both were in contact with Egyptian civilization. The rise of the Greek states was in some way due to the combined influence of Egyptian, Minoan,[3] and Phoenician civilization. Out of the Sidonian (early Phoenician) alphabet was evolved the Aramaic script. In Assyria as early as vii cent. B.C., and in Babylonia as early as vi cent. B.C., the Aramaic script began to supersede the earlier type. From the v cent. B.C. to i cent. B.C. the Aramaic script was commonly employed in international correspondence throughout Western Asia, and its development can be definitely traced. In the Aegean the Greeks came into contact with the Phoenician hieratic writing before they became acquainted with the Babylonian Aramaic script. Hence the Greek alphabet was developed from the older type of Phoenician, and not from the Aramaic.

The Greek and Aramaic alphabets are two branches of a pre-Hellenic and pre-Semitic signary through Phoenician. The Phoenicians were not so much the 'inventors' of the alphabet as the 'evolvers' of a script whose roots lie far

---

[1] At this village is the necropolis of ancient Memphis.

[2] *Vide* Winckler, in *Keilinschriftliche Bibliothek*, vol. v. (1896).

[3] From Minos, perhaps a mythical king, about whom many legends grew up; regarded as historical by Thucydides (i. 4. 8).

back.[1] It is quite possible that Babylonia was in possession of an alphabetic script, whose phonetics and other peculiarities were employed in the production of a Semitic language. Babylonian influence is apparent enough in Semitic, but the Semitic alphabet is not of Babylonian origin. Out of several elements an alphabet was developed among the Phoenicians about 1000 B.C. from some systems of linear signs inherited from their non-Semitic predecessors, and from the older inhabitants of the Mediterranean coast-lands. Through Phoenician activity this alphabet spread in two main directions : (1) to Greece and thence became the basis of all European writing; (2) to Aramaea—Mesopotamia and became the common script of Western Asia. Before 1000 B.C. the Phoenicians for a time used the cuneiform system, but this soon became too cumbrous and the evolved signary was generally employed for commercial purposes. But inevitably the earlier use of cuneiform left its mark on the superseding alphabetic systems.

VIII

DIRECTION OF WRITING

Generally we may accept the opinion that Phoenician writing was derived from Egyptian hieroglyphic or picture-writing through hieratic. This conclusion has to be some-what modified as a result of the researches in Egyptology, particularly those of Emanuel de Rougé.[2] He found the prototype of the Phoenician script in an older and ill-formed hieratic writing, which obtained in the time of the early empire, probably before the Hyksos kings. This ancient script has been preserved in the 'Papyrus Prisse,' now in the

---

[1] Lucan, in his famous epic *Pharsalia*, preserves the tradition that the Phoenician was the first alphabet invented :

Phoenices primi, famae si creditur, ausi
Mansuram rudibus vocem signare figuris.

Others attribute the origin of letters to Thoth (the Gk. Ἑρμῆς), and there-fore make Egypt the home of symbolic characters (Diod. Sic. *Lib.* i. ; Aelianus, *Hist.* I. xiv. 34 ; Pliny, *Hist. Nat.* I. vii. 36). *Vide* p. 80.

Mém. sur l'Origine Égyptienne de l'Alphabet Phenicien, 1874.

National Library at Paris. This MS is perhaps the oldest literary composition that has come from Egypt. It contains the proverbs of Ptah-hotep. *It reads from right to left.* It must be borne in mind that hieroglyphic writing ran both ways—from right to left on some monuments, and from left to right on others; hieroglyphic writing was never βουστρο-φηδόν. Originally it is probable that hieroglyphic writing ran from top to bottom, so the early Babylonian and the modern Chinese. With the development of hieratic writing from hieroglyphic came the change from perpendicular to horizontal writing. It was a matter of indifference or of a scribe's taste whether the linear script ran from right to left or *vice versa.* Hence, as stated, some ancient hieratic records proceeded in one direction, and others in the opposite direction. The 'Prisse' type prevailed and became the prototype of nearly all Semitic writings.

But how came the Greeks to write from left to right? If as generally supposed the Greeks imitated the Phoenicians, we should expect them to write from right to left. Now, it is probable that the Greeks were acquainted with Egyptian hieratic before they were influenced by Phoenician. Hence it is possible that they had some acquaintance with the two directions of hieratic writing. Phoenician activity may have influenced them towards right to left writing, and this is the direction of some of the earliest Greek inscriptions. The other direction, however, was not forgotten, and the two methods found expression in the unique βουστροφηδόν writing, which characterized the Greek inscriptions, notably in the vi cent. B.C. It is possible, perhaps, to find in somewhat earlier events a factor which tended to determine the direction of Greek writing. When the Greeks came into contact with Aegean and Asiatic tribes it was necessary to mark off one territory from another to prevent overlapping and conflict. This was done by the fixing of boundary-stones, which were commonly distinguished by some engravement. It is probable that the Pelasgi (? = Sidonians—Phoenicians) [1] were

---

[1] Some historical hints will be interesting here : The Greeks are called יָוָן (Is. 66[19], Ezek. 27[13], Zech. 9[13], Dn. 8[21], Joseph. *Ant.* i. 6. 1). The Chaldee paraphrase did not hesitate to substitute 'Macedonia' for 'Javan,'

commissioned to mark these boundary posts.[1] These people had been taught to write by association with west Asian Semites, while the Greeks were still a purely pastoral community, without any pretence to literary attainments. The Pelasgi had a script, which was in some sense peculiar, and which belonged to the pre-Homeric age. Diodorus, referring to Linus, says : 'This Linus, they say, wrote in Pelasgian (? Phoenician) letters the acts of the first Bacchus, and left other stories in his writings behind him. Orpheus, too, it is said, used the same characters, and Pronapides, Homer's master, an ingenious musician.'[2] In addition to some peculiarity of letter-forms, the Pelasgi writing probably perpetuated that type of hieratic inscription which was from left to right (vide supra). Moreover it possibly occurred to these stone-cutters, who of course held the chisel in the left hand, that it would be easier and more natural to begin the engraving on the side of the stone opposite the chisel, that is, on the left hand side, and proceed towards the right. To this period then we must look for the initiation of left to right writing among the Greeks. If the foregoing explanation be valid, the present mode of writing is due to the continuation and evolution of the innovation of the Pelasgi engravers.

Herodotus was acquainted with the two directions of writing—the Egyptian from right to left, and the Greek from

---

Gen. 10[2], and the LXX and Eusebius insert the term Ἐλισά, in addition to Ἰωύαν. The Athenians are called Ἰάονες by Homer (Il. xiii. 685), and Aeschylus (Prom. 175, 561). Now according to Herodotus (i. 56) the Ionians of Asia Minor were originally Pelasgi, and they inhabited Achaia in the Peloponnesus (ib. 145). Further, he says, the Athenians, being Pelasgi, were called Ionians, a name, however, which they resented (ib. 143, viii. 44). It was the Ionian type of Greek alphabet which became the standard for all the Greek States. In the cuneiform inscriptions in the time of Sargon (circa 709 B.C.), the name Yavnan or Yunan is used of Cyprus, where the Assyrians early came into contact with the Greeks. [Vide Max Müller, Asien u. Europa, 369 ff. ; Stade, Ausgewahlte Akademische Reden u. Abhandlungen (1899), 123–142.]

[1] Vide Diodorus (Siculus), Liber v.

[2] The original is : τὸν δ' οὖν Λίνον φασὶ τοῖς Πελασγικοῖς γράμμασι συνταξά-μενον τὰς τοῦ πρώτου Διονύσου πράξεις, καὶ τὰς ἄλλας μυθολογίας ἀπολιπεῖν ἐν τοῖς ὑπομνήμασιν. ὁμοίως δὲ τούτοις χρήσασθαι τοῖς Πελασγικοῖς γράμμασι τὸν Ὀρφέα, καὶ Προναπίδην τὸν Ὁμήρου διδάσκαλον, εὐφυῆ γεγονότα μελοποιόν (Lib. iii. sect. lxvi.).

2

left to right.   But he says nothing about the origin of these opposite methods; his language however is interesting: 'The Greeks write and cipher, moving the hand from left to right; but the Egyptians from right to left: and doing so they say they do it right-wards, and the Greeks left-wards. They have two forms of writing, one of which is called hieratic, the other demotic.' [1]

Another theory is worth notice, though by some it may be considered too ingenious to be satisfactory.   This theory connects the direction of writing with religious intuition. Many of the differences between Semites and Aryans were due to innate characteristics and original dispositions.   In all countries the priests were probably the first to represent words by signs, that is, were the first to reduce language to writing.   This was a sacred, a religious function, a divine inspiration.   The priests of the Southern hemisphere, that is, the priests of the black races—the Semites included—turned their faces towards the South as they traced their mysterious signs on stone, clay or skin; the hand was moved towards the East, the source of light and wisdom.   Hence they wrote from right to left.   The priests of the Northern hemisphere, that is, the priests of the white races—the Aryans—turned their faces towards the North, the home of their ancestors, when they were occupied in the sacred duty of writing; the hand, as in the case of the Semites and for the same reason, was moved towards the East.   Hence they wrote from left to right.[2]

IX

ROYAL COLLEGES

It is known that the kings of Babylonia and Assyria chose out from among the captives young men of noble birth

---

[1] The text is: γράμματα γράφουσι καὶ λογίζονται ψήφοισι, Ἕλληνες μὲν, ἀπὸ τῶν ἀριστερῶν ἐπὶ τὰ δεξιὰ φέροντες τὴν χεῖρα· Αἰγύπτιοι δὲ, ἀπὸ τῶν δεξιῶν ἐπὶ τὰ ἀριστερά· καὶ ποιεῦντες ταῦτα, αὐτοὶ μέν φασὶ ἐπὶ δεξιὰ ποιέειν, Ἕλληνας δὲ ἐπ' ἀρισερά, διφασίοισι δὲ γράμμασι χρέωνται καὶ τὰ μὲν αὐτῶν, ἱρά· τά δὲ, δημοτικὰ καλέεται, ii. 36.   Cf. Diodorus (Siculus), i. 81.

[2] Cf. Fabre d'Olivet, *Histoire philosophique du genre humain*, vol. 1.

from different nationalities, and trained them in schools connected with their palaces. The object was that these foreign representatives might assist the government in dealing with subjects of different races and languages. These captive students were placed in some official capacity in the palace, and received the best education possible at the time. The term of training usually lasted three years, after which the students were supposed to be proficient in the language, customs and ideals of their adopted country.[1] Daniel and other Hebrews were selected for a collegiate course by Nebuchadrezzar, in Babylon. Daniel already possessed a knowledge of Hebrew, and now he gained an acquaintance with the diplomatic language and script of Babylonia-Assyria. Whether Daniel studied the difficult arrow-headed writing of Assyria, or some intermediate hieratic script is not easy to decide. The story of the writing on the wall [2] suggests that the language was Aramaic, and that the script was unknown to the Babylonian magi.

The effect of these royal schools upon language constitutes a difficult problem, and up to the present has not received serious attention. One result was the change of name of the foreign students and other high personages.[3] The most familiar illustration is supplied by the Book of Daniel, but this practice was well established in the East.[4] This custom

[1] Vide *Cylinder of Bellino*, i. 13, from which we learn that Nebuchadrezzar had such a college at Nineveh. G. Smith, *Sennacherib*, p. 27 ; *Hist. of Assyr.* p. 111 ; *Records of the Past*, i. p. 23.

[2] *Vide* p. 36.   [3] 2 K. 24¹⁷.

[4] Dan. 1⁷. Here are four Heb. names, with the substituted Aram. (Babylonian) forms : (1) דניאל=בלטשאצר ; cf. the form on Babylonian inscriptions, *Balâṭsu-uṣur*. The name דניאל came into Nabataean (CIS ii. 258), but the form דנאל in Palmyrene (Vog. 93³) is doubtful. (2) חנניה=שדרך ; cf. the Babyl. *Šudur-Aku*. The form חנינו is found in Nab. (CIS ii. 201², 354¹). (3) מישך=מישאל ; cf. the Babyl. *Misha-Aku*. (4) עזריה=עבד נגו ; cf. the Assyr. *Nabû-šar-iddin* (CIS ii. 29). The word means 'servant of Nebo' (נגו should prob. be נבו). The Phoen. עזר בעל (CIS i. 453⁵ f.) has the same meaning ; cf. עזרתבעל (CIS i. 88³). The name of this god is frequent in Aram. proper names (CIS ii. 139 B² ; Eut. 4¹ ; Vog. 73²). It is suggestive that we find among Ezra's caravan persons of the three names מישאל (Neh. 8⁴), עזריה (Neh. 10²), חנניה (Neh. 10²³). It looks as if the author of Dan. has thrown back the contemporaries of Ezra more than a hundred years, in order to picture Jewish heroism at the time of the Captivity under Babylonian oppression. Cf. Cheyne, *Origin of the Psalter*, p. 107.

may explain the presence of foreign proper names in inscriptions and other literature. Persons sufficiently distinguished to have their names recorded may well have served in some capacity at a foreign court. The new name which was bestowed upon them in foreign service became their recognized cognomen, and afterwards was either employed alone, or superadded to their original name. The construction of names partly native and partly foreign belongs to another category, as also the formation of compound divine titles.[1] Many double names are due to bilingual districts and bilingual customs. This was the case in Palestine in the Graeco-Roman period.[2] The custom was known in Syria and other provinces as the Palmyrene inscriptions prove.[3] Much earlier the same thing is found in the Egyptian Papyri dating from the fourth century B.C.[4]

To institutions of a collegiate character must also be

---

[1] The word בעל is common to all the Semitic languages, but is rarely used alone. In itself it is almost colourless, meaning *possessor*, but not as owner of the worshipper, but as the proprietor of the place, or possessor of some special attribute. Hence the OT. titles: Baal-berith, Baal-hazor, Baal-peor, Baal-shamem, Baal-tamar, Baal-zephon, etc. Similar compounds are frequent in the inscriptions: בעל חמן (CIS i. 123a[2]); בעל שמם (CIS i. 7) perhaps of Heb. origin (cf. Lidzbarski, *Ephemeris für Semit. Epigr.* i. 248); בעל צלח (Sid. 4[2]) perhaps of Assyr. origin (cf. Cl.-Gan. *Études*, ii. 48). Other compounds are: עברסכר (Sid. 4[1]) possibly of Egypt. origin; *Sokari* (*vide* Maspero, *Hist. Anc.* 26, 412; cf. Hoffmann, *Zeitschrift für Assyr.* xi. 239 f.).—אשמנ־ארני (CIS i. 44[1]), perhaps Assyr.-Aram. The Phoen. ארן has here already become the Aram. אֲרָנִי (cf. Lagarde, *Bildung d. Nomina*, p. 188).

[2] Of this the NT. supplies several illustrations; many persons had two names, one Heb. or Aram., and the other Greek or Latin. *E.g.* Simon Peter (שִׁמְעוֹן Πέτρος, Mk. 3[16]), Simon Niger (שִׁמְעוֹן Νίγερ, Acts 13[1]); יוֹחָן Μάρκος (Acts 12[12]); יוֹסֵף 'Ιοῦστος (Acts 1[23]); שָׁאוּל Paulus (Acts 13[9]). The form Σαῦλος is the Hellenized Σαούλ).

[3] *E.g.* the royal name of Julius Aurelius is prefixed to at least three native Aram. names: יולים אורלים זברלא (Vog. 15[1]); יולים אורלים ענא (*ib.* 17[1.2]); יולים או(ר)לים נבובד (*ib.* 24[3]).

[4] These papyri, in one instance, seem to show the very time when a native name was supplemented, or supplanted by a Jewish name. Yedoniah is called the son of As-Ḥor (ירניה ומחסיה כל בני אסחיר, H 3), and he is again called the son of Nathan (ירניה בר נתן, J 3). Thus between the writing of H (420 B.C.) and the writing of J (417 B.C.), Yedoniah's father changed his Egyptian 'As-Ḥor' to the Jewish name 'Nathan.' He probably did so when he became a convert to Judaism. (Cf. Cowley, *Assuan Papyri*, J 3, note.)

attributed, at least in part, the hybrid nature of many eastern dialects. Where persons of different nationalities were associated in politics, literature or commerce, there would be a transference of words, phrases and idioms from one language to another. Doubtless Hebrew settlers left a linguistic deposit in Babylonia, as it is certain that Babylonia contributed something to the vernacular of Canaan. This process will tend to explain the presence of Egyptian words in Hebrew, as well as Arabic and Aramaic words in the same language. In the same way we find Phoenician words in Arabic and Aramaic, and Greek in many eastern dialects in the Graeco-Roman period. Persian words in Hebrew came naturally during the interesting period of Persian intervention on behalf of the Jews. Some of these words were doubtless introduced by officials in diplomatic circles. When Asia Minor was subject to Persian government, the satraps used Aramaic in correspondence with the western empire.[1] That Jewish scholars were employed by the Persian satraps is pretty evident; together they probably formed a small literary and advisory circle within the Persian administration. Through this channel royal names, legal terms, commercial and other expressions passed into Hebrew or Aramaic. Some of these, as might be expected, are found in the Book of Esther, and occasionally reappear in other Biblical books.[2]

---

[1] The character of some of the inscrip. in Asia Minor and Egypt (525–332 B.C.) is proof. Cf. CIS ii. 108, 122.

[2] *E.g.* אחשורש (Est. 1[1], Ezra 4[6], Dan. 9[1]), 'Ahasuerus.' The old Pers. *Khshayârshâ* is followed more closely in the inscription חשיארש (CIS ii. 122[3]), than in the Aram. Bibl. form. For the Gk. *vide* Herod. (vi. 98) : Δαρεῖος, ἐρξίης· Ξέρξης, ἀρήϊος· Ἀρταξέρξης, μέγας ἀρήϊος. Cf. אחשתרנים (Est. 8[10, 14]), 'royal'; from the Pers. *Khshatra*, 'lordship.' אחשדרפנים (Est. 8[9] 9[3], cf. Ezra 8[36]), 'satraps.' Pers. *Khshatrapâvan*; in inscriptions שרדפא (Müller, *Epigraphische Denkmäler*, p. 13). Gk. σατράπης. פרתמים (Est. 1[3] 6[9], cf. Dan. 1[3]), 'nobles.' Pers. *Fratama*=Skr. *prathama*, 'first,'=Gk. πρῶτος.

פתגם (Est. 1[20], Eccl. 8[11]), 'edict'; Pers. بيغام, =Syr. ܦܬܓܡܐ, =Gk. λόγος. פתשגן (Est. 3[14] 4[8] 8[13]; cf. פרשגן, Ezra 7[11]), 'apograph,' Pers. *Patğên*: cf. Syr. ܦܬܫܓܢ; a Pers. word through Aram. דת (Est. 1[8], Ezra 8[36]), 'law'; Pers. داد, *dáta*,=Syr. ܕܬܐ, *placitum*. Same meaning as כתבא (CIS ii. 198[10]), 'writ.' In Dt. 33[2] דת is appar. a corruption, perhaps for אש יקרת, 'a burning fire' (cf. p. 92). אגרת (Est. 9[29], 2 Ch. 30[1, 6], Neh. 2[8]),

Probably the Tell el-Amarna tablets supply the strongest evidence of the existence of ancient literary institutions, with scribal officials. These tablets indicate that a college of scribes was employed in middle Egypt at least 1400 B.C. This library, of which 350 clay tablets have been discovered, proves the wide extent of Babylonian influence. Two of these letters are from the Egyptian Pharaoh, one to the king of Babylonia, and the other to a vassal king of north Palestine. The points to be observed are : (1) these tablets are written in the cuneiform script and in the Babylonian (Semitic) dialect; (2) this character and language must have been the general means of inter-communication in all the regions of western Asia and Egypt; (3) to understand these diplomatic communications an acquaintance with Babylonian literature is more or less necessary. It would appear that lesson books prepared in Babylonian were used in the schools of Egypt. Among the Tell el-Amarna archives, tablets are found containing a Babylonian legend, written in Babylon in cuneiform, and in the Babylonian (Semitic) dialect, which were apparently used as school-books for teaching purposes in Egypt.[1]

X

LINE OF PRESENT STUDY

Discovery and exploration are more progressive along the line of history than of language. Archaeology is not adding light to the character of the speech of the Ancient East, as rapidly as it is reconstructing the times and movements of the primitive tribes. The study of the linguistic problem is a much duller undertaking than the investigation of the political, social and religious growth of nations. Yet the two phases—the historical and the linguistic—are closely linked,

'letter.' Pers. انكَرَه, ankarah=anything written, =Gk. ἄγγαρος. Cf. Palm. אגרתא (Tariff, ii. c⁵); אגורא, 'contractor' (of taxes), =Gk. τελώνης, μισθωτής, etc. (l.c.).

[1] Vide Keilinschriftliche Bibliothek, vol. v. (Tell el-Am. by H. Winckler).

and the latter cannot be quite separated from the former. Hence in the following work a framework of history will be found, within which the linguistic phenomena are set and illustrated. This at once suggests the character of the present study. It is not intended to be in any sense a comparative grammar of the Semitic languages, nor a syntactical comparison of the west Asian dialects. These subjects, however, could not be altogether ignored, and they are introduced so far as seems necessary to illustrate the types of language, which were in use in and around Palestine, during the period under discussion.

In the first place some statement is made of the great national and political movements represented by the Babylonian, Persian and Greek conquests, in order to indicate the contact of different languages, and the resultant deposit of idioms. A fairly complete analysis of the Semitic dialects is next introduced, which shows the genealogical connexion between the manifold branches of this great family of languages. This is followed by notes on the constructions which characterize the Semitic languages of western Asia. These notes are based mainly on the inscriptions—Phoenician and Aramaic—which are found during the period viii cent. B.C.–i A.D. In association with this section, a brief study is given of the inscriptions in relation to the language and ideas of the Old Testament. Then more particular attention is given to the coming of the Aramaeans and their connexion with the Hebrews. This section covers the period during which Aramaic superseded Hebrew as the vernacular of Palestine. The evolution and transition of the Semitic script is next considered. Here reference is made to the influence of the Aegean civilization. In the next section closer attention is given to the alphabet, pronunciation, vocabulary and abbreviation of Aramaic. Lines of study are here suggested, which could not be dealt with exhaustively. The Nabataean is next introduced as a fair representative type of the idiom and script of Aramaic at the beginning of the Christian era. Finally the Yemen MSS of Onkelos are discussed, as preserving the later Aramaic as it early emerged from Palestine.

II

EMPIRE AND LANGUAGE

BABYLONIA—PERSIA—GREECE

GENERAL STATEMENT

No people ever endured such momentous changes as the
Jews, and no people ever maintained such uniqueness of
character. From the time of their settlement in Canaan
(*circa* 1200 B.C.) till the Captivity they were not seriously
disturbed by outside forces.[1] But from the Exile they found
no truly abiding habitation. They were conquered, deported,
scattered, afflicted, and yet they congregated in considerable
colonies north, east and south, and always impressed their
influence on the regions in which they dwelt. These vicissi-
tudes had tremendous consequences for the political, social and
religious life of the Jews. These phases of the history, however, do not concern us here; we are looking rather for the
effect of these national changes on the language of the people.
The process of Hebrew deportation to Babylonian regions
went on from 739 B.C. under Tiglath-Pileser, to 586 B.C.
when Nebuchadrezzar finally captured Jerusalem. There
was another deportation of Jews to Hyrcania and Babylon
(*circa* 350 B.C.) under Artaxerxes Ochus.[2] As the result of
these deportations there must have been a considerable Jewish

---

[1] Among the earliest internal foes were the Amorites. In Egypt. in-
scrip. and cuneif. documents (Tell el-Am. etc.) it appears that ' Amorite'
(*Amurru*) was almost synony. with ' Canaan' (*Kinaḫḫi*), *i.e.* northern
Pales. (Cf. Wellhausen, *Die Composition des Hexateuchs u. der historischen
Bücher des Alten Testaments*, pp. 341 f.) Reference to the Hittites is
made in another place.

[2] Georg. Syncell., ed. Dindorf, i. 486.

population beyond the Euphrates. Here it seems the exiles gained some distinguished converts,[1] a fact which accentuated their influence in Babylonia. Judaism in these regions maintained its oriental and Semitic character with much zeal and fidelity. Here was one home for the preservation of the Jewish language and literature. Here great academic institutions sprang up, and here a great Targum had its origin.

Partly preceding and partly during the Persian period a considerable colony of Jews settled in Egypt. It is possible that as early as 663–609 B.C. Psameṭik (or Psammetichus) had a number of Jewish merchants and scholars in his service during a time of art and architectural revival.[2] It is evident that king Jehoahaz was exiled to Egypt by Nacho II. about the year 609 B.C. About twenty years later Jeremiah and a company of Jews migrated to north-east Egypt, to Tahpanhes. This place with Migdol and Noph (Memphis) became the three chief centres of the Jewish settlement in north Egypt. That Jews also settled in south or Upper Egypt is proved by the Biblical references to Pathros,[3] and by the Assuan papyri. The references to No-Amon[4] (Thebes) would imply that Jews were settled in this great south Egyptian city.

The beginning of the Jewish colony in Alexandria may date almost from the foundation of the city. Josephus assigns the settlement of the Jews in Alexandria during the time of Alexander the Great or Ptolemy I.[5] Some scholars, without sufficient reason, assign a much later date.[6] The frequent conflicts between the Ptolemies and the Seleucids probably

---

[1] Joseph. *Ant.* xx. 2–4.

[2] Letter of Aristeas: ed. in English by Lewis, London, 1715. This letter, however, is generally discredited by modern scholars. Whether Herodotus refers to Psameṭik I. or II. is uncertain. In any case his story is much exaggerated, ii. 30.

[3] Heb. פַּתְרוֹס: Is. 11¹¹, Jer. 44¹, Ezek. 29¹⁴ 30¹⁴. According to the special theory of Cheyne these references are not to a place of this name in Egypt; cf. *Crit. Bib.*; *Encycl. Bib. s.v.* 'Pathros.'

[4] Cf. Nah. 3⁸, Jer. 46²⁵, Ezek. 30¹⁴⁻¹⁶.

[5] *Apion*, ii. 4; cf. *Wars*, ii. 18. 7.

[6] Willrich, for instance, contends that there was no considerable Jewish community in Alexandria earlier than the second century B.C. But Josephus cannot be disposed of so easily. (*Vide* Willrich, *Juden u. Griechen vor d. makkabäischen Erhebung*, pp. 1–43, 126 ff.)

induced many Jews to migrate to Egypt, and chiefly to Alexandria, inasmuch as the Jews were much more partial to the Ptolemaic dynasty.[1] The Jewish settlement in north Egypt, especially at Alexandria, was very different from the settlement in Babylonia. In the latter country the surroundings were oriental and Semitic ; in Alexandria the environment was western and Hellenistic. This alliance with Hellenism had tremendous effects on the history of the Jews, and on the language of western Asia.[2]

We turn now to a fuller study of the three great movements alluded to above : The Babylonian-Assyrian invasion, which shattered the homogeneity of the Hebrew nation and language in Palestine ; the Persian intervention, which led to considerable international communication, and witnessed the establishment of Aramaic as the vernacular of Palestine ; the Greek eastern campaigns, which introduced new ideas and a new *lingua franca* into western Asia.

There have been epochs of linguistic unification, and three great types appeared in the pre-Christian world— Babylonian, Aramaic, Greek. These by the force of circumstances became international languages. Egypt and Assyria first realized the need for a common medium of communication. This was provided by the old Babylonian, *circa* 1400 B.C., as the Tell el-Amarna archives prove. In this ancient language was carried on the diplomatic correspondence of the Pharaohs Amenophis III. and IV. with the kings of Babylonia, Assyria, Mitanni, and the Egyptian rulers and vassals in Cyprus and Canaan. At first the Persian Empire had no uniform language to unite its far-flung area from the Indus to the Nile. The Court language was old Persian, a specimen of which is preserved in the Behistun inscription. But Aramaic was accepted as the language of diplomacy and became the international speech of the Orient. The linguistic bond between East and West, however, was Greek. But at

---

[1] Under the first three Ptolemies the Jewish community enjoyed peace, 306-221 B.C. But from about 200 B.C. the Jews voluntarily submitted to the Seleucid kings, and Judaea belonged to their kingdom.

[2] On the Palestinian settlers in Egypt *vide* Mahaffy, *The Empire of the Ptolemies*, 1895, pp. 86, 178, 358, *et al.*

first Greek was broken up into dialects, which rivalled one another for ascendancy. But growing cosmopolitanism, the breaking up of provincial autonomy, the exigences of commerce, the standardizing of Attic, and chiefly the conquests of Alexander, tended to a common tongue. The result was from the iv cent. B.C. a 'common language,' the Κοινή, or Hellenistic Greek.[1]

All change, civic and linguistic, is accelerated by some specific or adventitious circumstance. This is plainly the case with the process of civilization and colonization. The contact of different tribes, whether by migration or invasion, has almost invariably resulted in tribal transformation. 'It was thus that Greece was civilized by colonies from Egypt and Phoenicia; Italy by Asiatic and Grecian adventurers; our own country, in the first instance, by the Roman invaders, and the whole continent of America by the Europeans of modern times.'[2] Similar processes went on during the period between the Exile and the first century A.D. in western Asia. Smaller movements were almost lost sight of in the mighty invasions and deportations of Tiglath-Pileser, Shalmaneser and Sargon in north Palestine, and of Sennacherib, Esarhaddon, Assur-bani-pal and Nebuchadrezzar in south Palestine. The mighty movements of the people occupying the countries North, East and South of Canaan would inevitably accentuate the linguistic changes which became apparent at certain stages in the march of history. Into the *minutiae* of these changes we do not enter, but this study will indicate the influences at work, and the kind of linguistic deposit left in Palestine by the Babylonian-Assyrian, Persian and Greek conquests.[3]

[1] Cf. Angus, *The Environment of Early Christianity*, pp. 209-221.
[2] Tytler, *Elements of History*, p. 11.
[3] Some particulars will be found in the section on 'Semitic Constructions.'

A.—BABYLONIAN PERIOD

I

ANTIQUITY OF BABYLONIA

The discovery of the temple at Nippur enables us to trace the history of Babylonia back to *circa* 4000 B.C. The antiquity of Babylonia is rivalled only by that of Egypt. The great library unearthed in the palace of Assur-bani-pal at Nineveh contained thousands of tablets. Indirectly this library proves the early and advanced civilization of Babylonia. The tablets are largely educational, and the object of the library was to check the custom of sending the Assyrian youths to be educated in Babylonia, where they would imbibe ideas prejudicial to the political and social interests of their native country. There is an inscription in the British Museum, which refers to the reign of Sargon I., king of Akkad. The phrase 'king of Akkad' (Accad) probably means the city only, for at that early period the empire consisted of a collection of independent cities. Records of the Sumero-Accadian inhabitants of these city-states have been assigned to a date *circa* 2500 B.C. It is interesting to notice that the British Museum inscription referred to is a specimen of the 'scratched' or line-writing, as distinguished from the cuneiform method. The Semitic conquest of Babylonia had great influence on the language. The old Sumerians were not only subdued, but their language (of which little is known) was supplanted, and Phoenicians, Aramaeans and Arabians subsequently enter upon the scene. Of the many branches into which the original Semitic language grew the three main developments were Aramaic in the North, Arabic in the South, and Hebrew in the Middle.[1]

---

[1] Ethnologically Hebrew and Arabic are traceable to the same stock. The two sons of Eber were Peleg and Joktan (Gen. 10²⁵). (*a*) Through the former came Jacob (the links were פלג—רעו—שרוג—נחור—תרח—אברם—יצחק —יעקב, Gen. 10²⁵ 11¹⁸⁻²⁶ 21³ 25²⁶), and consequently the Israelites (cf. Gen. 32²⁸, Is. 27⁶, Nah. 2²). (*b*) Through the latter, יקטן, came the Arabians. Thirteen sons or races (cf. Gen. 10²⁵⁻³⁰, 1 Ch. 1¹⁹⁻²³) are attributed to Joktan. His descendants dwelt from Mesha to Sephar, 'the hill

Assyrian more than Hebrew preserved the simplicity of the vowels, but in the matter of consonants was more akin to Phoenician and Hebrew; Arabic preserved the greatest purity in both respects.

II

BABEL

The story of Babel (Gen. 11) looks like a symbolical representation of the earliest linguistic parting of the ways. Belief in the unity of the human race involves belief in one primeval language. By the nomadic movements and other circumstances attending the earliest human clans, slight differences of speech would arise. 'There are processes continually in operation which produce infinitesimal changes in all living languages.' There came a time when two great types of speech became clearly marked—Aryan and Semitic. The story of the 'confusion of tongues' may have behind it this great linguistic fact, which was not effected miraculously at Babel, but gradually through ages of which there is not one historical hint. The building of a tower may have initiated the building of the city—Babylon. By Jewish and early Christian writers, Nimrod is represented as taking a leading part in the building of Babel.[1]

The name 'Nimrod'[2] was perhaps at first an epithet to

country of the East.' משא in Assyr. inscrip. probably = *Mashu*, the Syro-Arabian desert; ספר probably = *Zafar*, the ancient capital of the Himyarites, the seaport of Hadramaut on the Indian Ocean. Perhaps the name Joktan is Sabaean, and represents the more ancient tribes of Arabia, and not the later, which were more closely related by origin and language to the Israelites. In the Arabic genealogies Joktan is identified with *Kaḥtan*, an ancient clan of south Arabia.

[1] Joseph. *Ant.* i. 4. 2; Cyril, *Julian*, i. p. 5; Augustine, *de Civ. Dei*, xvi. 4. The mythological character of this narrative is freely admitted, and similar stories are found in several quarters, whose origin cannot be traced. *Vide* Sayce, *Encycl. Brit.*,[9] *s.v.* 'Babel, Tower of'; Lüken, *Die Traditionen*, 318–322.

[2] נִמְרוֹד, lit. 'we will rebel.' Some have identified the name with *Nazimarattas* (14th cent. B.C.); Marattas is said to be the Kassite god of hunting. This would agree with the Biblical record, where Nimrod is said to be a son of Cush, if כוש = כש, which is the Babyl. *Kassu*; cf. Del. *Par.* 51, 72; Haupt, *Andover Review*, July 1884.

the earliest aggressive clans, which founded the states on the
Euphrates, which developed into the Babylonian Empire.
These founders of the historical Semitic nations of Babylonia
and Assyria were of a wild, warlike and lawless character.[1]
Their first centre was Babylon, the capital, just as Nineveh
was the first centre or capital of Assyria. From inscriptions
we learn that the real significance of ' Babel ' was not
' confusion,' but ' gate of god,' denoting that this was the
seat of the national deity, and the entrance to tribal re-
cognition.[2]

III

BABYLONIAN CAPTIVITY

The effect of Hebrew exile on the language of Palestine
was very great. It facilitated an Aramaic of a rather mixed
character as we shall see. There were three great captivities:
(a) Tiglath-Pileser (745–727) carried away northern Israel,
including Gilead, Galilee and all Naphtali (2 K. 15[29], Is. 9[1]);
also Ruben, Gad and the half tribe of Manasseh. These
were deported to the Assyrian regions of ' Halah, Habor,
Hara, and to the river of Gozen ' (1 Ch. 5[26]). In these
places some form of Aramaic, probably Chaldee, was spoken.
(b) Shalmaneser (727–722) took Samaria, and carried the
people away to Assyria ' and placed them in Halah, and in
Habor, on the river of Gozen, and in the cities of the Medes '
(2 K. 17[6]). These are apparently the same regions as those
mentioned above.[3] (c) Nebuchadrezzar (604–561) carried

---

[1] In Gen. 10[9], for Heb. צַיִד, Onk. has תַּקִּיף, perhaps ' arrogant.'

[2] The MT. connects בָּבֶל with בָּלַל, ' to confuse '; Aram. more easily
substitutes בַּלְבֵּל, so Onk. Gen. 11[9], cf. Olshausen, *Lehrbuch der heb.
Sprache*, 189a. Some make the word = بل باب, ' gate of Belus.'

Modern name *Hillah* or *Hela*, حِلَّة. There is still a mound *Bâbil*.

[3] Halah and Gozan were probably districts bordering on the river
Habor, a tributary of the Euphrates. ' Hara ' (1 Ch. 5[26]) seems to
correspond in some way with ' the cities of the Medes ' (2 K. 17[6]). It is
probable that הרא is a mutilated form of a longer phrase, such as הָרֵי מָדַי,
' mountains of Media,' or עָרֵי מָדַי, ' cities of Media.' (Cf. *Keilinschriftliche
Bibliothek*, etc., ii. p. 61).

away Judah to Babylon, 588 (2 K. 24, 25). The chief colony of exiles was at Tel-abib on the river Chebar (Ezek. 3[15]).[1] It is possible that the exiles were employed on the water-ways near the city of Babylon.[2] Here they would be brought into contact with the best vernacular Chaldee. The result of this contact will appear later in the character of the Judaean Aramaic.

The clans brought in to occupy the depleted province of Samaria were Babylonian subjects and spoke an Aramaic language. These were the Cuthites, Avvites, Sepharvites and Hamathites. The mixing of these clans with the remnant left in the country resulted in the community of Samaritans, who opposed the Judaeans and initiated their own religious cult, which had its centre on Mount Gerizim. The exact locality from which the invaders came from Babylonia is of no great importance. The point of significance is that they came from Semitic regions, speaking some form of Aramaic.[3] Some uncertainty attaches to the words Avva, עַוָּה, and Hamath, הֲמָת.[4] The former should perhaps be read עַזָּה = Gaza. We should then read: ' Where are the gods of Hamath, of Arpad, of Sepharvaim, of Hena and Azzah = Gaza ? ' That the language of this ancient city was Aramaic is incidentally suggested by the name of the local deity— *Marna*. This is evidently the same as מרנא,[5] ' our lord.' The earliest language of Gaza was perhaps similar to that of the Philistines when they took possession of Phoenicia.[6] By Hamath we must probably understand a royal city of the

---

[1] By a slight textual emendation כבר could be read חבור, ' Habor.'

[2] It now appears probable that ' the river Chebar ' is the same as *nāru kabaru*, a navigable canal mentioned in cuneiform documents of the time of Artaxerxes I. The word Chebar means ' great,' so that *nāru kabaru* = ' grand canal ' (*vide* Hilprecht's *Babyl. Exped. of the University of Penn.* ix. p. 50).

[3] Cuthah, כּוּתָה, is the *Kuta* of the cuneiform inscriptions, and is identified with *Tell-Ibrahim* in north-east Babylonia. In later Jewish writings, Josephus and the Talmud, the term Cuthites = Samaritans. (Cf. Winckler, *Gesch. Babyl. u. Ass.*) Sepharvaim, סְפַרְוַיִם, is no doubt Sippar in north Babylonia. Perhaps we should emend סְפַר מָיִם, ' Sippar on the stream.'

[4] Hamath, like Avva, may be wrongly inserted ; some scholars suggest כִּתִּים, ' Cyprus ' (cf. Cheyne, *Isaiah, Sac. Bks. OT.*).

[5] Nabataean form מראנא (CIS ii. 1. 201, 205).

[6] Cf. Calmet, *Dissertatio de origine et nominibus Philistaeorum.*

Hittites on the Orontes in Syria. That a Semitic influence early reached this province is fairly clear. The language, however, of the inscriptions found between Carchemish and Hamath is Hittite, and this has been pronounced to be of the Aryan type by Jensen. This scholar tried to show that the connexion between the Hittite and the Armenian was Aryan.[1] This is probably to be accepted, but the Hittite might be originally and fundamentally Aryan, though the proofs for a similar conclusion might fail in the case of the Armenian. The earliest portraits of Hittites (*circa* 1285 B.C.) have been considered by some to be Mongoloid. This conclusion is very precarious and rests upon very scanty evidence. The bearded figures on Hittite monuments, which are numerous, may with greater probability be regarded as of the Armenoid type. But from the ethnological point of view we are not entitled to pass with any degree of certainty to the linguistic. The Hittite characters bear a certain resemblance to Egyptian hieroglyphics, but this does not necessarily imply any basal connexion. Hieroglyph is at the foundation of Sumerian and Chinese, but we cannot trace any connecting link.[2]

IV

ARYAN BASIS OF HITTITE

One of the strongest evidences of the Aryan character of the Hittites is the fact that they worshipped the Aryan gods—Mithra, Varuna and the Heavenly Twins. Still it must be remembered that the form of some proper names in the Hittite inscriptions is apparently Semitic. At any rate they can · be best explained on the theory that they are Semitic. The Hittites of Hebron were Semitized at an early period, indeed the term Hittite in the Biblical traditions was sometimes a synonym for all the tribes of Canaan.[3] The Hittites of north Palestine and Syria were early intermixed with Semites

---

[1] *Hittiter und Armenier.*

[2] It is doubtful if any ancient writing was simply hieroglyphic—it was probably figurative, symbolical and phonetic in the same text. *Vide* Champollion, *Grammaire Egyptienne.* Cf. De Rouge, *Chrestomathie Egyptienne.*

[3] Jos. 1⁴: כֹּל אֶרֶץ הַחִתִּים.

and Egyptians.[1] The language of inter-communication became Semitic.[2] As early as 1500 B.C., Hittite art was indebted to Babylonian influence. In other words, Hittite artists were scarcely able to represent native ideas apart from Semitic models. It is now proved that the Hittite rulers of Cappadocia used the Babylonian (Semitic-Aramaic) language and script for diplomatic correspondence.

There is abundant evidence that Babylonian-Assyrian was the language of international documents in the East at the earliest historical period. It is now clear that the Hittites were acquainted with this language, at least it is evident that their officials were accustomed to prepare international covenants in this language. One of the oldest treaties of peace which has survived is that which was drawn up between Rameses II. of Egypt and Khetaser, king of the Hittites.[3] For some time this treaty was only known in an Egyptian translation. But among the later discovery of Hittite documents at Boghaz Keui is found this treaty with Rameses II. The title of Rameses as 'the mighty' in this tablet is suggestive of the Babylonian-Assyrian language. This title is not known to Egyptian convention, and as far as known at present it is not Hittite. The title in the contract tablet is, therefore, presumably due to a language different from the native languages of both the Egyptians and the Hittites, which was the medium of international correspondence. The Tell el-Amarna inscriptions show that this language was Babylonian-Assyrian. It is clear that 'the mighty' was a mode of address in Assyrian documents. Is it possible to refer the Biblical אל שדי to this source? In Assyrian *sadû* means 'high,' 'great'; and 'lord,' 'commander.'[4] The Israel-

---

[1] The ancient Hittite was gradually superseded by Semitic, in the same way as Hamitic Egyptian adopted multitudes of Semitic words in the course of its history. A similar process is going on in the Sudan at the present time. The old Hamitic dialect is dropping into oblivion before the advance of Arabic. Thus here, too, history repeats itself. *Vide* Thompson, *A Pilgrim's Scrip*, p. 225.

[2] Cf. Sayce, *The Hittites*; De Lantsheere, *De la Race et de la Langue des Hittites*.

[3] Cf. Müller, *Der Bündnis-vertrag Ramses II. und des Chetiterkönigs*, 1902.

[4] *Vide* Hommel, *Die altisraelitische Überlieferung*; Eng. trans. *Ancient Hebrew Tradition*, 1897.

ites came into contact with Babylonia-Assyria before, as well as during, the Captivity. This epithet, 'the mighty,' which was applied to an Assyrian presiding deity, might easily be taken over and appropriated by the Hebrews. The patriarchal *Yahveh* claims this title : 'The Lord appeared to Abram and said unto him אני אל שדי.' [1]

The later Hittite hieroglyphic inscriptions tend towards a more cursive form of the signs, and do not conform to such rules of writing as have been detected in the earlier Hittite inscriptions. There are certain apparent inaccuracies which are probably due to the writers' want of practice in the newer type of script. Even the Babylonian-Assyrian writing was already being superseded by a simpler alphabetic system, which was coming into common use. This newer every-day language, which may at once be termed 'Aramaic,' became the vernacular of Babylonia-Assyria long before Assyrian ceased to be the language of the government.[2]

NOTE ON אל-שדי

It is probably an error to suppose that the LXX word παντοκράτωρ was originally meant to translate אל-שדי. In Ex. 6³ this phrase is rendered θεὸς ὢν αὐτῶν ; in Gen. 17¹ and 35¹¹ merely ὁ θεός σου. In Gen. 49²⁵ the translation is ὁ θεὸς ὁ ἐμός ; in Job 6⁴ κύριος, ib. 8³· ¹³ ὁ κύριος ; but ib. 5¹⁷ παντοκράτωρ. In Ruth 1²⁰ the LXX has ὁ ἱκανός ; this is perhaps the truest equivalent of אל-שדי. This variety of translation shows that the phrase had no surviving meaning to the Greek scholars. On the other hand, παντοκράτωρ was probably introduced to render the Semitic יהוה צבאות. The form of the word was apparently based on the analogy of the astrological κοσμοκράτωρ. It primarily suggested that Yahveh was master of all evil powers (= malign constellations, the *caelestis exercitus* of the stars), which were generally believed in from the middle of the second cent. B.C. in the Hellenistic world. The κοσμοκράτωρες of astrology were vanity ; the

---

[1] Gen. 17¹. Though this passage is from P (Priests' Code), yet אל שדי is certainly pre-exilic (Gen. 49²⁵, Num. 24⁴· ¹⁶), but no satisfactory explanation has yet been given. The Rabbinic שׁ+די, 'who is sufficient,' is fanciful. Cf. Delitzsch, *Proleg. eines neuen hebr.-aram. Wörterbuchs zum AT.* 96 ; Hommel, *Ancient Hebr. Tradition*, 109 ff. *Vide* p. 184.

[2] Nöldeke, *Encycl. Bibl.*, *s.v.* 'Aram. Lang.'

παντοκράτωρ of the Jewish and Christian religions is 'Lord of hosts' and Judge over τὰ πάντα or τὸ πᾶν, the universe. Cf. reference to 'rulers' (ἀρχόντων) and 'powers' (ἐξουσίας) and 'world-rulers' of darkness (τοὺς κοσμοκράτορας τοῦ σκότους), 1 Cor. 2⁶⁻⁸, Eph. 6¹⁰⁻¹³. Note the use of Αὐτοκράτορος = 'Emperor,' in *Oxy. Pap.*, Nos. 255, 275, *al.*

V

THE SCRIPT

It has been shown ' that the language of the Assyrian and Babylonian empires, as handed down to us in this particular variety of cuneiform writing, was a member of the north Semitic group, closely connected with Phoenician and Hebrew, and only in a somewhat less degree with Aramaic.'[1] The Babylonian script in the time of Nebuchadrezzar for official purposes was probably similar to the earliest forms of Aramaic which have survived. But the dialect of Babylonia in the sixth cent. B.C. differed from the dialect in the third cent. When therefore it is said that the Aramaic of the Book of Daniel is the same as the language of Babylonia in the reign of Nebuchadrezzar there is an anachronism. It is quite evident from the inscriptions that the language of the Babylonians was Semitic, but differed in many particulars from S. Aramaic.[2] At the time of the Captivity the script of the Hebrews was akin to what we may call Samaritan, while that of Babylonia was akin to what we may call Aramaic. There was, however, some similarity between the earliest Aramaic character and the Samaritan script, both being derived from the Phoenician alphabetic forms.[3] The letter-forms of the *Assuan Papyri* (500–300) may suggest the character of the

---

[1] Wright, *Comp. Gram. Semit. Lang.*, p. 14.

[2] The use and form of the particles clearly indicate some of the differences between the Aram. 800–500 B.C. and the Bibl. Aram. The change of the older ז into the newer ד is quite noteworthy : thus די, זא, די=זנה, רא, דנה. In the *Assuan Papyri* די=רי rel. pron. and mark of the gen. *saepe* ; דנה=זנה (cf. זך, *iste*, C6, D8), A4, B7, C4, D11, *et al.*

[3] *Vide* Euting, in Chwolson's *Corpus Inscript. Heb.* Cf. Stade, *Lehrbuch der hebräischen Grammatik* (1879) ; Nöldeke, *Kurzgefasste Syrische Grammatik* (1898²), Eng. trans., 1904.

writing of the eastern section of N. Semitic at an earlier period.[1]

VI

PRE-SEMITIC—SUMERIAN

Recent discovery, however, takes us back to an earlier era. There was a Babylonian civilization before the inroads of Semitic hordes. For a long time we had no definite knowledge respecting the ' City-States ' into which ancient Babylonia was divided. It was thought that these archaic Communities were in many respects akin to the earliest historic Semitic clans. This raised the interesting problem concerning the rôle of the Sumerians. Were they essentially Semites ? Was their language a native non-Semitic speech, or a primitive form of Semitic ? The difficulty arose from two factors : (1) the earliest Sumerian inscriptions were thought to reveal traces of Semitic; (2) the earliest Semitic rulers employed the Sumerian system of writing. The problem is now solved, and it is known that the Semitic invasion superimposed itself upon the earlier Sumerian civilization. Sumerian played a great part in the ancient development of Babylonia, and it was used as a sacred language long after it ceased to be the vernacular. It was gradually superseded by Semitic from the time of the first Dynasty under the western Semitic kings. The interpretation of Sumerian signs has been made possible by their meaning in Semitic documents [2]

The pre-Semitic language of Babylonia was Sumerian. The ancient Sumerian inscriptions contain much interesting infor-

---

[1] If the writing on the wall (Dan. 5[25]) was Aramaic, written in Samaritan character, Daniel could easily read it, but the astrologers would be utterly puzzled by it. The words in Aram. (following the Assuan script) would appear something like this : 𐤀𐤀𐤀 𐤀𐤀𐤀 𐤀𐤀𐤀. The same in Samaritan character would look quite foreign : 𐤀𐤀𐤀 𐤀𐤀𐤀 𐤀𐤀𐤀. Both these types are clearly borrowed from the Phoen. 𐤀𐤀𐤀 𐤀𐤀𐤀 𐤀𐤀𐤀. The terms מנא תקל פרסם(ין) are prob. commercial=*number*, *weight*, *assessment(s)*, here treated as verbs.

[2] For interesting matter on the Sumerian lang. and lit., *vide* Langdon, *The Sumerian Epic of Paradise*, Philadelphia, 1915.

mation about the pre-Semitic occupation. Berosus and later Babylonian writers drew upon these early materials for some of their histories. A comparison of the Deluge story as found in the Sumerian inscriptions, with the later Babylonian epic of Gilgamesh, is most instructive both in the parallels and the divergences. It is now pretty clear that the Biblical account of the Creation and the Flood is to be traced back through Babylonian to Sumerian. In other words, the Genesis stories of the early history of the world were not primarily of Semitic origin. The Hebrews were acquainted with Babylonian legends long before the Exile, and some of their traditions may have been based directly on Sumerian sources. Sumerian Babylonian was probably indebted to Elamite enterprise, but Sumerian influence soon outstripped Elamite activity in all civilizing advancement. Sumerian was widely employed in the Euphrates-Tigris regions prior to the first Semitic incursions. That the Semitic Babylonians were preceded by a non-Semitic people speaking the Sumerian language is established by the tablets found at Nippur, one of the oldest cities of Babylonia.[1]

Thousands of inscribed tablets have been found within the Nippur mounds. They are written in Sumerian, the language spoken by the non-Semitic people whom the Semitic Babylonians conquered and displaced. It has been found that many of these tablets are grammatical, and were compiled by Semitic literati of the time of Hammurabi's dynasty to facilitate the study and knowledge of the ancient Sumerian speech. Since they comprise Semitic translations of Sumerian words and phrases, they are of great assistance to modern scholars in the study of the Sumerian language. These grammatical tablets are of special value in that they afford new information respecting the paradigms of the Sumerian pronouns, personal and demonstrative, and also the verbal forms. In some of the Nippur tablets containing the Sumerian Dynastic Lists, are found a few Semitic words and royal and proper names. These Semitic elements are not to be explained as reflections of a later date, but rather as Semitic infiltrations,

---

[1] Nippur or Niffer is 100 miles S.E. of Bagdad. Here *En-lil*, the Sumerian god, was worshipped in the great temple Ekur.

probably from Arabia.[1]   This point is interesting, and is an
early illustration of the way in which a later language in a
country may foreshadow itself upon an older tongue, which it
will eventually supersede.   Hence Aramaic elements in early
Hebrew, and Arabic in Aramaic.

The structure of the Sumerian language was agglutinative,
and with justice has been compared with Turkish, Chinese and
other Mongol languages, apparently indigenous to the high
plateau of central Asia.   At one period the Sumerian language
must have been widely spread, and its hieroglyphics must have
been among the earliest form of writing.[2]   This type of script
must have reached the American continent in very remote
times.   American archaeologists are investigating a series of
writings on the rocks of Round Valley, California.   It is concluded that these writings are not the work of the Indians,
and are believed to antedate all aboriginal traditions.   The
records have not yet been deciphered, but the characters are
said to resemble the hieroglyphics of ancient Egypt.   Since
there is a basal likeness between the early Egyptian script
and the Sumerian hieroglyphs, is it possible to connect in any
way these rock-writings of California with the ancient Sumerian
civilization ?   This type of script is certainly among the earliest
forms of written language known, and was far more widely
spread than has hitherto been supposed.

VII

PROCESS OF BABYLONIAN WRITING

Though Babylonia was so powerful and played so great a
part in history, yet its civilization contributed very little to
the art, science and literature of the world.   Its mud, baked
into dull brown bricks, did not lend itself to ornamentation and
architecture.   Its great use, however, was as a writing material,
and through this means we get hints of a momentous history.

---

[1] *Vide* Poebel, *Hist. Texts* and *Hist. and Gram. Texts* (Univ. of Penns.
Mus. Publ., Bab. Sect., vol. iv. No. 1, and vol. v.), Philadelphia, 1914.
[2] Cf. King and Hall, *Egypt and Western Asia in the light of Recent
Discoveries* ; Rogers, *History of Babylonia and Assyria* ; King, *Legends of
Babylon and Egypt in Relation to Hebrew Tradition*, 1918.

The earliest writings in Babylonia were scratched on the brick-surface by the sharp point of some instrument. These were picture-signs, which in the first instance represented objects, then sounds, and finally syllables. The scratching process was followed by impressing marks on the brick-shaped mud while it was still soft. These marks, as we have seen, were wedge-shaped, and this was the beginning of the cuneiform writing, which obtained for a long time in Babylonia-Assyria, and extended into the Persian era. With the introduction of impressed writing came the abbreviation of the picture-signs, which added to both exactness and celerity. The first scratched writing was arranged in perpendicular columns; the cuneiform was usually impressed in horizontal lines. This type of script was the normal form of correspondence between Babylonia and Egypt and the Syrian provinces as early as the eighteenth dynasty, *circa* 1400 B.C., as the Tell el-Amarna tablets of Upper Egypt prove. There was a much earlier cuneiform writing employed by the Sumerian population of Babylonia, as the Telloh tablets bear witness. This probably takes us back to *circa* 4000 B.C., and the inscriptions of Sargon I. cannot be more than two hundred and fifty years later. But the idiom of the old Sumerian language was non-Semitic. When did the dialect of Babylonia become Semitic?

Of the Semitic migrations something will be said in due course. It is remarkable that the earliest Semitic invaders succeeded in imposing their language on their new subjects in Babylonia. We know very little about the history of the Euphrates regions until the great 'Canaanite' migration, which initiated the 'Chaldee' regime in Babylonia.[1] In the inscriptions of Sennacherib the *Kaldû* are distinguished from the Arabs on the one hand, and from the Aramaeans on the other. But, as will be seen later, the founders of the 'Kassites' were of Semitic origin. They formed part of the great Semitic migration from Arabia, which branched off into

---

[1] In Assyr. inscrip. *mât Kaldû*, 'the land of the Chaldaeans,' was restricted to the country between the rivers, and consequently narrower than Babylonia, which included Mesopotamia. The *Kaldû*, or *Kašdû*, prob. = 'Kassites,' were the precursors of the 'Chaldaens' in Babylonia. These were perhaps a priestly caste: ὡς λέγουσι οἱ Χαλδαῖοι, ἐόντες ἱρέες τούτου τοῦ θεοῦ (Herod. i. 181 ; cf. 183.)

Syria, including Palestine; into Egypt, and established the
Hyksos dynasty; into the country beyond the Euphrates,
and founded the 'Kassite' or First Babylonian dynasty.
The language thus introduced into Babylonia was the
'Chaldee' cuneiform, which in grammar and vocabulary was
practically the same as Assyrian. The next wave of Semites,
the 'Aramaean,' a thousand years later, found fairly congenial
soil in the partly Semitized country between the rivers. With
their more advanced language, they had little difficulty in
widening the scope of the earlier dialect, and of developing
the Chaldee Semitic into the Babylonian Aramaic. This
latter was the common idiom in Babylonia at the time of the
Persian conquest.[1]

Until *circa* 4000 B.C., Sumerian was the only language
of the civilized states. From about this period the Semites
began to conquer and impress their influence upon the regions
of central west Asia. For a long time the old Sumerian
was accompanied by a Semitic translation, which has greatly
aided the decipherment of the older documents. The
Sumerian script was pictorial, after the manner of Egyptian
hieroglyphs. Curved lines could be made on papyrus and
parchment, but on clay it was simpler to impress plain
or straight lines. Something of the ancient pictorial character of the signs is preserved in the early cuneiform.
For instance, the sign for a 'fish,'   retains some
resemblance to a fish. To the Sumerians the signs were
always rather pictures of objects than symbols of sound.
This was entirely altered by the Semites: (1) they studied
the sound values of the signs; (2) they did not follow
the Sumerian vertical method of writing, but impressed
the signs along a horizontal line; (3) thus the old vertical
symbols were placed on their sides, the position of the

---

[1] In addition to the works already mentioned, the following among
the earlier and more modern literature may be named : Oppert, *Histoire
des Empires de Chaldée et d'Assyrie* (1865) ; Rawlinson, *Cuneiform
Inscrip. of W. Asia* (1857–84) ; Sayce, *Fresh Light from the Ancient
Monuments* (1885), and *Hibbert Lectures* (1855) ; Radau, *Early Babyl.
Hist.* (1900) ; Johns, *Babyl. and Assyr. Laws*, etc. (1904) ; Delitzsch, *Assyr.
Handwörterbuch* (1894–96).

signs being of no importance, since only their sound value counted.[1]

VIII

DEBT OF JUDAISM TO BABYLONIA

The debt of Judaism to Babylonian cuneiform writings is not yet fully realized. It has been shown that some institutions, at one time regarded as distinctly 'Jewish,' are really Babylonian. The scheme of the Mosaic legislation is proved to be largely indebted to the 'Code of Hammurabi.' The plaintive and penitential Psalms were not only composed during the Exile, but were to some extent imitations of similar Babylonian productions. The extent to which the Biblical historians were dependent on Babylonian civilization, history and literature, implies that they must have understood and studied the cuneiform documents. The chronological calculations, so characteristic of the authors of the Book of Kings, were undoubtedly prepared by the assistance of Babylonian records. The Jewish writers searched the cuneiform archives for information respecting their own land and people. Thus the Jews in exile not only acquired a new vernacular Aramaic, but they became more or less acquainted with the Babylonian cuneiform literature. This fact is becoming recognized by Biblical scholars, who are convinced that not the Jewish religion only, but practically the whole traditional civil and moral cult of Judaism, was inspired and elaborated during the Exile on the model of Babylonian worship and institutions.

NOTE ON אלהים

Is there any connexion between the Hebrew אלהים and the Sumero-Babylonian *iláni*? Both terms may be derivatives from the

---

[1] This can be seen in the early sign for 'man'   , compared with the later   , and in the early sign for 'reed,'   , compared with the later   .

same original, or the former may be the Semitized form of the latter. The Hebrew אֵל is the same as the Phoenician אל; sometimes אֵלֹן. The Assyrian equivalent is *ilu* (*vide* Delitzsch, *Assyrisches Wörterbuch.* Cf. Assyr. Cylinder seal, CIS ii. 77). Note the survival of the old Phoenician form in the Palmyrene votive inscription, אלן (Vog. 93). The earlier Aramaic was אלהן (CIS ii. 113, 145c. 7). In later Aramaic we should expect אלהיא (pl. emp. Jer. 10[11]). *Ilâni* is plural, 'the gods,' and in the Sumerian pantheon the assembled gods are apparently regarded as jointly concerned in the production of the universe. This is suggestively like the opening of Genesis, בראשית . . . ברא אלהים. The juxtaposition of the two names, *Anu-Enlil*, in the Nippur tablets strikingly suggests the Hebrew combination, *Yahveh-Elohim.* The former pair, however, did not come to be identified and unified as was the case with the latter. It is remarkable that in the Sumerian tablets, verbs and suffixes in the singular are seemingly employed when the reference is to *Anu-Enlil.* So in Hebrew we find the singular verbal construction with *Elohim* and with *Yahveh-Elohim* (*e.g.* Gen. 1[1], Ezek. 36[23] 39[5], Hos. 12[5]).

It is tempting to look for some connexion between the Sumerian *ilâni* and the Hebrew אני־אל (*e.g.* Is. 45[22]), and between the name of the god *Anu* and the simple pronoun אני (or אנכי, Yahveh's name to Israel, Ex. 3[13]). But for this speculation there is no warrant at present. Anu was the chief god of the Sumerians, he always heads the list in the pantheon. To him is ascribed the creation of heaven; he is described as 'the father of gods.' Throughout the Sumerian Deluge epic Anu and Enlil are the ultimate and supreme rulers of both deities and men. In concluding this note two things may be stated: (1) In tracing any connexion between Sumero-Babylonian and Hebrew, it should never be forgotten that the Babylonian pantheon and myth cycle were transformed by the Semitic editors of Genesis into a lofty monotheism. The elevated theology, the historical pragmatism, and the ethical depuration of Genesis reflect a much later stage in spiritual evolution. (2) The Genesis stories stand apart from the other Old Testament Scriptures, and scarcely come into the historical field in the ordinary sense of the term. These Genesis records are separated by four hundred years from the beginning of national history contained in Exodus.[1]

The attempt to get the derivation of Hebrew names from Sumerian or Babylonian sources is sometimes over-pressed. This is apparent in

---

[1] *Vide* the excellent commentaries on the Book of Genesis by Skinner, Ryle and Driver.

the case of the parallel epics of the Creation and the Flood.   From the available data it is difficult to see how definite conclusions can be advanced.   Wonderful ingenuity has been displayed by some scholars in the endeavour to find a parallel between the antediluvian kings of Berosus and the Hebrew names in the early chapters of the Book of Genesis.   The suggested equation between the pairs of proper terms is often quite fanciful, and sometimes demonstrably untenable.[1]   One is not entitled to be dogmatic in this field at present, but we should frankly face the possibility 'that the Hebrew parallels to Sumerian and Babylonian traditions are here confined to chronological structure and general contents, and do not extend to Hebrew renderings of Babylonian names.'

B.—PERSIAN PERIOD

I

SEMITIC AND INDO-EUROPEAN

The Semitic languages, even those most distant one from another, do not differ so widely as the members of the Indo-European group.   They all possess a clearly recognizable type of grammatical structure, and a considerable stock of words common to all of them.   The problem of defining the relation of the Semitic languages to the Iranian[2] is exceedingly difficult, because we do not know very clearly the date, place and circumstance of their origin.   To argue from the vocabulary, grammar, idiom and geographical distribution of the different nations is a most precarious method, and can only justify tentative conclusions.   The vocabulary and structure of a language may change very rapidly by migration into new provinces, contact with other languages, and intermixture of foreign ideas and customs.   It must not be assumed that the

[1] For some time scholars were content with the equation Ἀμμένων of Berosus = *Ummânu*, 'workman,' of Bab.   But now the Sum. tablets make it more prob. that Ἀμμένων = Sum. *Enmenunna*.   This makes it very doubtful whether Ἀμήλων = *amêlu*, 'man,' as gen. supposed.   The equation Ἄλωρος = *Aruru*, is far-fetched.   There is more prob. for Δάωνος ποιμήν = '*Etana*, a shepherd.'   From King, *Legends of Babyl. and Egypt in rel. to Heb. Trad.*, pp. 33, 34, 38.

[2] Zend, *Airyana* = land of the Aryans.   Cf. Herod. vii. 62.

earliest contact of different eastern people was synchronous with the earliest historical records. Iranians and Semites came into touch long before the rise of the Medo-Persian empire. This is proved by the presence of the names of Iranian gods and kings in Babylonian-Assyrian annals. Some Medo-Persian names, such as Teispes and Hystaspes,[1] are found in Babylonian and Assyrian inscriptions far earlier than we hear of Medes and Persians pressing into these regions.[2] When, therefore, we find the Persians writing in a cuneiform type, borrowed from the Babylonian-Assyrian civilization, it will be well to remember this period of unrecorded contact. The production of the simpler Persian alphabet from the Babylonian was not a sudden departure in historical times, but the result of long contact, sometimes friendly and sometimes antagonistic, during which the Iranians practically invented a new alphabet out of the complex Babylonian. It is doubtful if there ever was anything like a literature in this Medo-Persian language. The probability is that the traditions in verse, referred to by Pliny,[3] were handed down orally. It is quite uncertain whether there were any considerable writings in any idiom or script earlier than those of the Avesta. At any rate the language of international diplomacy during the Persian period, as we shall see, was not old Persian, but some form of Aramaic.

II

PRECURSORS OF OLD PERSIAN

Of the Sumero-Akkadian language no very clear knowledge is available. Sumerian differed from Akkadian only in its phonetic characteristics. There were twenty-two letters, or more precisely, eighteen consonants and four vowels. This language constituted one of the earliest forms of ideographic writing.[4] The Assyro-Babylonian alphabet is the same as the

---

[1] In Assyr. *Teušpa* and *Vištašpa*.

[2] So *Indra* and *Varuna* appear in the Boghaz-Keui inscrip. long before we have any history of the kingdom of the Ḫatti (Hittites).

[3] *Hist. Nat.* xxx. 1.

[4] *Vide* Brünnow, *Classified List of Cuneiform Ideographs*, 1889; *Indices*, 1897.

Sumero-Akkadian, but the phonology of the letters is more settled in the former. The accent, as in Italian, is almost invariably on the penultimate; when, however, the penultimate has a weak vowel the accent falls back on the antepenultimate. The Assyro-Babylonian, though written with syllabic signs, shows many of the phenomena exhibited by the other Semitic languages. This is due in reality to a common basal triliteralism. By those who spoke the language all words were considered as derived from a theme or root composed of three letters, usually consonants. These themes pictured to the speaker an abstract idea, and to give these themes worth and vitality vowels were added. All verbal forms were thus obtained by different vocalizations. Originally in this language, as in some other ancient dialects, the cases were distinguished by the use of mimation.[1] The Vannic language belongs to this group. The ancient city of Van is said to have been one of the residences of Semiramis.[2] There are at the present time many antiquities and cuneiform inscriptions in the neighbourhood. The Vannic syllabary was derived from Nineveh, and its alphabet is the same as in Akkadian and Assyrian. Indeed, Vannic was largely influenced by Assyrian, and the order of words in the sentence is practically the same. The Medic language shows some differences from Akkadian and Assyrian, indicating some development on the one hand, and some retrogression on the other. This language had two forms or tendencies, thus:

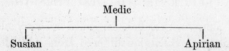

Susian was the language of the inscriptions of the old Elamite kings, and Apirian was the language of the inscriptions of Mal-Amir; both may be regarded as merely dialects of Medic. On the whole, Susian and Apirian are more archaic than

---

[1] *E.g.* Subjective *um*, Dependent *im*, Objective *am*. But these forms did not survive, and the final *m* was supplanted by a simple aspirate (=Sem. *st. emph.*), *Kaspa'* for *Kaspam*, 'the money.'

[2] One of two queens of Babylon; Herodotus, bk. i. 184.

Medic, and never became fixed as literary tongues. Medic was more systematized, a fact probably due to its use in the Court of the successors of Cyaxares. The old Persian [1] shows a still wider divergence from the other languages of the cuneiform inscriptions. It has many liknesses, especially in the verb-formations, to Sanscrit. Indeed it would be almost impossible to understand many of its constructions if we had not the clues and corresponding forms in Sanscrit and Zend. The order of words in all these old cuneiform languages is more or less the same, viz., subject—indirect object—direct object—complement—verb. There are, of course, many exigences of sentence-formation which require some deviation from this general rule. The language of Persia can be traced through several definite stages between 1200 B.C. and 1000 A.D., that is, from the old Bactrian of the Zend-Avesta to the modern form in the poems of Firdausi. Its early indebtedness to Assyro-Babylonian is considered below.[2]

III

NOTES OF HISTORY

The founder of the Persian empire was Cyrus.[3] He conquered Astyages, king of Media, 550 ; Croesus, king of Lydia, 545 ; Belshazzar, king of Babylon, 539 : and Cambyses, son and successor of Cyrus, conquered Amasis, king of Egypt, 527. With the conquest of Babylonia, Palestine came under Persian rule. Cyrus gave permission to the Hebrew captives to return to their native country and rebuild their temples.[4] Comparatively few availed themselves of this liberty. The greater part of the exiles preferred to remain in the lands where many of them had acquired considerable possessions. Here they established their religion, but not their sacrificial ritual ; they elected Exiliarchs, and built up schools of

---

[1] The home of the old Persians was *Iran*=Aryan (cf. Gk. Ariané).

[2] A brief but suggestive outline of the old Cuneif. lang. is that of Bertin, *Languages of the Cuneiform Inscriptions*, 1888.

[3] *Vide* Herod. i. 113 f., v. 11 ; Strabo, xv. 729. Cf. Schubert, *Herodot. Darstellung der Cyrussage*, 60 ff.

[4] *Keilinschriftliche Bibliothek*, iii. 2, 121 ff.

learning. Out of these schools grew the Babylonian Talmud.[1]

IV

RULING CLASSES

The list given in Ezra (4[7-9]) is not strictly historical, but quite suggestive. The Samaritans instigated a complaint against the Judaeans in connexion with the rebuilding of the Temple. This complaint was embodied in an official letter which was sent to Artaxerxes I., king of Persia. The authors of the letter were Rehum, the chancellor ; Shimshai, the scribe, with Bishlam, Mithredath and Tabeel, their secretaries. These officials had the support of certain Samaritan societies [2]—the so-called Dinaites, Apharsathchites, Tarpelites, Apharsites, Archevites, Babylonians, Shushanchites, Dehaites and Elamites. These are not to be regarded as ethnic terms, though apparently so understood by the writer of Ezra. They are rather to be considered as Samaritans, mostly of ultra-Palestinian origin, who formed certain clubs or colonies under the denomination of that part of the Babylonian empire from which they originally came. Perhaps they may be regarded as, in a sense, functionaries within the system of Persian government in Palestine. These titles may even stand for such ideas as 'judge,' 'magistrate,' 'scribe,' 'consul,' and other representative persons.[3]

[1] On this subject generally *vide* Kosters, *Het Herstel van Israel in het Perzische Tijdvak*, 1893 ; Germ. trans. *Die Wiederherstellung Israels*, 1895.

[2] Aram. כְּנָת, כנתא. Cf. Lidzbarski, *Nordsemitische Inschriften*, 298 ; Cook, *Gloss. Aram. Inscript.* 65. Syr. (Christ. Pal.) ܟܢܬ, 'associate.' Cf. Schwally, *Idioticon d. Christl. Paläst. Aram.* 46.

[3] Dinaites. Perhaps to be read דִּינָיֵא, 'judges,' the Aram. form of the old Persian *databhar* ; *vide* Meyer, *Die Entstehung des Judenthums*, 39 ; Marquart, *Fundamente israelitischer u. jüdischer Geschichte*, 64. The term is possibly derived from *Deinaver*, a Median city, or more probably from *Din-Sharru*, near Susa.

Apharsathchites. The term is probably to be understood as the title of certain officials under Darius, hence of Persian origin (Ezra 5[6]) ; compare old Persian *aparathraka*, 'lesser rulers,' 'magistrates.' *Vide* Hoffmann, *Zeitschrift für Assyriologie u. verwandte Gebiete*, ii. 54 ; Marti, *Grammatik d. biblisch-Aramäischen Sprache*, Glossary, 53.

Tarpelites. The word may represent מְפָרְיָא, the Aram. form of the

V

OFFICIAL LANGUAGE

The interesting fact is that the letter to Artaxerxes and his reply are both in Aramaic. The preference for Aramaic as an international language was probably initiated under the Assyrian empire, in which the great majority of people spoke Aramaic. This explains why it was so readily taken for granted that an Assyrian official could speak Aramaic, and why the leaders of Judaea appear to have acquired a knowledge of the language as early as 600 B.C. (cf. 2 K. 18[26] = Is. 36[11]). The Semitic inscriptions show that Aramaic had gained a footing in Arabia *before* the Persian period.[1] The

Assyr. *Dup-sarru*, 'table-writers,' hence 'scribes.' Cf. Andreas in *Marti's Aram. Gram.* 64 ; for other views *vide* Hoffmann, *l.c.* 55 ; Scheftelowitz, *Arisches im AT.* 86.

Apharsites. Perhaps intended for סָפְרַיָּא, 'recorders.' Some identify with אֲפַרְסַתְכָיֵא, *supra*, cf. Andreas, *l.c.* 53 ; others would translate 'Persians,' cf. Hoffmann, *l.c.*; Meyer, *l.c.* 38 ; Rödiger, *Additions to Gesenius Thesaurus Linguae Hebraeae*, 107. But we prefer סָפְרַיָּא(א), 'secretaries' (the א being dittogr. of preceding word), so Marquart, *l.c.*

Archevites. Not 'the people of Erech,' as Meyer, *l.c.* 40. The text is rather to be emended כּוּתָיֵא דִּי, 'who are Cuthaeans' (cf. 2 K. 17[24]), so Marquart, *l.c.* The reference is then to the preceding term, 'Apharsites who are Cuthaeans' (*i.e.* originally from Cutha, N.E. Babylonia). Or the relative might refer to all the parties previously named.

Babylonians. The presence of the term here is curious, inasmuch as many of the settlers in Samaria were of Babylonian origin. The reference may be to a party of Babylonian immigrants who kept apart from the native population of Samaria. Or possibly some official Babylonians are meant, who held a diplomatic position under the Persian government. To modernize the idea we might use the word 'consuls.'

Shushanchites. Some scholars think that the word has grown out of *Cushanaye*, 'Cushanites' (so Cheyne, *Critica Biblica*). But with greater probability the term has been identified with *Shushinak*, the name of the capital of Susiana on the Elamite inscriptions. Cf. Delitzsch, *Wo lag das Paradies?* 327 ; Calwer, *Bibl. Lex.* 876. If we are to think of Shushanites, we may have in the term a reference to representatives from the royal Persian city.

Dehaites. The form is probably a mistake for the pro-nominal compound דְּהוּא (not unlike דהיא of the text), 'which is.' The next term עֵלְמָיֵא, therefore, will stand in opposition to the preceding term and will be explanatory of it : 'Shushanites, that is, Elamites.' Cf. Hoffmann, *l.c.* 54 ; Marquart, *l.c.* 64 ; Meyer, *l.c.* 36.

[1] CIS², Nos. 113-121.

Aramaic monuments which come within the Persian period 'exhibit a language which is almost absolutely uniform.'[1] The Egyptian Aramaic inscriptions of the Persian period are as early as 482 B.C.[2] These inscriptions show Hebrew or perhaps Phoenician influence, which must be remembered when Egyptian Aramaic is studied as a source of the Palestinian vernacular. It is easily explained by the fact that in Egypt, besides a great many Aramaeans, there were many Jews and Phoenicians. The great mass of the Babylonian army was composed of Aramaeans (Jer. 35[11]), and the conflict with Egypt would result in the settlement of many Aramaeans in that land.[3]

The letter of the officials in Samaria to Artaxerxes I. 'was written in the Syrian *character*, and set forth in the Syrian *tongue*' (Ezra 4[7] RV.). The language was Aramaic, the common medium of international diplomacy. But the exact meaning of the passage is not clear.[4] The dialect in which the letters and edicts were written was the western or Palestinian Aramaic.[5] But what is meant by 'in the Syriac character'? We must understand this to refer to the kind of writing, the alphabet forms, that which we may call the *script*. The letters proceeding from Samaria, we might suppose, would be more naturally written in Samaritan (properly Hebrew) characters. The implication is that the Jewish community still employed the earlier Hebrew script. But these communications were written in the Babylonian Aramaic character, which later became the regular form of almost all Jewish writing. It is also suggestive that the replies of the Persian kings were found in the same kind of script. That the decrees kept in the royal archives at Babylon should be written in Aramaic characters is what we

---

[1] Nöldeke, *Encyl. Bibl.*, *s.v.* 'Aram. Lang.' col. 281.

[2] CIS², No. 122.

[3] Cf. Nöldeke, 'Die Namen der Aram. Nation und Sprache,' in *ZDMG*²⁵ 113 ff.

[4] The text is: וּכְתָב הַנִּשְׁתְּוָן כָּתוּב אֲרָמִית וּמְתֻרְגָּם אֲרָמִית. LXX: ἔγραψεν ὁ φορολόγος γραφὴν Συριστὶ καὶ ἡρμηνευμένην. Vulg.: Scripta erat Syriace, et legebatur sermone Syro.

[5] Driver, *Lit. OT.*² 516. On the genuineness of the Decrees of Artaxerxes, *vide* Stade, *Geschichte d. Volkes Israel*, ii. 153.

should expect.   The use of Samaritan letter-forms in Babylonia would be foreign and unintelligible.[1]   The period under discussion may mark the passing of the Samaritan letter-forms and the introduction of the Aramaic script into Palestine.

It is generally admitted that the Persian government issued its edicts to western Asia in Aramaic.   What then is the meaning of אֲרָמִית וּמְתֻרְגָּם ?   It might be taken to mean that the language was not Aramaic, but some other tongue, for example the Medo-Persian, used as the channel of diplomatic communication, and that this language was written in Aramaic letters, accompanied with an Aramaic translation.[2]   The word תֻּרְגַּם means 'translation,' 'interpretation,' 'opinion';[3] here it probably means that the sense was expressed in Aramaic.   The explanation already given, however, is to be preferred.   The official *communiqué* was not only in Aramaic letters, but also in the Aramaic language.

VI

BEHISTUN INSCRIPTION

This inscription is very interesting, and has attracted the attention of scholars for many years.   The history of its discovery and decipherment need not concern us here. It is introduced in this place to illustrate and support some opinions already expressed.   The few Persian inscriptions that have come to light seem to be, for the greater part, of royal origin and monographs of kingly exploits.   The famous inscription at Behistun is *par excellence* a monument of this order.   About 500 B.C. Darius caused his deeds to be inscribed on rock, so that men might know his prowess and extol his greatness for all time.   The long inscription is written on a sheer rock-face, and is one of the

---

[1] *Vide* reference to handwriting on the wall, p. 36.

[2] *E.g.* Tautes toi geneēs te kai aimatos euchomai einai, 'Of a truth both from this race and blood do I boast that I am,' is Greek in English letters with an Eng. trans.   For the opinion of a Medo-Persian lang., cf. Bleek, *Introd. OT.* 45-48; Hengstenberg, *Beiträge z. Einleit. ins Alte Test.* i. 310.

[3] Vide *Megillah*, fol. 3, col. 1.   Cf. Walker, *Hast. BD, s.v.* 'Targum.'

finest types of cuneiform engraving known. Above the inscription is a sculptured picture of the king, five feet and eight inches in height. Behind the king are two satraps, and before him nine captives bound together by the neck. Above all is the sun-god, the winged disk of Auramazda,[1] with lightning playing about him. The inscription is in three languages, Persian, Susian, Babylonian. An idea of the whole may be gained when it is stated that the Persian alone is in five columns, each twelve feet high. It contains the characteristic benediction for those who observe the monument and keep it intact. Our concern, however, is with the languages in which the inscription is written.

1. *Persian.*—The old Persians borrowed the idea of the wedge from the Babylonians or Assyrians, but they composed an independent alphabet, which was far simpler than that of Babylonia.[2] The Persians must have bestowed great care on the production and use of this new form of alphabetic writing, which seems to have been chiefly employed for royal documents and diplomatic annals. The official regulations for satraps and Iranian governors were presumably prepared in this language and script. But it is probable that translations into Aramaic, or even Greek, were made for practical service, especially in the case of the rulers in the west Asian and Egyptian provinces.

2. *Susian.*—It is not quite clear whether this term differed in meaning from 'Median,' which is a more familiar word. In the first place, it is probable that this language was rather younger than the old Persian, and was already superseding it in many parts of the Medo-Persian empire.

---

[1] The *Auramazda* of the inscrip. is the same as the *Ahura Mazda* of the Avesta. The younger Achaemenids were Mazda worshippers; Mazdaism is allied with Zarathustrianism.

[2] All that the Persians borrowed from the Babyl. were the three forms of the wedge : $\vert$, $\vdash$ and $\langle$; the written lang. was made up by a manipulation of these three forms. The Pers. rather complicated the Babyl. vowels, *a, i, u* ; for instead of 𝗬, 𝖤𝖤, and $\langle$ they wrote ⟋⟍, ⟋⟍, and ⟨⟋⟍. Cf. Bab. 𝖷 𝖤𝖨𝖨 𝖤 ; Pers. ⟨| ⟨𝗬 ⊢⟨⟨ ⟨𝗬 'Cyrus.'   *Kur - ra - ash*   *K - u - r - u*

Susian was not the language of the old rulers, who were Aryans, but was the dialect of the conquered territory.[1]   This would be natural if, as is probable, the native population considerably outnumbered the emigrant settlers.   This language should be termed 'Susian,' rather than 'Median,' because it was the dialect of the province in which the Persian kings had their chief palace—'Shushan the castle.'[2] If we are right in connecting the 'Susanchites' with Susan, then this idiom was brought into Samaria by the importations under Osnappar. This factor possibly contributed something to the peculiar and mixed dialect of the Samaritans.

3. *Babylonian.*—The script, as in the other cases, is cuneiform, but the idiom is different. The current language of Babylonia at the time was early Syriac or rather Chaldee. There is no question about its being an Aramaic dialect, but there may be a difference of opinion respecting the group of dialects to which it belongs. It may be safely said that it does not belong to the south Semitic, which includes Arabic, Himyaritic and Ethiopic. We do not think, moreover, that it can be classed with the west Aramaic section of the north Semitic branch, which includes Palmyrene, Egyptian Aramaic and Palestinian Aramaic. From an analysis of its construction and a comparison of its forms with other Aramaic dialects, we prefer to place it with the east Aramaic section of the north Semitic branch, and therefore in the same category as Syriac, Nabataean and Mandaean, with, of course, many local differences.[3] In this inscription, therefore, we have an illustration of the dialect prevalent throughout the northeast regions of western Asia at the beginning of the Persian period. Slightly variant idioms of Aramaic became common in other parts of the empire.

---

[1] In the Assyr. inscrip. the region is termed *Šušan*, and this must be the same as *Šušin* or *Šušun* of the Susian inscrip. This suggests that the difference between Assyr. and Susian was to some extent a matter of vowel-sounds.

[2] So prob. שׁוּשַׁן הַבִּירָה should be rendered (Est. 1[5]). Heb. בירה = Aram. בירתא (Ezra 6[2]), Nab. *ib.* (CIS ii. 164[3]); Assyr. *birtu.*

[3] The above conclusion is based on certain data made possible to the present writer through the courtesy of the Director of the Dept. of Egypt. and Assyr. Antiquities, British Museum.

VII

CYLINDER SEAL OF DARIUS

Any language may be written in cuneiform, and in some instances more than one language is found on the same cuneiform inscription. This is the case with the Cylinder seal of Darius (*c.* 521–486 B.C.), on which the phrase: 'I am Darius the king,' is written in Persian, Median and Babylonian (Aramaic).[1] The first line (*vide infra*) is old Persian, which was the royal language and conserved in the Court and priestly circles. The second line is in Median, perhaps the national language of the predecessors of Darius. Media shared the honour of sovereignty with Persia, and the phrases: 'the Medes and Persians,' 'Media and Persia' (even after the Persians gained the ascendancy, Est. 10²), are reminiscent of the original supremacy of Media. The third line is in Babylonian (Aramaic), which was the common language of international communication.

NOTES ON THE CYLINDER SEAL OF DARIUS

(1) The king referred to is probably Darius, son of Hystaspes, the real founder of the Persian empire. He had his great exploits recorded on the trilingual inscription at Behistun. (2) The word *ḥašayaṭaiya* is old Persian, and could mean either 'king' or 'great.' Phraortes, who lead a revolt in Media (*vide* Herod. i. 102), called himself *ḥašayaṭaiya* (or *Khashathrita*), which may mean the 'royal one (βασιλικός), or the mighty one' (ἰσχυρός). (3) The Median

inscription is in (what is sometimes called) the Susian dialect. The form *Tariyamauš* is Susian, and probably also the word *sunkik* (or *zunkuk*); compare the Susian: *anin šušinak gik sunkik anzan,* 'the Susian king, powerful ruler of Anzan' (Bertin, *Lang. of Cuneif. Inscrip.* p. 94). (4) The forms in the third line are Babylonian-Aramaic, but rare in Aramaic inscriptions. The lengthened personal pronoun, אנכי, is found in a Zenjirli inscription : ואנכי ברכב, 'And I (= as for me) Bar-rekub' (*Panammu*, l. 19). For שר רבא compare the Palmyrene inscription : שמש שרן רבא, 'Shemesh our great prince' (Vogüé, 135). In Babylonian *šar* is the *status constructus,* while *šarru* is the *status subjunctus.*

VIII

PERSIAN CUNEIFORM AN INVENTION

It will be well to re-emphasize the fact that the Persian cuneiform script was a pure invention to meet the ambitious claims of Darius. It was adapted from the Babylonian through the Elamite, in order to carve the deeds of the Persian kings. The new language differed grammatically from the older linguistic structure of the Sumerians, as later from that of the Semites. It could not therefore be written with the old hieroglyphic and syllabic script. It was, compared with Babylonian and Sumerian, a simplified syllabic writing, which served a specific purpose, but which had no general use. Apart from the few Persian inscriptions, this language never had a written development. The Persians, when they did not employ the Babylonian language and cuneiform script, commonly used the Aramaic as the language of imperial and commercial intercourse. The new Persian cuneiform script introduced by Darius to extol his exploits above those of his predecessors, had no history and contributed nothing to literary and general progress. Even the Avesta, the sacred book of the Ahuramazda religion, though found in a dialect allied with that of the old Persian inscriptions, was written in a literal alphabet adapted from the more volatile Aramaic, which was the *Lingua Franca* of the East during the Persian period.

Babylonia was more or less Semitized long before the Persian conquest. As early as 6000–5000 B.C. distinct traces

of a Semitic population are found taking possession of the
civilization of the Sumerians. The great wave of Semites,
however, came later, *circa* 2250, and established the 'Kassite'
or first dynasty in Babylonia. At the beginning of the Persian
period, therefore, Babylonia was thoroughly Semitized. As
early as viii cent. B.C. Aramaic writing was familiar in Babylonia. Inscriptions on bronze lion-weights found at Nineveh
are partly Assyrian and partly Aramaic. That is, the Assyrian
ideographs, in many cases, have Aramaic versions.[1] These
weights can be dated, inasmuch as they have the names of
Shalmaneser, Sargon and Sennacherib in the Assyrian inscriptions. The Assyrian language was the old royal language, and
retained on seals, coins, weights, etc. The Aramaic was the
international language, and perhaps the only one at this period
understood by the bulk of the people.[2]

IX

ABSENCE OF LITERARY REMAINS

The great plateau of Iran, the home of the Aryans, was
not so early disturbed as many of the neighbouring peoples.
There is much uncertainty about the claim of Cyrus to the
throne of Persia, and concerning the method by which he
achieved his end. But under this sovereign and his successor
Medo-Persian influence extended over the whole of western
Asia. The native language was written in a sort of cuneiform
script, which, however, does not seem to have been derived from
the Babylonian or Assyrian.[3] It consisted of thirty-six signs,
and was perhaps the earliest example of a definite alphabet.
It was employed for incising inscriptions on stone and clay

---

[1] CIS ii. 1-14. A cylinder seal from Assyria, viii–vii B.C., is in Aram. ;
vide CIS ii. 77.

[2] A lion-weight of the Persian period, found at Abydos, Asia Minor,
date *circa* vi–v B.C., is in Aram., but on the reverse side there is a mark
A, prob. = Gk. *Rhō*, poss. *Alpha*.

[3] The theory that the Persian cuneiform writing was introduced as late
as Darius Hystaspes (*vide* Weissbach, *Zeitschrift der Deutschen Morgenländischen Gesellschaft*, xlviii. 664) is not in harmony with the literary
monuments, and therefore untenable (cf. Meyer, *Geschichte des Alterthums*,
iii. 49).

tablets. This method of writing was too cumbrous for dispatches to provincial satraps and for international communications generally. For this purpose the Persians employed, not the old Pahlavi, which was of Parthian origin, but an Aramaic alphabet, probably akin to that used by the Babylonians and Assyrians in their official documents. On the whole, it seems best to conclude that the Persian cuneiform alphabet was really based on some old Aramaic prototype.[1]

Though the Persian empire comprehended the greater part of western Asia for more than two centuries, the native linguistic and literary contribution was surprisingly small. Some reasons are obvious. (1) Since there are no remains of a literature, in the proper sense, in the Medo-Persian language, it is to be concluded that no literature was ever written in that idiom. (2) The decentralization of power did not tend to the cultivation of letters. The viceroys were left largely to manage their own provinces without constant appeal to or from the central government at Susa. The people were hardworking and home-loving, and did not trouble much about arts and literature. (3) The Persians did not attempt to impose a religious creed upon the subject provinces. Their tolerance in this respect was very marked when contrasted with the social and religious oppression which characterized Babylonian-Assyrian rule. The cults being absent, there was no necessity for written stereotyped directions about worship— gods, temples and ceremonies. (4) Persian influence was not prominent in the dependencies, especially in the more remote. Some satraps had few, if any, Persian officials in their administrative councils, and in some of the provinces there were apparently no Persian soldiers to guard the interests of the imperial authority. The Persian dominance rested so lightly on the far-flung empire that it ' left hardly a single provincial monument of itself, graven on rock or carved on stone.' Besides some words in the later Old Testament writings, the Persian conquest did not materially affect Hebrew. Indeed,

---

[1] On the Persian cuneiform inscriptions *vide* Weissbach, *Die Achämenideninschriften zweiter Art* (1890) ; Benzold and Haupt, *Die Ach. Inschr. Babylon* (1882) ; cf. *Beiträge zur Assyriologie u. semitischen Sprachwissenschaft*, ii. 205 ff,

before the time of Cyrus the Persian language was restricted in geographical area. On the Assyrian and Babylonian inscriptions before the vi cent. B.C., no Persian word has been found, except the deific title *Mithra*. Anciently this term referred to the sun, the one object of Persian worship.[1]

C.—GREEK PERIOD

I

PRE-HELLENIC CIVILIZATION

The more carefully one looks into this subject, the more clearly is it seen that Greek culture owed a tremendous debt to the Aegean, and particularly to the Minoan civilization of Crete. This civilization had grown old, and passed away centuries before the period of Greek learning with which Homer has made us familiar. In the production of historical Greek civilization it is difficult to say which contributed more, the strong and severe Dorian and Achaean elements, or the mild and artistic genius of the Minoan golden age. We have been accustomed to look to the East—to Mesopotamia and Babylonia—for the beginning of Greek enlightenment, but probably when exploration has penetrated farther into the secrets of the Aegean, we shall find that the initial impulse came, not from the borders of the Euphrates, but from the islands and coast-lands of the Levant. The prosecution of this study tends to reverse the old conclusion respecting the relation of the Philistines and the Israelites. If the Philistines were early associated with the Minoan civilization, and the *Pulasti* were an Aegean people, it is to be concluded that in their first contact with the Israelites they were a more advanced people—the givers rather than the borrowers of a new culture. If we may identify the Zakkaru (or *Tikkarai = Teucrians*) with the Cretan Zakro, it follows that shortly after 1200 B.C. the whole coast-land of

---

[1] Hence the phrases: *Deo soli invicto Mithrae*; and *Omnipotenti deo Mithrae* (Spanhemius, *ad Jul. Caes.*, p. 144; cf. Herod. i. 131; Strabo, *Lib.* xv.).

Canaan was invaded by a race of Aegean origin that inherited the mighty Minoan civilization and traditions. These people were forced from their native island-home by the utter over-throw of Knossos (or Cnossus, the royal city of Crete), *circa* 1400 B.C., and after two centuries of migrations found a settle-ment on the shore-lands of Palestine, to which they gave their name—*Pulesti* or *Pulishta* (? *Pelasgi*) = Philistines = Palestine.

The language of the pre-Hellenic Aegean is still largely a secret; no key has yet been found which quite fits this linguistic lock. We need some Minoan Rosetta Stone—a bilingual inscription—to enable us to decipher the strange writing. The material is waiting, and abundant to supply information of a most important character, but the monuments are dumb. Intercourse was close and frequent for several centuries between Cretan and Egyptian officials and merchants. It is almost certain that bilingual contracts, treaties and diplomatic communications were drawn up between the two countries. Surely all have not utterly perished! Though past attempts to read the Minoan and Hittite inscriptions have not been altogether encouraging, yet we entertain the strongest hope that sooner or later the riddle will be solved.[1]

II

GREEK INSCRIPTIONS

These do not come within the range of the present study, inasmuch as Greek was never the language of Palestine at any time. That Greek had taken a strong hold on Antioch [2] and Alexandria is evident enough, but in both cases the circum-stances of history were quite exceptional. No doubt, too,

---

[1] *Vide* Dussand, *Les Civilisations Préhelléniques dans le Bassin de la Mer Agée*[2], 1914. Hall, *Ægean Archaeology*, 1914.

[2] Antioch in Syria was the most potent Hellenizing influence over Pales. iii–ii cent. B.C. It was the excessive Hellenizing ambition of Antioch which really saved Pales. from the dominance of this influence. Antiochus Epiphanes (175–164 B.C.) united the vanities of a Caligula with the immoralities of a Nero, and so paved the way for Antioch's decline. His policy of Hellenizing Pales. provoked the resolute and successful Hasmonaean revolt. *Vide* 1 Mac., and cf. Schürer, *Hist. Jewish People*, i. 162–290.

there were many Greeks and Greek-speaking Semites in Jerusalem and other Palestinian centres at the beginning of the Christian era. It is also to be noted that many Greek terms and idioms passed into the vernacular Aramaic of this period. But Greek has never been the language of Palestine, and at most it has only a very indirect bearing on the present discussion. The only point to be emphasized in the present connexion is that the old Greek alphabet was akin to Phoenician and Aramaic. Two facts support this statement: (1) The direction of the writing. Some of the ancient Greek inscriptions are found to run from right to left after the Semitic manner: others proceed from right to left and left to right, i.e. βουστροφηδόν writing. Finally, the left to right method became fixed. The fact that the earliest Greek inscriptions follow the Semitic order indicates some connexion with Phoenician. (2) The character of the script: many letters are similar to old Hebrew. This cannot be due to accident or coincidence, but to some organic association.[1] By turning some letters of the old Greek alphabet round to face the other way, they at once assume their later forms. The primitive contact of Semite and Greek language probably took place on the shores of the Levant and during the Minoan civilization. A comparative study will lead to the conclusion that the Phoenician, Aramaic and Greek alphabets were developed from one original.

III

CONTACT OF SEMITIC AND GREEK ALPHABETS

It is outside the scope of this work to discuss pre-Hellenistic influences, and the influence of Hellenism beyond Palestine. But before we speak of Alexander's eastern conquests, it will be interesting to point out a period in which the old Greek alphabet resembled in some respects the alphabet of Phoenician and old Aramaic inscriptions. The origin of Greek writing is as obscure as that of Semitic

---

[1] *Vide* Rochl, *Imagines Inscriptionum Graecarum Antiquissimae,* Berolini, 1883, No. 1. Cf. Driver, *Notes on the Heb. Text of Samuel*[2], p. v f. ; Roberts, *Greek Epigraphy*, pt. 1.

writing; both are lost in the myths of antiquity. The type
of writing in the Homeric age is not clearly defined, but the
practice of writing was quite familiar.[1] Different types of
writing were known to Egyptians and Sidonians in the
Homeric age, and the Greeks could hardly be ignorant of
some of these systems of writing.[2] It is commonly believed
that the Greeks originally gained a knowledge of writing
from the Phoenicians. This belief requires some explanation.
The art of writing is one thing, the art of writing by means
of an alphabet is another thing. This latter art received a
great impetus about 1000 B.C. In another place mention is
made of the civilization of the so-called 'Minoan' kingdom,
and a great Aegean wave over the coast-lands of western
Asia, which stimulated writing and characterized script in
different regions. Should the type of the old Greek alphabet
be associated in any way with this Aegean movement?

In the dedicatory inscription: לבעל לבנן (CIS i. 5), the
script is of the archaic character, akin to old Hebrew (e.g.
the Moabite Stone, 9th cent. B.C.) on the one hand, and to
old Aramaic (e.g. the Zenjirli inscrip., 8th cent. B.C.) on the
other. Now, it is found that the old Greek alphabet is of
the same general type, and some letters are almost identical.
This fact points to some movement which affected more or
less in common the Phoenician, old Aramaic and old Greek
scripts. The anterior movement could not have been far
back, otherwise these scripts would have developed greater
differences. The position, then, may be restated as follows:
The picture-writing of the Greeks in the pre-Homeric age
was derived from a Semitic source, circa second millennium
B.C., the type of alphabetic script which almost simultaneously
and rather suddenly appeared in Moabite, Aramaic, Cyprian
(Phoen.) and Greek, was due to a great Anatolian movement,
beginning circa 1000 B.C., which brought the Aegean into
close intellectual and commercial association with western

---

[1] E.g. the famous passage: πέμπε δέ μιν Λυκίηνδε, πόρεν δ' ὅγε σήματα
λυγρά, γράψας ἐν πίνακι πτυκτῷ θυμοφθόρα πολλά (Il. vi. 168–9). The 'graven
tokens' were undoubtedly some sort of picture-characters which could
be read, for Proetus asked to see these credentials when Bellerophon
arrived: καὶ τότε μιν ἐρέεινε, καὶ ᾔτεε σῆμα ἰδέσθαι (l. 176).

[2] Cf. Thumb, Die griechische sprache im Zeitalter des Hellenismus.

Asia. Writing among the Greeks in Homer's own time
(? 950–850)[1] was probably more advanced than has been
generally supposed.[2] On the other hand, written records in
the Aegean were apparently later than 1100 B.C. The
' Coming of the Achaeans ' (1250), the ' Trojan War ' (1194),
the ' Dorian Invasion ' (rather before 1100), mark the beginnings of Greek continuous history. But these great events
were handed down as traditions ; there were no contemporary
records.

IV

RESULT OF ALEXANDER'S CONQUESTS

In the year 335 B.C. Alexander was chosen Generalissimo
by the Greek States, and from this time Greek arms triumphed
in the East till the Roman conquests. But Greek thought
and language influenced the East long after Greece lost its
independence. The common language during the Greek and
Graeco-Roman period was influenced by certain definite forces
and tendencies, which may be named in the following order :

1. *The Septuagint.*—The Greek version of the Old Testament was the main factor in the Graecizing of Semitic
monotheism. As a force in the history of religion it has
been likened to Luther's Bible in modern times. The influence of the LXX on the language and literature of Palestine
may easily be exaggerated. The Bible of Jesus of Nazareth,
for instance, was Semitic, the earliest utterances and traditions
of the Gospel were Semitic. In so far as these are included
in the present Greek text of the Gospel, may they not be
regarded as translators' Greek ? The correspondences of the
New Testament with the LXX vocabulary and grammar are
not in themselves proof that the New Testament was primarily
written in Greek. One may almost unwittingly take for

[1] Herodotus (ii. 53) placed the age of Homer 400 years before his own
time : Ἡσίοδον γὰρ καὶ Ὅμηρον ἡλικίην τετρακοσίοισι ἔτεσι δοκέω μεῦ πρεσβυτέρ-
ους γενέσθαι, i.e. *circa* 850 B.C. But it is probable that Homer lived at a
somewhat earlier date.

[2] For arguments that the Homeric songs were not originally committed
to writing, *vide* Wolf, *Prolegomena ad Homerum* (1795). *Per contra*
Nitzsch, *Meletemata* (1830), and *Die Sagenpoesie der Griechen* (1852).

granted that quotations from the Old Testament which follow the LXX were originally cited in Greek, and that wherever the language of the New Testament conforms in structure to the LXX the same thing is to be concluded. Some portions of the New Testament, which were unquestionably first uttered in Aramaic, have correspondences with the LXX. Some of Paul's speeches, for instance, were given in Aramaic; so was Stephen's defence. How soon these were turned into Greek we do not know. Paul may have been his own translator, in which case he would naturally make what use he could of the LXX, especially in the matter of quotations. The dependence of Stephen's speech on the LXX is perhaps due to translation Greek, the translator attempting to bring his work into harmony with the Greek Old Testament.

The difficulties besetting the translators of the LXX were very great. It was almost impossible to reproduce the native inimitableness of a Semitic language in an Aryan tongue. They had to adopt new constructions, some lexical and syntactical forms which were foreign to the older Greek. Thus 'arose a written Semitic-Greek, which no one ever spoke, far less used for literary purposes, either before or after.' The LXX was a translation of Semitic matter into Egypto-Alexandrian Greek. The Greek was the type prevalent in the Ptolemaic age, but its forms were influenced by the language of the original and the character of the subject-matter. The translators, in order to make their work intelligible to Alexandrian Hellenists, sacrificed to some extent the meaning and genius of the Hebrew. The striving to make the Old Testament a book for Greek-speaking Jews may explain 'many peculiarities from which it might even be inferred that a text different from our own lay before them.' The translators of the LXX did not attempt to find a Greek word to correspond in sense with every Hebrew word or phrase. Sometimes they did not translate the original at all, but gave some substitute for it, whose meaning 'is, of course, to be ascertained only from Egyptian Greek.'

The LXX is a disappointing source for the purpose of this study. It throws no clear light on the real linguistic problem. The spoken language was more primitive than the literary. The work of the authors of the LXX was not only a translation, it was also a revised version. In all such translation work there is a concurrent process of modernization. The language of the LXX was not the literary Greek of the time; it was a new dialectic product coloured distinctly by the Semitic original. It was certainly not the spoken Greek, which was freer and less stilted. The LXX was a splendid monument of literature; it has had great influence on religious writing and history, and it is still a subject of immense importance and attractiveness. It can, however, aid us but slightly in the endeavour to discover the living, practical language of western Asia in the Ptolemaic age.

2. *Hellenization.*—Although the LXX itself was made into the best Greek of Alexandria, based upon the Attic dialect, and was not at first a book for the native peasantry or for the city proletariat, who at most could only speak a poor broken and mixed Greek patois, yet the Jews were increasingly brought under Hellenistic influence. In 40 A.D. Philo estimated the Jews at Alexandria at a million.[1] The bulk of the Jewish race remained in the old lands of the Captivity, beyond the Euphrates, where they were contracting Persian and Assyrian beliefs and culture rather than Greek. Still the Greeks were continually pressing their influence over western Asia, and the Jews were very numerous in the Greek-speaking cities of the Graeco-Roman period. Josephus says that 18,000 were slain in the war at Damascus alone, 66–70 A.D.[2] Antioch was full of Jews, so were the coast cities from Sidon southwards. Antiochus the Great placed 2000 Jewish families of Mesopotamia in Phrygia and Lydia.[3] There must have been a great surplus of population in Palestine at the beginning of the third century B.C., inasmuch as Ptolemy Lagos transferred 100,000 from Judaea to Egypt.[4] The widespread character of Jewish colonies may be gathered from a letter of Herod Agrippa to Caligula in 38 A.D. He says that Jerusalem was the centre of influence in the East, and that 'Europe and the islands generally were full of

---

[1] Philo, *in Flac.* ii. 523.   [2] *Jewish War*, vii., viii. 7.
[3] *Ant.* xii. 3. 4.   [4] Aristaea, *Epist.*

Jews.'[1]   This dispersion of the Jews in Greek-speaking regions meant considerable Hellenizing of the Jews. The process doubtless would have gone much farther in Palestine but for the check which it received by the Maccabaean revolt.[2]   This Jewish uprising, however, was not directly aimed against the Greek language, but against the attempt of Antiochus to enforce idolatry. The success of the revolt did as a matter of fact check the Hellenizing influence, and rekindled a passion for the national sacred language. If at the beginning of the return from exile the Jews had joined harmoniously with the Samaritans, they might have formed unitedly a strong barrier against the inroads of Greek speech and custom. But the jealousy and antagonism between these Semitic people made it all the easier for the growth of Greek influence in some of the centres of Palestinian life. But at no period did Greek become the language of Palestine.

It is not surprising that Greek influence should be evident in the Phoenician inscriptions found at Piraeus, the port of Athens. Here the Sidonians had a colony, perhaps as early as the fourth century B.C.[3]   These settlers maintained the religion and practice of their native province.[4]   But the inscriptions show how thoroughly they adapted themselves to Greek culture. Their records are given after the pattern of Greek inscriptions. Indeed, they appear sometimes to translate from exemplars in the Greek language.[5]   This study need not be extended here, but it deserves more careful investigation than it has yet received.

---

[1] Cf. Philo, *de Legat.* ii. 587.

[2] Against the Hellenizing attempt of Epiphanius to establish in Jerusalem a γυμνάσιον and an ἐφήβειον (2 Mac. 4 ; cf. 1 Mac. 1[14], 4 Mac. 4[20]).

[3] The character of the Gk. letters in CIS i. 115 suggests the fourth cent.

[4] *Vide* CIS i. 118, 119.

[5] Of such a character is the Piraeus inscription (vide *Corpus Inscriptionum Atticarum*, ii. 1[b]). Here דרכמנם is borrowed from δραχμαί ; אש עלתי משרת, if משרת be taken as ptcp. dependent on the suffixed עלתי, is an imitation of a Gk. idiom ; ישאן ז מצבת עלת ערב, if clause be dependent on the verb נשא, agrees with the Gk. form εἰς δὲ τὴν ἀναγραφὴν τῆς στήλης δοῦναι (cf. Michel, *Recueil d'Inscript. Grecques*, 118). To pay the cost of the *stele* from temple money is according to Gk. inscrip. (*ib.* 968,1003). In the Piraeus inscrip., CIS i. 119, the term רב כהנם is probably due to the well-known Gk. title ἀρχιερεύς ; Aram. פַּחֲנָא רַבָּא (Onk. Nu. 35[25]).

It is now fully proved that Greek had established itself in the chief centres of the Graeco-Roman period. It was in many cases the vernacular of Jews, who were scattered abroad, and its influence was apparent in the later writings of the Jews,[1] and even in Jerusalem itself. The post-Biblical literature contains many Greek loan-words.[2] On the Hasmonaean coins, Greek is found alóng with the Hebrew legends, while on the Herodian coins the inscriptions are in Greek alone. Every educated Jew probably understood Greek, and also many traders and travellers. Great numbers, of course, were bilingual. That Greek was cultivated among the Jews is implied in the later Rabbinic regulation prohibiting the instruction of children in this language.[3] The Jews in the remoter provinces of the empire commonly spoke Greek, and had no intimate acquaintance with Hebrew or Aramaic. The number of Greek-speaking settlers in Jerusalem warranted special synagogues.[4]

There was some knowledge of Greek in Judaea; the story of the Ἕλληνες[5] is interesting, it suggests that Philip spoke Greek. That the same was true of Jesus cannot be proved, but it is probable. His conversation with Pilate may have been through an interpreter. From the account of Titus giving an address in Jerusalem, we should not know that the Roman general had the assistance of an interpreter from any hint by the historian.[6] But Josephus in another place[7] says that on such occasions he acted as interpreter to Titus.[8] This

---

[1] In addition to several words in Dan., we find אפריון = φορεῖον (Cant. 3⁹); עשׂת טוב = εὖ πράττειν (Eccl. 3¹² 7²⁰ = Germ. *gut machen*); תחת השׁמשׁ = ὑφ' ἡλίῳ (Eccl. 1³ 2¹¹ 4¹ *al.*).

[2] *Vide* Krauss, *Griechische u. Lateinische Lehnwörter im Talmud, Midrasch u. Targum*, 1–2 (1898–99).

[3] *Sota* ix. 14.

[4] Acts 6⁹; Tōsephtā, *Měgillā*, iii. 6.

[5] John 12²⁰ff. These Ἕλληνες were born Gentiles, probably 'proselytes of the gate' (cf. Ex. 20¹⁰); this suggested by the pres. ptcp. ἀναβαινόντων, 'were accustomed to go up' to worship at the feast.

[6] Joseph. *Bell. Jud.* v. 9. 2.

[7] *Bell. Jud.* vi. 2. 5.

[8] Possibly Titus spoke in Latin. Though Gk. was included in the training of every educated Roman, yet Lat. was specially employed in legal, official and military affairs. The emperor Claudius, himself an admirer of Gk., insisted on Lat. (Suet. *Claud.* 16, 42). Notices in the

last reference makes it quite clear that the inhabitants of Jerusalem generally were not familiar with Greek.

The Nabataean and Palmyrene inscriptions show how Greek was making itself felt in the literary monuments in the regions bordering on Palestine, and we know the same was true, though in a less degree, in Palestine itself. The inscriptions have not yet been fully examined with a view to discover the presence of Greek influence. This new investigation is full of interest, and the following statements are sufficiently attested. Some forms in the Aramaic inscriptions are simple transliterations of Greek terms;[1] others are transcriptions with slight terminal differences due to difference of language.[2] Some phrases are apparently due to Greek forms, especially those of an official and regal character.[3] But when full allowance is made for this Greek influence, the inscriptions retain their distinctive Aramaic features. Greek was still a foreign language to the tribes that moved behind these inscriptions. In general it may be said that Greek no more changed the Aramaic in the two centuries preceding the

temple at Jerusalem were sometimes in Lat. (Joseph. *Bell. Jud.* v. 5. 2, vi. 2. 4). But Lat. had no hold on Jerusalem.

[1] In the following terms Aram. וס =Gk. ος; occas. υς: תידרום, *Theodoros*, *i.e.* Θεοδώρος (Vog. 5¹); אלכסנדרום, *Alexander, i.e.* Ἀλέξανδρος (Vog. 15³); גרמטוס, *scribe, i.e.* γραμματεύς (Vog. 16²). This is clearly due to the Gk., inasmuch as the Aram. is סלוקוס ספרא, *Seleukus, i.e.* Σέλευκος (Vog. 17²).

[2] Other transliterations are: שאילא, *She'eila, i.e.* Σεειλᾶ (Vog. 17³). The consonantal use of א is unusual; cf. מאכסמום, *i.e.* Μάχιμος (Constantine, Afr. 1⁴). בסלקא, *basilica, i.e.* βασιλικός (Vog. 11³). חימרא, *theatre, i.e.* θέατρον (CIS ii. 163²). קיסר, *Caesar, i.e.* Καῖσαρ (CIS ii. 170²); the insertion of י is clearly due to Gk.; cf. the Palm. קסר (Vog. 15³). בסםא, *i.e.* βάσις (CIS ii. 199¹).

[3] *E.g.* בולא ודמס, 'the council and the people'; this is merely a transliteration of the Gk. ἡ βουλὴ καὶ ὁ δῆμος (Vog. 1¹ 2¹). חרתת מלך . . . רחם עמה, 'Harethath, king . . . lover of his people' (CIS ii. 197⁴⁻⁵). Prob. due to Gk., since Aretas III. when ruler of Damascus, 85 B.C., struck coins with the legend: βασιλέως Ἀρέτου φιλέλληνος.

In אלן א(ח)ם, 'the divine brethren' (Phoen. Ma'sûb, line 7), it is doubtful whether there is any connexion with the Ptolemaic inscriptions with θεῶν ἀδελφῶν (*vide* Michel, *Recueil d'Inscriptions Grecques*, 551); cf. עברת אלהא (CIS ii. 354¹), and the Gk. Ὀβόδης ὁ βασιλεύς, ὃν θεοποιοῦσι (Müller, *Fragmenta Historicorum Graecorum*, iv. 525). The same uncertainty exists respecting ארן מלבם, 'the Lord of kings' (CIS i. 3¹⁸ 7⁵); the Ptolemaic title is same, κύριος βασιλέων. Cf. מלכא וי מלכיא, 'King of kings' (CIS ii. 122³).

Christian era, than Aramaic changed the Greek in the two centuries following.

3. *Jewish Diaspora.*—The beginning of the non-Palestinian Jewish communities is rather obscure. A Jewish colony was established at Damascus in the reign of Ahab.[1] Probably the alliances of David and Solomon with Phoenicia resulted in similar colonies there. Sargon transplanted from Samaria hosts of Hebrews and settled them in Mesopotamia and Media. The real dispersion, however, began with the Babylonian captivity. The flower of Judaean Jewish families Nebuchadrezzar carried into Babylonia.[2] From this centre Jews radiated to many parts of the East, and reached Media, Persia, Cappadocia, Armenia and the Black Sea. The Jewish colonies in Babylonia were maintained till *circa* 1000 A.D. Here, after the beginning of the Christian era, the Babylonian Talmud was compiled. That Jewish colonies were early established in Egypt is proved by the discovery of Aramaic Papyri, and by the testimony of Josephus.[3] In the first century B.C., Jews were scattered into all regions, Syria, Arabia, Greece and Rome. Besides the chief centre of Jewish religion and literature at Jerusalem, there were several other great centres—'Susa in Persia, Nehardea in Babylonia, Assuan and Tahtanhes in Egypt, Bethel in Samaria; all these, we have documentary evidence, were orthodox, and highly sensitive to the religious life in Palestine.'[4] In Rome there was a great Jewish community, dating from the time of the Maccabaean princes.[5] Later, when a deputation came to Rome from Judaea to complain of the misrule of Archelaus, at least 8000 Roman Jews joined themselves to it.[6] Perhaps five Synagogues are referred to as existing in Rome.[7] In Cyrene a quarter of the inhabitants consisted of Jews.[8] In Alexandria, two of the five divisions of the city were occupied by Jews.[9] The mention of the *Synagoga Alexandrinorum* in the Talmud [10] suggests its importance. There was a considerable community

[1] 1 K. 20³⁴.   [2] 2 K. 24¹²⁻¹⁶.
[3] *Jewish War*, ii. 18. 8 ; cf. *Apion.* ii. 4.
[4] Hodes, *Studies in Sidoor*, pp. 72–73.   [5] 1 Mac. viii., xii., xiv.
[6] Joseph. *Ant.* xvii. 11. 1 ; *War*, ii. 6. 1.   [7] Acts 6⁹.
[8] Joseph. *Ant.* xiv. 7. 2, xvi. 6. 1 ; cf. *Apion.* ii. 4.
[9] Ib., *Ant.* xiv. 7. 2, xix. 5. 1 ; *War*, ii. 18. 7.   [10] *Megilla*, 73. 4.

of Jews in Cilicia, of which the chief town was Tarsus; hence Paul was a Cilician Hellenist.[1] That multitudes of Jews were scattered over the whole of western Asia and south-eastern Europe is certain.[2] With few exceptions the Jews of the Diaspora were loyal to the religion of the home-land; and at the great Feasts, pilgrimages to Jerusalem were undertaken from all parts of the world.[3] Contact with the world gave

[1] Acts 21³⁹ 22³ 23³⁴.

[2] Joseph. *Ant.* xii. 3. 4; Cicero, *Pro Flacco*, xxviii.; cf. Ramsay, *Cities*, i. 2, 667.

[3] This is suggested by the mixed races that came to Pentecost (Acts 2⁹⁻¹¹). Six nationalities are mentioned, and a greater number of dialects. The nationalities may be tabulated thus:

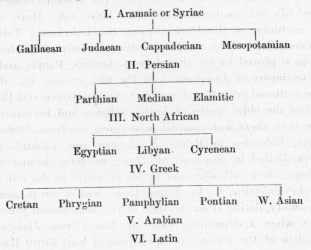

I. Aramaic or Syriac

Galilaean Judaean Cappadocian Mesopotamian

II. Persian

Parthian Median Elamitic

III. North African

Egyptian Libyan Cyrenean

IV. Greek

Cretan Phrygian Pamphylian Pontian W. Asian

V. Arabian

VI. Latin

The connexion is not in every case racial, but sometimes only linguistic. Thus (*a*) the Elamites had no racial connexion with Persia. They were a foreign people who had early associations with the Semites (*vide* עֵילָם, Gen. 14¹ff.). Their country owed allegiance to Babylonia, and later became subject to Persia. Thus probably the people acquired a knowledge of the Persian language. Persian kings assumed the hereditary title of 'princes of Anzan,' the Babylonian name for Elam. Cyrus was the fourth of these princes (*vide Inscrip. of Nabonidus, circa* 548 B.C.). (*b*) The Phrygians were not a Greek race, and the native Phrygian language belonged to a separate family. These people came from Macedonia across the Hellespont into the extreme west of Asia Minor. The region of north Macedonia was termed by the Greeks Thraco-Phrygia. Perhaps Phrygia here is the same as Galatia (*i.e.* Phrygia Galatica), and these Phrygians did no doubt speak either Greek or Latin, probably the former. The inscriptions on

these non-Palestinian Jews a wider outlook, and they conceived the idea of converting the world to Judaism. For aiding this project the *Sibylline Oracles*, and other types of literature calculated to attract Graeco-Roman readers, were produced.

The case of the Phrygian language is of some illustrative importance. It shows that a native tongue may be spoken, especially by the proletariat, long after a foreign language has been adopted by the educated classes. Take, for example, the city of Iconium. The people reckoned this city to be Phrygian, yet as early as the middle of the first cent. A.D. the language of public business was Greek, and not Phrygian. The educated part of the community spoke Greek, but the uneducated certainly used the Phrygian speech. Probably many Iconians were bilingual. The same condition of things was no doubt true of other west Asian centres. The instructed people spoke Greek, and the uninstructed the native language. The aristocracy (ἀριστο-κρατία) formed another community, not characteristic of a Greek city, but of a Roman *colonia*. It is interesting to remember that the Pauline Christian converts were not gained from the aristocracy (where these existed as a class), nor from the lower superstitious class, but from the educated middle class. This was probably one reason why Paul wrote in Greek and why his epistles were disseminated in Greek, and not in the native languages, which still survived among the peasantry in rural districts and among the illiterate in urban centres. The inscriptions, however, prove that the Phrygian language was in existence as late as the third cent. A.D., and was then probably spoken among the humbler people. One inscription described by Ramsay 'can hardly be earlier than A.D. 240, and may be even later.'[1] Naturally some Phrygian words

---

Phrygian tombs are in Greek, but the character of the language and the customs alluded to are largely Semitic and Jewish; cf. especially the phrase : ἔσται αὐτῷ αἱ ἀραὶ ἡ γεγραμμέναι ἐν τῷ δευτερονόμῳ (*vide* Ramsay, *Expos. Times*, Jan. 1915, pp. 168 ff.). (c) Possibly Latin was spoken at Lystra; the earliest tombs here have Lat. inscrip. (Ramsay, *Expos.*, Sept. 1905); so the coins, 'Colonia, Julia, Felix, Gemina, Lustra' (*Corpus Inscrip. Lat.* 3[6956]).

[1] *First Christian Cent.*, p. 167. Cf. Calder, *Journal of Hellenic Studies*, 1911, pt. ii.

passed into Hellenistic Greek.[1]　The same conditions and processes, as will be shown later, apply to the relation of the old Canaanite languages to the later Semitic and Aryan invasions.

4. *Semitization.*—While Greek was imposing itself upon the provinces in the East, it suffered something in the process. If the Jews were Hellenized, it must be remembered that the Greeks were Aramaized.　Scholars who reject the notion of ' Semitisms ' in the Greek Bible seem to ignore an important factor.　To show that the vocabulary of the LXX and the New Testament was drawn from the Greek language as spoken at the time, is not *ipso facto* to banish all ' Semitisms.' It simply puts the question back one step.　These linguistic peculiarities did exist, and they are found in the Greek Bible, though not, of course, restricted to this literature.　How did Semitic terms and idioms get into the vernacular of the Graeco-Roman age ?　The classical language is free from these peculiarities.　It was developed in another atmosphere, by the genius of another people, and employed for the expression of different ideas.　The purity of Greek was fairly maintained till the West began to conquer the East.　With the progress of Greek arms came the decline of the Greek language.　Some dialect of the Semitic family was spoken in nearly all the eastern regions subdued by Greeks and Romans.　The influence of the Jewish colonies in the chief centres of commerce was strong and tenacious, and in the main it was a dogmatic religious influence.　The Greek language in taking possession of these centres lost something of its own purity, and took on something of Semitic colouring.

---

[1] It is said that the terms πάπας and μάμμη were of Asiatic origin, and were introduced by Phrygian slaves into Athenian nurseries (*vide* Wilamowitz, *Griechisches Lesebuch*, i. p. 396, ii. p. 260).　These terms are found in a letter-fragment discovered at Herculaneum.　It was written by Epicurus (*circa* 270 B.C.), and addressed to an orphan, and is simple in style and artless in character : εὖ δὲ ποιε(ῖ)s καὶ σὺ ε(ἰ) (ὑ)γιαίνεις καὶ ἡ μ(ά)μμη (σ)ου, καὶ πάπαι . . . πάντα πε(ί)θη(ι), ' It is well if you too are in health and your grandmother, and (your) grandfather . . . in all things obey.'　The word μάμμη was used in the same sense in later Gk. (cf. 2 Tim. 1[5]; Joseph. *Ant.* x. 11. 2 ; Herodian, v. 3. 7 ; Plutarch, *Agis*, 4) for the earlier τήθη (cf. Lobeck, *Phrynichus*, pp. 133 f.).　The word βεκός (=ἄρτος) is said to be Phrygian (Herod. ii. 2).

The mixing of languages in the different provinces at this time will tend to explain the peculiar terms and formulae found in Aramaic and Greek inscriptions and papyri dating from the Imperial age. Many of these linguistic idioms may still be properly called 'Semitisms,' though no longer found exclusively in the LXX and the New Testament. We may reject the notion of a 'Judaeo-Greek' dialect, but the Greek received something of its prevalent form 'by its passage through the Semitic mind.'

One reason why so many 'Semitisms' seem naturalized in Greek, is that some eastern idioms, in the process of the contact of Semite and Greek, silted through into the Κοινή. No doubt some forms of Semitic expression were fundamentally analogous to forms in Greek. These would easily pass into the latter language, and appear like native constructions. It must further be admitted that the LXX did render some terms and idioms familiar which previously were unknown in Greek. But whether the Semitic colouring of some portions of the New Testament Greek is due to the influence of the LXX, or to the Aramaic of Palestine, is not easy to decide. No doubt both elements contributed to the general result. To the vernacular of Palestine must be attributed the Hebraic tone and form of the teaching of Jesus in the first instance. The same may be said of writings composed in Palestine, or based immediately on Palestinian sources. Other New Testament writings may owe their Semitic tone more directly to the LXX.

The Greek papyri show how Semitic influence was perpetuated in Greek-speaking regions. Many 'Semitisms' silted through into the Κοινή, and became naturalized in the Greek vernacular.[1] It is obvious that if a race of people wander far and wide, and be thrown into contact with foreign languages, the changes in its own speech will be marked and inevitable. The one element that would to some extent retard this process, would be the possession of a literature which by the dispersed people was held inviolate and sacred. This was the case with the Jews in the centuries immediately preceding and following the Christian era. The Jews never

---

[1] For relation of papyri to NT. and Κοινή, *vide* Robertson, *A Gram. of the Gk. N.T.*, 3rd ed. (1919).

lost their Semitic constitution, they never forgot that Hebrew
was the tongue of their nation, and they never ceased to
think in Hebrew even when they spoke in Greek. This line
of study, we think, more naturally and satisfactorily accounts
for the 'Semitic idioms' in the popular Greek of the Graeco-
Roman period than the statement of Harnack, that 'a very
large portion of the supposed Semitic idioms . . . should be
regarded as natural productions of the Κοινή that more or
less accidentally coincide with Semitic forms.'[1] With this
view Moulton's judgment on 'Semitism' agrees, that locutions,
correct enough as Greek, became prominent through 'the
accident of their answering to Heb. or Aram. phrases.'[2]
This is probably the case with some words and phrases
which characterized the Κοινὴ διάλεκτος.[3] But even in these
instances the prominence and frequency of such words and
phrases must be attributed to a nearer or more remote
Semitic influence. Other instances can hardly be regarded
as natural developments of the Greek, or as accidental coinci-
dences with Hebrew or Aramaic. They must be explained
rather as Hellenic adaptations to a Semitic environment.
The point is that such forms are not native to the genius
of the Greek language, but the Greek language readily
accommodated itself to their reception.[4]

5. *Super-Hellenization.*—Recent discussions have scarcely

[1] *Acts of the Apostles*, p. xxxvi.

[2] *Prolegomena*, ch. i. Cf. Meisterhans, *Grammatik der attischen
Inschriften*, 1900.

[3] Forms like δύο δύο (*vide* ἔρε κατὰ δύο δύο, *Oxy. Pap.* 886, ed. by
Grenfell and Hunt, vi. pp. 200 f.) ; ἐρχόμενος δὲ ἔρχου (*vide Tebtunis Pap.* ii.
p. 298, ed. by Grenfell, Hunt, and Goodspeed); ἐρωτάω in the sense of 'ask,'
'peto' (*vide* Ἐρωτᾷ σε Ἀντώνιος, *Oxy. Pap.*, ed. by Grenfell and Hunt, iii.
p. 260) ; πληροῦσθαι in reference to time (*e.g.* μέχρι τοῦ τὸν χρόνον πληρωθῆναι,
Oxy. Pap. ii. pp. 262 ff., ed. Grenfell and Hunt) ; ἰδού with a nominative
simply (cf. Luc. *D. Deor.* 20. 10 ; Timon, 11; but these are not true parallels.
Moulton's remark, that ἰδού is a 'good Attic interjection,' *Proleg.* p. 11,
needs support); καθαρὸς ἀπό . . . (cf. ἀπὸ δὲ τάφου καὶ ἐκφορ(ᾶς) . . . καθαροὶ
ἔστωσαν, and other ref. in Deissmann, *BS*, p. 196. The phrase, γένονται
καθαραὶ πώποτε, *Paris Pap.* 51, is more idiomatic) ; and many other forms
are possible Gk. emphasized by corresp. with Semitic constructions.

[4] In illustration the following may be quoted : βλέπε ἀπό . . . (*e.g.*
βλέπε σατὸν ἀπὸ τῶν Ἰουδαίων, *Griechische Urkunden*, Berlin, 1079[24-26]. The
redundant pronoun (=σεαυτόν) is Semitic ; ἀπό=מֵן, as מִן קְרָמוֹהִי אִיסְתַּפַּר, Onk.
Ex. 23[21] ; מִן קֳרָמָא אִסְתַּמְּרוּ, Jon. b. Uzz. Josh. 6[18]) ; ἐκ τεσσάρων ἀνέμων (*e.g.*

succeeded in veiling the writers' bias. The latest tendency is towards a super-Hellenization of western Asia. This is partly a reaction against the earlier attempt to discover 'Semitisms' in the Greek of the eastern empire. There is a specious danger, which few escape, of confusing the language of the conqueror with that of the conquered. It has sometimes happened that small cabinets of strong rulers wield effective government over considerable populations, without imposing their language on their subjects. This was the case with the Satraps and their secretaries in the outlying countries of the Persian empire. This, too, was a familiar condition of affairs with Greek rulers in some eastern provinces. Princes, generals, and other officials in foreign service, who had Persian or Greek names, did not necessarily administer local affairs in the Persian or Greek language. A later analogy has been noted in the case of the Norman princes who bore Teutonic names, but governed the people of Normandy in the Norman-French language.[1] This fact must not be overlooked even in the case of the centres which were most affected by Greek. Alexandria was permeated with Greek thought and speech, but Greek was not the language of lower Egypt. Antioch was largely a Greek city, but Greek was not the language of Syria. It is quite unwarrantable to argue from the discovery of official and other Greek documents that Greek was the vernacular of any Semitic or foreign region.

[γείτο]νες ἐκ τεσσάρων ἀνέμων, *Corp. Papyr. Raineri*, etc., cxv. 6. This is a thoroughly oriental expression : Heb. אַרְבַּע רוּחוֹת הַשָּׁמַיִם, Zech. 2¹⁰ ᴴᵉᵇ·; Aram. אַרְבַּע רוּחֵי שְׁמַיָּא, Dan. 7² ; Arab الرياح الاربع السماوات ; Syr. ܐܪܒܥ ܢܣܝܡ ܕܫܡܝܐ ; ἔνοχος ἔστω with dative of tribunal infliction (*e.g.* ἔνοχος ἔστω τοῖς ἴσοις ἐπιτε[ί]μοις, *Oxy. Pap.*, ed. Grenfell and Hunt, ii. pp. 262 ff. Wellhausen thinks this constr. *ungriechisch*, *Einl.* pp. 33 f. It is equivalent to אִתְקְטָלָא יִתְקְטִיל, LXX θανάτῳ ἔνοχος ἔσται, Onk. Gen. 26¹¹) ; υἱός followed by a genitive (*e.g.* υἱὸς τῆς πόλεως, υἱὸς τῆς γερουσίας, *et al.* Paton and Hicks, *Inscrip. of Cos.*, pp. 125 f. If not un-Greek, the constr. is usually avoided even in bilingual inscr. [Palm. and Gk.] which have בר in the Aram. text ; cf. ובידא בר מקימו, Gk. Ζεβείδαν Μοκίμου, Vog. 4² ; Eut. 102¹). These and many other forms found in Gk. inscr. and papyri could scarcely have come into the Κοινή except through Semitic.

[1] The reverse order is also found, as in the case of the old Parthian kings, who took Iranian names and governed in the Iranian language, but who in reality were Turks. Are not the present Shahs of Persia Turks?

Egypt was in some sense anomalous.   Cities and even villages which were largely under a foreign influence rather readily attempted to utilize the language of the invaders.   But we must not be mislead by the abundance of papyri discovered in Egypt.   Considerable Aramaic literature has been found at Elephantiné, but this was mainly a Jewish settlement.   Vast stores of Greek papyri have been brought from Oxyrhynchus, but a considerable Greek community had migrated to this district.   How far native Egyptians in either case employed the foreigners' language is not easy to decide.   The probability is that the Aramaic at Elephantiné was almost wholly restricted to the Semitic settlers, and the Greek papyri at Oxyrhynchus largely written by emigrants of Greek extraction. No doubt some of the illiterate specimens were imitative products of native Egyptians.   In the case of Palestine, in spite of Epiphanes, Hellenism never took serious root.

The tendency of modern scholarship is to overestimate the influence of the Greek language and the prevalence of Greek ideas in the Semitic literature of western Asia in pre-Christian times.   It is unfortunate that the Semitic originals of *Ecclesiasticus, De Bello Judaico*, and some apocalyptic Jewish writings are no longer extant.   The Greek translations tell us nothing about the presence of Greek influence in the originals. In the case of *Ecclesiasticus*, written by Jesus ben Sirach of Jerusalem, *circa* 209 B.C., a few fragments of the Hebrew original have been discovered.   As far as can be ascertained, these fragments do not contain a single word derived from the Greek.[1]   It is doubtful whether the vernacular of Palestine admitted any Greek element prior to the Christian era.   Even in the Greek form of the teaching of Jesus of Nazareth, there is not a single idea traceable to a Greek source.   The Greek language, however, did influence the Aramaic language before Greek ideas influenced Jewish and Christian thought.   Greek terms and Graecized Semitic words are found in the later Old

---

[1] These fragments deserve careful study: some were published by Cowley and Neubauer, with Gk. Lat. and Syr. texts (1897).   The Genizah Fragments were published by Schechter and Taylor (1899); the British Museum Fragments by Margoliouth (1899).   Other leaves were published by Schechter in the *Jewish Quarterly Review*, 12[456-465].

Testament writings, in the Apocrypha, and in Semitic inscriptions. But this far from proves that the vernacular of Palestine was to any appreciable extent infected with Greek. It is possible that a few Aramaic terms and idioms in the Synoptic Gospels were influenced by the growing presence of Greek in western Asia. The appearance of Greek inscriptions on Palestinian coins, though somewhat later, show that Greek was gaining a footing in the very centre of Judaism. But these considerations do not by any means prove that the Aramaic of Palestine at the beginning of the Christian age was materially affected by Greek. The present text of the Synoptic Gospels affords no data for discovering how far Greek had penetrated and changed the Aramaic vernacular of Palestine. With regard to the ideas of primitive Christianity, it must be unhesitatingly admitted that they are almost entirely allied with Hebrew conceptions, and only slightly influenced by Greek teaching. Hellenistic influence came later, and in the fourth cent. Christianity was rooted in it.[1]

V

CHIEF CONTRIBUTION OF EAST TO WEST

The chief contribution, after all, of the East to the West was not linguistic, but religious; similarly the main contribution of the West to the East was not linguistic, but philosophic. It is easy to find some Semitic idioms in the Greek and some Graecisms in the Aramaic of the age. But Greek remained Aryan, and Aramaic remained Semitic. It was the blending of the Semites' religion of philosophy with the Greeks' philosophy of religion, which was the permanent factor of the contact of East and West. The fusion of these elements was first clearly represented by Zeno, a Phoenician of Cyprus, and afterwards strikingly exemplified by Saul, a Jew of Tarsus. For the culture and religion of the western world, this blending of Semitic religiosity and Greek philosophy was of unspeakable significance. It prepared the way for the Christian religion, which alone can satisfy the moral craving of mankind.

[1] Cf. Hatch, *The Influence of Greek Ideas*, etc., 8th ed. (1901).

III

LINGUISTIC GENEALOGY

I

TABLE OF LINGUISTIC RELATIONS

PRIMAL RACE

(' Caucasian—Tauranian ')

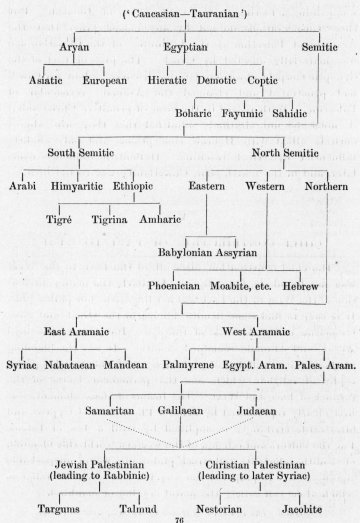

II

TABLE OF ETHNIC SOURCES

NOAH [נח = 'Rest']¹

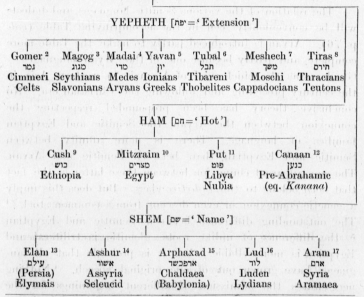

YEPHETH [יפת = 'Extension']

Gomer²	Magog³	Madai⁴	Yavan⁵	Tubal⁶	Meshech⁷	Tiras⁸
נמר	מגוג	מדי	יון	תבל	משך	תירס
Cimmeri	Scythians	Medes	Ionians	Tibareni	Moschi	Thracians
Celts	Slavonians	Aryans	Greeks	Thobelites	Cappadocians	Teutons

HAM [חם = 'Hot']

Cush⁹	Mitzraim¹⁰	Put¹¹	Canaan¹²
כוש	מצרים	פוט	כנען
Ethiopia	Egypt	Libya	Pre-Abrahamic
		Nubia	(eq. *Kanana*)

SHEM [שם = 'Name']

Elam¹³	Asshur¹⁴	Arphaxad¹⁵	Lud¹⁶	Aram¹⁷
עילם	אשור	ארפכשד	לוד	ארם
(Persia)	Assyria	Chaldaea	Luden	Syria
Elymais	Seleucid	(Babylonia)	Lydians	Aramaea

---

¹ The names in Gen. 10 are mostly ethnic, notably those which end in the Sem. pl. *im*, and the Aryan ('Gentilitian') adj. *ite* (*vide* vv.⁴⁻⁶, ¹³⁻¹⁴, ¹⁶⁻¹⁸). The Table has no conclusive historical value, but with the notes below indicate the ancient identifications.

² *Vide* Homer, *Od.* xi. 14; Herod. i. 6. 15, 103; cf. *ib.* iv. 1. 11–12; Joseph. *Ant.* i. 6. 1. Cf. Bochart, *Phaleg.* iii. 8.

³ *Vide* Herod. i. 103–106; Joseph. *Ant.* i. 6. 1.

⁴ *Ib.* vii. 62; cf. *ib.* iv. 37, 40; Joseph. *Ant.* i. 6. 1.

⁵ *Vide* Homer, *Il.* xiii. 685; Herod. i. 56, 143, 145, viii. 44; Aeschy. *Prom.* 175, 561; Joseph. *Ant.* i. 6. 1.

⁶ *Vide* Herod. iii. 94, vii. 78; Joseph. *Ant.* i. 6. 1.

⁷ *Vide* Strabo, xi. 497–499; Herod. iii. 94, vii. 78; cf. *ib.* i. 652–653.

⁸ *Vide* Herod. v. 3; Joseph. *Ant.* i. 6. 1; cf. Bochart, *Phaleg.* cap. 2.

⁹ *Vide* Strabo, xvii. 817; Joseph. *de Bell. Jud.* iv. 10. 5; Pliny, *Hist. Nat.* vi. 35.

¹⁰ *Vide* Herod. *passim*; cf. Bochart, *Phaleg.* iv. 24.

¹¹ *Vide* Joseph. *Ant.* i. 6. 2; cf. Bochart, *Phaleg.* iv. 33; cf. Smith, *Anc. Hist.* i. p. 47.

¹² *Vide* Herod. vii. 89; cf. Hengstenberg, *Christol.* i. 28; Müller, *A. u. E.* 206 ff.

¹³ *Vide* Joseph. *Ant.* i. 6. 4; Smith, *Anc. Hist.* i. ch. ix.; Müller, *Sci. of Lang.* 380.

¹⁴ *Vide* Strabo, xvi. 507; Ptol. vi. 1; cf. Smith, *Anc. Hist.* i. ch. ix.

¹⁵ *Vide* Joseph. *Ant.* i. 6. 4; Ptol. vi. 1; cf. Bochart, *Phaleg.* ii. 4.

¹⁶ *Ib.*, *Ant.* i. 6. 4.

¹⁷ *Vide* Homer, *Il.* 783; Hesiod, *Theog.* 304; cf. Müller, *Sci. of Lang.* 381.

III

GENERAL STATEMENT

The relation of the various Semitic languages and dialects will be conveniently seen in the accompanying Table (*vide* p. 76). Aryan is introduced partly to make the Table more complete, and partly because one of the Aryan languages— Greek—was the chief rival of Aramaic in western Asia in the century preceding and following the Christian era. No conclusive theory has been propounded respecting the connexion between the Aryan, the Semitic and Egyptian families of language. There is more affinity between Semitic and Egyptian, than between Semitic and Aryan. The one apparent connexion between these latter is the fact that both belong to the *inflective* class. But does this imply a genetic connexion or even descent from a common stock ?[1] The outstanding difference between Semitic and Egyptian is the difference of unlike roots—Semitic is triliteral and Egyptian is monosyllabic. Yet it is probable that all languages have grown out of one original speech. 'Nothing necessitates the admission of different beginnings for the formal elements of the Tauranian, Semitic and Aryan branches of speech.'[2] The primitive unity of language is suggested by the persistence of root-words, with the same fundamental ideas, in all the great linguistic families. Different tribal and national speeches arose gradually by the introduction of different forms, structures and pronunciations, induced by new climate, occupation and objects of thought. The Onkelos Targum rendering of the passage in the Book of Genesis (11[1]) is suggestive : והוה כל־ארעא לישן חד וממלל חד, 'and the whole earth was of one tongue, and of one word.' Though this passage has no historical value, it probably contains a truth. The phrase ממלל חד may mean the *material* of language, which must remain common to all ages and races ; לישן חד may denote the *manner* of utterance, which must vary with change of place, time and condition.

---

[1] Whitney, *Study of Lang.*, Lect. viii.
[2] Müller, *Science of Lang.*, First Series, p. 342.

On the whole, both ethnological and philological considerations
point in the direction of an ultimate racial and linguistic
unity.[1]

IV

RELATION OF EGYPTIAN

Whether Egyptian is to be classed among the Semitic
languages is a problem which scarcely enters our present field
of inquiry. It is apparently impossible to settle this question
from any examination of the hieroglyphic monuments. Nor
can we gather much more light from the deposit of Egyptian
words in other languages, for instance, the Egyptian words in
the Hebrew of the Old Testament. It is almost certain, however, that in the 'spoiling of the Egyptians' the Hebrews
carried away some linguistic booty.[2] We have this early
hint of the way in which a foreign element found its way
into the language of the Israelites. Other foreign elements
from various sources came later, as will appear in the progress
of this study. Egypt remains a dark and mysterious background all along the line. The only conclusions we care to
state on the problem of Egyptian are these: (a) Egypt was
the home of writing, the mother of arts, the cradle of
learning, the inventor of letters, i.e., symbolic characters.[3]

---

[1] Cf. on origin of races, Prichard, *Physical Hist. of Mankind*; Topin-
ard, *Eléménts d'Anthropologie Générale*; Peschel, *Races of Man*.
On origin of language, in addition to those already named, Wedgwood,
Origin of Lang.; Renan, *Histoire Générale des Langues Semitiques*;
Sayce, *Introd. to the Science of Lang.*

[2] Proper names like פרעה and פענח צפנת (? 'saviour of the world,'
Gen. 41[45]) are Egyptian. The following seem to be from the same source:
אחו, LXX ἄχει; יאר, LXX ποταμός; אברך, LXX κῆρυξ; שש, LXX βύσσος (Gen.
41[1, 2, 43], Ex. 26[1]). It is uncertain whether the pers. pron. אנכי came from
an Egypt. or an Assyr. source, i.e. from *anek* or *anak*. This pronoun-
form is found also in Phoen. and Moabite, i.e. אנך, but does not appear
in Arab. or Aram. But as Ⲧ- (*Ku*) appears as the suffix of the first pers.
pron. in Ethiop. (ⲰⲀⲖⲦ-, *walad-ku*), the form אנכי points to a north
African source, prob. therefore Egyptian. Cf. p. 54.

[3] According to Lucan, i. 3. 222, stone-writing preceded papyrus:
Nondum flumineas Memphis, contexere biblos
Noverat, et saxis tantum volucresque feraeque
Sculptaque servabant magicas animalia linguas.

(*b*) From Egyptian writing the Phoenicians constructed an alphabet which passed into world-literature.[1]

From various sources it has been computed that the ancient Egyptians used about 500 characters in their picture-hieroglyphic writing. These characters were phonetic and ideographic: some signs were alphabetic and others syllabic; some were generic and others specific. This may be represented in tabular form thus:

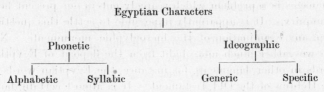

The ideographic characters were pictorial representations of the objects referred to, they were added immediately after the phonetic characters as 'determinatives' or representative symbols. The generic ideographs determined a class, and the specific ideographs determined an individual. There seems to have been no rule governing the direction of the script. It proceeded (1) from right to left, or (2) from left to right, or (3) in columns. The more correct arrangement was from right to left in horizontal lines. It is probable that the other methods, from left to right and in columns, were at first for ornamental effect. The lines or columns were read *towards the face* of any animal depicted. This hint will be found useful in the attempt to decipher the Hittite inscriptions, which still baffle the archaeologist.

No modern transliteration of ancient Egyptian represents with any certainty, or even tolerable accuracy, the native

---

[1] Herodotus attributes the transliteration of Phoen. letters into the Gk. alphabet to Cadmus, a Phoenician, celebrated in Grecian history :

Οἱ δὲ Φοίνικες οὗτοι οἱ σὺν Κάδμῳ ἀπικόμενοι, τῶν ἦσαν οἱ Γεφυραῖοι, ἄλλα τε πολλὰ, οἰκήσαντες ταύτην τὴν χώρην, ἐσήγαγον διδασκάλια ἐς τοὺς Ἕλληνας, καὶ δὴ καὶ γράμματα οὐκ ἐόντα πρὶν Ἕλλησι, ὡς ἐμοὶ δοκέειν· πρῶτα μὲν, τοῖσι καὶ ἅπαντες χρέωνται Φοίνικες· μετὰ δὲ, χρόνου προβαίνοντος, ἅμα τῇ φωνῇ μετέβαλον καὶ τὸν ῥυθμὸν τῶν γραμμάτων. Περιοίκεον δὲ σφέας τὰ πολλὰ τῶν χώρων τοῦτον τὸν χρόνον Ἑλλήνων Ἴωνες· οἳ παραλαβόντες διδαχῇ παρὰ τῶν Φοινίκων τὰ γράμματα, μεταρρυθμίσαντες σφέων ὀλίγα, ἐχρέωντο· χρεώμενοι δὲ ἐφάτισαν, ὥσπερ καὶ τὸ δίκαιον ἔφερε, ἐσαγαγόντων Φοινίκων ἐς τὴν Ἑλλάδα, Φοινικήϊα κεκλῆσθαι.
V. 58.

pronunciation.[1] The Coptic is the latest form of the Egyptian language. This form, along with the Greek transcription of Egyptian names, furnish the only means of attaining anything approaching the vocalization of the Egyptian language. Coptic spelling affords the earliest stage of the language which suggests some idea of the original and native pronunciation. While Coptic orthography thus supplies an important guide to philologists in restoring the word-forms of ancient Egyptian, it must be remembered that there is a great linguistic span between it and the older Egyptian dialects. Indeed, the true pronunciation of all the archaic languages is irrecoverably lost. Modern scholars usually pronounce Egyptian words phonetically, that is, as they are spelt.

V

EGYPTIANS AND HAMITES

It is customary to speak of the aboriginal Egyptians as ‘Hamites,’ but the meaning of the word חם, *cham* (? = *chemi*), is not clear. An interesting suggestion is that ‘Ham’ is a shortened form of *Ḥammu-rabi*, king of Babylonia. The most important point at the moment is the relation of the Hamites to the Semites. Canaan is said to be the son of Ham, which may mean ethnically that Ham was the father of the Canaanites,[2] in the same sense that Shem was ‘the father of all the children of Eber.’ Were Hamites in occupation of Canaan when Abraham entered the country? We must perhaps look in this direction for an explanation of the Hamitic element in Hebrew. If the Hamites at this period in Canaan spoke Hebrew, they must have learnt it from an earlier Semitic population. In this case they passed on

[1] In the Tell el-Amarna letters Khattu-shili, the Hittite king, gives the full name of Ramses II. as *Uashmuaria Shatepuaria Riamashesha mai-Amana*. This probably gives the approximate pronunciation of the name, slightly accommodated to the Babylonian speech and script. It is doubtless more original and correct than the conventional reading: *User-maa(t)ra Setepeura Ramses mari-Amen*.

[2] The phrase, ‘the father of Canaan’ (Gen. 9²²), may be a redactional insertion. Cf. Haupt, *Sacred Bks. of the OT*.

6

Hebrew through the Canaanite tribes, but with a certain linguistic filtration from the earlier Hamitic invasion. From the time of Abraham's migration, the languages of Canaan were for all practical purposes one, *i.e.* they were but dialectical varieties of the same basal speech. Hence (1) the Israelites in all their Canaanite wanderings never employed interpreters; (2) interpreters were first required by those Hebrew clans who ventured into Egypt; (3) the main difference between the spoken dialects of Canaan was accentual.

In the poetry of the Jews 'the land of Ham' evidently means 'Egypt,'[1] but when Mizraim is said to be the son of Ham, the reference is perhaps more geographical than ethnic. The modern Kaffir races of South Africa are historically and, it would seem, ethnically connected with the Hamitic Egyptians. Both their customs and their language point in this direction. Some of these tribes observe circumcision, the distinction between clean and unclean, certain marriage rites, and in one case, the Makalakas, the holding sacred of a seventh day. The Semitisms in their language are partly due, no doubt, to their association with strong and ruling Arab influences. The probability, however, is that the Kaffir races are fairly direct descendants of the ancient so-called 'Hamites.' The ancestors of the Kaffirs made large contributions to the Semitic invasions of Europe by Hannibal, and later they aided the great incursions of the Moors in the Middle Ages. The ancient Numidians,[2] the Copts and Berbers were in all likelihood of the same 'Hamitic' blood, and the southern Kaffirs are later prodigals.

---

[1] *E.g.* Ps. 105[23], where we have the equations :

ויבא ישראל מצרים

ויעקב גר בארץ־חם

[2] Numidia corresponded in a general way with the modern Algeria. The Greeks gave the name Λιβύη (*Odyss.* iv. 84) to the greater part of N. Africa, including Egypt. Herodotus says: νομάδες εἰσὶ Λίβυες.

Anciently the lang. of the Libyan tribes (Arab. لُوبِى = לובי) was Hamitic, inasmuch as they were αὐτόχθονες, while the Phoen. and Gks. were ἐπήλυδες (Herod. iv. 187, 197).

VI

TWO MAIN SEMITIC BRANCHES

The Two Main Branches—

Semitic Languages

North Semitic   South Semitic

The various Semitic dialects have many features in common, but between the northern and southern groups the difference is much greater than between any two members of the same group. In a general way it may be said, from a geographical point of view, that the north Semitic group includes Babylonian and Assyrian, Canaanite and Hebrew, and the Aramaic dialects ; the south Semitic group includes the Arabic and Ethiopic dialects. In this analysis it is really impossible with any consistency to follow either a geographical or historical line, and this for two reasons : (*a*) The political history of the early clans was very confused. There was conquering and recapturing of certain regions from time to time, and the line of triumph did not often follow any direct or consecutive course. (*b*) The people who earliest played a great part in history had not always the most ancient or developed language. Sometimes nations which came into prominence much later possessed a language far more characteristic of the primitive type. It is to be expected that in the 14th and 13th centuries B.C., the Semitic languages differed from each other much less than in later times. Nomadic tribes in the regions between Syria and Arabia, Canaan and Mesopotamia, could often understand one another in those early times.[1] The best representative languages of north and south Semitic are Hebrew and Arabic respectively. In its classical form Arabic is of later date than Hebrew, but in its ancient form akin to Hebrew and Aramaic, certainly as old, perhaps older.[2]

---

[1] The Israelites understood the Midianites (Judg. 7[9-15]) ; Jacob and Laban understood both Heb. and Aram. (Gen. 31[47]).

[2] The phases בני־קדם (Job 1[3], Judg. 7[12]) and ארצה בני־קדם (Gen. 29[1]) may refer to Arab clans allied in pursuit and language with the Midianites,

1. *South Semitic Branch—*

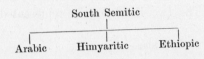

Originally the word עֲרָב was not an ethnic term, but came to be so through certain stages: (*a*) It stood for *waste, desert, uncultivated steppe.*[1] (*b*) It was the name of the deep gorge, extending from the N. of the Dead Sea to the Red Sea.[2] (*c*) It reached a transition meaning—passing from the notion of *waste land* to that of *community.*[3] (*d*) It came to mean the Arabians as distinguished from other clans.[4]

There are two distinct Arabian types of people, both traditionally descended from Shem. The better known are the 'Ishmaelites' of the northern part of the Arabian peninsula. But by Arab ethnologists these are the 'derived' or 'impure' Arabs, inasmuch as there is some Hebrew strain. The other stock is the 'Joktanic,' constituting the indigenous tribes of Yemen and the Aden hinterland. These are considered the 'original' or 'pure' Arabs, but they have lost

Amalekites and others. The reference to חכמת כל־בני־קדם (1 K. 5[10 Heb.]) is no doubt to magicians of Arabia, as well as to those of Chaldaea. The simplest explanation of the word חמשים (Judg. 7[11]) is that it was borrowed from the Arab clans which were *in battle array*. The term is thus derived from خميس, *army*; cf. خمال, *military valour*. The √ חמש seems common to nearly all the Semitic languages as a numeral—five. When employed in reference to battle it suggests the disposition of the warriors into five attacking divisions. This connotation of the word is probably of N. Arabic origin, and thus indicates the influence of Arabic on Hebrew in remote times (cf. Ex. 13[18], Jos. 1[14] 4[12], Num. 32[17]).

[1] Hence we translate מַשָּׂא בְּעַרְב בַּיַּעַר בָּעֲרָב תָּלִינוּ אֹרְחוֹת דְּדָנִים, 'the oracle on the waste: encamp in the thicket, in the waste, ye Bedouins of Dedan' (Is. 21[13]).

[2] The modern name of the entire Jordan-valley is *El-Ghôr* (cf. Dt. 1[7], Jos. 11[2. 16]); the modern name of the depression S. of the Dead Sea is *Wady el-Araba* (cf. Dt. 2[8]).

[3] It is uncertain, *e.g.*, whether the terms עֲרָבִי (Is. 13[20]) and כְּעַרְבִי (Jer. 3[2]) should be taken as proper names of the Arabians, or simply as denoting prairie clans.

[4] The term was extended to the dwellers of the whole N. Arabian peninsula as early as Herodotus: ἔστι δὲ τῆς Ἀραβίης χώρης (ii. 11); cf. Neh. 4[1], 2 Ch. 22[1]; Euting, *Sin. Inscrip.* 463.

something of their characteristic features by intermarriage with immigrant Ishmaelite Arabs, and also by the presence of local taints. The two lines may be represented graphically thus :

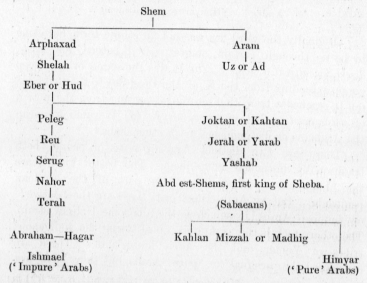

Shem

Arphaxad   Aram
Shelah   Uz or Ad
Eber or Hud

Peleg   Joktan or Kahtan
Reu   Jerah or Yarab
Serug   Yashab
Nahor   Abd est-Shems, first king of Sheba.
Terah   (Sabaeans)

Abraham—Hagar   Kahlan Mizzah or Madhig
Ishmael   Himyar
('Impure' Arabs)   ('Pure' Arabs)

These genealogical steps are tribes rather than individuals. Jerah, son of Joktan, is said to have been the progenitor of Yemen (S. Arabian) Arabic, and to have first separated the old Arabic from ancient Hebrew. He, too, was the reputed founder of the Sabaean kingdom in Yemen on the ruins of the old Minean dynasty, which probably dates as early as 3000 B.C. The Sabaean kingdom merged into the Himyaritic dynasty as the table shows. It is not possible to decide whether the language of the so-called 'Ishmaelite' tribes was more akin to Arabic or Hebrew. The fact that in an Assyrian inscription [1] the name of the god of Kedar is *Atar Samaïn* favours the former. *Atar* is the Arabic *'Athtar*,[2] and not the Hebrew *'Ashtar*; *Samaïn* is probably the Arabic plural of *Samā*, 'heaven.' From the Aramaic and Arabic proper names in the Ituraean inscriptions no

---

[1] Vide *Keilinschriftliche Bibliothek*, etc., vol. ii. 216.
[2] Sabaean עתתר, CIS iv. 40[4] 41[2] 46[5] 74[12] *el al*.

conclusion can be drawn respecting the nationality and language of the people concerned.[1]

For long ages the Arabic branch of the Semitic family slumbered in inaction and insignificance in the plains of Arabia. Then suddenly at the call of a new prophet the tribes awoke and spread in irresistible numbers over Asia, Africa and parts of Europe. Arabic, of course, is far older than Islam ; it was the spoken language of the tribes which occupied the central steppes of the country. The contributory elements to the united Arab nationality were possibly the early Ishmaelites, Midianites, Amalekites and other kindred clans, who wandered southward from the scene of Hebrew activity. At the beginning of the seventh century B.C. all trace of these nomadic bands had disappeared. They were then in the heart of Arabia forming a new nationality with a common speech. All the constituent tribes were of the purest Semitic blood, and they were less affected by foreign influence than any other member of the Semitic family. This explains the purity and homogeneity of their national tongue. The Arabic language has had a great history, and in many respects is more remarkable than any other Semitic speech. With the rise of Muhammadanism, Arabic entered upon a history almost comparable with that of Latin itself. In any Semitic study, Arabic is a most useful adjunct, inasmuch as it often indicates the true significance of words where the Hebrew, Syriac and other dialects are faulty or doubtful. For the understanding of primitive Semitic vowel-sounds a study of Arabic is almost indispensable. The meaning of many grammatical forms can only be discovered by tracing the vowels back to their original sounds. In Hebrew and Aramaic the vowels have undergone vast modifications, whilst in Arabic they have retained to a large extent their primitive purity and simplicity. In its ruggedness Hebrew seems an older language than Arabic, but some Arabic forms are certainly older than the corresponding Hebrew. The influence of ‘Arabic on the language of Palestine was mainly in vocabulary. This is seen to some extent in the

---

[1] On subj. generally, cf. Redhouse, *Chronological Synopsis of Arab. Hist.*; Huart, *Histoire des Arābes* ; Sale, *Introduction to the Koran.*

text of the Old Testament, and especially in the Book of Job.[1]
It is also and more clearly evident in the Aramaic and other
inscriptions of Asia Minor and Arabia.

Himyaritic was the dialect of south Arabia, and extended
from the strait of Bab-el-Mandeb on the West to the mouth of
the Persian Gulf on the East. This dialect is proved by the
numerous inscriptions discovered in Yemen to have been the
ancient speech of kindred tribes in the area named.[2] Probably
the province of חצרמות, the modern *Hadramaut*, was peopled
by a Himyaritic clan.[3] This dialect was apparently intermediate between the Arabic of central Arabia and Ethiopic. Its
modern representative, the *Hakili*, bears a strong resemblance
to the later developments of Ethiopic. Tradition says that the
Himyarites became the dominant race in Yemen about 3000
years before Muhammad. They spread in one direction to the
Euphrates, and in another to Abyssinia. Their most prosperous
period was from 100 B.C. to 629 A.D.[4]

It is not necessary to dwell on Himyaritic and Ethiopic,
as these did not affect to any appreciable extent the language
of Palestine. The likeness of Ethiopic to Arabic suggests an
original tribal affinity. The Cushites of Arabia Petraea were
probably the primitive stock. From Arabia a section of
Cushites emigrated to Africa and settled in the province

---

[1] The text of the Book of Job constitutes a very interesting problem.
The LXX differs widely from the Massoretic text. A little less than one-fifth
of the Heb. text is wanting in the LXX (*i.e.* 400 lines out of a total 2200).
It is sometimes contended that the Heb. text has been augmented, or that
the LXX has been abbreviated. More frequently it is argued that the
two texts are from different Hebrew sources. No scholar has seriously
suggested that the text behind the LXX was in Arabic, and that this
Arabic version was briefer than the Heb. A study of the Arabic words
and colouring of the Book of Job would provide much in favour of this
view.

[2] This dialect in Arab. is called حِمْيَر = הִמְיָר.

[3] Cf. Gen. 10²⁶· Strabo calls these S. Arabian tribes χατραμωτῖται
(xvi. 4. 2) ; modern Arab. حَضْر مَوت, *enclosure of death*. The Sabaean
form is same as Heb. LXX Σαρμώθ (Gen. 10²⁶), ᾿Αραμώθ (1 Ch. 1²⁰). For
inscriptions, *vide* Glaser, *Skizze*, 2. 20, 423 ff.

[4] The modern *Mahrah*, مهره, tribes of south Arabia are the lineal
descendants of the ancient Himyarites.

called Ethiopia.[1] If this relation between the Cushite tribes existed, it would give an explanation of the similarity of their dialects. Ethiopic must be traced ultimately to Arabic.[2] In its simplicity of construction, however, it is more akin with Hebrew and Aramaic, a fact due to the influence of the Himyaritic of Yemen. Ethiopic was the living national language of Abyssinia, till it was superseded by the modern Amharic, which took its definite form in the thirteenth century A.D. But there were stages marked by distinctive dialects of Ethiopic. (*a*) The old Ge'ez was early supplanted by the Tigré in the outlying provinces of the country. (*b*) Tigrina was the contemporary dialect of the province of Shoa, of south-east and of central Abyssinia : it formed a link between the Tigré and the Amharic. (*c*) Amharic was the language of the district of Amhara. This form of Ethiopic is probably as old as the other two dialects, but it has gradually gained ground in south and central Abyssinia. It is now the vulgar tongue as well as the court language.[3]

---

[1] On Egyptian inscriptions Ethiopia is termed *Kesh*. Probably this 'Cush' is meant in Is. 11¹¹ 18¹ 20⁴. In Jer. 13²³ the reference is almost certainly to Ethiopia proper. The word כוש, prob. = כור, means *furnace*, as Arab. كّ,, Eth. **ከሠረ**, *swarthy*; cf. Aἰθίοψ = αἴθω, *to burn*, and ὤψ, *face* ; hence כושים = 'the sun-burnt people.' Cf. Herodotus, iii. 94, vii. 70.

[2] Perhaps Ethiopic is more correctly *Ge'ez*. The word **ግዕዝ** is said by some to signify *original speech*, and by others *migratio*. We suggest, however, that the original Eth. root was **ግዘo**, *to cut in two* (cf. Arab. جَزَ, *to cut off*), the reference being to the division of the Cushite clans into two great sections, as indicated above.

[3] Many words came into Heb., including some proper names, which were of Egyptian origin. A few may here be compared with the Coptic forms :

מֹשֶׁה	ⲙⲱ-ⲟⲩⲭⲉ	אַבֶּה	ⲉⲃⲟⲩ
פַּרְעֹה	ⲡⲟⲩⲣⲟ	אַיָּל	ⲉⲓⲟⲩⲗ
רַעְמְסֵס	ⲣⲏⲙⲥⲥ	יְאֹר	ⲓⲟⲣ
שִׁישַׁק	ϣϣⲕ	אֵיפָה	ⲱⲓⲡⲓ
פַּתְרוֹם	ⲡⲉⲧⲣⲏⲥ	אֹן	ⲱⲛ
פְּתֹם	ⲡⲓⲑⲟⲙ	נֹעֶה	ⲛⲁ
פּוּל	ⲡⲟⲗⲟ	שָׁשָּׁה	ϣⲟⲛⲧⲉ

2. *North Semitic Branch—*

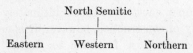

North Semitic

Eastern   Western   Northern

This branch is best considered under three sections, inasmuch as each section is sufficiently distinct to claim separate reference. At the same time it is difficult to know exactly where to fix the dividing line between some of these northern dialectic offshoots. The eastern section includes the provinces of Babylonia and Assyria. The western section includes the lands of Phoenicia and adjacent Canaanite regions. The northern section includes the localities in and around Syria, and dialectically Palestine, Edessa and parts of Egypt.[1]

Eastern Section of North Semitic Branch—

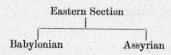

Eastern Section

Babylonian   Assyrian

It is impossible to make a clear distinction between Babylonia and Assyria. The people were the same,[2] the religion was the same, arts, crafts and customs were the same, and the language was the same. If any distinction can be made, perhaps Babylonia in some sense led the way. Politically the association is just as indistinct ; sometimes Assyria is a province of Babylonia, and sometimes Babylonia is a

---

[1] A different arrangement is sometimes found : ' I. The old Babyl. and Assyr. . . . From this the Aram. dialects derive their origin. II. The old Canaanitish, of which the Heb. and Phoen. were important dialects. III. The old Arabic, of which the Ethiopic and Abyssinian are offshoots. . . . IV. The old Egyptian, which is a deposit of some ante-historical Semitic idiom. . . . It is represented in a modern form by Coptic. V. The Berber dialects scattered over the whole of Africa," . . . (*Ency. Brit. s.v.* ' Philology'). The present study will amplify, and to some extent modify, this outline.

[2] In Gen. 10²², Elam and Asshur are sons of Shem. The Elamites were not originally Semites, but their earliest history is closely interwoven with Babylonia. Berosus, a native Chaldaean historian, seems to regard the Elamites as Cushites, and of an Assyrian dynasty in Asia, and gives priority in time to the former. *Vide* Payne Smith, *Anc. Hist.* i. ch. 11.

province of Assyria. But the difference scarcely appeared to
the historian who called Nebuchadrezzar, king of Babylon,
'King of Assyria' (2 K. 23²⁹), who went out against
Pharaoh-Necho at Megiddo.¹ The three terms—Babylonian,
Assyrian, Chaldaean—were no doubt distinctive in origin, but
they became to some extent interchangeable in later history.
Babylonia was so named from the chief town;² Assyria was
probably so called from a supposed connexion with Asshur;³
Chaldaea was originally a province S.-E. of Babylonia proper.⁴
Whatever ethnological distinction may have existed between
these tribes in pre-historic times, they emerge on the scene
with one language, which was certainly Semitic, and must be
characterized as Aramaic.

Western Section of North Semitic Branch—

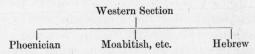

The home of the Phoenicians has not yet been definitely
ascertained, and early accounts differ.⁵ On the whole it is
probable that the primitive clans came out of Chaldaea from a
region on the Persian Gulf. Their first great migration, it
may be conjectured, was about the time of the call of Abram,
when there was a momentous journeying of the Semitic tribes
up the Euphrates valley.⁶ This movement was perhaps
simultaneous with the great migration of tribes from north

¹ Nabopolassar was really king, but Nebuchadrezzar was acting against
Egypt. The 'Magdolum' of Herodotus is probably the same as Megiddo ;
vide bk. i. 17. 18, 25, ii. 159.

² בבל, Ass. *Bab-ilu* (Delitzsch, *Par.* 212 ; but cf. Jensen, *Cosmologie der
Babylonier*, 498). Other names in Gen. 10¹⁰ are confirmed by Ass. inscript.:
ארך=*Arku*; אכד=*Akkadi*; שנער=*Sanhar* (Tell el-Amarna); אור=*Uru*(Gen. 11²⁸).

³ The phrase in Gen. 10¹¹ is uncertain. It is corrected by Onk. מִן־אַרְעָא
הַהִיא נְפַק אֲתוּרָאָה.

⁴ כשדים, Ass. *Kaldū*. These people spoke a Semitic language, and they
provided an early dynasty of Babylonia. Nabopolassar, who refounded
Babylon (*circa* 626), was a Chaldaean, and from his time Chaldaea was
synonymous with Babylonia. For ancient references to Chaldaeans, *vide*
Xen. *Cyrop.* iii. 2. 7 ; *Anab.* iv. 3. 4, v. 5, viii. 8. 14.

⁵ *Vide* Herodotus, i. 1, vii. 89 ; Strabo, xvi.

⁶ Cf. Rawlinson, *Herodotus*, iv., Essay ii.

Arabia, along the shore of the Persian Gulf and the Euphrates valley. The outcome of these migrations was the formation of two important dynasties—the Kassite dynasty in Babylon, and the Hyksos dynasty in Egypt. The Phoenicians were originally Hamites, and in the Old Testament are frequently called 'Sidonians,'[1] and *Chna* (= Heb. כנען) was the original name of their country.[2]

The old question, How did the Phoenicians come to employ a Semitic language ? has no longer any force. When the Phoenicians were simply described as 'Hamites,' it was usual to affirm that they changed their language after their settlement along the coast-lands of Canaan. Before they appeared on these borders, we have no clear knowledge of their history. If there was any foundation for the statement of Herodotus (i. 1, vii. 89) that they came from the Persian Gulf, we should still be without knowledge of their speech. It is quite possible that the Phoenicians were a composite people, made up of Hamitic and Semitic elements. But when they appear in contact with Canaanite tribes, they are found to speak with an analogous tongue. There were slight dialectic differences between them, but no linguistic barrier. For the Canaanite tribes, the Phoenicians were the pioneers of the alphabet and of writing in the more modern sense. Whether the Phoenicians produced their alphabet from an adaptation of Egyptian hieroglyphs, or from a reconstruction of Babylonian cuneiform, or from contact with Aegean civilization, or from a concurrence of all these factors, is considered in another place. It is certain that 'Phoenician' became the type of all subsequent script in western Asia and Europe. In this type of script the greater part of the Old Testament was written.

That there should be a Phoenician element in Old Testament Hebrew was to be expected. The compilers of some of the Jewish books probably had access to some Phoenician sources,[3] as much later Josephus gained information about

[1] *Vide* Gen. 10[6, 15] : חם—כנען—צידן.
[2] Tell el-Amarna=*Kinaḥna*. Found on a Phoen. coin : לארכא אש בכנען 'Laodicea which is in Canaan'=Phoenicia (v–ii B.C.).
[3] *Vide* Ezek. 27–28, Is. 23.

Nebuchadrezzar's siege of Tyre from Phoenician writings.[1]
The following statements will indicate a line of study which
could be greatly extended, but scarcely belongs to the present
investigation.. Some Old Testament passages should perhaps
be emended in the light of the Phoenician script. The word
we select for illustration is איש, in Hebrew 'man'; the
Phoenician form is אש.[2] But אש in Hebrew may be 'fire'
(אֵשׁ), or the substantive particle 'there is' (אֵשׁ or יֵשׁ). Moreover, the Phoenician אש is also the relative pronoun = Hebrew
אשר.[3] Have these forms led to some confusion in the Hebrew
text?

In Ezek. 8[2] it is almost certain that אש = איש: thus the
phrase דמות כמראה־אש should be rendered 'a likeness as the
appearance of a man.' This seems necessitated by the following reference to מתניו, 'his loins,' which could hardly be
applied to fire. In Ezek. 21[37] (Heb.) a similar case occurs:
לאש תהיה לאכלה should be read, 'To man thou shalt be for
food' (cf. Is. 9[18]). In Ezek. 1[4] אֵשׁ possibly stands for יֵשׁ or
אֵשׁ. The Hebrew is difficult: ענן גדול ואש מתלקחת ונגה לו סביב,
but may be translated 'a great cloud, and *there was* a
continuous involution (Hithp.), and a brightness surrounding
it.' In Dt. 33[2], אֵשׁ may = the Hebrew substantive particle
יֵשׁ, or the Phoenician substantive אש (= Heb. אִישׁ). The text
stands: מימינו אשדת למו, and is probably corrupt. The reference appears to be to the writing of the law on Sinai by the
hand of Yahveh (Ex. 31[18]). The term אשדת is *ἅπαξ λεγ.*,
and דת is Aramaic of the Persian period denoting *law, decree*.
Now a 'fire of law' is an anomaly, though figuratively it
might stand for the scene of the law-giving. We may
translate either (*a*) 'At His right hand *there was* a law (שׁ דת)
for them' (cf. Is. 62[8]), or (*b*) 'At His right hand (was) *a man*
of law (איש דת) for them' (cf. Dt. 31[4. 29], Jos. 1[7] 22[2]; איש ימינך,
Ps. 80[17], John 1[17]). In Is. 64[1] there is perhaps an
instance of the Phoenician relative pronoun אש (= Hebrew

---

[1] *Ant.* x. 11.

[2] Old Heb. was the same, אש נר, Moab. St. l. 10; cf. CIS i. 86[9].

[3] *E.g.* אֲשֶׁר הִיא שְׁנַת=אש שת הא, CIS i. 93[2]; *ib.* 139[1]. So on Phoen. coins,
e.g. as already quoted: לאארכא אש בכנען, 'Laodicea *which* is in Canaan'
(Plate ix B8. Brit. Mus.). Occasionally in Heb. איש=אש in proper
names, *e.g.* אשבל=בעל איש (Gen. 46[21], Num. 26[38]).

אשר) being read for the Hebrew אֵשׁ, *fire*. There is apparently corruption of text, but it reads : בקדה אש המסים מים תבעה אש. Possibly the first אש may be taken as a noun and the second as a pronoun, and the passage read : 'Like *fire* kindles the sticks, *which* (or when it) boils the water.' In Lev. 22⁴, and like passages, the second איש might be translated as a pronoun (Phoen. אש or Heb. אשר), thus : 'What man of the seed of Aaron, *who* is a leper . . . ?' In Ezek. 31³ it is pretty certain that אשר has been mistaken for a substantive. The text stands : הנה אשר ארז בלבנן. The pointing is אַשֶׁר = אַשּׁוּר, 'Assyrian,' and so generally read by scholars. But the whole reference is to Egypt, not to Assyria ; to Pharaoh, not to Nebuchadrezzar. The question of v.² is answered in v.¹⁸, and we should probably read : 'Behold, *he who was* (as) a cedar in Lebanon.'

It is perhaps too precarious to suggest a Phoenician form, אשם, in the passage : . . . אם־תשים אשם נפשו יראה זרע (Is. 53¹⁰). Some idea is wanted to harmonize with the phrase, 'He shall see a seed.' Now a 'seed' must be *begotten* or produced, and this idea is not foreign to the verb שׂוּם.[1] But what is the meaning of אשם ? The Phoenician for איש, *man*, is אש, and the plural is אשם.[2] Can this Phoenician form be accepted in the present instance ? That there is a foreign element in the Hebrew passage is suggested by the Aramaic form החלי.[3] The 'seed' is attributed to the life-struggle of Yahveh's Servant : מעמל נפשו, 'from the anguish of His life.' This involved the shedding of His life-blood : הערה למות נפשו, 'He exposed to death His life.' That a righteous seed might be ordained, begotten, Yahveh crushed Him, 'He made Him sick,' דכאו החלי. But following His agony, there shall appear a generation of chosen, reborn men, and with the result shall come the Sufferer's felicity. Hence we may translate : 'When He

---

[1] *Vide* וישימו בנים, Ezra 10⁴⁴ ; cf. Gen. 13¹⁶. The verb has also the idea of 'designate,' 'appoint,' 'determine' ; cf. CIS ii. 113⁴.

[2] Cf. the Phoen. pl. שמם, 'heavens.' This form of pl. is not unknown in Heb. העינם (Jos. 15³⁴) ; the form קרתן (Jos. 21³²) is more Aram., the Heb. is קריתים (1 Ch. 6⁶¹). Both endings are found on Moab. St., הצהרם, מאהן (ll. 15, 20). For Phoen. inscrip. cf. . . . לאשם אש, 'To men who . . . ' (CIS i. 86A ⁹).

[3] For Heb. *Hiphil* החלה.

(lit. His life) shall beget (lit. set up; ordain, renew) men, He shall see a seed, He shall long live, and the purpose of Yahveh shall succeed through His instrumentality. From the toil of His life He shall see it (the reborn race), He shall be satisfied.'

The Moabites and other Canaanite tribes were closely allied with the Phoenicians in language. It is probable, however, that the Canaanite dialects were more akin to each other than to Phoenician. The difference between these dialects was largely one of local accent or pronunciation.[1] The Old Testament recognizes slight dialectic differences between the Canaanite tribes themselves, and between them and neighbouring tribes. Among the dialects referred to are Moabite (practically = Hebrew), Hittite, Amorite, Phoenician (probably = Sidonian), Ashdodite [2] (apparently = Philistine), Aramaic, Judaean.[3] By 'the language of Canaan' (Is. 19[18]) is meant the original tongue of the settlers, that which is designated 'Hebrew.' [4]

The relation of Moabite to Hebrew was so close that no distinction of language must be conjectured. The likenesses are so many and unmistakable that the two forms certainly belong to the same stock, and differ but slightly when they emerge upon the historic scene. The variations are easily explained by the different conditions and regions into which the different branches of the common stock wandered. Whether, therefore, Moabite was a dialect of Hebrew,[5] or Hebrew a dialect of Moabite, is no longer a problem to be solved. They are rather to be regarded as dialectic differences of one and the same language. Moabite did not differ from Judaic Hebrew in so many respects as the north Israelitish dialects.[6] In a general way it may be said that

[1] *E.g.* the Gileadites said שבלת, and the Ephraimites said סבלת (Judg. 12[6]); the Sidonians said שרין, and the Amorites said שניר (Dt. 3[9]). There may be an accidental transposition of letters in this word, but the termination ין suggests a later linguistic stage. The clan of Sidonians here referred to may have been an offshoot from the Amorites.

[2] The מדבר אשדורית (Neh. 13[24]) = the speech of Philistines. Cf. p. 152.

[3] The term יהורית (Neh. 13[24]) means 'the Jewish language, but perhaps more specifically the language of Judaea' (cf. 2 K. 18[26]).

[4] Lit. שפת כנען means the 'lip of Canaan'; cf. לשון = speech.

[5] *Vide* Grove, Smith's *Dict. Bibl. s.v.* 'Moab.'

[6] Later known as 'Samaritan,' 'Galilaean,' etc.

Moabite agrees with Hebrew and Phoenician, and the north Israelitish dialects with Aramaic and Arabic.[1] But in some particulars the variants are curious. Sometimes Moabite agrees with Hebrew against both Phoenician and Aramaic.[2] Sometimes Moabite agrees with Phoenician against Hebrew and Aramaic.[3] Occasionally Moabite agrees with Arabic in a manner scarcely to be expected.[4] Again, Moabite sometimes agrees with Hebrew and Phoenician against Aramaic and Arabic.[5] Some Moabite forms agree with Aramaic against Hebrew and Phoenician.[6] These variants are dialectic, they indicate the affinity and commingling of Semitic peoples in western Asia in the second millennium, B.C. It must always be remembered that the inscriptional type of language may have been different in many respects from the commonly spoken dialect. The actually spoken tongue of a people almost invariably shows considerable deviation from the language of literature.

Hebrew and Arabic ethnologically are traceable to the same stock. The two sons of Eber were Peleg and Joktan. Through the former came Jacob, and consequently the Israelites;[7] through the latter came the Arabians. The descendants of Joktan dwelt from Mesha to Sephar, 'the hill-country of the east.'[8] It is clear that Joktan is repre-

---

[1] Cf. Driver, *Introd. OT.* 422 n. ; *Heb. Text Bks. of Sam.*[2] xciii.

[2] *E.g.* the impf. with *vav* conversive : וָאֶלְחַם בְּקִר וָאֹחֲזֶה, 'And I fought against the city and took it' (Moab. St. l. 11) ; the rel. pron. אשר (Phoen. אש, Aram. די, י, ו, Syr. ?). Does אשל=אשר, *i.e.* אשר לי (cf. CIS i. 7[4]) ? Thus it is a rel. *sign=as to which, as to whom.*

[3] *E.g.* the form שת, 'year' (Moab. St. l. 2) is the same as Phoen., and =Heb. שנה, Aram. שנא.

[4] The most notable un-Hebrew feature is the insertion of ת after the first radical, on the analogy of the inf. of the 8th Arab. conj., *e.g.* בהלתחמה (*l.c.* l. 19)=בְּהִלָּחֵמֹה, lit. 'in the to fight,' *i.e.* 'while he fought.'

[5] An illus. is אנך, with Heb. and Phoen. (and Old Aram.) ; Arab. Eth. and later Aram. give אנא.

[6] This is seen in the pl. ending, ן, for Heb. and Phoen. ים, ם, thus : ארבען, 'forty' (*l.c.* l. 8) ; קרן, 'cities' (l. 29), cf. Aram. קרין (Onk. freq. קרויא). *Vide* Schröder, *Die Phönizische Sprache* (1869).

[7] The links were : יעקב—יצחק—אברם—תרח—נחור—שרוג—רעו—פלג (*vide* Gen. 10[25] 11[18-26] 21[3] 25[26] ; cf. Gen. 32[28], Is. 27[6], Nah. 2[2]).

[8] Probably משא, in Assyr. inscrip. *Mashu*, is the desert land between Syria and Arabia. Probably ספר=*Tsafar*, the ancient capital of the Himyarites, the seaport of Hadramaut on the Indian Ocean, S. Arabia.

sented as the ancestor of the older Arabian clans, the pure
Arabs as contrasted with the Ishmaelite Arabs. Thus Eber
was the ancestor of both the Israelites and the Arabians,
and this fact helps to explain the similarities between the
Hebrew and Arabic languages. In a sense Hebrew holds
a middle position between Aramaic and Arabic; it is wider
in scope than the former, and less comprehensive than the
latter.[1]

Of the three languages the Arabic exhibits, in some
respects, the oldest features, but Hebrew and Aramaic did
not grow out of Arabic. Each language had an independent
development from an earlier common speech, which cannot
be traced with any degree of certainty. Graphically the
position may be represented thus:

Common
Source.

In this figure A represents Aramaic, and
B Hebrew; these gradually diverged from C, *i.e.*
Arabic. After the Exile, Hebrew as a spoken
language was lost in the continuous stream of
Aramaic (D), which became the vernacular of
Palestine. Arabic never came into serious con-
tact with Hebrew, but after the rise of Islam,
Arabic moved towards Palestine, and superseding
Aramaic, became the common speech (E). Natur-
ally Aramaic (D) took along some Hebrew,[2] and
Arabic (E) took along some Aramaic.[3]

The influence of the further East on the Hebrew language
has not yet received the attention which it deserves. It is
customary to refer certain names of articles of luxury to an

Thus הר הקדם will point to a mountainous region in Arabia, 'the east
country' (cf. Gen. 10³⁰ 25⁶).

[1] These linguistic positions were due partly to geographical movements,
and partly to intellectual attainments.

[2] *E.g.* Aram. words like אחרית, *end*, נביא, *prophet*, צדא, *purpose*, ניחוח,
soothing, אנשים, *men*, are apparently due to Heb. influence.

[3] Some modern Arabic words in Palestine are found in the earlier
Aram., *e.g.* جدر, *fold*, Aram. נדירא; بير, *pit*, Aram. בארא; بركة, *pool*,
Aram. בריכתא; طل, *dew*, Aram. מלא; وعر, *forest*, Aram. יערא; تبن, *straw*,
Aram. תיבנא.

Indian origin. Possibly some terms of a regal character are due to Sanscrit, but in these instances an Arabic source may be suggested. It is always important in tracing the origin of anything to distinguish the primitive source from the medium of communication. For instance, it is usual to attribute the signs for numbers to the Arabs, but the Indians were the first to deviate from the ancient custom of making their letters stand for numbers. Strictly the Sanscrit letters have no specific and separate names, and consequently could not conveniently represent numbers. Hence the Indians invented the ten numerals,[1] though they have come to us through Arabic influence. The discrepancy between Semitic and Indo-European spelling is often due to alphabetical differences and deficiencies.[2]

It is probable, however, that some words which the earlier philologists attributed to a Sanscrit source are more naturally explained by a reference to Arabic, or, as some modern scholars suggest, to Assyrian. The title רוֹזֵן, or רָזוֹן (Prov. 14[23]), 'prince,' 'ruler,' will serve as an illustration of the general subject. In Hebrew there was no necessity for this term, it was a mere poetical embellishment used synonymously with מֶלֶךְ (once with שֹׁפֵט, Is. 40[23]). It was evidently a borrowed word, and, like many others in Hebrew,[3] may be

---

[1] The Arabs admit the Indian source by the name رقم هندى or خروف هندى, 'Indian signs.'

[2] *Omnis illa variatio et discrepantia in defectum Alphabetorum Europaeorum et gentilium Indicorum est rejicienda.* Gr. *Samscridamica,* Romae, 1790.

[3] Familiar among these words are the following :—'Almug-trees': San. *Valgu, Valgum* (or *mocha*); Heb. אלמגים, prob. = 'sandalwood'; Gk. πελεκητά. 'Aloes': San. *aguru*; Ass. *âlu*; Arab. هيل, 'tent'; Heb. אהלים; Gk. ἀγάλλοχον, 'eaglewood.' Note: such words beg. with אל sugg. the Arab. art. ال, 'the.' 'Apes': San. *kapi*; Heb. קפם; cf. Gk. κῆπος (Egypt. κυφι). 'Ophir': San. *Abhira?* Heb. אפיר; Σώφειρα (Joseph. *Ant.* viii. 6. 4); accord. to Hitzig (*Philistäer*, p. 217) = Indian *Sauvira.* 'Ivory': San. *ibhas* (cf. *danta*); Ass. *sinnu*; Arab. سن, 'tooth'; Heb. שן (cf. שנהבים, lit. 'ebony-teeth,' 'elephants'; prob. corrupt). 'Peacock': San. *sikhin*, or Tamil *tokei, togai*; Heb. תכיים. 'Topaz': San. *pita*; Heb. פטרה; Gk. τοπάζιον. 'Girdle-of-state': Heb. אבנט, 'priests-girdle'; no doubt a loan-word whose source is unknown; Gk. ἀβανήθ (Joseph. *Ant.* iii. 7. 2).

traced with some plausibility to either Sanscrit or Arabic.[1]
If the former, it may be related to the Sanscrit word for
king—*Rawjan* = רוֹ. The Sanscrit has no letter corresponding to the Hebrew ז, but uses a letter whose sound more
resembles the Arabic ج (*Jeem*); but ז nearly = Arabic ز.
This will explain some apparent discrepancies in the transliteration of Sanscrit words in the Semitic tongues. If the
title came from an Indian source, it would mean that
prophets and poets in Israel in pre-regal times had a term
applied to them equivalent to Nabob and Mogul. On the
other hand, רוזן might very well come from the Arabic
root رزن, 'gravity,' 'dignity,' which became associated with
precedence and honour.[2] The word in an adjectival form
occurs in the *Arabian Nights*, in the saying of the barber's
fifth brother: اشدة عقلي ورزانة عقلي, 'with dignified dis-
cretion and majestic wisdom.' In cases of uncertainty the
probability always is that the derivation of Hebrew loan-words
is from the Arabic rather than Sanscrit.

VII

ARAMAIC: EAST AND WEST

Northern Section of North Semitic Branch—

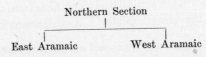

Northern Section

| | |
| East Aramaic | West Aramaic |

The division between east and west Aramaic must not
be pressed too sharply. It may, however, add to clearness

[1] The Ass. *ruzzunu*, 'prince,' should not be overlooked, having much
the same form and meaning (vide *Journal Bibl. Lit.* xvi. 175 f.).

[2] The term רוזן is derived from the obs. root רזן, and not from רזה, رزح,
to make lean. The word רוזין in a Palm. inscrip. suggests a composite
idea. It is prob. from רוא, رزي =*impoverishment by generosity* (cf. Gk.
δαπαναί); hence the phrase וחסך רוזין שניאן may be rendered: 'and bestowed
most lavishly.' (For inscrip. vide Vogüé, *La Syrie Centrale*, 15.)

to separate the north Mesopotamian [1] type of Aramaic from the Palestinian type. This separation is largely geographical; dialectically there is considerable overlapping. East Aramaic includes Syriac, Nabataean, and Mandaean; west Aramaic includes Palmyrene, Egyptian Aramaic, and Palestinian Aramaic. The real problem is to evolve from these dialects the one type which best represents the language of Palestine between 100 B.C. and 100 A.D. Meanwhile we must consider the supersession of Hebrew by Aramaic which followed the Exile.

At a very early date a considerable portion of the population of Babylonia-Assyria was Aramaean, while Assyrian was still the language of the government. The earliest hints are certain Aramaic writings on weights, and other inscriptions. This early form of Semitic language is certainly Aramaic, but differs considerably from Biblical and Egyptian Aramaic. It more resembles Hittite (Hebrew-Canaanite), and in some respects it resembles Assyrian. That the Assyrian and Aramaic languages were closely associated in the seventh century B.C. is suggested by the description of Nebuchadrezzar's army as 'the army of the Chaldaeans and of the Aramaeans,' and also by the Assyrian-Aramaic inscriptions on the bronze weights found at Nineveh.[2] These hints do not prove that Aramaic had its origin in Babylonia-Assyria. Assyrian and Aramaic had long separate histories before the time of Nebuchadrezzar. But the evidence shows that these languages came into contact with each other in Babylonia-Assyria. Each assimilated something from the other, but Aramaic was the greater debtor. Assyrian was already a

---

[1] The N. Mesopotamian includes, as will appear later, the Syriac of Edessa. Possibly Edessa is to be identified with אור, ‎ܐܽܘܪܗܳܝ. This region is called אור כַּשְׂדִּים (Gen. 11[28]), either (a) because N. Mesopotamia formed an original base of Chaldaean activity, or (b) because they extended their empire thus far North after its establishment in Babylonia. It must, however, be stated that most scholars identify אור with the old Babylonian city of Uru (cf. Delitzsch, Wo lag das Paradies? 226 f.).

[2] The Zenjirli (زنجيرلو, a village N.W. Syria) inscriptions belong to 8th cent. B.C. Assyr. influence is seen in the form אל (cf. אלהו), ilu; in N. Sem. inscrip. almost exclusively in compounds (vide Cooke, N. Semit. inscr. p. 165). The Aram. כלמו, totality, is Assyr. kalamu (ib. p. 184). In the Nineveh inscr. (CIS. ii. 1), the form מלך is due to Assyr. influence; the usual Aram. would be מלכא.

declining force, and Aramaic soon prevailed in most of the provinces included in the Babylonia-Assyria zone. From these regions Aramaic came into Palestine and supplanted Hebrew.

Among the districts and cities which were mixed up with the history of Israel, and whose inhabitants were apparently Aramaic-speaking people, were Damascus,[1] Maacah,[2] Geshur,[3] Rehob,[4] and Zobah.[5] These are among the facts which seem to show that several Aramaean tribes dwelt near or within the northern limits of the tribes of Israel. In the region of Ḥarran, too, Aramaic and Hebrew tribes apparently dwelt in close proximity.[6] Aramaic influence extended, without serious opposition, as far as Damascus, and from Damascus it inevitably reached northern Palestine.

East Aramaic Subsection—

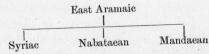

The Aramaean tribes very early (*circa* 1300 B.C.) made their appearance in the Euphrates valley, and rapidly migrated westward. Their main country was the region between Ḥarran,[7] east of the Euphrates, and the Ḥauran,[8] south-east of Mount Hermon.[9] The north-east portion of this region was termed Mesopotamia,[10] probably meaning the land between the Euphrates and the Chaboras.[11] In the reign of Sen-

---

[1] In time of David we read of אֲרַם דַּמֶּשֶׂק (2 S. 8⁵; cf. 1 Ch. 18⁵).

[2] Perhaps אֲרַם מַעֲכָה (1 Ch. 19⁶) should be מֶלֶךְ מַעֲכָה (2 S. 10⁶).

[3] Reckoned Aramaean : נְשׁוּר בַּאֲרָם (2 S. 15⁸; cf. 1 Ch. 2²³).

[4] *Vide* אֲרַם בֵּיתדחוֹב (2 S. 10⁶; cf. Num. 13²¹).

[5] Cf. אֲרַם צוֹבָא (2 S. 10⁸; 1 Ch. 19⁶).

[6] The writer J identifies Ḥarran with the city of Nahor (Gen. 24¹⁰), and as the home of Laban (Gen. 29⁵). The writer P calls Laban an Aramaean (Gen. 25²⁰). Abraham appears to come from the same locality (Gen. 12¹ 24⁴⁷).

[7] *Vide* Mez, *Gesch. der Stadt Ḥarran*, 1892. *Sin*, the moon-god of Ḥarran, is mentioned in the Nerab inscript. Cl.-Gan. *Études*, ii. 222.

[8] The worship of the Arab goddess *Allath* extended to Ḥauran, CIS ii. 170, 182, 198. Cf. Wetstein, *Ḥauran*, 1860.

[9] In Assyr. *Aramu* is never applied to the people W. of the Euphrates; these are termed *Ḥatti*, vide *Cuneiform Inscrip. and the OT.*, Gen. 10²²; cf. Delitzsch, *Wo lag das Paradies?* 257.

[10] Cf. ארם נהרים in title of Ps. 60 = 'Syria between the two floods.'

[11] For more details *vide* Dillmann, *Genesis*.

nacherib, Aramaic made its impression on the language of Babylonia, as the inscriptions clearly testify.[1]

In Babylonia, Aramaic became a serious rival of the older Chaldee at an early date.[2] The form of Babylonian Aramaic differed in some respects from Syrian Aramaic. This is shown by the inscriptions which have been found in the different localities.[3] It is also confirmed by some Old Testament passages, which say that the Jews while they were able to speak Aramaic could not understand the Babylonians.[4] In the Aramaic which afterwards prevailed in Babylonia one of the great Talmuds was written. The Aramaeans made themselves more and more felt in the territory between Aleppo in north Syria and the Euphrates. This region was occupied by the Ḥatti, Hittites, until they were overthrown by Assyria. The weakening of the Hittites enabled the Aramaeans to extend their influence in Syria. The Aramaic of Syria, that is more specifically 'Syriac,' deviated considerably, as time went on, from the Babylonian type. In this Syriac language from the second century a considerable literature grew up and continued till after the Crusades. This subject does not fall within our period, yet at least indirectly Syriac helps us to discover something of the older type of Aramaic behind it. Syriac is specially valuable to the Biblical and ecclesiastical scholar, but it has value for the linguistic student as well.

It will be sufficient to notice the following points: (a) As a member of the north Semitic group, Syriac is a later development of Aramaic, and therefore shows the changes which take place in the evolution of a language. (b) It is not without significance as well as interest, that through the channel of Syriac literature the thought and Christian teaching of the West were conveyed to Arabia and Persia,

---

[1] Cf. the name שנורב (Nerab inscr. loc. cit.) with Sin-aḥe-erba, on Assyr. inscrip. Vide generally G. Smith, Hist. of Sennacherib.

[2] The Tell el-Amarna letters (circa 1400 B.C.) mention the Aḥlamu, i.e. Aramaean nomads. Ramman-nirai I. and Shalmaneser I. were in conflict with Aramaic bedouins in Mesopotamian regions. Still later (circa 1100) Tiglath-pileser I. fought with the Aḥlamu who had pressed into Mesopotamia.

[3] Cf. Memphis (CIS ii. 122), Nineveh (CIS ii. 1), Zenjirli (Lidzb. Nordsem. Epigr.).

[4] Vide, e.g., Is. 33[19], Jer. 5[15].

and in a less degree to India and China. (*c*) The language, though much altered by Arab influence, is yet employed in the district around lake Urumiyah in Persia, in parts of Kurdistan, and in the Lebanon regions of north Palestine, anciently known as Coele-Syria. (*d*) The dialectic differences which developed between the eastern or Nestorian branch and western or Jacobite branch, are very suggestive in tracing the original pronunciation. (*e*) When a Hebrew or Arabic word fails to reveal its own meaning, an examination of its use in Syriac will sometimes elucidate the difficulty; the latter language having retained and perpetuated an older meaning. (*f*) Since the earliest Syriac was in many features like the Aramaic of Palestine, it cannot be neglected in any attempt to describe the language of that country in pre-Christian times.[1]

The section of Aramaeans that pressed its way from the Euphrates southward, and drove the Edomites out of Petra, was afterwards known as Nabataean. These Syro-Arabian people had a dialect differing somewhat from both Syriac and Arabic. Remains of this language are found in inscriptions in the Sinaitic peninsula and elsewhere, dating from the Persian period. The older form of this language is represented in the Babylonian Talmud, that is, within the framework of the Talmud many ancient forms are perpetuated. The later form of the

---

[1] As the later history of Syriac forms no part of this discussion, the following notes may be added here : (1) The oldest type of Syriac writing is the ' Estrangelo' ($\sigma\tau\rho o\gamma\gamma\acute{u}\lambda\eta$ $\chi\epsilon\acute{\iota}\rho$). The Sinaitic and Curetonian versions were written in this form, and it is the character used by the Nestorians. The newer type of writing is the 'Serta' (ܠܝܼܣܐ = $\kappa\epsilon\rho a\acute{\iota}a$). The Peshitta was written in this form, and it is the character used by the Jacobites and Maronites. It grew out of the earlier form as an easier and more cursive hand. (2) The Estrangelo pointing is the ancient system of indicating the vowels by the different positions of one or two points; the Serta pointing is borrowed from the Greeks. (3) Pronunciation slightly differs, *e.g.*—

Nest.	ܪܝܫ,	pron.	*reesh*.	Nest. ܡܫܪܟܘܢ,	pron. *mashrakun*.
Jacob.	ܪܝܫ,	,,	*rish*.	Jacob. ܡܫܪܟܘܢ,	,, *mashrikun*.
Nest.	ܫܠ,	,,	*shel*	Nest. ܬܟܣܐ,	,, *taksa*(o).
Jacob.	ܫܠܝ,	,,	*sheli*	Jacob. ܬܟܣܐ,	,, *teksa*(o).

Nestorian punctuation has ā frequently where Jacobite has ō, and in many cases ō where Jacobite has ū. The Eastern system is more exact, and on the whole more in harmony with ancient pronunciation; the Western has the advantage of greater convenience.

dialect is termed *Nabatee* by Arab authors.[1] The significance of Nabataean for our study is considered in another place.

Mandaean appears to be a later form of Nabataean. The centre of the Mandaean community was Bassorah in Asiatic Turkey, the ancient 'Athens of the East.' They were a sect of religionists rather than politicians, and professed to follow the teaching of John the Baptist. Hence the name 'Sabaeans' = Baptists. They had a goddess, whose name apparently was not pronounced, just as the Phoenicians had a 'goddess of Gebal,' whose real name was hidden, possibly from a religious sentiment.[2] Their religion retained many pagan elements which were of Babylonian origin; in some respects their teaching was tainted with Manichaeism. The Mandaean dialect in a general way occupies a place between Babylonian and Syrian Aramaic. It is inconsistent in the use of gutturals, often incorrect in spelling, and deficient in grammatical forms. Its letter-forms resemble the older Syriac, that is, the Estrangelo character. It is, however, considerably coloured by Arabic. Its likeness to Nabataean and the Babylonian Talmud makes it valuable in this study.

West Aramaic Subsection—

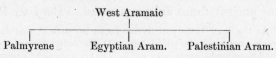

Though the identity of Palmyra with Tadmor has been

---

[1] That is نَبَطِي. It is probable that we should identify the *Naba-aiti* (*Keilinschriftliche Bibliothek*, ii. 216–222) with the Arab clan termed נבית (cf. Gen. 25¹³, Is. 60⁷, 1 Ch. 1²⁹). So Joseph. *Ant.* i. 12. 4. The Apostle Paul regarded the Sinaitic Peninsula, which was part of the Nabataean kingdom, as in Arabia (Gal. 4²⁵). The desert into which the Apostle withdrew near Damascus was under the dominion of the Nabataean king (ἐν Δαμασκῷ ὁ ἐθνάρχης Ἀρέτα, 2 Cor. 11³²). The 'Arabians' who came to Pentecost (Acts 2¹¹) were probably Nabataeans from this region. They would have no difficulty in being understood at Jerusalem, since their popular language was similar to Palestinian Aramaic.

[2] The title in Sabaean is בעלת מיפע (CIS iv. 172); for Phoen. בעלת גבל (CIS i.), cf. Nab. דושרא, 'lord of Shara' (Wellhausen, *Reste Arabischen Heidenthums*², p. 51). The name 'Sabaeans' is from صَبَغ, צְבַע, to *dip*. They were Gnostics, as the name 'Mandaean' implies—מַנְדָע, which is the Heb. מַדָּע, where *dd* is resolved into *nd* after the Aram. mode.

proved by many inscriptions, there is no clear connexion
between the two terms.   The Palmyrene dialect was a modification of the early Hebrew, and its alphabet was among the
first to diverge from the more ancient letter-forms towards
the later character.   In other words, Palmyrene may be
regarded as an alphabetic link between the Samaritan and the
Jewish or Aramaic square character.   Many Palmyrene words
resemble Hebrew, but a far greater number resemble Aramaic.
There must have been a good deal of overlapping and inter-
influence among the Aramaic dialects during our period.
Some words were apparently influenced in form by the corresponding Hebrew term,[1] and others were perhaps influenced in
meaning by the corresponding Hebrew root.[2]   In many cases
the vowel-letters are omitted in Palmyrene where they are
found in Hebrew, and final א is more usual than Hebrew ה.[3]
The likenesses of Palmyrene to Biblical Aramaic are quite pronounced, and show that the two forms are essentially one.[4]

Egyptian Aramaic is found in a number of inscriptions,
some of them dating from the Persian rule in Egypt, with

---

[1] *E.g.* Heb. מלכיאל, Gen. 46[17]. Palm. מלכבל, Vogüé, *La Syr. Centr.* 3.

                צפור, Num. 22[2].   צפרא, Vog. *ib.* 11[2].

                עלין, Num 24[16].   עלינא, Vog. *ib.* 11[1].

                עמוד, 1 K. 7[15].   עמודא, Vog. *ib.* 9[4].

                אלנתן, 2 K. 24[8].   עתנתן, Vog. *ib.* 30[a2].

                ברכאל, Job 32[2].   בלברך, Vog. *ib.* 117[3].

                לחית, Is. 15[2].   לחיתו, CIS ii. 196[4].

[2] *E.g.* Heb. rt. משה, Num. 3[25].   משחא, Vog. *ib.* 16[3].

                גרב, 2 S. 23[38].   גריבא, Vog. *ib.* 141.

                קרב, Ps. 73[28].   קרבתא, CIS ii. 122[1].

                עוד, Ps. 119[61].   עידא, Cook, *Gloss.* 90.

                בשם, Is. 3[24].   בשימא, *ib.* 34.

                נהר, Is. 60[5].   נהירא, Vog. *ib.* 22[2].

[3] *E.g.* Heb.   בית, Ex. 12[30].   בת, Vog. *ib.* 64[1] *al.*

                חמור, Gen. 22[5].   חמרא, Vog. *ib.* 146.

                אנוש, Is. 8[1].   אנש, Cl.-Gan. *Étud.* i. 121.

                שבעה, Gen. 41[2].   שבעא, Vog. *ib.* 11[3].

                שאול, 1 S. 9[2].   שאילא, Vog. *ib.* 17[3].

[4] *E.g.* Bib. Ar. קדמיא, Dan. 7[4].   קדמיא, Cook, *Gloss.* 103.

                בריך, Dan. 3[28].   בריך, Vog. *ib.* 75[1].

                צבו, Dan. 6[18].   צבו, Vog. *ib.* 1[4].

              (בנה(א, Ezra 5[11].   (בנה(א, Vog. *ib.* 16[5].

                חזו, Dan. 2[19].   חזי, CIS ii. 137[a5].

                מלח, Dan. 3[28].   פלחא, Vog. *ib.* 22[4].

fluctuations between 525–332 B.C.[1] These inscriptions may
with confidence be attributed to Jewish settlements in Egypt.
From them we gather that the new colonists used their own
Aramaic language, which was also the official language of
Persian diplomatists.[2] The discovery of papyri confirms the
fact that Aramaic was spoken in certain regions of upper
Egypt in the fifth century B.C.[3] These papyri, extending
from 471 B.C. to 411 B.C. 'are quite sufficient to prove that
the Aramaic spoken in 500 B.C. from Babylon in the north to
Assuan in the south of Egypt was identical with what has
been popularly styled the Biblical Aramaic.' The differences
are due to differences of locality and provincial pronunciation.
Unless we are seeking exact variations of form, the differences
between Egyptian and Biblical Aramaic need not detain us.
A few terms in Egyptian Aramaic are apparently foreign to
the language, probably due to Persian influence.[4] A few
words are ἄπαξ λεγόμενα, but they may have been quite
familiar and general, though not found in the scanty literature
that has survived. Many words and phrases are absolutely
identical, others are practically so.[5] Some portions of Biblical

---

[1] The most important inscriptions are the Memphis (CIS ii. 122, 123)
and the Elephantina (CIS ii. 137, 138). The Carpentras Stele (v–iv B.C.)
is interesting as showing in the form of many letters the change from the
old Aram. towards the square alphabet (CIS ii. 141).

[2] Cf. the official certificate on a trade-weight found at Abydos in Asia
Minor (vi–v B.C.): אספרן לקבל סתריא די כספא, 'certified according to the
keepers of money' (vide CIS ii. 108).

[3] Vide Aramaic Papyri discovered at Assuan, London, 1906. Edited
by Sayce and Cowley; Drei aramäische Papyrusurkunden aus Elephantine,
Berlin, 1907. Edited by Dr Sachau.

[4] E.g. חור (CIS ii. 122[1]), common in Nab. = حَوُر; עריה (ib.) = عَادِيَا. In
the Assuan pap. אבינרנא (H 14, J 15) looks like a Persian legal term; הנרו
(E 4) = اَنداِزِ, perh. measurer; חצן (G 16) = حَضَـتَ, ivory; אגר (A 4, 5, al.) =
اَجَرَّة, brick, besides several proper names.

[5] The following will illustrate:

          כהל, A 6, B 12, F 7; cf. כהל, Dan. 2[26].

          כוין, J 6   כוין, Dan. 6[11].

          עמר, G 7, 10   עמר, Dan. 7[9].

From the Papyri, ed. by Sachau:

בלכיא cf. כלבים, Heb. 1 K. 14[11].   מן־קרמת דנה cf. קרמת דנה, Dan. 6[11].

זכרין דכרונה, Ezra 6[2].   מרבחא די בית בית מרבחא, Ezra 7[17].

Aramaic were written, like the Egyptian Aramaic, during the Persian period. The Aramaic source used in the compilation of Ezra was probably written *circa* 450 B.C. Ezra lived in the reign of Artaxerxes I., Longimanus (464–424 B.C.). The compiler lived long after the time of the events recorded in his Book. Some parts of the Aramaic source are cited verbally (4^{8-22} 5^1–6^{16}). These parts may therefore represent the Aramaic of Palestine 450 B.C., that is, the Palestinian Aramaic which was contemporary with the Egyptian Aramaic. Other Aramaic passages, which were fashioned by the compiler himself, and therefore two hundred years later, may represent the Palestinian Aramaic which was contemporary with the earlier Nabataean inscriptions. The Aramaic of Daniel is rather later than that of Ezra. No doubt some parts of the Aramaic narrative are borrowed from older sources, but the compilation as a whole belongs to *circa* 166 B.C., and therefore contemporary with the golden age of Nabataean influence. The Book of Daniel was bilingual from a very early date, as the LXX version proves.[1] The Persian words not only point back to the Persian period, but show that certain Persian official terms persisted in later Aramaic.[2] The few Greek words indicate that the Book was written in the Greek period, and that Greek was already pressing itself into Aramaic-speaking provinces.[3] The important facts are that the dialects of Ezra and Daniel are practically identical,[4] both belong to

---

[1] The LXX rendering of Daniel, especially the Aram. portion, was considered so unsatisfactory that Irenaeus adopted Theodotion's translation; so did Jerome, and ecclesiastical writers generally. Note the confusion of שָׁבְעִים and שְׁבָעִים ($9^{24f.}$).

[2] Among Persian words are the following: אדרא, adj. *assured* (Dan. 2^5 *al.*); ארדנור, *counsellor* ($3^{2, 3}$); אחשדרפן, *satrap* (3^2 *al.* 6^2 *al.*); רתבר, *judge* ($3^{2, 3}$); גדבר, *treasurer* ($3^{2, 3}$); פתגם, *command* (3^{16}); הדבר, *lawyer* (6^8 *al.*). The termination בר is the Persian ﻟﻪ, which is used to form possessives.

[3] The three Greek musical terms certainly do not prove that Greek had really affected the Aram. language. The terms are: סומפניה = συμφωνία (Dan. 3^{10}); in Palm. ספון = σύμφωνοι (*Tariff*, ii. b. ^{46}). פסנטרין = ψαλτήριον (3^7 *al.*); the oriental ן — becomes ιον in Gk., *e.g.* סנהדרין = συνέδριον. קיתרס = κίθαρις (3^5 *al.*); perh. same as כנור (cf. Joseph. *Ant.* vii. 12. 3).

[4] There are small differences like המו (Ezra 4^{10}) and המון (Dan. 2^{34}); לכם, להם (Ezra 5^3) and להן, לכן (Dan. 2^{35} 3^4); נולו (Ezra 6^{11}) and נולי (Dan. 2^5); גובריא (Ezra 7^{21}) and גדבריא (Dan. 3^2). The terminations ן and י are indications of a somewhat later stage than ם and ו.

the western Aramaic section, and are therefore representative of the Palestinian Aramaic.

VIII

EGYPTIAN AND PALESTINIAN ARAMAIC

The relation of Egyptian Aramaic to the language of Palestine was very close, but the position is not quite clear. It is known that not a great many years after the destruction of Jerusalem by Nebuchadrezzar a company of Jews settled on the southern frontiers of Egypt. The simple historical facts are fairly plain.[1] The first caravan of Jews returned from exile and began the rebuilding of the Temple 535 B.C. A hundred years later Nehemiah received his commission as Governor over Judaea, 444 and 433 B.C.[2] The Elephantine Jews addressed a petition to Baghoi,[3] Persian Governor of Judaea *circa* 408 B.C. The petition asked assistance to rebuild their Temple to Yahu, which the Egyptians had destroyed. This Temple had been built nearly one hundred and twenty years earlier, that is, just before the conquest of Egypt by Cambyses, son of Cyrus, in 525 B.C.[4] The question is, how the Jewish settlers in Egypt were connected with Palestine. Did the Aramaic language of Assuan come directly from Babylonia, or *via* Palestine? Certainly Babylonian forms and proper names suggest some connexion with Babylonian Aramaic.[5] It is quite probable that some members of the Jewish colony in Egypt came from the Euphrates regions. If, however, these settlers had ever been in northern exile, their acquaintance with Judaean Governors and with

---

[1] *Vide* Sayce, *Aram. Pap.* (Assuan), Introd. pp. 9–14.

[2] The oldest Assuan Aram. Papyrus is dated 'the 14th (15th) year of Xerxes,' *i.e.* 471 or 470 B.C. (A 1).

[3] Cf. 'Bagoas,' Joseph. *Ant.* xi. 7.

[4] Herodotus, i. 214, respecting last days of Cyrus, is uncertain.

[5] The following are interesting : The Babyl. form ארתחששש, 'Artaxerxes,' is always used, not the Persian *Artakhshathrá* (B 2 *al.*). דין ורבב is a Babyl. legal formula, 'suit or process against,' but the words are Aram. (B 12). וטיב לבבי, a common Heb. and Aram. phrase, but as a legal formula, 'and my heart is satisfied,' it is Babyl. (F 5). The name (נ)בוזראבן is Babyl., but his son's name, עתרשורי, is Aram. (C 16). This suggests that the remnant of Babylonian language was giving place to the newer form of Aramaic.

the Jerusalem priesthood, suggests that they came into Egypt through Palestine. The position may be reconstructed as follows: This colony of Jews returned from Babylonia to Palestine. This will explain the Babylonian names in the records. Being dissatisfied with the condition of affairs in Palestine, and joined by a company of disaffected Samaritans, this colony left Palestine and journeyed to southern Egypt. This will explain the Samaritan element in the Jewish settlement at Assuan. This connexion with Babylonians and Samaritans will explain why the Jews in upper Egypt did not feel altogether bound by the Hebrew cult, and did not regard the altar at Jerusalem as the only valid altar to Yahu. These conclusions have important bearings on the question of language. The Egyptian Jews, like the Palestinian, acquired a knowledge of Aramaic in the countries of their captors. The Palestinian Aramaic was influenced by Samaritan; a similar influence was present in the Jewish settlement at Assuan.[1] Thus we are justified in using the Egyptian Aramaic literary remains in discussing the language of Palestine.

The Palestinian Aramaic in general is not to be distinguished from the Aramaic portions of Daniel, Ezra and the Targums in their original form. The Nabataean and Palmyrene inscriptions are found in a language practically the same. This may be termed the 'literary language' of Palestine which extended over the whole country. This language, owing partly to climate and partly to a foreign environment, became poor in vowels and rough in enunciation. Compared generally with Aramaic, Hebrew was bold, pithy and expressive, and

---

[1] The evidence for the Samarit. influence is found in the Papyri edited by Sachau. In the first we read : ' We have also all sent (concerning) the affairs in a letter in our name to Delaiah and Shelamiah, the sons of Sanballat, the Governor of Samaria.' This is restated in the second papyrus, which, however, is imperfect : 'For information we have sent a letter in our name to Detayâh and Shelamyâh, the sons of . . .' Sanballat is often mentioned in Nehemiah as 'the Horonite' (perh. 'native of Beth-Horon') ; once he is called a 'Samaritan' (Neh. 4[1. 2]). It may be supposed that the Samaritans in Egypt would desire to appeal to Sanballat, their fellow-countryman, and this may be the reason why the authorities at Jerusalem at first hesitated to assist the Jewish settlers at Elephantine. But the Samaritans claimed kinship with the Jews, and possibly this induced the Jerusalem officials afterwards to afford some help (cf. Joseph. *Ant.* xi. 8. 9).

Arabic was rich, sonorous and elegant. Aramaic suffered by conquest and became ultimately a mixed and corrupt tongue. At the beginning of the Christian era there were marked differences between the popular dialects of north, middle and south Palestine, but finally the north Palestinian became pretty general. It was the Moslem conquest that suddenly brought to an end the ascendancy of Aramaic in Palestine after it had lasted for more than a thousand years. During its golden age it suppressed Hebrew in Palestine, Phoenician in the regions of Tyre and Sidon, it took possession of the provinces of the Edomites and Moabites, and it spread over ' the entire Nabataean kingdom, which stretched from the Elamitic gulf to the vicinity of Damascus.' This is the language we shall presently characterize more definitely. Meanwhile we may notice its Palestinian provincial patois.

IX

DIALECTS OF PALESTINE

Palestinian Aramaic

| Samaritan | Galilaean | Judaean |

The distinction between the Palestinian dialects must not be pressed too far. Zahn is scarcely prepared to admit any real dialectic difference between the speech of north and south Palestine : ' With all due respect for the learning and thorough- ness with which of late Dalman has been at pains to distinguish Judaean from Galilaean Aramaic, one may question whether the separation of the sources which underlies this work furnishes a sufficiently secure foundation for such an under- taking.' [1] Dalman, however, has certainly adduced sufficient proof of dialectic differences more or less,[2] and we shall incidentally support this conclusion as we proceed. Differ- ences in Aramaic appeared in different provinces long before the Christian era. The period from the Exile to the end of the first century B.C. afforded ample time for the growth of new terms and idioms in distinct, though adjoining provinces.

[1] *Introd. NT.* i. p. 28.　　　　[2] *Gram. d. jüd. pal. Aram.*

This would be the case particularly where there was but little intercourse between the separate members of the same tribe or nation. We cannot state even approximately the time required for the production of new forms of speech. But it is certain that they appear with surprising quickness among non-literary and uncultivated people. It is safe to say that the speech of Palestine at the end of the first century B.C. was sufficiently one throughout the country for a dweller in the south to be understood in the north, and *vice versa*. It is needless to imagine that a Galilaean changed his dialect when he journeyed through Samaria to Judaea. He would be understood with readiness at Caesarea, at Sychar, and at Jerusalem. Syntactically the Aramaic of Palestine was homogeneous, and from this point it would be difficult and quite needless to compile separate grammars for Samaritan, Galilaean and Judaean.

There were, however, differences. The uncouth accents of the North grated on the more refined southerner. This is really a clue to the chief difference between the colloquial speech of Galilee and the national speech of Judaea. The difference may he described as twofold—pronunciation and vocabulary. The former was the more distinctive feature, and resulted in many instances in a changed orthography. The whole difference may be traced ultimately to a provincial use of the gutturals and the vowel letters. A similar difference is to be observed between Hebrew, Phoenician and Moabite in more ancient times, and between Nestorian and Jacobite in more recent times. The differences of both accent and vocabulary are to a large extent due to geographical position and the intrusion of a foreign element. Differences of vocabulary are sometimes found in the variant spellings of the same terms, and sometimes in entirely new terms in one dialect or the other. It does not, of course, follow that a term in Judaean not found in any Galilaean literature was really absent from the latter dialect. The argument here *e silentio* is very precarious, inasmuch as the remnants of Galilaean are very limited. The following outline of the characteristics of the Palestine dialects is all that is necessary in this place.[1]

---

[1] In any complete statement it would be necessary to distinguish the vernacular and the literary language of Palestine. The first heralds of the

1. *The Samaritan Dialect.*—Samaritan was a very early
form of Aramaic. Its alphabet and letter-forms were almost
identical with Phoenician and ancient Hebrew. Samaritan
as now generally understood, was formed among the Phoenicians and other tribes that occupied the habitations of the ' ten
tribes ' when they were carried into captivity by Shalmaneser
and Esarhaddon. The best specimens of Samaritan are found
in the Samaritan Targum and some early liturgies. It may
be compared with the Aramaic of the Jerusalem Talmud and
with the Palestinian Syriac. On the whole it was more akin
to Galilaean than to Judaean, but was closer to Hebrew than
either.[1] The confusion of letters that are similar in form
(*e.g.* ד and ר, ו and י, ה and ח) is due to a degenerate literary style,
and indicates a somewhat late period in the history of the
language. Samaritan pronunciation differed in some respects
from other Aramaic dialects. The Samaritans appear to
have differed from their neighbours in the sibilant sounds,
and there was perhaps some uncertainty in the use of
lingual and dental sounds.[2] It is probable that the Greek
form of certain Semitic words was due to this peculiarity
of Samaritan.[3] The Samaritan Targum often resembles

Εὐαγγέλιον used their native Galilaean, but Judaean more nearly represented the literary language of the period. So little is known of the local
dialects that the attempt to render the words of Jesus from the Gk. into
Aram. is practically impossible. For the recovery of the language of the
Pales. Jews the Onkelos Targ., in the judgment of the present writer, is
on the whole a better guide than the Pales. Targums. Dalman thinks
otherwise (*Gram. d. jüd. pal. Aram.*), but see the section on the Yemen
MSS of Onkelos discussed later.

[1] The following will indicate some points in which Samaritan differed
from Hebrew. (1) The Samaritan supplied the quiescent letters (אהו,
matres lectionis). (2) It completed verbal forms that were wanting in
Hebrew. (3) It changed the apocopated future into the full form. (4) It
omitted the paragogic letters at the end of nouns. (5) It arbitrarily put
genders to nouns which were of common gender in Hebrew. (6) It reduced
proper names to a uniform spelling where the Hebrew has different forms.
(7) It altered the poetical forms of the pronoun into common ones. (8) It
turned the infinite absolute into a finite verb. (9) It changed Hebrew
idioms into Samaritan.

[2] Not only did the Samaritans pronounce שׁ like ס, but ת (particularly
final) was probably sounded like שׁ or ס. Hence Hebrew שִׁבֹּלֶת was possibly
pronounced *sibboles*.

[3] *E.g.* פַּרְשִׁישׁ and אַשּׁוּר are words in which the medial שׁ becomes ס in Gk.

Onkelos, a fact which, in the judgment of the present writer, is attributable to the use of Onkelos by the authors of the Samaritan Targum. Some scholars explain the fact by referring both Targums ' to an oral tradition current in Palestine at the time when Aramaic was the common language of the people, and that they were subsequently reduced to writing independently, and with local variations.' This may have been the case in the third or fourth century, and still the Samaritan may have been influenced by Onkelos later.

2. *The Galilaean Dialect.* — The peculiarities of this dialect were due partly to the geographical position, and partly to the large admixture of Gentiles. Amongst the inhabitants of Galilee are named Egyptians, Arabians, Phoenicians, and later Greeks and Romans. The vernacular was the common Aramaic, with some peculiar forms, and particularly a provincial accent. We gather from Jewish authorities that the rough northern brogue of the Galilaeans was quite distinguishable from that of Jerusalem, and was a subject over which the Judaeans made merriment. By the southern provinces the northern dialect was considered corrupt and barbarous. The cultivated sense of the metropolitan Jew was often offended by the rough and ready speech of the Galilaean. According to Rabbinic writings, Galilaean was characterized by a vague or indistinct utterance of certain letters, and by the confusion or suppression of others, especially the gutturals.[1] The softening of the gutturals was probably not so advanced in Galilee as in Samaria, but this is a phase of the subject which probably belongs to a later period. When out of their native province, the Galilaeans sometimes so blended or divided words as to render them unintelligible. Thus they were frequently supposed to say things entirely different from what they intended.[2]

Galilaean must not be regarded as a later and more degenerate form of Judaean, any more than Aramaic itself

---

Hence Ταρτησσός (cf. Herod. iv. 152 ; Ταρσήιον is, however, the form in Polyb. iii. 24. 2) ; 'Ατουρία (in Gk. of Alexandrian period, cf. Strabo, xvi.; but 'Ασσυρίη in Herod. iv. 39, *et al.*).

[1] *E.g.* א with ע, ח with ה; apparently sometimes ט with ת.

[2] Cf. Buxtorf, *Lex Talmudicum*, pp. 435–436, 2417.

must be regarded as a corrupt form of Hebrew. Certain influences were at work in Galilee which tended to change and deteriorate the speech of the people. An intrusion of words and phrases came from the North and East, from Syria and Babylonia. The Aramaic of Babylonia had become less consistent and more illiterate during the Persian epoch and the Greek ascendancy. The trade route from Babylon, through Palmyra and Damascus, to Nablus would inevitably bring many linguistic changes into Galilee. On the other hand, the conquest of Alexander resulted in the introduction of many Greek forms, which sometimes entered the common speech to the exclusion of some of its native terms.

It is more difficult to get specimens of Galilaean than of Judaean and Samaritan. Forms of the two latter may be seen in the Onkelos and Samaritan Targums respectively. No literature, however, preserves exactly the colloquial speech of a province; there is always some difference between the written language and the spoken dialect. The following extract from the Mishna (*Kethuboth*, ii. 5. 26°) is perhaps as near an approach to the common speech of Galilee as we are likely to get. The present writer is responsible for the vocalization and the translation :

אִיתְּתֵיהּ דְּרַבִּי יוֹסֵי דְּגְלִילֵי הֲוַת מְעִיקָה לֵיהּ סַגִּין · סָלֵיק רַבִּי לְעָזָר בֶּן עֲזַרְיָה לְגַבֵּיהּ · אָמַר לֵיהּ רַבִּי שִׁיבְקָהּ דְּלֵית הִיא דְּאִיקָרָךְ · אָמַר לֵיהּ · פּוּרְנָהּ רַב עֲלַי · אָמַר לֵיהּ רַבִּי לְעָזָר אֲנָא יָהֵיב לָךְ פֻּרְנֵהּ וְשַׁבְקָהּ · יְהַב לֵיהּ פֻּרְנֵהּ וְשַׁבְקָהּ · אֲזָלַת וּנְסִיבַת לְטַסוֹרָא דְּקַרְתָּא · אִיתְנַחַת מִן נִיכְסוֹי וְאִיתְעֲבֵד סַנְיָא נְהוֹרָא וַהֲוַת מְחַזְּרָא לֵיהּ עַל כָּל קַרְתָּא וְלָא אִיתְיְהַב לֵיהּ כְּלוּם · אָמַר לָהּ לֵית הָכָא שְׁכוּנָה תּוֹרִין · אָמְרָה לֵיהּ אִית הָכָא שְׁכוּנָה דְּמַשְׁבְּקִי וְלֵית בְּחַיֵּילִי עַיֵּיל לָהּ תַּמָּן · שָׁרֵי חָבֵיט לָהּ · עֲבַר רַבִּי יוֹסֵי הַגְּלִילֵי וּשְׁמַע קָלוֹן מִתְבַּזְיָיא בְּשׁוּקָא · נַסְבוּן וְיַהֲבוֹן בְּגוֹ בֵּיתָא מִן דִּידֵהּ · וַהֲוָה מַפֵּיק לוֹן מְזוֹנִין כָּל יוֹמִין דַּהֲוָוֹן בְּחַיִּין :

'The wife of Rabbi José of Galilee used to worry him greatly. Rabbi Laezar (Elaezar) son of Azariah went to (see) him. He said to him, "My master, divorce her because she does you no credit." He replied, "(I cannot) there is too much dowry to pay her." Rabbi Laezar replied, "I will give you the dowry, and you divorce her." He gave him the dowry and

8

he (R. José) divorced her.   She went and got married to the guardsman of the town.   The latter became poor and also blind, and she had to lead him from town to town to beg, but he could get nothing.   One day he said to her, " Is there not another place round about ? "   She replied, " There is the neighbourhood where my former husband (lit. the one who divorced me) lives, but I cannot (lit. it is not in my power to) go there."   He, therefore, smote her severely.   Rabbi José of Galilee passed by and heard her voice raised in disgraceful fashion (or possibly, raised in misery) in the street.   So he took them and gave them one of his houses, and provided them with food as long as they lived.' [1]

3. *The Judaean Dialect.*—This form of Palestinian Aramaic was akin to Nabataean and Palmyrene.   The Aramaic portions of Ezra and Daniel, and the Targum of Onkelos, were written in a dialect very similar to Judaean. In its earliest form the language shows a striking affinity in grammar with the Sabaean, a south Arabian dialect; in vocabulary it agrees remarkably with Phoenician and the older Hebrew.   Judaean Aramaic is in no sense a mixture of Hebrew and Syriac, but it has affinities in both directions. Its likenesses to Hebrew are mainly in orthography and punctuation; [2] to Syriac, are chiefly in grammatical forms,

---

[1] This quotation is a comment on ומבשרך לא תתעלם, 'and hide not thyself from thine own flesh' (Is. 58[7]), to which the Tal. adds : אפלו גרושתו, 'even if she be divorced.'   The phrase דלית היא דאיקרך, may mean, 'it is not to your honour to quarrel with her.'   The expression, פורנה רב עלי, lit. 'the dowry is much above me,' simply means, 'I cannot afford it.'   The term פורנה is less generally used than כתובה, *i.e.* the *written* agreement to give back to the wife in case of divorce twice the amount she brought with her. The construction, אזלת ונסיבת, 'she went and she married,' is according to the rule that ו couples like tenses of verbs ; the pf. is the narrative tense. In למסורא, the prefix is the sign of the acc.   The foll. circumlocution is thoroughly Galilaean : איתנחת מן ניכסי ואיתעבד סגיא נהורא, lit. 'he was deprived of possessions and the use of much light.'   The idiom should be noted : שרי חבט לה, lit. 'he allowed beating to her,' *i.e.* 'he began striking her.' שרי is the vernacular behind the Gk. ἤρξατο in many Gospel passages.

[2] The points where Judaean Aram. corresponds with Hebrew may be outlined as follows :

(1) Tendency to employ the clearer vowel-sounds, *e.g.* אֱלָהָא, rather than אֱלָהֹן ; קְרָא, rather than כְּרֵי ; כֹּל, rather than כֹּל.

(2) Use of long vowels, i and o, rather than diphthongs, ai and au.

syntactical structure, and vocabulary. This latter statement will be more fully considered when Palestinian Aramaic is definitely discussed.

It is evident that at no period between the Exile and the Christian era was there one homogeneous language in Palestine. But during practically the whole period, Aramaic in some form was the general language. The influence of Hebrew was greater at the earlier period, and the influence of Syriac was greater at the later period. No one dialect became the sole dialect of any province, but there were over-lappings of speech in almost every direction. Hence the difficulty of defining the character of the language of the country and the dialect of a province at any given period. The conclusion based on the inscriptions and literary documents found in one region, are often invalidated by inscriptions and other literary remains found in another region. Not infrequently the inscriptions and literary documents found in the same region and in the same age, show quite striking differences among themselves.[1] From the Exile, Aramaic suffered through its own success, and there no more existed a definite and uniform system of orthography or even of construction.

Towards the close of our period the vernacular of Palestine was broken into a number of local patois, as we have seen. A knowledge of Hebrew was cultivated in Judah down to a comparatively late date, as the later writings of the Old Testament bear testimony. The foreign elements in

(3) Absence of מ preformative in the inf. of all conjug., except Peal.

(4) The preformative י of 3rd pers. sing. and pl. impf., rather than Syr. ܢ.

(5) The system of doubling letters, other than gutturals, cf. קֵטֵּל, ܩܛܠ.

(6) Accenting the ultimate, e.g. מַלְכָּא, Syr. ܡܲܠܟܵܐ.

(7) Preference for the *scriptio plena*.

[1] Cf. such simple forms as בריך (CIS ii. 122¹) and בריכה of same date (CIS 141¹); the use of the conj. פ in פמו (Zenj. *Hadad*, l. 3), פהא (Zenj. *Bar-rekub*, l. 18), פא (Zenj. *Hadad*, ll. 17, 33; *Panammu*, l. 22); cf. the forms מו (Zenj. *Hadad*, ll. 4, 22), מחוה=חֲוָה (ptep.) + מָה (*Nêrab*, 2, l. 5). Cf. the transpos. אשרה (*Nêrab*, 1, l. 8), אתרא (*Cilicia*, l. 6).

Hebrew came mainly from Aramaic sources, though other influences are evident. Behind and along with the language of the Hebrew Scriptures there was a common speech—the vulgar tongue—which frequently obtruded itself into the sacred language. The best remnants of Judaean Aramaic are found in Ezra, Daniel and the Palestinian Targums. The speech of Galilee was a quicker development of Aramaic tendencies. Foreign elements had penetrated deeper, and Hebrew had earlier ceased to be a retarding force. The stories embedded in the Palestinian Talmud, which best represent the speech of the peasantry, suggest that rural Galilaean was something of a colloquial jargon.[1] There was probably a larger admixture of Greek in Galilee than in any other Palestinian province. There were Greek towns, Greek mercenaries, and Greek diplomatic communications. But the inhabitants of Galilee as a whole knew no language but Aramaic. Neither Edessan Syriac nor Macedonian Greek had supplanted the Aramaic vernacular in the wide pasturable areas.[2] No doubt many Galilaeans were bilingual before the Christian era, as we know many were afterwards[3] In Samaria there was a type of speech which in a sense stood between that of Judaea and that of Galilee. The inhabitants of Samaria seem to have perpetuated a form of Chaldee, hence their dialect had some likenesses to Babylonian Aramaic. This is partly explained by the simple fact that heathen (Chaldee) settlers possessed much of the country. The Samaritans were conservatives in the matter of script, preserving the Phoenician type after Judaea and Galilee had accepted the Aramaic character. Samaritan was in some respects akin to the Peshitta Syriac, and this Version we know had many affinities with Chaldee. Syriac, however, was not a prominent element in the language of Palestine in pre-Christian times, and therefore belongs to a later study.[4]

[1] Cf. Deutsch, *Remains: The Talmud*, p. 42.
[2] *Vide* Neubauer, *Studia Biblica*, i. pp. 39-74.
[3] Cf. Abbott, *Essays on the Original Texts of the Old and New Test.*, p. 162. Proof of the bilingual character of the time is found in the Palm. inscrip.—Aram. and Greek.
[4] *Vide* discussion in Zahn, *Introd. NT.*, chs. 1 and 2. Cf. Hort, *Epistle of James*, posth. ed., p. iii.

IV

SEMITIC CONSTRUCTIONS

GRAMMATICAL—SYNTACTICAL

I

LANGUAGE OF THE OLD TESTAMENT LIMITED

THE Israelites in adopting Aramaic during and after the Exile, were in reality returning to the language of their tribal originators. Without expressing any opinion on the historical character of the Abraham-story, there is nothing *a priori* inconsistent in the theory that certain Hebrew clans came into Canaan from Ḥarran and Ur-Kasdim. On their arrival in Palestine they gradually dropped their native Aramaic, and adopted the language of the Canaanites, which was in many respects allied to their mother-tongue. They naturally retained some forms of their primal speech when the ' lip of Canaan '[1] became their common dialect. These traces of Aramaic, however, ultimately disappeared almost altogether, and in the period immediately preceding the Exile little evidence was left of the Mesopotamian language of the Hebrew tribes. But the Captivity brought back Aramaic once more to the Israelitish community, after they had ceased to employ it for 1500 years. Association with Babylonia, Assyria, Damascus and other regions after the Exile had the effect of reintroducing Aramaic peculiarities, which characterized the language in the pre-Canaanitish age. This statement adequately explains the phenomena of some Aramaic forms occurring in the earliest Old Testament

[1] שְׂפַת כְּנַעַן = Hebrew, Is. 19[18].

117

fragments, then disappearing, and again being introduced in the latest Old Testament books. [*Vide* König, *Alt. Test. Studien*, Heft ii.]

The language of the Old Testament, however, is a very limited guide to the composite language of Palestine in the pre-Christian age. The Zenjirli inscriptions supply far more suggestive criteria, and show how cautious we must be in coming to conclusions respecting the unity of the Aramaic language. These inscriptions are in many ways more akin to Hebrew and Assyrian than to Aramaic. This is perhaps most clearly shown by the consonantal equations, which commonly agree with Hebrew and Assyrian against the usual Aramaic equivalents.[1] The explanation is threefold : (1) The Zenjirli inscriptions belong to an early period of Aramaic, before the language had thoroughly established itself in Syria. (2) These inscriptions belong to a type of Aramaic, which, though found in different regions, was comparatively restricted. These regions —Nerab (N. Syria), Babylonia, Egypt—were peopled with very mixed Semitic races. (3) The dialect was probably influenced by Assyrian,[2] which may be regarded as the chief foreign element fashioning the language, perhaps in part through Hebrew.

---

[1] Thus : Zenj. ו=Aram. ר, Heb. ו, Arab. ذ (cf. וי, *Hadad*, l. 1=רי, Bibl. Aram., Nab. CIS ii. 221¹, Palm. Vog. 16²).

Zenj. צ=Aram. ט, Heb. צ, Arab. ظ (cf. כיצא, *Bar-rekub*, l. 19=קיטא, Aram. *summer*, Tal.).

Zenj. ש=ת, Aram., Heb. ש, Arab. ث (cf. אשר, *place*, *Hadad*, l. 27= אתר, CIS ii. 145 C⁴). That is, Zenjirli has *z*, *ṣ*, *sh*, as is the rule in Heb. and Assyr., and not *d*, *t*, *th*, as in Aram., and as the slightly variant sounds of *th* in Arab., as ذٰ, ظِـيَ, أُثْـر. Even more interesting is the fact that Zenjirli inserts ק instead of ע (as in other Aram. dialects) to represent Arab. *ḍ* and Heb. *ṣ*. This is easily illustrated by the familiar word for 'earth': Arab. أرض, *ar'd*, Heb. ארץ, and Aram. (usually) ארעא; but Zenjirli ארק (*Hadad*, l. 5), ארקא (*Panammu*, l. 14). In a very mixed Biblical passage both forms appear—the older ארקא, and the later ארעא (Jer. 10¹¹).

[2] *E.g.* the following are almost pure Assyr.: אל, *ilu* (*Hadad*, l. 2) ; פחי, *paḳâti* (*Panammu*, l. 12) ; כלמו, *kalâmu* (*Bar-rekub*, l. 17). The word כלמו is of uncertain meaning, but the phrase בית כלמו (*loc. cit.*) should perhaps be translated, 'house of completeness.' Cf. Tal. כְּלָם, *anything*.

II

PLACE AND VALUE OF INSCRIPTIONS

The reason why the Hebrew of the Old Testament is not more fully considered in this work is obvious—it was in no real sense the language of Palestine during our period. The later writings of the Old Testament were composed in a degenerate type of Hebrew, often made more difficult by the introduction of archaic words and expressions. The attempt to make the literature appear old in form and classical in idiom is evident in many of the religious songs, and in some of the solemn prophetic utterances. The secular poetry, however, made no such pretensions to imitate the ancient grandeur of the Hebrew sacred Psalms. The *Canticles*, for instance, manifestly belong to a late period of Hebrew literature. This is shown by the general character of the language, the absence of archaisms, and the readiness to modernize its form to the age of its composition. All these writings, however, render but very limited aid in the attempt to discover the living language of Palestine. They were written by Jews, who sought with indifferent success to preserve the national language, after it had been superseded by a foreign though kindred tongue. After all we have but specimens of Hebrew literature in the Old Testament and in the pseudepigrapha. Of the latter writings we possess no specimen earlier than the third cent. B.C. It must be presumed that only a fragment of the literary product of that age has come down to us. All extra-Biblical writings, which must have been composed in the great days of the two kingdoms, have disappeared. It is to be concluded that they were lost, never to be recovered, during the tragic dissolution of Israel and Judah between viii–vi cent. B.C. Such later writings as were rescued owe their preservation in many instances, not to their intrinsic or literary worth, but to the fact that they were issued under the aegis of the great names of national patriots and religious teachers.

The pseudepigrapha or extra-canonical literature cannot greatly assist us here. Many of these were written in a late

Hebrew, which was never a spoken language, though perhaps
it was sometimes attempted in religious assemblies.   Others
probably written in Aramaic have survived in another
language, or in an Aramaic which is considerably removed
from the original.   Of these latter the Book of Tobit may
be taken as a type.   Its author, its age, its subject-matter,
and its language, are all interesting and suggestive.   Tobit
was an exile in Nineveh, who clung to his Judaism, and
enjoined fidelity to God and to ancestral ties.   The Book
was probably written rather more than 200 years B.C. in a
dialect of Aramaic, slightly coloured by Babylonian influence.
The present Chaldee text cannot be regarded as the original,
nor the text which Jerome had before him when he translated Tobit from Chaldee into Latin.[1]   Probably the Chaldee
text known to us dates from the second cent. A.D., but has been
edited and emended several times.   It is simple, idiomatic,
and generally free from any attempt to imitate archaic
forms.[2]   The argument of Neubauer for a Hebrew original,
based on the use of certain proper names, is of little force.[3]
A Jewish author, well acquainted with the nomenclature of
his own people, might easily introduce familiar Hebrew
names into his Chaldee story, especially, as in the present
case, when the appeal is to compatriots of the Diaspora.[4]

For the character of Aramaic between the Exile and the
Christian era we are indebted more to inscriptions than to
other writings.   Any conclusions, however, based on the
Semitic inscriptions must be accepted with considerable
caution.   These inscriptions exhibit only skeletons of the
spoken language.   They do not contain vowels, or only in
rare cases, and then in the most primitive and uncertain
manner.   Still less do the inscriptions indicate the finer
phonetic modifications, such as the difference between *a* and

---

[1] *Opera*, ed. Vallarsi, Verona, 1740, tom. x.

[2] The Prologue will indicate the style : הוא בתוב במדרש רבה דרבה פרשת
ויצא יעקב פרשתא ע נבי וכל אשר חתן לי עשר אעשרנו לך · עשר תעשר אם להם משה עשר
ברכות חמלו אם תעשרו וכן יעקב אם וכל אשר חתן לי עשר אעשרנו לך עשר ברכות שחתן לי
כמו שברכנו אבי בזכות מה בזכות אעשרנו לך:

[3] *Book of Tobit*, pp. xv–xvi.

[4] The form טוביה is Aram. as well as Heb., *e.g.* עדיה (CIS ii. 122[1], cf.
2 K. 22[1]) ; פלליה (Egypt. *Pap.* C 17) ; אוריה (*ib.* D 7).

o, the doubling of consonants, etc. Probably, therefore, as spoken languages Moabite and Judaean differed considerably more than the written monuments suggest. The utmost that can be said from the available evidence is that during the period of the Aramaic inscriptions there was something approaching a common phonetic system.

The following notes will indicate some differences between Phoenician and Aramaic, and between Aramaic dialects at different times and in different localities. At the same time the uncertainty of many forms will appear, and the insuperable difficulty of writing an adequate grammar or syntax of the language during the period under discussion. Incidentally comparison will be made with Biblical texts, and occasionally the inscriptions will throw light on Biblical passages.

III

SEMITIC IN TWO TYPES

The Semitic language preserved in the inscriptions is known in two main forms—the Phoenician, including the Punic and Neo-Punic, and the Aramaic, including Nabataean and Palmyrene. The inscriptions cover a wide area, as the following table will show :

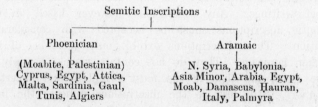

Semitic Inscriptions

Phoenician	Aramaic
(Moabite, Palestinian) Cyprus, Egypt, Attica, Malta, Sardinia, Gaul, Tunis, Algiers	N. Syria, Babylonia, Asia Minor, Arabia, Egypt, Moab, Damascus, Ḥauran, Italy, Palmyra

These two forms of the language cover much of the same period. The Phoenician extends from the v cent. B.C. to i cent. A.D. [The Cyprus inscription *Baʿal Lebanon* (CIS i. 5) dates from the viii cent. B.C. and is the oldest specimen of Phoenician writing known.] The Aramaic extends from the viii cent. B.C. to the iii cent. A.D. The fact that these inscriptions overlap in place and time is itself evidence of the movements and mixtures of the Semitic tribes in the regions named.

In the foregoing table the Moabite Stone and the Siloam inscription are bracketed. It may, however, be stated that Moabite was more akin to Hebrew than to any other Semitic dialect. But where Moabite differed from Hebrew the difference pointed to Phoenician on the one side, and to Arabic on the other, rather than to Aramaic. This is explicable from the geographical position of Moab, between the Philistines and the Edomites. The *scriptio defectiva* is the rule in Moabite. The most remarkable peculiarity is the *vav* conversive with the imperfect as in Hebrew. The Siloam inscription is more flowing than the Moabite, but it belongs to the same archaic type. It, too, has the *vav* conversive with the imperfect. One noticeable difference is that the third masculine singular suffix ends in ה' in Moabite, and ו' in Siloam. *E.g.* בארצה ויחלפה בנה, ' with his land. And his son succeeded him ' (Moab. St. ll. 5, 6) ; רעו, ' his fellow ' (Siloam inscr. ll. 2, 3, 4).

IV

CONSTRUCTIONS: GRAMMATICAL AND SYNTACTICAL

1. The *ARTICLE* is less frequent in Phoen. than in Heb. Cf. משכב · על (CIS i. 46²), and על־המשכב (1 K. 1⁴⁷). Where the pronoun follows the noun, Phoen. omits the article with the pronoun : האדם הא (CIS i. l. 15), Heb. האדם ההוא (cf. Num. 9¹³). Sometimes Phoen. omits the article with the noun as well : ממלת הא (CIS i. 3¹¹). The absence of the article and the use of the *status emphaticus* are signs of the supersession of Phoen. and the advancement of Aram. The Zenjirli inscriptions show that about the time of the Exile these Aram. characteristics were becoming evident. Thus : ארקא, ' the earth '; ביתא · זנה, ' this house ' (*Bar-rekub*, ll. 4, 20). But the article is not found in these inscriptions. The *status emphaticus* is frequent in Nab. and Palm., but in most instances it has lost the sense of the definite article. *E.g.* פסלא, ' mason ' (CIS ii. 201⁵, 208⁹); אתרא דנה, ' this place ' (CIS ii. 217⁷); תגרא, ' merchants ' (Vog. 4³). In a phrase like אלהא טבא ושכרא,

'the good and generous god' (Palm. Votive inscr., Littman, 2 B[4]), the form may or may not signify emphasis. [In one instance the *st. emp.* appears to end in ה' : קישה (CIS ii. 197[5], 198[4]), but is found in regular form קישא (CIS ii. 209[9]). Possibly in the former instance it is not the *st. emp.*, but the absolute form of the proper name.] In late Aram. חד, חדא, or אחד is used occasionally as indefinite article = Gk. εἷς or τις (*vide* Ezra 4[8] 6[2], Dan. 2[31] 6[18] 7[16]). This is rare in the inscriptions ; cf., however, חד · מלכן · רברב, either 'one of the powerful kings,' or 'any of the powerful kings' (Zenjirli : *Bar-rekub*, l. 13 ; cf. *Hadad*, l. 27 ; *Panammu*, l. 5). This use is not found in Onkelos, but חד is employed for 'each one,' 'every' : רבא חד ליומא, 'each leader on his day' (Targ. Num. 7[11]) ; . . . לאמרא חד, 'for every lamb' (*ib.* 28[11]) ; תרין סמכין תרין סמכין תחות דפא חד, 'two sockets under every board' (Targ. Ex. 36[30]).

2. The construction of the *PRONOUN* with the participle is found in Phoen. much the same as in Heb. *E.g.* שכב אנך, 'I lie' (CIS i. 3[3], cf. Jer. 38[14]). This construction is far more common in Aram. and Syr. *E.g.* דאין אנא, 'I judge' (Onk. Gen. 15[14]) ; ܩ̣ܛ̣ܠ ܐܢܐ, 'I slay'; ܙܟܝܐ ܐܢܐ, 'I am innocent' (Pesh. Mt. 27[24]). The use of the personal pronoun after the relative is common to Phoen. (=Heb.) and Aram. *E.g.* אש הא=אֲשֶׁר הִיא (CIS i. 92[2]) ; Heb. אשר־הוא (Hag. 1[9]) ; Bibl. Aram. די אנין (Dan. 7[17]) ; Targ. Onk. די־היא (Dt. 20[20]) ; cf. the construction הא זא, 'this which' (CIS ii. 113[15]).

The form of the relative changes from the Phoen. ש to the Heb. של and to the Aram. ד. By this particle the genitival idea is expressed. Thus : שלא=אֲשֶׁר לָהּ, 'which to her' (N. Punic, Louvre, 130[3]) ; שבדמלקרת, 'of Bod-melqarth' (CIS i. 139[2]) ; Heb. כַּרְמִי שֶׁלִּי, 'my vineyard of me,' *i.e.* which is mine (Cant. 1[6]). In some early inscriptions Aram. retains the Phoen. ש, *e.g.* ששנזרבן, 'of Sin-zir-ban' (*Nêrab*, 1, l. 1), שאאנבר, 'of Agbar' (*ib.* 2, l. 1). In later Aram. ד or די is the common usage, *e.g.* the Palm. קברא דנה די עתנתן, 'this tomb is that of 'Athē-nathan' (Vog. 30[a1. 2]). The same form is characteristic of Pales. as it is found in Bibl. Aram and Targ. *passim.*

The change of the form of the demonstrative pronoun can be traced through the inscriptions from the earliest Phoen. ז to the latest Aram. ד.   The forms ז, mas. and fem.; זן, mas.; זא, fem.; אז, mas. and fem.; זת, fem.; אל and אלא, pl. are all found in Phoen. inscrip. (*vide* CIS i. 3³, *ib.* 60¹; CIS i. l. 4, *ib.* l. 6; CIS i. 44¹, *ib.* 91¹, *ib.* 14⁵; N. Punic, 66⁴). The oldest Aramaic has most of the same forms (*vide* Zenjirli: *Hadad*, l. 3; *ib. Panammu*, l. 1; CIS ii. 113¹³); cf. Egypt. Aram. אלו (Rabb. *ib.* = Heb. אלה), *these* (CIS ii. 138²). The form אלה, *these*, Egypt. Aram. (Pap. E 13, K 13), Nab. (CIS ii. 207³), and Ezra (5¹⁵), Jer. (10¹¹), is a peculiarity of these dialects. The usual Aram. is אלין, Pales. (cf. Targ. Onk., Ps.-Jon. Gen. 2⁴). With the foregoing cf. the late Palm. דה (Vog. 31¹), דא, fem. (CIS ii. 332¹), also Bibl. Aram. and Nab., דנה, mas. (Constantine: Afr. 1¹), also Bibl. Aram. and Nab., = Pales. דין. The Palm. pl. is אלן (Vog. 1¹), Bibl. Aram. אלך (Ezra 4²¹ *al.*, Dan. 3¹² *al.*); *Tal. Babli* אלין, *these* (proximate); אלך, *those* (distant).

The form זי, relative and genitival, in Aram. passed into די probably about iii–ii cent. B.C. In the Aram. inscrip. of the iv cent. B.C. זי is employed as relative, *e.g.* מלך יאדי זי הקמת נצב זן, 'king of Ya'di, who set up this pillar' (Zenjirli: *Hadad*, l. 1); זי מת(כ)תב, 'which is written' (CIS ii. 146 A¹). It is also used as the sign of the genitive, *e.g.* תמנחא זי אוסרי אלהא, 'devotee of the divine Osiris' (*ib.* 141¹). In the Egypt. papyri זי is the common form (in one only, E 7, 11, 16, *circa* 446 B.C., is די found). But in the earliest Nab. inscrip. (beginning with i cent. B.C.) די has become thoroughly established. Here it is used as relative, *e.g.* קברא די עבד עידו, 'the tomb which 'Aïdu made' (CIS ii. 197¹), and as the sign of the genitive, *e.g.* צלמא די עבדת אלהא די, 'the statue of the divine 'Obedath, which . . .' (where די is used in both senses, *ib.* 354¹).

When the dem. or pers. pronoun is used with the rel., the former is frequently added for emphasis. Thus: וכר זנה הא, 'and a memorial this (it) is' (Zenjirli: *Panammu*, l. 22). So in Pales. Aram., *e.g.* הלא דא היא בבל רבתא, 'Is not this (it) great Babylon' (Dan. 4²⁷); כל-רחשא דהוא חי, 'every crawling thing which (it) is living' (Onk. Gen. 9³); ארעא די-הוא עברא, 'a land which (it) is flowing' (Onk. Num. 14⁸). This use of the pers.

pronoun, it will be noticed, is before an adjective or participle. This is the rule, as, *e.g.*, further : עַל־קרתא די־הוא עבדא עמך קרב, 'against the city that (it) maketh war with thee' (Onk. Dt. 20²⁰).

The Phoen. form of the pronoun הא is used for both masculine and feminine. Thus : mas. כ מלך צדק הא, 'for a righteous king he is' (CIS i. l. 9); fem. אש הא שת = אֲשֶׁר הִיא שְׁנַת, 'which (it) is the year' (CIS i. 93²). In early Aram. הא is used as mas., *e.g.* אבי לו בעל כסף הא, 'my father whether he possessed gold . . .' (Zenjirli : *Panammu*, l. 11 ; cf. the emphatic use of הא, Palm. *Tariff*, ii. c. ⁶). In later Aram. the two forms — או and הי — are used to give emphasis as ὁ αὐτός in Gk. (*vide* Nab. CIS ii. 198¹⁰; Palm. Vog. 36 b; *Tariff*, ii. b. ⁶, c. ¹⁰). The neutral or common character of הא in Phoen. sufficiently explains the use of הוא in the Pentateuch for both genders. The old Heb. was probably הא (cf. Moab. St. ll. 6, 27), and הוא was introduced later when it was felt necessary to distinguish the masculine from the feminine. Originally the context, *i.e.* the gender of the antecedent, would decide the gender of הא and הוא. In Bibl. Aram. Targ. and Tal. the forms הוא and היא are regularly employed. The transition stage to these final forms in Aram. is seen in the Egypt. Aram. הו and הי (*e.g.* mas. Pap. A 1, B 1, C 1, *al.*; fem. Pap. A 4, C 9, D 25, *al.*).

3. The *SIGN OF THE ACCUSATIVE* in Phoen. was את or אית, perhaps vocalized אֵית (*vide* CIS i. ll. 7, 8). In the earliest Aram. inscrip. the form ות is found (Zenjirli : *Hadad*, l. 28), and later in Nab. the familiar ית (CIS ii. 198⁵). This particle ית is found once only in the Palm. inscrip. (Vog. 15⁴, ית לגינא, the legions; λεγεῶνας, cf. Vog. 22⁵), and this may indicate its vanishing from the Aram. dialects generally. Its frequent appearance in the Targ. is in imitation of the Heb. את. It is rare in Bibl. Aram. (cf. די מנית יתהן, Dan. 3¹²). This particle, though not essentially Aram., was probably retained in Pales. Aram. as the Yemen (Onk.) MSS suggest. In Syr. ܠ is very rare, ܠ being preferred. In the Targ. Samarit. ית is found much as את in Heb. In Palm. Aram. as a rule no sign indicates the accusative, though sometimes ל is found as in Syr. (*vide* Vog. 132). The Heb. form את is perhaps taken directly from the Phoen. shorter form את (*vide*

CIS i. l. 3, *ib.* i. 28⁴, *ib.* 95⁴, *ib.* 165²¹). The Aram. form
יח perhaps from the longer Phoen. form אית, by omitting the
initial א (*vide* CIS i. l. 15, *ib.* i. 3¹⁹, *ib.* 86 A⁹, *ib.* 132¹·³;
Carthage, l. 3). The accusative particle is very rare in the
Aram. inscrip., and in Egypt. papyri it never occurs.

4. The *ORDER OF WORDS* is found to change as we pass
from Phoen. to some later dialects. For instance, in Phoen.
we have מלך תבנת, 'King Tabnith' (CIS i. 3²). In Nab. and
Pales. Aram. the order is reversed; thus: חרתת מלך, 'King
Harethath' (CIS ii. 199⁹), נבוכדנצר מלכא (Dan. 3¹, cf. 5¹),
מלכי־צדק מלכא (Onk. Gen. 14¹⁸). In the case of numbers in
Phoen. the ten precedes the unit, *e.g.* עסר וארבע, 'the fourteenth'
(CIS i. 3¹). Observe the rather awkward method of expressing the ordinal: בשנת עסר וארבע, 'in years fourteen'; there
was no special form for the ordinal in Phoen. The same
order is followed in Nab., *e.g.* שנת עשר ותלת, 'the year of ten
and three = 13th year (CIS ii. 199⁹), and in Palm., *e.g.*
[עשר ושת], 'ten and six' = 16 (*Tariff*, ii. b.²⁰). Pales. Aram.
seems to reverse the order: ארבע־עשרי שנין, 'fourteen years'
(Onk. Gen. 31⁴¹); חמש עשרי אמין, 'fifteen cubits' (Onk. Gen.
7²⁰); ביומא תרי עשר, 'on the twelfth day' (*ib.* Num. 7⁷⁸). So
the Syriac: ܐܪܒܥܣܪ, 'fourteenth' (Pesh. Acts 27²⁷). Cf.
ܟܣܢ ܡܬܡܐܝܢ ܘܐܪܒܥܡܐܐ ܠܫܢܬ, 'to the year (of) four hundred
and twenty-one' (Aphraates, *Homilies*, 475, 2, Wright's ed.).

5. There seems to have been no uniform method of expressing numbers and dates. In Phoen. inscriptions they are
sometimes expressed in words, *e.g.* בת שמנם שת, lit. 'daughter
of eighty year(s)' (Neo-Punic: *Shershel*, 1, l. ⁶); רב שני,
'second official' (= under-prefect, Phoen. *Sidon*, 4, l. ²).
More often signs are employed, *e.g.* Ⅲ ⁓z, '33ʳᵈ' (Phoen.
Larnax Lapēthos, 2, l. ⁵); ⁓ⅢⅠⅠ\, '15ᵗʰ' (ib. *Piraeus*, l. ¹).
Perhaps more frequently both words and signs are found
together, *e.g.* ⁓Ⅲ Ⅰ, בשנת עסר וארבע, 'in the year fourteenth,
14ᵗʰ' (CIS i. 3¹); ⁓ʌ, בשנת שלשם, 'in the year thirtieth, 30ᵗʰ'
(Phoen. Brit. Mus. Cyprus Room, No. 252, l. ⁵). Rather
strangely three methods are found together in an early Aram.
inscription (Nineveh, viii–vii B.C.): ⁽ᵃ⁾ ⁓Ⅲ Ⅱ, ⁽ᵇ⁾ ||||||||||||||,
⁽ᶜ⁾ חמשת עשר (= 15, CIS ii. 1). As a rule, in the earlier
Aram. inscriptions the numerical signs are employed. In

Nab. we find both words (CIS ii. 199[9], 202[4], 196[6. 8], 170[1]) and signs (CIS ii. 205[11], 354[4], 161 col. iii., 174[3]). In Aram. Sin. the method is mixed, מאה ‎וֹ6, 'one hundred (and) 6' (Euting, *Nabatäische Inschriften*, 457, l. [1]). Palm. commonly employs signs, but occasionally words, *e.g.* חמש מאה וארבע, 'five hundred and four' (Müller, *Palm. Inschr.* 46[15]).

6. It is doubtful whether *vav* conversive with the imperfect was a Phoen. idiom. It is found in Moabite (Moab. St. l. 5), but this may only show how closely this dialect was related to Heb. The form ויספננם, 'and we attacked them' (CIS i. 3[19]), is apparently the imperfect with *nun* demonstrative, a common construction in Arabic. If this is really an instance of *vav* conversive with the imperfect (Stade, *Morgenländische Forschungen*, 310), it is ἅπαξ λεγ. in Phoen. The construction *vav* conversive with the perfect is found in a few Phoen. inscriptions (CIS i. 165[4. 6. 8. 10], *ib.* 167[4. 5], *ib.* 170), and is used much as in Heb. to indicate the place and force of the predicate (cf. Driver, *Heb. Tenses*, §§ 122, 123). In Phoen. the usual tense for historical narrative is the perfect with *vav* unconversive, *e.g.* חדש ‎ופעל, 'renovated and made' (CIS i. 175[1]). The idiom of *vav* conversive is not known in Aram., but in *Talmud Babli* the imperfect with *vav* continuing an imperfect with modal force is found (*vide* Margolis, *Lang. Babyl. Tal.*, p. 78). Apart from the Heb. Scriptures the data are scarce, meagre in bulk and doubtful in character. Even in late Bibl. Heb. the use of *vav* consecutive was less pronounced, and soon after its conversive character was entirely lost (cf. Olshausen, *Heb. Gram.*; Böttcher, *Lehrbuch d. Hebr. Sprache*). The origin of *vav* consecutive is by no means clear. In Heb. alone did it come into prominent use. It is doubtful whether this construction was originally as frequent or consistent as the MT. would suggest. The pointed text stereotyped a pronunciation and accentuation which obtained in the latest stages of the language. It is hardly to be supposed that the OT. writers had in mind all the nice distinctions and constructional mechanisms that modern scholars often attribute to them. The original use of the *vav* consecutive was probably much simpler than generally imagined. It first

appears among the Canaanite tribes, Moabites, Hebrews, and no doubt others. It is clearly associated primarily with the impf. The intention of the speaker by this device was to indicate that the further statement was not only connected with, but was the sequence of the previous statement. In this method of expression was involved the *desire* of the speaker, and the *tendency* of his thought or of the action. Hence grammarians distinguish the two modifications of the impf.—the jussive and the cohortative. Originally these shades of meaning were expressed by intonation or the place of the accent. When speech was reduced to syllabic writing, it was not unnatural to express the *direction* of the speaker's *feeling*, and the connexion between the second verb and the first, by the use of the copulative or consecutive particle *vav* joined to the second thought or action. The idiom really looks like a primitive attempt to vary the nuance of a single tense. If this suggestion could be supported it would throw new light on the origin of this peculiar construction. It is pretty certain that the Assyrian Chronicles reveal but one tense—corresponding to the Heb. impf. [cf. Hommel, *Geschichte Bab. u. Assyr.* 1885–1889; Delitzsch, *Assyr. Gram.*, 1889; Bezold, *Kurzgef. Ueberblick über die Bab.-Assyr. Literatur,* 1896]. The Assyrian language was based on the Babylonian, and in the Babylonian dialect the vassal princes of Palestine wrote the letters found among the Tell el-Amarna tablets. It is probable, therefore, that the Palestinian tribes adopted the impf. as the annalistic or historic tense, and developed from it, by the *vav* consecutive, the method of expressing continuation and consequence. The pf. with *vav* consecutive is simply the counterpart of the foregoing idiom. As the retracting of the tone (intonation) in the impf. indicated association with what went before, so the projecting of the tone in the pf. indicated association with what was to follow. This construction is later than *vav* with impf., it is not found in Moabite, and the cases in Phoen. are not free from suspicion (cf. Cooke, *North Sem. Inscr.* 118 f.).

7. The use of ל with the imperfect in the Zenjirli inscriptions (vide *Hadad*, ll. 23, 24, 30, 31) is the earliest occurrence of this construction yet found in Aram. Here

ל has clearly a jussive force, and the cohortative conception of the passive itself may explain the construction. It is rare, but appears in S. Semitic (*e.g.* Sabaean, CIS iv. 74[10ff.]), N. Semitic (*e.g.* Mandaean, *vide* Nöldeke *Mand. Gram.* §§ 166, 196), Bibl. Aram. (only with היה), Targum (Ps.-Jon.), and *Talmud Babli*. It does not appear in Phoen. inscriptions. No satisfactory explanation of this construction has been given. In the opinion of the present writer the probability is that the form is due to the infinitive. Some ancient writers in a rather original, but inexact way attempted to express *purpose*, in some of its many phases, or even object, by the imperfect prefixed by the infinitive particle ל. For instance, והדד חרא לותכה, 'and let (or may) Hadad wreak anger upon him,' *i.e.* 'let Hadad mete out wrath *to* him' (Zenjirli : *Hadad*, l. 23). In general it may perhaps be said that wherever ל with the imperfect is found the infinitive idea is involved. Gesenius indeed regards להוא (Dan. 5[22]) as infinitive instead of למהוא, and basis his conclusion on the analogy of the frequent use of the infinitive for finite tenses in Hebrew. It is probably unwise to look for any connexion between the imperfect with ל and with נ, though the two forms in Mandaean point in this direction. It must be confessed that there is not sufficient evidence to lead to a conclusion on this point (*vide* Duval, *Traite de Gram. Syr.* § 181 ; Kautzsch, *Bibl. Aram.* § 47). The common interchange of ל and נ for phonetic reasons may sufficiently account for the two forms in different Aram. dialects. It is worthy of note that there was a tendency in Semitic to substitute נ for י, *e.g.* נאה=יאה (Prov. 17[7], Ps. 33[1]); נצב=יצב (Ex. 8[16], 1 S. 22[9]); נקש=יקש (Dt. 15[14], 2 K. 12[10]). In Syriac this tendency hardened into a rule in the third person imperfect. (Contrast the foregoing suggestions with Driver, *Heb. Tenses*, § 204, Obs. 1.) The construction of the inf. absol. with ל, *e.g.* לזבח, 'to sacrifice' (CIS i. 165[14]), in which the inf. with ל fills the place of the predicate, is an idiom common in late Heb. (cf. *Aboth*, iv. 22). The use of the impf. with cohort. ל is found, *e.g.* פלכתשה, 'Let him fight him' (*Hadad*, l. 31), פא(פא)+ל+כתש=, with ה 3 s. m. suffix. The conj. פ is so used in Nab. (*e.g.* CIS ii. 198[7. 10]), and Palm. (*vide* Müller, *Palm. Inschr.*, No. 46).

9

8. The Aram. imperf. 3 sing. of ל״י verbs ends in ‫ֶ‬‫ה‬ in many inscriptions, e.g. ירקי, ירשי, תלעי (Zenjirli: *Hadad*, ll. 22, 27, 32, et al.). This is the case in Pales. Aram., e.g. אֹודִי (Targ. Is. 12¹), תֶּחֱזֵי (Targ. Mic. 4¹¹), and Targum generally. In Bibl. Aram. א‫ֶ‬ is usual, as ‫ֶ‬‫ן‬ in Syriac. The normal termination of the imperf. 3 pl. is ן׳, but the final ן was probably at first either not inserted in writing, or not sounded in speech. The Zenjirli inscript. seem to indicate the transition period. Here we find יתנו (*Hadad*, l. 4), יסחו, יהאבדו (*Nêrab*, 1, ll. 9, 11), ולשמו (*Nêrab*, 2, l. 6). This form is found in Egypt. Aram., e.g. יאכלו (CIS ii. 137 B³), but ן׳ is also found, e.g. יכהלן (Pap. D 15, H 11). The inscriptions with termination ו׳ were probably influenced by Phoen. or Moabite. In the later inscriptions (v cent. onwards) the ן׳ is commonly added, e.g. יתכנשן (CIS ii. 145 A⁸), יהון (*ib.* D³, cf. Onk. Gen. 1¹⁶). In Nab. it is usual, e.g. יתקברון (CIS ii. 205⁴, *ib.* 209³), יזבנן, ימשכנן, יוגרן, יכתבון (CIS ii. 212⁴). This was the Pales. Aram. form, e.g. יתברכון (Targ. 2 S. 7²⁹), יבאשון (Targ. Is. 11⁹), יטלון (Targ. Jos. 6⁶), יתנפחן (Targ. Eccl. 12⁵, *et ubique*).

In Phoen. final י in verbs was frequently not written, but was probably pronounced, e.g. קראת, 'I called' (CIS i. l. 7); פעלת, 'I wrought' (CIS i. 3¹⁹); יטנאת, 'I erected' (Hifil, CIS i. 46²); יתת ויקדשת, 'I gave and consecrated' (Cyprus inscr.: *Larnax Lapêthos*, 2, or *Narnaka*, l. 9). For fuller illustration *vide* Schröder, *Die Phönizische Sprache*, 204. In earlier Aram. final י in verbs was not pronounced, and frequently not written, e.g. ורצת, 'and I ran' (Zenjirli: *Bar-rekub*, l. 8); מתת 'I died' (*Nêrab*, 2, l. 4); חזית, 'I saw' (CIS ii. 137 A²). For instances in later Aram. (Palm.) *vide* Vogüé, *Syrie Centrale*, 79⁴, 92, 103. In the first pers. sing. perf. the י is similarly omitted in the Egypt. Aram. In the Pales. Aram. the endings חי׳ and ת׳ are found (e.g. Ps.-Jon. Gen. 3¹⁰. ¹³ 31³⁹; 2 S. 7⁷. ¹⁵). There was some uncertainty in the writing and the pronunciation of this final vowel in the vernacular of Pales. This may possibly explain certain readings and phrases in the Greek Gospels, e.g. Ταλιθὰ κούμ, or Ταλιθὰ κούμι, i.e. טליתא קום, or טליתא קומי (Mk. 5⁴¹). Final vowels in other constructions were also liable to confusion, hence perhaps Ἀββᾶ, ὁ πατήρ=אבא אבי (Mk. 14³⁶). *Vide* p. 218.

9. The inscriptions seem to prove that in Aram. the *PASSIVE* was properly expressed by the reflexive forms, *e.g.* די מתקרא, ' who is called ' (Nab. CIS ii. 158[2]; Palm. Vog. 17[2]); מתכתב, ' was written,' ויכתב, ' and be written ' (Palm. *Tariff*, i. ll. 5, 8); די יזבן, ' who shall be sold '; תהוא מתזבנא, ' it shall be sold '; הוא מזבן, ' it shall be sold ' (Palm. *Tariff*, ii. a.[4], c.[32. 33. 37]). The Biblical Aram. Hofal forms (Dan. 4[33] *al.*) were probably Hebraisms, and such forms were not normal in the living Pales. dialect. The assimilation of ת in some of the foregoing terms should be noted. Since the Palm. inscriptions are late, we cannot conclude from these data that this assimilation was general in Pales. Aram. a century or two earlier. In the earlier Nab. ת is usually found, *e.g.* יתשנא, יתזבן, יתקבר (CIS ii. 208[3. 4], *ib.* 350[4]). Observe in Nab. the ת in these conjugations stands before the sibilant; cf. the correct Pales. form ישתנא (Dan. 2[9]). In the case of ד, ז takes the place of ת in the passive, *e.g.* מזדבנין, יזדבן, אזדבן, etc. (Talmud, *saepe*), but the inscriptions pay little heed to these correct forms.

The Phoen. verb יתן (perf. 3 sing. mas.) is found in several inscriptions (CIS i. 3[18], *ib.* 5[a], *ib.* 10[3] *al.*). This form is not to be explained as the Hifil of נתן (as Winckler, *Altorientalische Forschungen*, i. 69 f.), since there is no evidence whatever that י ever takes the place of ה in this conjugation. Indeed the evidence is the other way, as the inscriptions and other Aram. authorities show, *e.g.* נפק, not only retains ן in Hifil, but ה as well, hence יהנפק (CIS ii. 113[21]); cf. תהנפק, הנפקת, (Ps.-Jon. Gen. 1[13. 24]) יהנזיק (*ib.* Ex. 11[7]); *vide* הנפק (Ezra 5[14], Dan. 5[2]), הנפקו (Dan. 5[3]), יהנפקון (Egypt. Aram. Pap. D[15. 17] *al.*). In some Aram. inscriptions the ן is retained in the imperf., *e.g.* ינתן (CIS ii. 145 D[1]); אנתן (Egypt. Aram. Pap. A[7]); so in later Nab. (CIS 197[3]). In others the ן is dropped, *e.g.* יתנו (Zenjirli: *Hadad*, l. 4); יתן (Palm. *Tariff*, ii. a.[5], b.[20]). No certain conclusion can be reached on this point respecting the Pales. dialect. Bibl. Aram., which is one of the best guides, generally retains the ן (Ezra 4[13] 7[20], Dan. 2[16] 4[15]), but Targums usually omit (Onk. Gen. 17[2] 26[3]; Targ. Jos. the Blind, Ps. 110[1]). In Targums, the Preterite, Participle and Imperative are commonly rendered by the verb יהב, which

occasionally appears in inscr. (CIS ii. 146 A[4], 147 B[2], *ib.*
209[9]; in 199[6] יהב is impf. for ינתן, which is the usual form,
CIS ii. 197[6]).

10. Phoen. frequently terminates in א where later dialects
discriminate between ה, י, ו. Thus : קלא רפיא, ' his voice (and)
healed him' (CIS i. 143[2]), for קולו רפאו; קלא יברכא, ' his voice :
let him bless him' (CIS i. 181[5]), for קולו יברכו ; אמא, ' his
mother' (Neo-Punic, 130[4]), for אמו; כלא, ' for him' (Neo-
Punic : *Shershel*, 2, l.[6]), for פי לו. But occasionally correctly,
זרעו, ' his seed' (CIS i. l.[15]). כא, ' for' (Punic : *Carthage*, l.[3]),
for כי; אדני, ' his lord' (Phoen. *Sidon*, 4, l.[2]), for אדנו, but אדני,
' my lord,' correctly (CIS i. 7[7]). שלא, ' which to her' (Neo-
Punic, 130[3]), for שַׁאֲר לָהּ (= Aram. די לה).

A final י sometimes appears where א might be expected.
In מרתי (CIS ii. 158[2]; Vog. 13[1]) the י really looks like the
first pers. pron. suffix, ' my lady'; but this reading does not
quite harmonize with the form of the sentence. More naturally we should expect מרת (as 1 K. 17[17]). Possibly the י is
euphonic to distinguish the proper name from the titular
מרת, and this passed into the א *status emph.,* With this the
Greek form of the name in the inscr. Μάρθειν (acc.) agrees.
From the Aram. מרתא came the Gk. Μάρθα, just as from
the Aram. מריא came the Lat. *Marius* (Vog. 22[4], unfortunately
the Gk. of this Palm. inscr. is defective).

11. In Egypt. Aram. (v–iv cent. B.C.) the dual form
differed from the plural by the omission of י in the latter,
e.g. מצרין, ' Egypt'; ביומן אחרנן, ' in after days'; שנן, ' years'
(CIS ii. 145[8, 4, 9]). With regard to the last word it should be
noted that the sing. is written שת (= שנת), and the plural שנת
(*vide* Clermont-Ganneau, *Recueil d'archeologie orientale*, ii.
§ 75). It is probable that many Heb. duals were formed from
Phoen. (or Moabite) sing. forms, and not from forms which
were originally dual. *E.g.* צהרים, from Moab. צהרם; כהנים,
from רב כהנם, ἀρχιερεύς (*vide* CIS i. 119[2]; *Carthage*, l. 8[bis]).
On the other hand, it looks as if there is some connexion between the Moabite dual in ֵן, the Heb. ִים, and the Aram. ִין.
Thus מאתן, ' two hundred' (Moab. St. l.[20]), מאתים, מאתין (Heb.
and Targ. Ps.-Jon. Gen. 1[27]). In Pales. Aram. both dual and
plural forms were alike, ִין. The pointing of the dual in Bibl.

Aram, יִ֫ן_ is a Hebraism, *e.g.* יָדִין (Dan. 2³⁴) should be יְדִין
(Egypt. Pap. G 8); רַגְלִין (Dan. 7⁴) should be רַגְלִין (Targ.; cf.
Palm. *Tariff*, ii. b. ³⁰); קַרְנִין (Dan. 7⁷) should be קַרְנִין (*Tal.
Babli*); מָאתָין (Ezra 6¹⁷) should be מָאתִין (or מָאתָן, Targ. Ps.-Jon.
Gen. 1²⁷); עֵינִין (Dan. 7⁸· ²⁰) correctly (as Targ. עַיְנִין, Ps.-Jon.
Gen. 2⁷; עַיְנִין, Onk. Gen. 3⁶ *al.*).   In the Targums the form of
the plural is used for the dual, and where necessary תרין is
added, *e.g.* תְּרֵין נְהוֹרַיָּא, ' two lights ' (Onk. Gen. 1¹⁶); so in Nab.
e.g. תלתין תרין, ' two-thirds ' (CIS ii. 213⁴).

It is doubtful whether some titles are sing. or plural, *e.g.*
אלם (Phoen. *Piraeus*, ll. 2, 5, 6 ; CIS i. 119² ; Neo-Punic :
Maktar, A i. ⁴); אדנם (CIS i. 276, 293).   These terms are
used with sing. meanings, though the forms are plural, *i.e.*
honorific plurals.   The forms אלם and אדנם are more abstract
than the sing. אל and אדן.   The Heb. plurals could easily
come from these Phoen. forms, hence אדנים, אלהים.   The latter
word is not found in Aram., except perhaps a trace in the
proper name בלאדן, a Chaldee title (2 K. 20¹²).   The form
אלהו (Zenjirli : *Hadad*, l. 2) is ἄπαξ λεγ. in inscriptions.   It
suggests the proper name אל, suffixed by the personal pronoun
הו (which often has the meaning of ὁ αὐτός = Syr. הֹסֹ; cf.
CIS ii. 198¹⁰; Palm. *Tariff*, ii. a. ⁶).   Hence קמו עמי אלהו הדד,
may be rendered : ' stood by me the god himself Hadad.'

12. The idea of ' any,' ' certain ' is frequently expressed
by some form of repetition, *e.g.* יֹם מֹד יֹם, ' day by day ' ;
ירח מד ירח, ' month by month ' (Phoen. *Larnax Lepēthos*,
2, ll. 11, 12).   The word מד is peculiar, possibly it is the
source of the Heb. מֻדֵי, ' from ' (cf. 1 S. 7¹⁶, Is. 66²³) ; or it may
be equivalent to the Aram. מִן־דִי, where the relative is really
redundant.   It is just possible that מד is a mistake for עד,
which is often used with time, *e.g.* עַד־יוֹמָא (Onk. Gen. 19³⁷· ³⁸).
Against this is the fact that עד is not found in Phoen. inscriptions, but *adû* is found in Assyrian.   Simple repetition is
found in all Aram. literature, *e.g.* מן מן בני, ' any (= whoso-
ever) of my sons ' (Zenjirli : *Hadad*, l. ¹⁵) ; בזבן זבן, ' at any
time ' (Palm. *Tariff*, i. l. ¹⁰), cf. ܘܒܙܒܢ, ' at a certain time '
(Pesh. Jno. 5⁴); יום יום (Onk. Gen. 39¹⁰, Ps. 68²⁰) ; שתא שתא
(Onk. Dt. 14²²), or שתא בשתא (*ib.* Dt. 15²⁰).   The circumlocu-

tion בזמניה מזמן לומן, ' in his time from time to time ' (Onk. Ex.
13[10]), is unusual.

The repetition לי . . . לי (Zenj. : *Panam.* 1.[11]) is uncertain.
Some take it as = Phoen. אי, Aram. אין, *if, whether*, but prob.
here it = לא. The inscr. should perhaps be rendered : ' My
father possessed neither silver nor gold.' The usual Pales. for
neither . . . nor was לא, . . . לא, and for *whether . . . or* was
או . . . או (Onk. Lev. 13[48]), or אין . . . אין (Targ. Eccl. 12[14]).

13. The use of כל with suffixes is idiomatic in Aram.
dialects. It is found in the earliest inscriptions (Zenjirli :
Panammu, ll. 17, 19). It is frequent in Nab. (*e.g.* CIS ii.
350[5], cf. 219[5]), in Syriac (Nöldeke, *Syr. Gram.* § 218), and
in Arabic (Wright, *Arab. Gram.* ii. § 82 a). The Targums
use it (*e.g.* Ps.-Jon. Gen. 2[3]) and the Talmud, *e.g.* לכולי תלמודא
(*Sabbat*, 63[a]), כוליה האי (*Berakot*, 7[b]; the Munich edition of this
Tractate reads כולי, due probably to the non-pronunciation of
the final ה). The form כלה is usually distributive (cf.
כלה . . . כלה, CIS ii. 205[5]; אנוש כלה = ' any one,' *ib.* 209[5];
כלה מחר = ' without exception to-morrow,' Egypt. Pap. G 20).
This must have been a very common usage in Pales. Aram.
(cf. Dan. 2[38] 7[19]; Onk. Gen. 11[6] 25[25] 43[34], Ex. 25[36], Lev.
13[13], Num. 13[33] 16[3], Dt. 1.[22] 4[4] 5[3]; Ps.-Jon. Gen. 2[3]; Targ.
Ps. 8[2], Warsaw ed.).

HEBRAISMS are rare in the Phoen. and Aram. inscriptions
and papyri. We find such forms as איש (CIS ii. 141[2], 145[2]) ;
לקח in the inf. לקחת, which is same as Heb. (CIS i. 166[5]) ;
אבד אבד עלם (inf. absol. with finite verb), ' perish utterly for
ever ' (Moab. St. l. 7 ; this inscript. is allied to Heb.). In the
pap. לאמר, ' saying ' (A 3, *al.*) ; נשחט (Niph. G 10), the root
שחט is not found in Aram.

14. The inscriptions indicate the period when the Phoen.
feminine ending ת' passed into the Heb. ה', and this again into
the Aram. א'. In the Moabite inscription the Phoen. ת is
employed : הבמת, ' the high place,' *i.e.* ' the altar ' (Moab. St.
l. 3) ; המכרתת, ' the trench ' (*ib.* l. 25) ; המסלת, ' the highway '
(*ib.* l. 26) ; משמעת, ' obedience ' (*ib.* l. 28). During the next
150 years (*i.e.* between 850 B.C. and 700 B.C.) the Phoen. ת'
became ה', as is shown by the Siloam inscription : הנקבה, ' the
boring ' (ll. 1[bis], 4) ; הברכה, ' the pool ' (l. 5) ; אמה, ' cubit '

(l. 5). This change was due partly to the general law of tone, which lengthened the vowel of ת׳ final under the accent from *Pathak* to *Kametz* (*i.e.* ת׳ַ to ת׳ָ), and partly to the Heb. tendency of aspirating or heightening the ending ת׳ to ה׳. The feminine ending in ה׳ in Aram. is generally a Hebraism. This usage came into Aram. through Jewish influence after the Exile, but it was again lost as Aram. became the regular dialect. The inscriptions suggest the transition period when the Hebraism ה׳ was superseded by the truer Aram. א׳. For instance, the Nerab inscriptions have both forms : ארצתה and ארצתא (*Nérab*, 1, ll. 4, 7, 12) ; צלמה and צלמא. (*ib.* 2², *ib.* 1³· ⁶). Cf. ברה and ברא (Egypt. Pap. F 8, 9), suggesting little distinction in pronunciation.

15. The absence of the neuter gender in Semitic is peculiar, and its explanation is perhaps psychological. The apparent irregularities of gender are not always grammatical inaccuracies. Some words which in the older period of the Hebrew language were used for both masculine and feminine, were really of common gender. When we find similiar phenomena in Aramaic and Syriac they are not necessarily vulgarisms, but possibly classical characteristics of these languages in their primitive age.[1] The mental outlook and temperament of a people are reflected in the construction of their speech. The Semites could use the future of the historic past and the preterite of the prophetical future. This idiosyncratic outlook is consonant with people who are impulsive rather than deliberative, poetical and symbolical rather than logical and dialectical. People of such emotional and idealistic temperament vivify every object of nature, and every object thus endowed with life is regarded as male or female. The absolutely impersonal, the real neuter, is inevitably excluded.

---

[1] The Pentateuchal (Kethib) use of הוא for both genders is referred to in another place. The word נער is of com. gender (cf. Gk. παῖς) ; the San. *nara* is apparently mas. = ἀνήρ. In Heb. נער is generally mas., נערה is the fem. form ; but the pl. נערים is both mas. and fem. Two pl. forms are found with a fem. sense : נערים (Ruth 2²¹), נערות (Prov. 9³). For נער Onk. has often עולימא or רביא. The root עלם, ܓܠܐ, غُلَم, is of com. gender, though in practice its use is almost invariably fem. In an inscrip. רבא, 'mistress,' is found with suffix רבתי (CIS 146 B 4⁴).

This means that abstract conceptions are not native to the Semitic mind. Purely intellectual ideas are expressed by metaphors, mental qualities and moral dispositions are' represented by concrete terms and bodily movements. Everything in the universe was by the Semite likened to some concrete thing with which he was acquainted. There existed in nature but two sexes, and consequently for him there were but two genders, and of these the feminine predominated. Nothing was indifferent or neutral, but was intuitively classed with one or other of the two great distinctions of nature. Probably the absence of a neuter in Semitic and its presence in Indo-European, are grammatical phenomena due to some extent to theological differences. The Semite was instinctively theistic, and the Deity cannot be neutral; the Aryan was materialistic or hyloistic, and to him things real or possible could be neutral.[1]

16. The *NEGATIVE PARTICLES* in Phoen. were sometimes joined, perhaps for emphasis. This usage is found in inscriptions of the Punic type in Gaul and Carthage. The combination איבל may be compared in a general way with οὐ μή, but the Semitic particles have not the same precision as the Greek. The negatives joined in this word are אי and בל; of these אי is probably the earlier. It occurs in the OT. (1 S. 4[21], Job 22[30]), often in Rabbinic and in inscriptions (Sidon : *Tabnith*, l. 4 ; *Eshmun-'azar* ; CIS i. 3[5]). בל is found separately (CIS i. 165[15], *ib.* 167[6]), and joined with אי (*ib.* 165[18. 21] 167[11]). The negative לא (Heb. and Aram.), though contemporary (cf. CIS ii. 137, b.[4]), does not appear in Phoen. [It is interesting to note in view of Is. 9[3] that לו=לא in a Phoen. inscrip. : לא טנא ת המאש זת מכפזן . . ., ‘Mikipzan . . . to him erected there is this statue’ (Neo-Punic : *Shershel*, 2, l. 3).] In Aram. לית (=אית, *is*, and לא, *not*) is usually taken for a simple negation. In Egypt. Aram. the particles are kept separate, לא איתי (Pap. D 10, G 17–18, 20–21, N 2). The Pales. was apparently לית or ל ית (*vide, e.g.*, Onk. and Ps.-Jon. Gen. 2[5]; Onk. Ex. 33[15], Num. 5[8]; also with suffix, *e.g.* Onk.

[1] Cf. *Wisd.* 13[1], οὐκ ἴσχυσαν εἰδέναι τὸν ὄντα (*i.e.* God) ; τὰ γὰρ μὴ ὄντα ἐκάλεσεν εἰς τὸ εἶναι, Philo, *de Creat. princip.*, p. 728 ; τὰ μὴ ὄντα ὡς ὄντα, Rom. 4[17] ; τὰ μὴ ὄντα, ἵνα τὰ ὄντα καταργήσῃ, 1 Cor. 1[28].

Dt. 1[32]). This form is not found in Bibl. Aram., but became common in Targ. and Talmud (*vide* Dalman, *Aramäische Gram.*, pp. 107 f., 219).

17. The *SCRIPTIO DEFECTIVA* is the rule in Phoen., *e.g.* איש=אש, 'man' (Moab. St. l. 10; CIS i. 86 A[9], B[7], *ib.* 93[2]; Plate xi. No. 5, Semit. Room, Brit. Mus.). From this source came the Heb. איש, and probably the same word in the Aram. inscriptions (CIS ii. 141[2], *ib.* 145, A[2]). But איש in Aram. is really a Hebraism. The more frequent Phoen. word is אדם (in the plural, אדמם, CIS i. 3[6. 11. 22], *ib.* 86, A[5]; *Piraeus*, ll. 4, 7; CIS i. 165[16]), the plural of which is not found in Heb. The construction אש אדה לזבח, 'which a man (is inclined) to sacrifice' (CIS i. 65[14]), is quite Hebraic and several Biblical constructions are in harmony with it (*vide* Is. 10[32], Hos. 9[13], *al.*). In Aram. inscript. אדם does not appear, and probably is not an Aram. word. The common term is אנש (Zenjirli: *Panammu*, l. 23; CIS ii. 113[20]; Palm. *Études*, i. 121; *Tariff*, i. 11), or אנוש (CIS ii. 197[2], *ib.* 209[5], *ib.* 350[5]), which is the usual Nab. (CIS ii. 206[6], *ib.* 212[7] *al.*). This, too, is the Egypt. Aram. form אנש (Pap. K 8, 10), and with this the Pales. forms agree : אנש (Dan. 2[10], Targ. Jon. b. Uzz., 2 S. 7[14]), אנוש (Dan. 4[13]), אינש (Targ. Onk., Ps.-Jon. Gen. 2[5]). The form בר נשא (Targ. Ps. 8[5]), or בני נש (Targ. Ps.-Jon. Gen. 1[2]) is perhaps Galilaean ; the form בר אנש (Dan. 7[13]), or בני אנשא (Targ. Jerus. Gen. 1[2]) is probably Judaean. The *scriptio plena* is the rule in Aram.

V

ELEMENTS OF UNCERTAINTY

The foregoing notes will have sufficiently indicated the uncertainty of the orthography and construction of the Semitic dialects in western Asia. Changes were constantly taking place in the number and use of words. These processes so evident in the dialects round about Palestine, were not less certain in the dialects of Canaan. When the Semitic settlers began to write, they doubtless tried to express themselves in the language common to all. But in the process of writing, each tribe would introduce some novelty, and while preserving many of the old forms would abandon others. These differences were accelerated with the movements and fortunes of the tribes, but down to the latest date of their history the Canaanite communities could readily understand one another. The Hebrew clans constituted no exception to the general processes taking place. When these tribes became united into an empire, it is probable that there was an attempt to make the dialect of Israel, rather than that of Judah, the official language. From this time the literary language of Palestine presented something like uniformity. But the scientific element failed the Hebrew author completely. The Israelite could no more systematize the modes of speech, than he could codify the laws of nature. Some Hebrew writers could doubtless appreciate what they would regard as correct speech, but this apparently did not go beyond intonation and conventional pronunciation. Where the most 'classical' writers of the Old Testament are recording ordinary and familiar events in common terms and daily constructions, the grammar is fairly regular. But immediately they attempt some new conception, and new forms and turns of expression are required, the grammar is confused and the syntax unique and irregular.

It must never be forgotten that the books of the Old Testament, as we know them, do not represent the language of Palestine as spoken at any one time or in any one place. These books are compilations, embodying extracts from older documents, and ideas from foreign sources. In their present form they are more the work of schools and editors, than of individuals expressing their own notions in their own language. So that such uniformity of grammar and composition as these books present, is more or less artificial and late. From the books themselves we are not able to fix with any certainty the original dialect, time or place in which they were written. It is impossible without further MS evidence to say what features are due to the pecularities of the writer, or of his sources, and what idioms are due to the locality. The elaborate attempts, by means of extensive emendations, forced etymologies and fanciful reconstructions, to reproduce the primitive language of the Hebrews and the dialect in which the Old Testament books were written, certainly reflect great credit on the assiduity and erudition of the scholars, but leave the reader in as much uncertainty as before. All this is conceded in effect by Margoliouth : ' It seems likely that if there had been Hebrew grammarians as well as writing-masters in any pre-Christian century, the sphere of the optional in Hebrew grammar would have been reduced to narrower limits.' Hence it must be concluded that the grammatical and syntactical ' rules ' in ancient Hebrew are mostly tentative and should be received with caution. A small volume could easily record all the proved rules of Canaanitish Hebrew, but a large volume would be required to express all the exceptions to these rules.[1]

[1] Cf. the foll. works : Winckler, *Geschichte Israels* ; Delitzsch, *Heb. Lang. in the Light of Assyr. Research* ; Schröder, *Phönizische Sprache* ; Marti, *Kurzgefasste Grammatik d. biblisch-Aramäischen Sprache* ; Wright, *Comp. Gram. Sem. Lang.* ; *Records of the Past*, New Series, iii. v. vi. (1890–1894) ; Stade, *Morgenländische Forschungen*.

V

ARAMAEANS AND HEBREWS

I

ARCHAEOLOGICAL PERIODS

THE different periods at which the Semites invaded
Palestine are marked in a general way by the archaeological
remains. The arrival of the Semites is indicated by the
introduction of the use of metals and of the potter's wheel.
As far as inscriptions are concerned, they are divisible into
Phoenician, Graeco-Phoenician, Roman, Christian and Arabic.
Archaeologically the divisions should be marked rather
differently. The pre-Semitic Troglodytes used flint tools, had
little inventive or artistic genius; they cremated their dead.
With the coming of the Semites various arts and developments came into Palestine, due, however, mainly to foreign
influence. This may most easily be seen by the following
tabular outline.

FIRST SEMITIC PERIOD: *circa* 2500–2000 B.C.

On the whole this period was free from foreign influence.
Some marks on the rude pottery occasionally resemble old
Hebrew letters; but this is a mere coincidence, since the
earliest Phoenician script was much later.

SECOND SEMITIC PERIOD: *circa* 2000–1400 B.C.

Egyptian and Cypriote influence quite marked in this
period. Scarabs are found, and seal-impressions on pottery,

but writings had not yet become general in domestic and industrial affairs.

THIRD SEMITIC PERIOD: *circa* 1400–1000 B.C.

This was a time of Egyptian and Aegean influence redivivus. At this period geometrical and animal figures appear on pottery and elsewhere. There was scarcely anything new in this period; it was reminiscent and repetitional. Very few scripts have survived from this age to reveal the character of the pre-Israelite language in Canaan.

FOURTH SEMITIC PERIOD: *circa* 1000–500 B.C.

The Israelite occupation was roughly correspondent with this period. The foreign influence at this time came chiefly from Cyprus, and there were faint beginnings of the influence of Greek culture. Seals with Hebrew inscriptions were common, and inscriptions on pottery and metal were associated with manufacture and building. The principal Hebrew (or Phoenician) inscriptions on stone belong to this period.

FIFTH SEMITIC PERIOD: *circa* 500 B.C.–622 A.D [1]

This was the age of Hellenistic and Byzantian influence, showing itself in social life, in architecture, and to some extent in language. Many stone inscriptions are in Greek, some with both Greek and Hebrew letters. Extra-Semitic influence becomes increasingly pronounced.[2]

The facts to be noted in the foregoing outline are these. (1) From the beginning of the Semitic invasion of Palestine extraneous elements appear, and these betray contact with foreign people. (2) The Semite occupiers of Palestine did not invent anything, but their lack of initiative was to some extent counterbalanced by their aptitude for assimilation. (3) They were sufficiently open-minded to accept from the

---

[1] To make the *Hijra* the *terminus ad quem* is quite arbitrary.
[2] Cf. Bliss–Macalister, *Excavations in Pales.*, pp. 53–55.

foreigner—Egyptian, Babylonian, Hittite, Minoan, Greek—almost any change in the ordinary commercial and secular affairs of life, as evidenced by the variety of the archaeological remains. (4) Their conservatism was most pronounced and insistent in the matter of religion, and in the preservation of their language. Though false gods occasionally obtruded, yet the worship of Yahveh was always central and pre-eminent. So, too, after Aramaic began to supersede Hebrew as the vernacular, the religious scribes tried to perpetuate the Hebrew of the Law, and the poets and prophets still sang and uttered their oracles in the sacred tongue. (5) Adhesion to the same factors has kept the Hebrew people together as a Community, though scattered and persecuted in every land. They are still distinct from all other races in pedigree, religion and language.[1]

II

SEMITIC MIGRATIONS

It will be seen presently that the home of the historic Semites was Arabia. But there is no clear connexion between Arabia and the primitive Semitic element in Babylonia. It is probable that in the remotest times the language of Babylonia was non-Semitic, and possibly akin to that known as 'Sumerian.' It may, however, be assumed that the original dialect of Babylonia lent itself more readily to Semitic influence than the dialect of Elam and adjacent regions. This postulated 'Sumerian' may have been Semitized both by Babylonian and Arabian interaction, arising from nomadic conditions and trade factors. But when and how the Semitic tone and colour first infected Babylonia, we have no means of knowing. The earliest Babylonian language of which there is any sufficient trace, is Semitic in its characteristic construction. Its Semitism is, however, interspersed with a non-Semitic element, due apparently to

---

[1] *Yiddish* (=יהודית, ܐ ܝܺܘܿܕܠ, *Judisch*) is a corrupt form of Heb., but really a polyglot jargon, used for intercommunication.

the dialect of the original inhabitants of Babylonia. The influence exerted by the primitive dwellers in Babylonia on their Semitic Over-lords was indelible, and all through the subsequent literature words of a non-Semitic type are frequent and unmistakable. While some of the inscriptions of this earliest period are Semitic in character, the majority are written in a non-Semitic dialect, now usually termed 'Sumerian.' This term, we think, represents a distinct language, and not a mere patois.

The coming of the Semites is an important part of this study. The great outstanding movements of the Semites may be represented graphically—

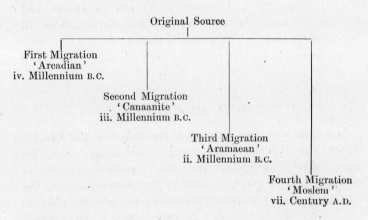

The name 'Arcadian' is here given to the first Semitic movement simply to denote its antiquity (ἀρχαῖος). The relation of Babylonian to Sumerian speech during this period has not yet been sufficiently elucidated.[1] The fourth Semitic movement does not, of course, form any part of the present investigation.

SEMITIC MIGRATIONS.—The available evidence leads to the conclusion that the Semites originally moved out of Arabia. There were apparently earlier and later migrations. The former were more restricted, and only the barest hints

---

[1] For the language, *vide* Haupt, *Die akkad. Sprache,* 1883; Hommel, *Die Sumero-akkad. Sprache,* 1884; and for the history, *vide* Winckler, *Gesch. Bab. u. Assyr.,* 1892; Maspero, *The Dawn of Civilization,* 1896.

remain; the latter were more far-reaching in territory and
influence. Of the earliest invaders of Babylonia and the
Euphrates regions there can only be speculation and tentative
suggestions. But what may be regarded as the second great
wave of Semites, overran ancient Syria with ' Canaanites,'
and resulted in the ' Hyksos ' dynasty in Egypt, and the so-
called ' First' dynasty in Babylonia. It is not yet clear
whether the name ' Canaan' originally belonged to the
emigrant Semites, or to the land to which they came, or to
the primitive inhabitants of the land. The same uncertainty
surrounds the term ' Amorite,' which by Egyptians and
Assyrians was often applied to some inland regions of
Canaan. Of this second wave of Semitic migration there
are perhaps echoes in the Genesis story of Abraham, and
' Amraphel, king of Shinar,' is probably the same as
Hammurabi, king of Babylon.[1]

The ' Hyksos ' invasion of Egypt cannot be placed earlier
than 1800 B.C. Can the Joseph story of Genesis be fitted
into the Hyksos period? There is a very suggestive hint
supplied by a comparison of Manetho's history and the
Biblical record. Speaking of the Hyksos,[2] the old Egyptian
historian says : ' they made one of their leaders king, who
was called Salatis.' This term seems very much like the
Egyptian ' Shallit,'[3] a title which Joseph received from
Pharaoh. Putting aside, as without sufficient foundation, the
legendary theory of Joseph, and the attempt of some scholars
to bring his supposed existence down to a later date, it is
most probable that the Israelitish period in Egypt came
within the Hyksos Dynasty.

---

[1] *Temp. circa* 2250 B.C. Possibly אמרפל=חמרבי. Cf. Schrader, *The Cuneif.
Inscr. and the OT.* ii. 299 f. ; Hommel, *Geschichte Babyloniens u.
Assyriens*, 169.

[2] Manetho derives Hyksos ('Υκσώς, pl. 'Υκουσσώς) from *Hyk*= ' king,' and
sos= 'shepherd.' The word is probably *Hyku-Shasu*, ' princes of Shasu,'
where *shasu*= 'spoilers' or Bedouins. Cf. Joseph. *Contra Apion*, i. 14.

[3] The form שליט (Gen. 42⁶) is adj. but used as subst. *ruler, Sheik, Sultan*
(cf. Arab. سلط, سليط, *be strong, overcome*). שלים is prob. an Aram. word
(*vide* Onk. Targ. Gen. 42⁶), and late in Heb. In Aram. inscrip. שלטן= 'rule '
(CIS 196⁵); cf. Syr. ܫܘܠܛܢܐ (*vide* Cook, *Glossary*, p. 113).

The points to be clearly kept in mind here are the following :

(1) The Semite emigrants who settled in north Babylonia with their centre at Accad (or Akkad), annexed the Sumerian South, crossed the Tigris and occupied Elam. Afterwards, when the Nabataeans overran this region and pushed their way as far as Damascus, they were on soil which long before had been Semitized.

(2) Both in Babylonia and Elam the Semite invaders successfully imposed their own language. This was really their chief deposit, for besides this the Semites in those remote times contributed very little to the intellectual and commercial advancement of Babylonia and Elam. In Babylonia a Semitic language became the regular dialect of the people, and superseded the old Accadian and Sumerian speech, which was probably non-Semitic. Only the most rudimentary knowledge of the old language has been preserved by some learned writers in Babylonia and Assyria, who compiled vocabularies of Accadian words with Semitic equivalents. But these have little more than an antiquarian value, indeed the very existence of ' Sumerian ' has been doubted.[1]

In Elam the old 'Sumerian' was not so completely supplanted; it existed for a considerable time alongside the invading Semitic. The latter became the official language, the language of literature, commerce and diplomacy. Sometimes important documents were issued in both languages.

(3) From these regions Semitic tribes entered Canaan. When it is said that the Semitic language of Palestine came from Babylonia-Assyria, it is to be understood in the sense stated above. All Semitic languages are perhaps ultimately traceable to Arabia, but this type of speech came into Canaan *via* Babylonia-Elam. The Aramaic-Canaanite, however, came with a later wave of Semites in the twelfth century B.C.

Josephus says that the Elamites were the ancestors of the Persians.[2] They were no doubt of the same Aryan group and

---

[1] For information on the controversy, *vide* Weissbach, *Die sumersiche Frage* (1898). Vide *Keilinschriftliche Bibliothek*, ii. 240.

[2] *Ant.* i. 6. 4.

language. The native rulers of this province called themselves 'lords of Anzan,' and even Cyrus at first took the title of 'king of Anzan.' But when the 'Great King' subdued all formidable rivals, he assumed the title 'King of Persia,' of which country he claimed to be a native. The capital of Elam was Susa = Shushan.[1]

The 'Aramaean' migration is sometimes regarded as the third great Semite movement from north-east Arabia. As early as 1350 B.C. they are found invading the whole Euphrates region. In 1300, Shalmaneser I. speaks of the 'Arimi' harrying the frontiers of the upper Tigris. They repeated in many respects the methods of the second or 'Canaanite' invaders of Harran a millennium earlier. The 'Hittite' occupation of the regions in and around north Syria came between these two great Semitic movements, and the 'Ḥatti' developed into a great power in westernmost Asia as early as the fifteenth century B.C. The Hittite kingdom disappears and the territory is taken by the Aramaeans, who gain possession of the main desert routes. The 'Syrians' who came into conflict with Israel in David's time and later, were in reality these Aramaeans now settled and powerful. The 'Aramaeans'[2] rapidly spread over north Syria including the region between Phoenicia and the Euphrates, Palestine including the country southward, Phoenicia and Damascus which lay between and formed a strategic central province. Only through the sacred Books of the Jews do we know more of Palestine than of the other regions invaded by Aramaeans. Into the southernmost region of the Syrian coast entered those clans which called themselves 'Children of Israel,' while surrounding peoples called them 'Hebrews.'

At this time Syria was in a state of confusion, without unity or power of resistance. The strong Ḥatti power had ceased to direct in the north, and the intermittent Egyptian influence was withdrawn from the south. Into this disintegrated and depleted land came various wandering Semitic

---

[1] *Vide* Loftus, *Chaldaea and Susiana* ; Rogers, *Hist. Bab. Ass.* i.

[2] It is possible that Ἐρεμβοί in Homer (*Od.* iv. 84) may mean 'the inhabitants of Aram.'

clans from the steppes west of Mesopotamia, and from the desert plateaux north of Arabia. One of the oldest tribes among the new invaders made its centre at Zenjirli, to use the modern name, and left inscriptions which throw considerable light on both the history and language of the people. Other centres were at Hamath and Damascus, commanding important trade routes. These clans formed new Aramaean states, and their geographical position combined with their natural trade aptitude soon placed them in control of much of the eastern commerce. Their language, too, was so pliable and practicable that it was adopted for international purposes from Babylonia to Egypt, and from Asia Minor to Arabia. The original 'Syrians' were included in the 'Aramaean' migration.

The primary factor behind the Semitic dialectic differences needs clearer emphasis than it has yet received. All the great Semitic migrations had their starting-place in Arabia, thrust out perhaps by desert drought and aided by a desire for trade. Four momentous migrations have been noted:[1] the 'Accadian' (?), perhaps as early as Sargon I., *circa* 3800 B.C.; the 'Canaanite,' perhaps resulted in the Hyksos dynasty in Egypt and the Kassite dynasty in Babylonia, *circa* 2300 B.C.; the 'Aramaean,' probably referred to in the inscriptions of Shalmaneser I., *circa* 1350 B.C.; the 'Moslem' in the vii cent. A.D., which does not fall within this study. It will be seen that there was roughly a millennium between the first three of these migrations. Here is the real secret of the dialectic differences between the Semitic tribes of western Asia. That the desert march and contact with foreign people tended to accelerate differences of speech and custom must be evident enough. But the fact of chief importance, and so often overlooked, is that these great migratory clans, with a thousand years between them, moved out of Arabia already in possession of the main dialectic differences which characterized their later history. The native language of the people who remained in Arabia was slowly changing, and each millennium was long enough to produce a practically new dialect in the absence of a written language.

[1] *Vide* tabular representation, p. 143.

III

LINGUISTIC PARTING OF THE WAYS

Though the Semitic tribes came out of Arabia, Hebrew and Aramaic were not variations of Arabic. All three were variant products of an earlier type which has disappeared. Many elements contributed to the diversifying of language. (a) When a clan is divided into two or more groups, and the regions into which these sections move are discontinuous and communication is cut off or seriously interrupted, local dialectical variants invariably arise. (b) New conditions, such as contact with foreign tribes and fresh pursuits, would tend to add to the vocabulary of a dialect, and in some instances result in the non-use of old terms. (c) Native people who acquire the new language of the invaders would certainly change its character in accent, orthography and construction. (d) When an attempt is made by one tribe to communicate with another in a distant region, the available writing material would naturally have some effect on the character of the writing, and ultimately on the dialect itself. The impressions on Babylonian clay would differ from the writings on Egyptian papyrus, and the engravings on Cyprus stone would differ from the carvings on Zenjirli metal. (e) In its turn the style of writing would tend to vary the character of the language. As in Egypt the hieroglyphic picture-writing was superseded by the hieratic cursive hand, so in Babylonia the scratched picture-signs were superseded by the impressed cuneiform mark. In both cases the object was greater speed and accuracy. But with these changes of caligraphy there would be introduced minute differences in spelling and vocalization.

To return to the statement at the beginning of this section, the original language of the descendants of Abraham was not Aramaic, which was changed to Hebrew when the tribes of Israel entered Canaan. The 'Habiri' brought their Hebrew type of dialect with them into Canaan, and this dialect had much in common with the dialect of the earlier settlers—Phoenicians and Canaanites. While 'Hebrew' was becoming the vernacular of Palestine, 'Aramaic' was spread-

ing in Syria. Taken in a broad sense 'Syria' included
Palestine and the whole narrow strip of land running from
Asia Minor and Armenia southward towards north Arabia,
bounded on the west by the Mediterranean Sea and on the
east and south-east by broad desert tracts. Here later came
the tribes with the Nabataean dialect in the south, and the
Palmyrene dialect in central north-east. Through this
country passed the great trade routes, and all nationalities and
all dialects met and mingled in this busy passage between
north and south-western Asia. This was the home of Laban,[1]
and he spoke the language which came with that great
Semitic migration from Arabia, which we have called the
Chaldaean or Aramaean, which first found a settlement in
Babylonia and Syria, and later in Africa. It was to be
expected that in this country, with the juxtaposition of clans
and dialects, a type of language would be developed, differing
slightly from Hebrew on the one hand, and even less from
Aramaic on the other. And this is precisely what exploration
has confirmed. The Zinjirli inscriptions discovered (1890–
1891) in the extreme north of Syria, are written in a dialect
which has many points of likeness to Hebrew, but which on
the whole most resembles Aramaic.[2]

IV

RELATION OF ARAMAIC TO HEBREW

The relation of Aramaic to Hebrew can never be quite
definitely stated. The general statements, considered more
fully in another place, are that the 'Canaanite' migration
from Arabia preceded the 'Aramaean' migration, that Hebrew

---

[1] At this period, and probably long before, Hebrew and Aramaic had
separate histories; cf. the double name of the Covenant-cairn, Gen. 31[47].
The reference Dt. 26[5] is probably to Jacob, but it does not necessarily mean
that Jacob was an Aramaean. The Heb. text has possibly been slightly
distorted, and the sense is preserved in Onk. לבן ארמאה מעא-לאובדא ית-אבא,
'Laban the Aramaean endeavoured to destroy my father.'

[2] On the character of the Zenjirli inscrip. *vide* Lidzbarski, *Handbuch
der nordsemitischen Epigraphik*, 440 f. Cooke, *Text-Book of North Semitic
Inscriptions*, 159–185.

was in some sense included in the former, and that something like a millennium separated these two migrations. Both migrations came into contact with Babylonia and Egypt. The Hebrews were perhaps a secondary offshoot of the 'Canaanite' migration, just as the Abyssinians were a secondary offshoot of the Arabian-Sabaeans. It is found that the Egyptian language has an appreciable admixture of Semitic, which was derived ultimately from Arabia. There is some evidence that the Canaanites lived together with the Babylonians for a longer period than did the Aramaeans. This conclusion is based on a comparison of the Hebrew and the Aramaic languages with Babylonian. It is found that Hebrew, on the whole, is phonetically more closely related to Semitic-Babylonian or 'Assyrian' than Aramaic. This suggests that the Canaanites lived for a longer period in association with the Babylonians than did the Aramaeans. Thus the original differences of idiom between 'Canaanite' and 'Aramaic,' arising from the millennium which separated these migrations, were accelerated in both cases by association with Babylonia, but more so in the former case than in the latter.

As far as we can discover, Aramaic is as old as Hebrew; for a long period, of which there is no clear knowledge, these languages had parallel histories. Since Aramaic did not come into Palestine until after the Babylonian-Assyrian conquest of the country, it was not known to the early Israelites, and did not affect their literature till after the Exile. It cannot be stated definitely when 'Aramaisms' first appeared in Hebrew. From the inscriptions it appears that Aramaic was understood and used both commercially and officially by Assyrians, Babylonians and Persians in the eighth century B C.[1] A verse in Jeremiah (10^{11}) in a peculiar Aramaic dialect suggests (a) the use of the language in the seventh century B.C., and (b) the contact of Aramaic and Hebrew in Palestine.[2] This, however, probably did not mean that

---

[1] *Vide* the Nineveh inscrip. (CIS ii. 1–14). These Babyl. weights have Assyr. as well as Aram. inscrip. ; they belong to the viii–vii cent., since they have the names of Shalmaneser, Sennacherib, etc.

[2] The verse in Jer. is probably the intrusion of a marginal gloss, it may, however, represent the Babyl. vernacular at the time.

Aramaic had made any real progress among the Israelites at this early date. The Jews could not understand the Babylonian language, but their nobles understood Aramaic.

The time when Aramaic began to supplant the Canaanite dialects can be approximately fixed. The historical line can be traced from the literary monuments, and may be summarized as follows: The earliest dwellers in Canaan were subjugated by Hittite tribes. Later Canaanites, including the Hebrews, contended against powerful hordes of Hittites, who, however, left traces of their language and cult in Canaan. In turn the Hittites were overthrown by strong and progressive tribes of Aramaeans. The latter, however, did not continue their march directly against the Hittites into Syria, but moved in a more easterly line towards the Euphrates. They took possession of Mesopotamia, crossed the Euphrates, and then turned back towards central Syria. At Carchemish Tiglath-pileser I. thrust the Aramaeans back across the river, and the Hittite centres of Syria were not taken by Aramaeans till a later period. It was, therefore, in the Assyrian time that Aramaic really supplanted the 'language of Canaan.' Aramaic writing probably first appeared in Syrian regions about the time of Tiglath-pileser IV., or possibly in the reign of Tiglath-pileser III. [Assyr. form *Tukulti-Pal-Essara*, the פלא of 2 K. 15¹⁹], in the viii cent. B.C. Specimens of this script are preserved in the Zenjirli inscriptions.

Aramaic in some form extended over a very long period. A dialect akin to Aramaic was used in the cuneiform script of Assyria-Babylonia from the earliest historical times. The Tell el-Amarna library in middle Egypt proves the use of this language, in cuneiform script, as early as 1400 B.C. The country north of Palestine is termed 'Aram' in the Old Testament, and its inhabitants were the 'Aramaeans.'[1] Much later, when these people became Christians, their name was often confounded with 'heathen,' hence they called their land by the Greek name Συρία, ܣܘܪܺܝܰܐ, themselves by the name

---

[1] For the geographical connotation of *Aramu* and *Ḥatti* in inscriptions, *vide* p. 100; cf. p. 156.

'Syrians,' and their language 'Syriac.' The Christian Aramaic of Palestine became known as 'Syriac.' This dialect was related to the literary or Edessene Syriac much as Doric was related to Attic Greek.[1]

From the Captivity the Jews began to lose the purity and use of their language, though Hebrew was well known and employed in certain circles long after the Exile. Among the post-exilic prophets, Hebrew was preserved, and Aramaic was for a considerable time exceptional. The Hebrew inscriptions are practically all pre-exilic,[2] and do not shed much light on the language of Palestine after the Captivity. From a very interesting passage in Nehemiah (13[24]) it would seem that Hebrew was normally spoken in Jerusalem about 430 B.C. But partly as the result of mixed marriages several dialects were in use, which were to some extent unintelligible to each other.[3]

The periods which marked the changes in the Hebrew language are indicated in the Old Testament literature. Three periods are marked with sufficient clearness : 1. The Mosaic, the archaic period. The language in this age was distinguished by its antique character, partly recognizable in ancient terms and forms, and partly in original poetry and the poetic tone of the prose. 2. The Davidic, the period of high development. This period began about the time of

---

[1] If Jesus of Nazareth had spoken Edessene He would have said :

ــاٰهَصܘ ܠܶܡܳܢ, and not למא שבקתני (the Gal. Aram.) = λεμά σαβαχθανεί.

This sugg. that the Gal. pronunciation of שׁ was שׂ, or rather ס, as the Ephraimite or Samaritan (Judg. 12[6]). The Rabbinic pronunciation of ת sometimes approaches the ס sound.

[2] The Moabite Stone, circa 850 ; Siloam, circa 700.

[3] The references are to (a) Ashdodite, a Philistine dialect. As early as the time of Amos (760–746), the Ashdodites made slave-raids upon Judah. (b) Ammonite, a dialect akin to Heb. and therefore similar to Moabite. (c) Moabite, an older form of Heb. and one of the dialects of the 'language of Canaan.' Though these dialects were similar, the tribes were usually hostile. Nehemiah also mentions among his opponents הָעַרְבִי גֶּשֶׁם (2[19] 6[1]). This was about the time of the Nabataean migration, and probably this Arabian was a Nabataean. The form נשמו (prob. שֵׁמוּ, 6[6] ; Sin. Inscr. 58, 167, 345) suggests this, inasmuch as final ו in Nab. proper names is characteristic ; cf. Arab. جَشَمُ.

Samuel and extended to Hezekiah. Under the united
monarchy the language attained its meridian; its wealth of
utterance appeared in the lyric and prophetic books of the
time. 3. The Exilic, the period of decline. From the time
of the Assyrian and other invasions, Hebrew began to
deteriorate, as seen in Ezra, Nehemiah, Esther and the
Chronicles. Though Hebrew ceased to be the vernacular
of Palestine soon after the Exile, yet some of the great
post-exilic writers continued its use from sacred scruples and
associations.[1]

The Jews acquired gradually the use of Aramaic, first
from their neighbours in exile, and afterwards from their
neighbours in Palestine. The position may be outlined thus:
(a) During the long Captivity the Hebrews became familiar
with the Aramaic language of their captors. (b) Concurrently
Aramaic was being spoken in Palestine by the Chaldaean
and other tribes brought in to occupy the land. (c) When
the Jews returned from Captivity, not only were they in
possession of a new language, but they found Aramaic already
in possession of their country. (d) Earlier than the Exile a
very mixed movement of captives between the central regions
of Canaan and Babylonian-Assyrian provinces resulted in the
'Samaritans,' whose dialect was a corrupt, but by no means
an unintelligible form of Aramaic. These people were
strongly entrenched in Samaria when the Jews returned
from Exile.[2] (e) Together the foregoing factors naturally
and inevitably resulted in the supersession of Hebrew as a
spoken language, and the establishment of Aramaic as the
vernacular of Palestine.

---

[1] *Cum scriberent historiam aut prophetias ad Judaeos pertinentes,
voluerunt uti eadem lingua, qua priscae eorum historiae et prophetiae
jam fuerant conscriptae, si excipias pauca quaedam loca ad res Chaldae-
orum aut Persarum pertinentia* (Clericus, *ad Neh.* 13²⁴).

[2] There was probably a strong Israelitish element among the Samaritans. This would explain their desire to participate in rebuilding the
sacred city. The phrase, עֲלֵיכֶם אָתֵי לִירוּשְׁלֶם (Ezra 4¹²), implies that the
Samaritans were accustomed to worship at Jerusalem before the Jews
returned from Captivity.

V

HEBREW CLANS

The particular origin of the Hebrew tribes is quite uncertain. They no doubt moved out of Arabia with some of the earlier migrations from that great Semitic reservoir. They were strong and adventurous clans, closely knit together in nomadic pursuits and religious rites. They made early incursions into Egypt, and from the south-east deserts raided the frontiers of the Phoenicians and the Philistines. These bold and aggressive tribes were related to, if not the same as, the ' Habiri ' mentioned on the Tell el-Amarna tablets.[1]   As early as 1400 B.C. these tribes seriously contested the land of Canaan and adjacent regions. The old Sumerian or Accadian inhabitants of Canaan were in part dispersed or assimilated by these invaders at an early date. The Book of Judges recalls some of the struggles, not only with Canaanites, but also with Amorites,[2] and later with Aramaeans. The Philistines for a time checked the movements of the ' Hebrews,' and pressed right up to Galilee. Under a powerful chieftain, Saul, whose religio-despotic spirit gained for him the title of ' King,' the Philistines were driven out of Palestine, and the country became the settled home of the Hebrews [3] till the new troubles with Assyria and Babylonia.

[1] Except on these Tablets the word ' Hebrews ' has not been found in the early monuments of the east. This identification is still doubted by some scholars.

[2] This shows that the ' Canaanites ' and the ' Amorites ' are not synonymous terms. The latter were the older and belonged to the more warlike times (cf. Wellhausen, *Die Composition des Hexateuchs*, 341 f., and Winckler, *Gesch. Is. in einzeldarstell.* i. 52 f.).

[3] The names of these Semitic clans are obscure in origin, and no attempts at explanation can as yet be regarded as final. The suggestions in the following note are submitted with hesitation. The *Jacob-Israel* story (Gen. 32^{28-30}) probably preserves a certain element of historical reality. *Jacob-el* was a place-name in Palestine according to an inscription (Thothmes III., *circa* 1500, *vide* Müller, *Asien u. Europa*, 162). *Isra-el* or (with common Semitic prefix בני) *Children of Isra-el*, was the name of the confederated tribes united under the Semite god El. Some allied clans bore this name before they entered Canaan (cf. Paton, *Syria and Palestine*, 103 ff.). *Hebrew* was originally the name of some trans-Euphrates clans, and became a general name for the confederate tribes after they crossed the Jordan. Abraham represented one of these clans : אברם העברי.

This early 'Habiri' confederacy is clearly intimated, for besides Abraham other allied chieftains are mentioned : וְהֵם בַּעֲלֵי בְרִית־אַבְרָם (Gen. 14¹³).¹ The use of the word עבר = *trans*, is found in a Sidonian inscription : רב עבר לספת, 'governor of the other side of the river-bank' (SFT = סוף, 'stream,' or שפה, 'boundary'). The verbal form העבר (part.) is found in an Aram. inscription : והעבר אבי מן דמשק, 'and transferred my father from Damascus' (Sid. 4, l. 1, Louvre ; Zenjirli, *Panam.* l. 18). In the latter instance, the form תעבר (impf.), given by Cook, *Gloss. of Aram. Inscrip.*, is apparently incorrect.

The meaning of the word ישראל is as much discussed as ever. Two explanations are suggested by the Genesis story (Gen. 32²⁴⁻³⁰), one direct and the other implied. The latter is perhaps the older and may be stated first. An old analysis of the word is : יש(א) = *man* ; ראה = *saw* ; אל = *God* ; hence 'the man who saw God.' This agrees with the name of the place, and the reason why the name was given : 'And Jacob called the name of the place *Peniel* (פני אל), for *I have seen God face to face.*' The other analysis, שרה אל, 'God rules,' is perhaps later, and represents an idea read into the term by the Hebrews who accepted the sovereignty of El, and witnessed His triumphs among them. In this case vv.²⁷⁻²⁸ must be regarded as a later addition, when the Hebrews explained their origin in the light of their history.

VI

AMORITES AND CANAANITES

Another ethnic relationship which involves some difficulty is that between the Amorites and the Canaanites.² The term 'Amorite'³ is sometimes 'the general name of the pre-Israelitish population of both west and east Palestine.'⁴

---

¹ For general history, *vide* Peters, *Early Hebrew Story* ; Barton, *Semitic Origins.*

² The genealogical phrase, האמרי . . . ילד כנען (Gen. 10¹⁵, ¹⁶), is of no historical value.

³ LXX : 'Αμορραῖοι, and their land by Joseph. 'Αμωρῖτις, 'Αμορία.

⁴ Driver, *Introd. Lit. OT.*, p. 112.

The Babylonian, Egyptian and Hebrew usage was to call the pre-Israelite Semites collectively 'Amorites.' Flinders Petrie would reserve the name 'Canaanite' 'for the neolithic troglodytes, the aborigines of Canaan.'[1] Of the two great 'Syrian' peoples figured on Egyptian monuments, the *Amurru* were the more southern, and the *Ḥatti* the more northern. The former included Canaan and Philistia, and the latter Cappadocia and Mesopotamia. The great *Amurru* civilization, which preceded the Israelite occupation of Canaan, was largely influenced by Babylonian culture. All the tablets found in Syria, dating from these early times, are in cuneiform, and correspondence with Egypt was conducted in cuneiform (Babylonian) script. This was rendered possible by the presence of a Babylonian secretary at the Egyptian court, who translated the communications from Syria, and composed the replies.

VII

SOURCES AND CHARACTER OF CANAANITE

On the theory adopted in this work the Hebrews originally came out of Arabia in some association with the 'Canaanite' migration. Ancient Arabic, therefore, may naturally be regarded as the chief source of the Hebrew language. The same theory most easily accounts for the likeness of Hebrew to other Canaanite dialects.[2] The hints which have been noticed of some Canaanite deviations from Arabic[3] suggest either (*a*) a vulgarization of the classical source, or (*b*) an infusion of foreign elements. In a general way it may be

---

[1] *Eastern Explor.*, p. 24.

[2] It is important to notice that the Canaanite dialects, which are allied to Arabic, are the only Semitic languages which have in regular use : (1) an article prefixed ; (2) a letter and a syllable prefixed with interrogative force ; (3) passive conjugations [Bibl. Aram. shows signs of (2) and (3)] ; (4) a Niphal conjugation [perh. also in Assyr.] ; (5) something approaching cases ; (6) an infinitive plan ; (7) a system of moods (Margoliouth, *BD*, *s.v.* 'Lang. OT').

[3] Such as : (1) an abbreviation of the alphabet ; (2) a peculiar interchange of letters ; (3) a confusion of gutturals and sibilants leading to much uncertainty in pronunciation ; (4) a transposition of consonants, which frequently renders the identity of words difficult or impossible.

said that Canaanite differed from the earlier Arabic [1] in three main directions : (1) In the absence of final vowels, which in the classical prototype had the force of syntactical constructions. (2) In the tendency to over-emphasize the accent, which resulted in the depreciation or supersession of some letter-vowels, and the toning-up or heightening of others. (3) In the less complex method of expressing ideas, a simplification of form, which characterizes all languages in the process of degeneration. If by some such process the Hebrew language gained boldness, it lost beauty ; if by this means it became a better channel for the expression of spiritual impulses, it became a less suitable vehicle for the transmission of general literature.[2]

While it is to be admitted that the chief source of the Canaanite languages (including Hebrew) was early Arabic, other elements came into their composition. It is rather surprising that Hebrew does not exhibit a larger Egyptian element, indeed this element is exceedingly small. It is pretty evident that the Biblical historian of the Exodus was unacquainted with Egyptian, though a few Egyptian terms had become Hebraized.[3] Assyrian, however, did contribute a recognizable element to Canaanitish. In the xv cent. B.C., though the Canaanites had a native language, the official medium of international diplomacy, with Babylonia and Egypt in particular, was Assyrian. It is found that Assyrian and Canaanite have certain terms in common, which are not found in other Semitic languages. Inasmuch as there is some evidence of a pre-Canaanite Assyrian supremacy in Palestine, it is probable that Canaanite was indebted to Assyrian for at least a modicum of its vocabulary.[4] In addition to the

---

[1] Arabic was earlier in (1) its system of orthography ; (2) its form of accidence ; (3) its scheme of syntax.

[2] A book which may still be consulted with interest and profit is Böttcher, *Ausführliches Lehrbuch* (1866).

[3] The terms חרטמם, *magicians* ; שרי מסים, *princes of gangs=taskmasters* ; אחו, *bulrushes, Nile-grass* ; יאר, *river*, especially *the Nile* ; שש, *linen*, later בוץ, βύσσος ; אברך, *Bow the knee! Hail* ! are prob. of Egypt. origin, but all Semitized. The term 'Pyramid,' πυραμίς, does not occur in the Bible, though there is a possible reference in חרבות (Job 3[14]). Cf. p. 79.

[4] *Vide* Delitzsch, *Assyrisches Handwörterbuch* ; Karppe, *Journal Asiatique*, Series 9, vol. x.

sources named, it is probable that Canaanite gathered up some words from the aboriginal tribes of Palestine, among these there was perhaps a Hittite element not yet clearly defined.[1]

It is not easy to specify the 'Canaanite' phrases which are definitely attributable to Assyrian. But a few expressions can be traced to Assyrian sources which pre-date the 'Canaanite' invasion, or rather which are independent of that invasion. To 'reveal a secret' is expressed by נלה אזן (1 S. 9¹⁵ 20² et al.), and is found in Assyrian.[2] The symbol of irretrievable ruin is שבר נבל יוצרים, 'the smashing of a potter's vessel' (Is. 30¹⁴ et al.), and is common in Assyrian, especially in the Sargon inscriptions.[3] Epithets like ישב בשמים, 'he that sitteth in the heavens' (Ps. 2⁴ et al.); טוב לב, lit. 'good, or glad, of heart' = 'cheerfulness' (Dt. 28⁴⁷, Is. 65¹⁴), go back to Assyrian times. Occasionally Aramaic has preserved an Assyrian phrase, which is not known in Canaanite (Hebrew). For example, the Tell el-Amarna letters give the expression אכל קרצי, 'accuse slanderously,' which occurs in Biblical Aramaic (pl. Dan. 3⁸ 6²⁵). It appears to represent the Assyrian Karṣe akâlu, but Hebrew has no exact equivalent.[4]

VIII

CHARACTER AND INFLUENCE OF HITTITE

The ancient inhabitants of Canaan, it seems, had no native writing, just as the aboriginal tribes of central Africa have no written language. One confirmation of this statement is the existence of the Tell el-Amarna tablets. About 1400 B.C. the Canaanite rulers conducted their diplomatic correspondence with the Egyptians in the Babylonian language and character. That this correspondence was not in the cuneiform character of Egypt was due perhaps partly to the ignorance of the Canaanites of the Egyptian script. That it

---

[1] Cf. Jensen, Hittiter u. Armenier.

[2] Cf. Keilschrifttexte Assurbanipals, Heft i.

[3] Vide Winckler, Keilschrifttexte Sargons, 1889. On Sargon, Is. 20¹, cf. Schrader, Keilinschr. u. d. Alte Test. ad loc.

[4] Vide for other illustrations, Budge, Rabban Hormizd.

was not in the language of Canaan was due most likely to the absence of a written speech. A written language may have been introduced into Canaan by the Ḥatti, and of its character the Hittite inscriptions bear testimony. The tribes denoted by the general term 'Hittites' were probably not all of one stock, nor did they speak one entirely homogeneous language. They formed, however, an important linguistic link between Egypt and Canaan. The Hittites adopted the Egyptian hieroglyphics, which probably had many affinities with their native script. Hittite proper names appear in both Egyptian and Assyrian inscriptions. The Old Testament shows the close contact with the Israelites. The Hittite language seems to have accommodated itself in several directions—*pictorial* towards Egyptian, *conventional* towards Babylonian-Assyrian, *linear* towards Phoenician and Hebrew. The following tabular representation may be useful :

Original source of 'Hittites'
Non-Semitic and Non-Indo-Germanic
|
Mitanni
(Possibly N. Syria and N. Mesopotamia)
overthrown in 14 c. B.C. by Assyria
|
Khatti
(A single tribe that afterwards gave
its name to all the 'Hittites')
Centre at Kharkhemish = Jerabis

Kummukh
(= Kommagene = Komana)

Related to
(a) Muski (= Phrygia)
(b) Kaski (= Armenia)
(c) Tabal (= Cappadocia)

Lukki
These gave name to
(a) Lycia, (b) Lycaonia

Khilakku
These gave name to
Cilicia

Hittites
(First Capital Boghaz Keui ; second city, Kharkhemish)
These formed the Fourth great Power, by the side of
Lydia, Media, Babylon

The above Table is geographical and chronological, rather than ethnological. It is impossible to discover how the different 'Hittite' tribes were genealogically related. It is probable that in the ground-stock of the Hittites in Asia Minor the Turanian type prevailed, yet there is clear evidence of a Semitic element.   [*Vide* Jensen, *Hittiter und Armenier*, 1898.]

It is difficult to state exactly what progress has been made in the decipherment of Hittite records. With the hieroglyphic texts very uncertain results have been achieved. These hieroglyphs, known as early as 1736, differ from the hieroglyphs of Egypt,[1] and cannot be translated by the same general principles. Many attempts have been made to unravel their secrets, but the decipherers have gone widely, and sometimes fantastically, apart, and no very sure or definite conclusions have yet been attained. More advancement has been made with the Hittite cuneiform tablets. The latest work in this field is an attempt to confirm the Indo-Germanic traces embedded in the language.[2] These attempts, and also the attempt to find comparisons between the ' Arzawa '[3] tablets and Doric Greek,[4] are quite arbitrary in procedure and results. What may be stated with some confidence, based on the Boghaz Keui tablet library, is easily expressed. Some of the Boghaz Keui tablets were written in Babylonian Semitic, with reversions into Sumerian ; others were written in the language of the ' Arzawa ' tablets, with reversions into both Babylonian Semitic and Sumerian. The latter type must at present be presumed to be Hittite. After following with some critical closeness the philological analyses and findings of the foremost scholars in this field, we shall be fairly safe to conclude that the Hittite language was a resultant, having in the background Sumerian, Babylonian Semitic, Indo-European, and perhaps Egyptian.[5]

[1] *Vide* Wright, *Empire of the Hittites*, 1886.

[2] Cf. Hrozný, *Die Sprache der Hethiter*, Leipzig, 1917 ; Marstrander, *Caractère Indo-Europeen de la Langue Hittite*, Christiania, 1919.

[3] Two tablets found at Tell el-Amarna and doubtless related to the Boghaz Keui library.

[4] Hempl, *Trans. Amer. Philol. Assoc.*, 1913, 185.

[5] From known parallels (*e.g.* ancient Egyptian) it is quite possible that Hittite retained such basal elements as case-endings, verb-forms and suffixes from the original common source, and borrowed or incorporated roots from later associations. Whatever the primal form of a language, it will be inevitably changed in process of history by local circumstances of all sorts. Although Egyptian, *e.g.*, is not considered to be a Sem. lang., yet its pers. pronouns, pers. suffixes, the fem. termination *t*, fem. pl. *wt*,

Though no certain conclusion can be drawn from our present knowledge of Hittite history and language, yet from a study of the few hints available we put forth the following new suggestions :

(i.) Hittite script shows a number of sign-faces ; the inscriptions are to be read as a whole *horizontally towards the faces*. Frequently there are signs one above another ; these may represent letters, syllables or even words, and are to be read *perpendicularly*. Whether some of these signs indicate words to be pronounced, or simply ideas to assist the speaker, it is impossible at present to decide. Many Hittite inscriptions begin with a sign-face, with arm and hand upturned, the fingers pointing towards or touching the mouth. Probably this representation means, ' I am . . .,' or ' I proclaim,' ' so speaks . . .,' or ' I . . . declare.' Possibly we have here the source of the Semitic formula : . . . אנך, e.g. אנך משע (Moab. St. l. 1) ; אנך יחומלך (Phoen. CIS i.) ; אנך פנמו (Zenjirli : *Hadad*, l. 1) ; אנה נבוכדנצר (Dan. 4[1]) ; אני יהוה (Ex. 6[2]) ; כה אמר יהוה (Is. 50[1]) ; אני יהוה דברתי (Num. 14[35] ; cf. Onk. אנא יי גזרית־במימרי). This formula is not usual in the Hellenistic papyri, which frequently begin, ' To . . .,' or ' . . . to . . .' Thus : Βασιλεῖ Πτολεμαίῳ (*Paris Papyri*, 26[1]) ; Ἀμεννεῖ βασιλικῶι γραμματεῖ (*Tebtunis Papyri*, 40[1]) ; Πολ[υ]κράτης Φ[ιλ]οξένωι χαίρειν (*Gk. Pap. fr. Cairo Museum*, ed. Goodspeed, p. 8).

(ii.) According to the Tell el-Amarna tablets the pirate ships of a Hittite people searched the waters between the southern coast of Asia Minor and the island of Cyprus (*Alašia*, in the Amarna tablets). These adventurers are termed the *Lukki*, and they gave their name to the provinces of Lycia and Lycaonia. Here two points are suggested : (*a*) when the Phoenicians entered Cyprus, they found a people already in possession. The arts and literary fragments show that these people were closely akin to the earlier tribes of Asia Minor. It is known that branches of the Hittites had

dual in *i*, and certain verbal forms, are unquestionably similar to Semitic (*vide* Erman, *Ägypt. Gram.*, 1911). The similarities between Egypt. and Sem. are explained by reference to some early connexion or common origin. It is probable that in the same way, the apparent likenesses between Hittite and Indo-Germanic must be explained by reference to some distant common source.

spread themselves over the greater part of Asia Minor. It is therefore probable that the old Cypriote language was due largely to Hittite occupation and influence. (*b*) What was the speech of Lycaonia (*Λυκαονιστί*, Acts 14[11])? It was not Greek, which was the language of commerce, nor Latin, which was possibly used in the garrison towns. It was the dialect of the native population in the rural provinces and remoter towns. Its origin was quite unknown to the early writers, and this indicates its antiquity. We venture to attribute this native speech to the piratical Lukki (Hittite) invaders. The few inscriptions in this obscure language (vide *Journal of Hellen. Studies*, ii. 157) bear some resemblance to what is known of the Hittite speech in sentence form. It is clear that some of the Phoenician inscriptions of Cyprus begin with the formula . . . אנך (which is possibly Hittite, *vide supra*), *e.g.* אנך עבדאסר (CIS i. 46[1]).

(iii.) The Indo-European element in Hittite was probably superimposed. The latest theory is that Hittite was an Indo-European language, allied to the western half of the group, which includes Greek, Italic, Germanic and Keltic. This theory is based on an examination of the script discovered at Boghaz Keui, the site of the ancient capital of Cappadocia.[1] The archives of Boghaz Keui probably belong to the xiv–xiii cent. B.C. It is impossible to say how much earlier the language of these scripts had its beginning. It has been said that the verb-flexions, pronouns and adverbs of the language were largely according to the Aryan type, and that the vocabulary, so far as ascertained, was indicative of the Indo-European stock. This, however, is very different from proving that the primitive language of Cappadocia was Indo-European and that Hittite belonged to the same family. The Semitic element in these literary discoveries is unmistakable and overwhelming. There are Babylonian-Assyrian, Horite,[2] Mitanni and Chaldee features, which are not easily explained on the above theory. The early Aegean migrations into western

---

[1] Vide *Milleilungen der Deutschen Orient Gesellschaft zu Berlin* for December 1915 (No. 56).

[2] The Ḥarri, חרי, חרים, are commonly explained as *cave-dwellers*, 'Troglodytes'; but see Jensen, *ZA.*, 1896, p. 332.

Asia may have left a deposit of an Indo-European element, which became a part of the structure of a more ancient native tongue. It has yet to be decided whether the Indo-European character of the language was superimposed upon an earlier Semitic basis, or *vice versa*. Until new light is thrown on the whole problem, the present writer adheres to the former theory. It is certainly interesting to discover an Indo-European literary vein in the peoples bordering on Palestine prior to the Israelitish age. How far the Iranian influence goes back we have no means of discovering. The probable position is—(1) that originally Sumerian-Akkadian tribes occupied Cappadocia;[1] (2) that the Semitic basal elements of the old language were developed by the inroads of Mitanni and Aramaean clans; (3) that the Indo-European features of the language were introduced by the early incursions of Minoan and Iranian civilization.

IX

HEBREW OCCUPATION OF CANAAN

The Hebrews occupied Canaan in a much more restricted sense, and their language was much more limited in extent than has been commonly imagined. This has arisen from the prominence given to the Jews' sacred writings, long before scientific research brought to light some of the incontestable facts of history. Nearly 2000 years B.C. King Hammurabi succeeded in fusing a number of conflicting tribes and warring provinces, and thus consolidated the Babylonian Empire. From the Code of Hammurabi the Israelites probably derived some of their ethical enactments. They understood, it may be supposed, the language of this Code, and Babylonian words and ideas readily came into Hebrew writings from this source.[2] The civilization of Egypt

---

[1] Herodotus tells us that before the Persian Conquest the Cappadocians were subject to the Medes: Οἱ δὲ Καππαδόκαι ὑπὸ Ἑλλήναν Σύριοι ὀνομάζονται· ἦσαν δὲ οἱ Σύριοι οὗτοι, τὸ μὲν πρότερον ἢ Πέρσας ἄρξαι, Μήδων κατήκοοι (i. 72).

[2] *Vide* Edwards, *The Hammurabi Code*, 1904; Cook, *Laws of Moses and the Code of Hammurabi*, 1903. On the general subject of the indebtedness

preceded that of Babylonia, and was on the wane when
Hebrew tribes touched the Egyptian Delta.   Both Egypt and
Babylonia have passed their meridian when the Medes and
Persians rise from obscurity and fill the eastern picture.
Where do the Israelites enter upon the scene ?

The opinion that Israelites were settled in Canaan before
the Hebrew clans came out of Egypt, that is, before the
' Exodus,' does not rest upon mere conjecture.   At Taanach,
for instance, among the Canaanite remains, some cuneiform
tablets were discovered addressed to Ishtar-Washur, ruler of
Taanach.[1]   One of the tablets was written by *Ahi-ya-mi*,[2]
which is probably the same as the Hebrew ' Ahijah,' אֲחִיָּה,
' brother or friend of Yahveh.'[3]   The syllable *yâ* or *yô*, in
the early Canaanite inscriptions, is best explained as the
abbreviation of the Hebrew sacred name יהוה.   If, then,
this name *Ahi-ya-mi*, which goes back as early as the
xv century B.C., can be attributed to the presence of Semites
(Hebrews), it affords considerable evidence that some factions
of the Israelite tribes found their way into Canaan about the
same time that other factions wandered into Egypt.   This
consideration makes it easier to understand two things :
(*a*) how the Hebrew tribes under Joshua and the early Judges
so successfully met and overthrew the aboriginal inhabitants ;
(*b*) how the dialect of the Hebrews so soon and so easily
became the language of Canaan.

X

TESTIMONY OF TELL EL-AMARNA TABLETS

The letters from the vassal Asiatic governors to the
Egyptian Pharaoh (Tell el-Amarna tablets) show clearly the
presence and influence of the *Habiri*, ' Hebrews,' in and
around Canaan.   A royal captain, named Abdi-Kheba, sent

of Christianity and Judaism to Babylonia, *vide* Jeremias, *Babylonisches im
Neuen Testament*, 1905.

[1] On the discoveries at Taanach, *vide* Sellin, *Tell Ta'annek*.

[2] Is the termination *mi* descriptive of tribe or place, *i.e.* ethnic?

[3] Other Heb. names were discovered at Samaria, but of later date,
800-700 B.C.

a message to the Egyptian king imploring help lest 'the royal cities fall a prey to the *Habiri*.' Another letter from Rib-Addi, of Gebal, pours out bitter complaint against Aziru and his father Abd-Ashera. He writes: 'To Amanappa, my father. . . . Canst thou not rescue me from the hand of Abd-Ashera? All the *Habiri* are on his side.' In yet another letter, Itakama, prince of Kadesh, complained that Namyauza, his rival, had enlisted the *Habiri* in his army, and he wrote: 'Behold, now Namyauza hath delivered up to the *Habiri* all the King's cities in the land of Kadesh and in Ube.'[1] Thus Hebrew hordes already overran parts of Canaan. Since a city *Shakmi* is sometimes mentioned, it appears they also possessed Shechem.

XI

HEBREWS IN EGYPT

In all the Egyptian monuments there is no trace of the Israelites in Egypt, or of Joseph, or of the great Exodus This fact does not invalidate the Hebrew Scriptures, but suggests a reconstruction of the history. Somewhere between 3000 and 2000 B.C. a great movement of tribes (perhaps from Arabia) brought Phoenicians and Canaanites to Palestine, where they subdued and supplanted the older inhabitants, and founded a new civilization. A thousand years later another great invasion (probably from Mesopotamia) brought the Amorites, Moabites, Edomites, Israelites and other tribes into contact with this Canaanite civilization. The new invaders wandered into different regions. The Moabites and Edomites settled beyond the Jordan; the Israelites and others spread over the south of Palestine, stretching to the frontier of Egypt. That certain Israelite tribes crossed the border and entered Egyptian pasture land

---

[1] Ube = ' Hobah,' חוֹבָה, Gen. 14[15].

In a very interesting and important tablet from the region of the Jordan, the following names (among others) occur : *Ayab* and *Yashua*. These = the Heb. אִיּוֹב, ' Job ' [יֹב], in Gen. 46[13], is prob. an incorrect reading for יָשׁוּב, Num. 26[24]], and יֵשׁוּעַ (contracted form of יְהוֹשׁוּעַ or יְהוֹשֻׁעַ), ' Joshua.'

near the Sinai peninsula is probable. Most likely these nomads would be compelled to work for Egyptian taskmasters after the custom of the age. That they should seek to escape eventually for greater freedom across the peninsula is natural enough. All this is in general harmony with the underlying pilgrimage which forms the background of the Book of Exodus. Having escaped to the desert of Sinai, these tribes joined other Hebrew clans, including the Midianites, and formed the important community known as the 'Children of Israel.' Whether Yahveh was the mountain-god of Sinai or Horeb is not a question to be discussed here. But led by their tribal God the united Hebrew clans attacked Moab and Edom, and gained possession of a considerable part of Canaan. This was about one hundred years after the clans escaped from Egypt, and about 1200 years before the Christian era.

Relatively the Canaanites were a cultured and active people, as Egyptian and other literary remains prove.[1] From them the Israelites probably gained some knowledge of letters. The earliest forms of this Canaanite-Israelite language known to us are found in the Phoenician and Moabite inscriptions. The Israelites were settlers in Canaan about 300 years before they attempted anything like a written account of their wanderings, laws and exploits.

XII

HEBREW IN OLD TESTAMENT WRITINGS

A few Hebrew fragments may date from early times, such as the Song of Deborah, and some ceremonial rites

---

[1] The most remarkable are the Tell el-Amarna tablets, which were found (1888) in the tomb of a scribe of Amen-hotep III., about 180 miles south of Memphis. The tablets are written in Babylonian cuneiform, the language of the Pharaoh's foreign dispatches. There is a mixture of Canaanite words and phrases ; the composition is often inaccurate, suggesting a faulty knowledge of the languages involved. These tablets contain dispatches from princes of N. Syria, Assyria, Babylonia, and from vassal kings in Jerusalem, Megiddo, and other places. The standard translation is by Winckler, *Die Thontafeln von Tell-el-Amarna*, 1896.

attributed to Moses. The stories twined about the names of Saul and David were probably compiled before 900 B.C. But the literary period began after the separation of the tribes into south and north. The outlines of the history of the south—the Kingdom of Judah—were collected sometime preceding 800 B.C. The outlines of the history of the north—the Kingdom of Israel—were collected sometime before 750 B.C. The significant fact here is that only a mere fragment of Hebrew literature, as we know it in the Old Testament, was written during the occupation of Palestine by the Israelites. The ethical and priestly teaching, the prophetical books in their edited form, and the development of the historical writings, belong mainly to post-exilic times. That is, Hebrew literary activity began when the Israelites no longer possessed Palestine, and when Hebrew was no longer the vehicle of common parlance. This explains why there are no Hebrew inscriptions during this period,[1] and why the later Old Testament writings are characterized by Aramaic elements, and why some of them look like translations from Aramaic originals. This is notably the case with the Ecclesiastes, which is one of the latest books in the Jewish canon. In many respects its language resembles that of the Targums and the Syriac. It has, indeed, some striking similarities to the Mishna, whose compiler, Jehudah ha-Nasi, died *circa* 220 A.D. Its general language belongs to the same type as that of Chronicles, Ezra, Nehemiah and Esther, but on the whole it is farther removed from the classical Hebrew.[2] The writer of this book, like the authors of other late Hebrew Scriptures, thought and

---

[1] A small number of Heb. inscriptions have been found, dating from i B.C. to iii cent. A.D. *Vide* Chwolson, *Corp. Inscr. Heb.* The inscriptions on Jewish coins, dating from the Hasmonaean princes, 135 B.C., to the second revolt against the Romans, 132-135 A.D., were furtive attempts to revive the national language. They are found written in the archaic character, which had long ceased. Cf. Madden, *Coins of the Jews.*

[2] Already the *vav conversive* is very rare ; the pregnant constructions of the older language have given place to less condensed forms ; the style has become distended and degenerate by the introduction of new particles, and nominal and verbal forms. *Chronicles, e.g.,* reveal many novelties, which suggest much uncertainty in the literary language of the time. (*Vide* König, *Syntax der hebr. Sprache.*)

spoke in Aramaic. His knowledge of Hebrew was a purely literary acquirement. This may easily be proved by comparing the diction of these later books with the easy and almost perfect style of the writer of Ruth. Probably the writing of Ruth and the compilation of Esther were separated by at least 300 years.

From the foregoing statements it will have become evident that the problem of linguistic origins is by no means easy. The conclusion here stated respecting the source of the Hebrew language and writing is perhaps not the one generally accepted. Several possibilities have been named and advocated by different scholars. (*a*) That when the Israelites settled in Canaan they adopted the language of the old inhabitants. (*b*) That after the Israelites settled in Canaan they enlisted the services of Phoenician linguists and scribes to instruct in these and other arts. (*c*) That the Israelites before they migrated to Canaan spoke a language which was akin to that of the earlier settlers. The first theory is perhaps the most popular; the last has probably most in its favour. Possibly there is some element of truth in all three views. The Israelites certainly did learn something from the civilization which they found in Canaan; it is probable that Phoenician *savants* were employed to instruct them in many arts and crafts; but most of all their migration from the same original home as the *Kinaḫḫi* and the *Amurru*, ensured a similar language among these earlier Semitic tribes. Writing was employed in Canaan long before it was used by the Israelites. The older settlers were probably acquainted with some form of hieroglyphic or cuneiform script. It cannot be shown that the Israelites had this knowledge. The earliest Old Testament document was perhaps written *circa* 1000 B.C.

VI

INSCRIPTIONS AND THE OLD
TESTAMENT

I

RELIGIOUS TONE OF INSCRIPTIONS

THE sources and effects of the sacred language of the Jews
constitute a wide and difficult problem. That problem is
raised in many ways in the course of this study, but no
attempt is made to discuss it fully here. The object of this
section is to indicate the possible source of some ideas and
phrases in the Hebrew Scriptures by comparison with similar
ideas and phrases in early Phoenician and other Semitic
literature, and further to suggest the possible influence of
these ideas and phrases by comparison with some apparent
parallels in contemporary and later Semitic documents. We
take the north Semitic inscriptions as the basis of this comparative study. We select the inscriptions because they have
not suffered a change of text; the writing is sometimes
incomplete and illegible, but there has been no corruption
through transcription. Differences of orthography and construction mark inscriptions from various regions. Any
adequate comparative grammar would necessarily take these
differences into consideration. A brief grammatical and
syntactical outline is given in another section of this work.
Our purpose, however, is rather to state and illustrate leading
principles in the dissemination of linguistic influences and
tendencies.

The Jewish tone and colour of some of the north Semitic
inscriptions must not be taken as proof that these inscriptions

are of Jewish origin. But the moral sentiment, pietistic and
religious character of some of these documents are probably
due to the ubiquitous Jew. The Hebrews often impressed
their unique influence where they could not establish their
language. This they could do readily through two linguistic
channels—Phoenician and Aramaic. Their native language
was closely allied to the former, and they had acquired a
knowledge of the latter after the Exile. This may be
regarded as the simple and direct explanation of the
Phoenician and Aramaic elements in the sacred Books of the
Jews. Some of the idioms found in the inscriptions are not
only paralleled in the Hebrew of the Old Testament, but
occasionally protrude through the Greek of the New Testament. In the following notes the inscriptions are not
necessarily quoted in chronological order; sometimes a
sequence of subject is observed.

A common formula in Phoen. inscriptions is the personal
pronoun followed by the proper name. Thus: אנך משע, ' I am
Mesha' (Moab. St. l. [1]); אנך יהומלך, ' I am Yehu-Milk' (CIS i.
l. [1]); אנך עבדאסר, ' I am Abd-osir' (*ib.* i. 46[1]); אנך אספת, ' I am
Asapt' (*ib.* i. 119[1]). So in the Zenjirli inscriptions: אנך פנמו,
' I am Panammu' (*Hadad*, l. 1); אנה בן[ר]רכב, ' I am Bar-rekub'
(*Bar-rekub*, l. 1). In later Aram. this formula is rare, and is
scarcely to be found in Nab. and Palm. inscriptions. Its use
in the Canaanite group of dialects suggests the origin of the
Biblical אני יהוה, or אנכי יהוה; אנכי האל, or אני אל (cf. Gen. 31[13]
15[7], Ex. 6[2], Lev. 18[5], Num. 3[13], Is. 42[8] 45[22], Jer. 32[27], Mal.
3[6]). This formula is almost absent from Egypt.-Aram., but it
occurs twice in one papyrus, אנה ידניה, ' I, Yedoniah' (J 9, 12).
The connexion between the Jews in Assuan and in Babylonia
was close, as they were branches of kindred Semitic migrations.
In the Egypt. papyri the 'Jews' are frequently called
' Aramaeans,' partly because they spoke Aram., but chiefly
because the western part of the Persian Empire was officially
known as Aramaean (cf. Sayce, *Assuan Pap.*, p. 10). The
Semitic formula appears in the Apoc. (22[16]): ἐγὼ Ἰησοῦς =
אנא ישוע.

II

USE AND SUPPRESSION OF THE 'NAME' OF DEITY

It is suggestive to find in some Phoen. inscriptions (*circa* 500–200 B.C.) that the names of certain gods and goddesses were not pronounced.   Thus: בעלת נבל, 'mistress of Gebal' (CIS i. l. [2]); this was probably 'Ashtart' (= עַשְׁתֹּרֶת of OT.), worshipped among all Semitic people, except the Arabs. Possibly the 'house of the Ashtaroth' (1 S. 31[10]) is the same as the temple at Ashkelon (ἐν Ἀσκάλωνι πόλι, Herod. i. 105). A similar expression is בעל צדן, 'lord (baal) of Sidon' (CIS i. 3[18]), and בעל צר, 'lord (baal) of Tyre' (CIS i. 122[1]), but in this last case the name מלקרת is given.   In instances where the name of the deity was known, its pronunciation was apparently often withheld, doubtless out of reverence to the local deity.   But different localities possessed different degrees of sentiment, and in some places the name was pronounced, in others omitted.   The same statement applies to the name יהוה among the Jews.   At one period the pronunciation of the name was forbidden (*vide* Philo, *Vit. Mosis*, tom. iii. pp. 519, 529).   Rather later it was perhaps uttered in an abbreviated form.   The processional at the 'Water Feast' commenced with the recitation of . . . אנא יהוה הושיעה נא (Ps. 118[25]).   According-ing to Rabbi Jehuda the processional cry was אני והו הושיעה נא (M. Suc. iv. 5).   If we compare another saying of R. Jehuda, ה" והו שמו של הקב "ה (b. Sab. 104[a]), which is almost unintelli-gible, it will perhaps appear that he declared the Name was pronounced.   In the former of the quotations from R. Jehuda the words אני והו no doubt stand for אנא יהו, and this suggests *Jahu* as the pronunciation of the Name.   This form is attested for the Jewish colony in Egypt in the Assuan Papyri (B 4, 6, 11, J 6).   In later and more degenerate times, a longer form of the word was apparently used. Plutarch says that the Jews invoked *Evohé* in the temple (*Symp.* iv. 6. 2), and this suggests that the full Name יהוה was pronounced.

It will be appropriate to notice here the absence of the term יהוה from the inscriptions, and the presence of מרא.   Now

in the Aram. portions of the Bible יהוה does not occur, but
מרא appears (in Dan.) where at first we might expect the
former term.   This fact is perhaps due to the strong Babylonian influence in these Biblical sections.   These selections
from Babylonian sources naturally did not originally contain
the name of the Israelitish Yahveh, but the distinctively Aram.
מרא.   There were, no doubt, good reasons why the writer of
Daniel did not introduce the name of the God of Israel into
the incorporated Aramaic sections.

Another phrase in the inscription referred to above is
interesting, as showing the Semitic background of another
Jewish expression.   It is this : עשתרת שם בעל, 'Ashtart the
name of Baal' (CIS i. 3¹⁸).   Here שם has the meaning of
'representation' or 'epiphany.'   So פן in a Carthaginian
inscription : תנת פן בעל, 'Tanith face of Baal' (CIS i. 181¹).
This probably means 'the display of divine attributes,' i.e.,
'the self-revelation' of the deity's nature.   It is probably to
be inferred that 'Tanith' was in some localities a synonym for
'Ashtart'; cf. לרבת לעשתרת ולתנת בלבנן, 'To the mistress (or
mistresses) Ashtart or Tanith at Lebanon' (Ref. Cooke, North
Semit. Inscr., p. 127 ; Clermont-Ganneau, Recueil d'archéologie
orientale, iii. pp. 186 ff.).   In the Hebrew Scriptures the
Name of Yahveh is often employed for His person, presence
or attributes (cf. Ex. 3¹⁵ 23²¹ 33¹⁴, 1 K. 8¹⁶, Is. 18⁷ 63⁹).

The expression 'make mention of the name' in a Zenjirli
inscription sounds quite Jewish.   The phrase is : יזכר אשם חדד,
'make mention of the name of Hadad' (Hadad, l. 16).   Hadad
was the supreme deity of the Aramaeans, and is found in a
few compounds in the OT. (2 S. 8³, 1 K. 20¹, Zech. 12¹¹).
Cf. the Heb. הזכיר שם יהוה (Is. 26¹³).   The Targ. has same
idea : מלצלאה בשמא דיי, 'to invoke in the Name of the Lord'
(Onk. G 4²⁶).

Among many ancient people the 'name' was a part of
the person, in some instances corresponding to the function
which is termed the 'soul.'   In Egypt many persons,
especially the elect ones in the divine pantheon, had two
names—the 'great' name and the 'little' name.   These
corresponded with the 'true' name and the 'good' name ; the
latter was made public, but the former was strictly con-

cealed.[1] It is not without significance that the 'name' of the God of the Hebrew tribes was among the first questions raised after the Exodus from Egypt. The sacred and public names of the God of Israel may be traceable to Egyptian influence.[2] The distinction was preserved by the Jews, who pronounced יהוה, the incommunicable ' Name,' by the secular term אדני.[3]

The name ' Yahveh ' was probably familiar to the tribes on the Egyptian side of the Sinai peninsula. Here Kenites, Midianites and other tribes commingled. Originally the name ' Yahveh ' may have been no more divinely communicated than ' Chemosh ' among the Moabites, or ' Milcom ' among the Ammonites, or ' Hadad ' among the Edomites, or ' Jupiter ' among the Greeks and Latins. The name ' Yahveh ' was certainly known in pre-Exodus times.[4] The story in the Book of Exodus is the poetic institution of the Name as the signal of a tribal rally and the centre of national worship. The influence of this Name, with all it came to imply for Israel, cannot be estimated. Moab, Ammon and Edom disappeared hopelessly into the sand, but Israel remained and continues the living evidence of Yahveh's greatness. The prophets of Yahveh raised the faith of Israel from the present temporal dispensation to the Messianic and eternal age.

NOTE ON יהוה

For the Rabbinic teaching on the use of the sacred Name we must consult the Talmud [5] and the Midrashim.[6] Of the Targums

---

[1] Lefébure, *La Vertu at la Vie du Nom en Egypte.*

[2] *Vide* the interesting passage Ex. 6[3].

[3] Accord. to the Tal. ' those who utter the name of God accord. to its sound have no position in the world to come,' *Sanhedrin*, x. 1. Philo says, ' He who utters the name of the Lord at an unfit time shall die,' ii. 166. For use of the ' Name' by the priests, *vide* Buxtorf, *Heb. and Ch. Lex.* 2432.

[4] The passage, Gen. 4[26], is suggestive : אָז הוּחַל לִקְרֹא בְּשֵׁם יְהֹוָה (cf. Onk. בְּכֵן בְּיוֹמוֹהִי־חָלוּ־בְנֵי־אֲנָשָׁא מְצַלָּאָה בִּשְׁמָא דַּיָי, lit. ' therefore in his days began the sons of man to pray in the name of Yahveh '). The phrase, ' to call on the name,' or ' to pray in the name,' is a synonym for divine worship. This act distinguished the descendants of Seth from the race of Cain ; hence probably the former are meant by the בְּנֵי הָאֱלֹהִים, and the latter by the בְּנוֹת הָאָדָם (Gen. 6[2]). The use of the ' Name' in the NT. is worthy of careful study (*vide* Mt. 6[9] 28[19], Acts 9[14], Rom. 10[13]).

[5] *Sanhedrin*, 90[a]. [6] *Pesikta*, 50[a].

that of Onkelos is our best guide.   When the Tetragrammaton refers
to God, Onkelos writes יי, and when it refers to man, רבוני.   In the
Jewish Samaritan Targum, when the name is sacred it is written
מרי, מאריא, and when secular רבי.   The Samaritan pronunciation of
the Tetragrammaton is uncertain, but some have represented it by
איו, *Ayoo* (perhaps more accurately אַיָא, *Aya*).[1]   The Jewish Rabbis
say that the sacred Name has not changed in form, יהוה, or in pronunciation, אדני, since the time of Ezra.   The form אדני is not
general in the Semitic languages.   It is found in Phoenician in
Ἄδων, Ἄδωνις, as the name of an idol.[2]   There is probably a trace
of the word in the Assyrian *adunnu*, 'strong.'

In the Phoenician inscriptions the compound is sometimes found
אדנבעל,[3] but more frequently the simple אדני.[4]   With these forms
should be compared the name *Marduk-bal-iddina*,[5] perhaps equal to
'Merodach-Baal is mighty.'   The latter part of the term is not
unlike בעלאדן, lit. 'Baal is Lord.'   Compare the Neo-Punic אדנבעל,
which according to the Latin transcription is pronounced *Idnibal*.

The pointing of יהוה is uncertain.   The common pointing יְהֹוָה
is grammatically incorrect, inasmuch as consonantal ו cannot have
two vowel-signs—its own proper vowel and the cholem of a preceding open syllable.[6]   No doubt the pointing יְהֹוָה is intended to
represent the pronunciation אֲדֹנָי, and hence should be written יְהוָֹה.[7]
A more correct pointing is found in many ancient MSS, יַהְוֶה,[8] which
more nearly conveys the generally accepted pronunciation *Yahveh*,
and is accurately preserved in the Rabbinic abbreviation יְ.

III

WORDS AND PHRASES WITH AN OLD TESTAMENT ECHO

The word צדק usually has the meaning of 'equity,'
'justice,' 'righteousness.'   Compare the quite Jewish expres-

---

[1] For authorities, *vide* מבשרת ציון לו ('Zion's Glad-tidings'), p. 36[b].   This
work was written in German by Eleazar Levi in 1835, and was translated
into Hebrew by A. M. M. Mohr.   Both Levi and Mohr are held in Jewish
circles as very reliable scribes.

[2] Rendered by Aeschylus, *e.g.*, by κύριος.

[3] CIS i. 149[1] *et al.*   [4] CIS i. 5[a] *et al.*

[5] The MT. is wrong בְּלְאדַן בַּלְאֲדָן ; the LXX Μαρωδὰχ Βαλαδάν is right,
and appears based on another source.

[6] *Vide* König, *Lehrgebände*, i. 44–49.

[7] As on title-page of AV. 1611.   [8] E.g. *Cod. Edinburgensis.*

sion concerning ' Yeḥaw-Milk, king of Gebal,' כ מלך צדק הא,
' for he is a righteous king' (CIS i. l. [9]) ; cf. מלכי־צדק, ' king
of righteousness' (Gen. 14[18], Ps. 110[4]). Until further light
is thrown on this name, we may suppose that צדק was the
name of an old Accadian (Phoen. or Canaanite) deity. Cf.
צדקא on an old Heb. seal of the vii–vi cent. B.C. (Levy, *Siegel
und Gemmen*, No. 7, p. 39).

It is more interesting to find that the noun צדקתא was
used in the sense of ' gift,' ' grant,' ' religious due' in the v
cent. B.C. (CIS ii. 113[15]). The word had the same meaning
in Arabic, ' charity,' ' endowment.' In the ii cent. B.C. Pales.
Aram. employed the term with a similar meaning, as is
shown by the LXX rendering of צדקה by ἐλεημοσύνη (Dan.
4[24]). If צדקתא was the Aram. behind Mt. 6[1], then the
rendering δικαιοσύνη is too literal. It means ' practical
righteousness,' therefore = charity, almsgiving ; cf. Syr. וֹכמֹ|
= ἐλεημοσύνη, ' beneficence' (Pesh. Acts 10[2]). In the Tal.
צדקתא = *Almosen*, ' almsgiving.' In the Targg. צדקתא is often
best rendered by ' righteousness' (*e.g.* Ps. 97[2. 6]). Frequently
the Heb. צדקה is rendered in the Targg. by זכותא, ' innocence,'
' justice' (Onk. Dt. 6[25] ; cf. Targ. Ps. 110[4]).

The word רכבאל, ' chariot of El' (Zenj. *Hadad*, l. 2 ;
Panammu, l. 22; *Bar-rekub*, l. 5), is interesting in view of some
OT. phrases. The picture of רכב אלהים (Ps. 68[18]) is thoroughly
Jewish (cf. 1 K. 8[12], Ps. 18[11] 19[1-7], Hab. 3[8]). The figure in
Heb. was probably due to Hittite. The Palestinians usually
associated chariots with the Egyptians and the Hittites
(2 K. 7[6]). It is true, battle scenes in Hittite sculptures are
rare, yet war-chariots are found, and charioteers are seen
riding in the lion hunt (cf. Messerschmidt, *The Hittites*, p.
55 ; *Encycl. Bibl.*, *s.v.* ' chariot'). Perhaps, too, the Hittites
supplied the symbol of the ' eagle.' It is interesting to find
the ' double-eagle' in Hittite art. From this source came
the symbol of the two-headed eagle found among the Seljuk
Sultans, *circa* 1217, and later, 1345, it adorned the es-
cutcheon of the German Emperors. The LXX renders נשר
by ἀετός ; we may suppose the Aram. נשרין behind ἀετοί
(Mt. 24[28]). In view of the word Ἀκελδαμά (Acts 1[19]), it is
suggestive to find the vernacular for ' field' supported by

a v cent. inscription, חקלא (CIS ii. 113¹⁸).   The NT. word is distinctly said to have been according to the local brogue— τῇ ἰδίᾳ διαλέκτῳ αὐτῶν—it was therefore : חקל-דמא.

The following are phrases which have an echo in Old Testament Heb.: כתעבת עשתרת הדבר הא, 'for an abomination to Ashtart is that thing' (Phoen. *Tabnith*, l. ⁶); cf. כי תועבת יהוה אלהיך הוא (Dt. 7²⁵ 17¹ 18¹² 24⁴ *al.*).   Onk. employs another word, טרחקא, but תועבא is the general Aram.

The wide world was expressed by the 'four parts' of the earth, *e.g.* מדא רבעי ארקא, 'from the four parts of the earth' (Zenj. *Bar-rekub*, ll. 3, 4) ; רבעהארק, 'earth's quarters' (*ib.* *Panammu*, l. 14).   The same idea is expressed by the 'four winds,' 'four corners' (Ezek. 7² 45¹⁹, Dan. 11⁴).   So Aram. מארבע רוחי ארעא (Targ. Is. 11¹²), ארבע רוחי שמיא (Dan. 7²).   Our Lord would find words ready at hand for the idea rendered : ἐκ τῶν τεσσάρων ἀνέμων (Mk. 13²⁷).

'To sit at the feet' of a superior is a familiar Semitic expression ; also 'to follow at the feet.'   Compare בלגרי מראה, *lit.* 'at the feet of his lord,' i.e. *following* (Zenj. *Panammu*, l. 16), and the Heb. ברגליו, 'at his feet' (Judg. 4¹⁰).   In the case of הם תכו לרגלך, Onk. avoids the anthropomorphism : אנן דמדברין תחות עננך (Dt. 33³).   *Vide* idiom לרגלי = 'at my approach' (Gen. 30³⁰).   In Egypt. Aram. רגל, רגלא = *clientela* (A 2, B 3, C 2, *al.*).   Cf. πρὸς τοὺς πόδας τοῦ κυρίου (Lk. 10³⁹).

The expression לסכר ושם נעם, 'for a memorial and a good name' (CIS i. 7⁶ ; cf. שם טב, *Nêrab*, 2, l. 3), should be compared with Is. 56⁵ ; *Berakoth*, 17ᵃ.   The phrase תחת פעם אדני, 'under the foot of my lord' (CIS i. 7⁷), is a thoroughly eastern figure of subservience (cf. 2 S. 22³⁹).   The term מליץ הכרסים, 'interpreter of thrones' (CIS i. 44²), is peculiar, but doubtless refers to the dragoman, who was employed in eastern palaces to interpret between one foreign court and another.   The Heb. Scriptures abound with the words אכל ושתא, 'eat and drink' (Zenj. *Hadad*, l. 9).   The symbolic act אחז בכנף מ[ר]אה, 'lay hold of the skirt of his lord' (Zenj. *Panammu*, l. ¹¹), is quite familiar to the Bible writers (cf. 1 S. 15²⁷, Zech. 8²³).   The idea of royal succession is expressed in the usual way, על כרסא אבי, '(to sit) upon the throne of my father' (Zenj. *Bar-rekub*, ll. 6—7).   The double terms for 'posterity,' זרעה ושמה, 'both his seed and his name' (CIS ii. 113[14]), are found together in Heb. (*e.g.* Is. 66[22]). The Aramaic phrase להיי נפשה (CIS ii. 114[4]), 'for the life of his soul,' may be compared with לנפש חיה (Gen. 2[7]). The word ביד, 'by the hand of' (CIS ii. 122[4]), is the common method of expressing instrumentality (Ex. 4[13], Lev. 8[36], *saepe*). Compare ויתקלנהי בלבה, 'and let him weigh it in his heart' (CIS ii. 145 A[6]), with same Biblical idea (Is. 57[1], Jer. 12[11]; cf. Lk. 2[19]).

The catalogue of offerings and revenues in an inscription found at Marseilles, but probably of Carthaginian origin, dating *circa* iv cent. B.C. (CIS i. 165, cf. 167), bears considerable likeness to the Mosaic-Levitical cult. The word כלל = 'whole-offering'; צועת = 'prayer-offering'; שלם כלל = 'whole peace- (or thank-) offering'; מנחת = 'meal-offering.' That the 'sin-offering' (חטאת, חטאתא), and 'the guilt-offering' (אשם, אשמא), should be absent from the Punic inscriptions suggests that the sense of personal transgression was not so vivid among the settlers in the Phoen. colonies as among the Jews. That many of the sacrificial rites of the Hebrews were survivals of early Canaanite and Phoen. ceremonies is more than suggested by inscriptional evidence. Tribal and communal sacrifices and offerings occupy practically no place in Aram. inscriptions. That offerings were made by individuals to local deities is proved by an Egypt.-Aram. inscription (CIS ii. 146).

In another Phoen. inscrip. we find the phrase: אדרנם ועד צערנם, 'the greatest of them even to the least of them' (*Carthage*, l. 5). The usual Heb. reverses the order: מקטנם ועד-גדולם (Jer 31[33] 44[12]; Jonah 3[5], however, is like the inscrip.). Cf. the order ἀπὸ τῶν πρεσβυτέρων ἕως τῶν ἐσχάτων (John 8[9]).

In a bilingual inscription we find the phrase: לענת עז חים, 'To Anath, the strength of life' (CIS i. 95[1]). The Greek text has Ἀθηνᾷ Σωτείρᾳ, which shows that the Phoen. phrase was not familiar in Greek. It has, however, its parallel in the OT.: יהוה מעוז-חיי (Ps. 27[1]). The idiom חי חים, 'the life of life' (N. Punic: *Shershel*, 2[1]), is unusual. In the OT. חי is familiar in association with Yahveh: אל חי (Jos. 3[10]), חי יהוה (Ps. 18[47]), אלהים חי (2 K. 19[4. 16]), אלהים חיים (Dt. 5[23], 1 S. 17[26]).

12

The expressions : כ שמע קל, 'because he heard his voice' (CIS i. 88[7], 90[2], 122[3. 4]; Phoen. *Tamassos*,1.[6]), and בשמע קל דברי, 'because he heard the voice of his words' (CIS i. 123[5. 6]), are suggestive of the source of some OT. language. Thus: וישמע יהוה את־קול דבריכם (Dt. 5[25], Dan. 10[9]). The following sentence is quite Jewish in conception : שמ[ע] [ק]לא רפיא, 'he heard his voice (and) healed him' (CIS i. 143[1. 2]). Cf. the Heb. : וישמע יהוה . . . . וירפא את־העם, 'And the Lord heard . . . and healed His people' (2 Ch. 30[20]).

Another OT. expression is illustrated in מקדש בת עשתרת, 'the sanctuary of the house (= temple) of Ashtart' (CIS i. 132[3]). The temple of Ashtart was at Sidon (cf. 1 K. 11[5. 33]), but the cult was established in other places. With the expression compare : מקדשי בית יהוה (Jer. 51[51], cf. Ezek. 48[21]).

The inscriptions throw some light on the application of the word כלב, 'dog,' to persons. From the Tell el-Amarna letters we learn that the Assyrian *kalbu* was a common term addressed to inferiors, indicative of humble deference on the part of suppliants. In some early Biblical passages the word has an unfavourable meaning, 'Sodomite,' '*κίναιδος*' (cf. Gen. 38[21], Dt. 23[18]); כלבים suggests the same class of persons as קדשים, perhaps = 'devoted to the service' of Ashtart or other deities. In Phoen. inscriptions הקדשת, הקידש, הקדש, קדש (prob. all adjectives, CIS i. 165[12], 166[2. 4], N. Punic: *Maktar*, A i.[4]) are used in the Heb. sense of 'sacred,' 'holy.' In some documents the term 'dog' is found in a proverbial sense, often suggesting reproach (cf. Tell el-Amarna, 75[36], 86[19] *al.*; 2 K. 8[13], Rev. 22[15]). But the word has not necessarily this connotation, *e.g.* לכלבם ולגרם, lit. 'to the dogs and whelps' (CIS i. 86 A[15], B[10]). This probably means the 'suppliants and clients,' perhaps in some instances 'foreigners,' 'sojourners' (cf. גור, *to sojourn*, 1 K. 17[20] = *ἀγείρω*; גר in Phoen. may = 'friend,' 'guest,' CIS i. 47[2]; so in Palm., Littmann, *Journal Assyr.*, 1901, ii. 374–390). Later the word was applied to people who were not Jews (*Niddah*, 77[a]; *Baba Kama*, 49[a] *al.*). Our Lord's word to the Syrophoenician (*τοῖς κυναρίοις*, Mk. 7[27]) was probably the vernacular לכלבם or Syr. ܠܟܠܒܐ.

Divine appellations in the Old Testament have many

analogues in inscriptions. We find such names and titles as : בעשמם (for בעלשמם), 'Lord of the heavens' (CIS i. 139[1], *ib.* i. 7[1]; later Palm. Eut. 4[1], Vog. 73[1]); עזמלך, 'Milk is strong,' or 'Milk is my strength' (Phoen. *Tyre*, l. [3]; cf. עזבעל on Phoen. coins, Babelon, *Les Perses Achéménides*, No. 670). Notice the two forms בעלמלך (Phoen. coins, Babelon, *l.c.*, Nos. 647, 679), and מלכבעל (CIS i. 123 a[1, 2]): 'the lord is king,' 'the king is lord.' With these terms compare : 'God of the heavens' (Ps. 136[26], Ezra 1[2]), 'Lord strong and mighty' (Ps. 24[8]), 'the Lord is King' (Ps. 10[16]), 'the Lord my strength' (Ps. 18[1]).

Some divine epithets in Palm. inscriptions may have been influenced by Jewish associations. For instance : מרא עלמא, 'Lord of eternity' (Vog. 73[1]), cf. Targ. אלהא דעלמא (Onk. Gen. 21[33]), אלהא דמלקדמין (Onk. Dt. 33[27]). Another phrase equally Jewish is : לבריך שמה לעלמא, 'To him whose name is blessed for ever' (Vog. 76[1]); cf. the Bibl. Aram. להוא שמה די אלהא מברך מן־עלמא ועד־עלמא (Dan. 2[20]). Observe the Persian title : מלכא זי מלכיא, 'King of kings' (CIS ii. 122[3]), and cf. the Phoen. אדן מלכם, 'Lord of kings' (CIS i. 3[18]). In OT. used of Nebuchadrezzar (Ezek. 26[7]); it is also applied to God : מרי מלכין (Onk. Dt. 10[17]).

Some other phrases may be noticed here as appropriately following the last named. The Palm. is reminiscent of OT. phraseology : בריך שמה לעלמא, 'Blessed be his name for ever' (Vog. 79[1], cf. 75[1], 76[1]). Cf. יהי שם יהוה מברך (Job 1[21], Ps. 113[2] *al.*).

The following sentence has a thoroughly Jewish ring : לרחמא טבא ותירא, 'to the compassionate one, the good and the merciful' (Vog. 93[3, 4], cf. 79[1, 2], 75[1, 2]). Cf. רחום וחנן יהוה (Ps. 103[8] *al.*), כי טוב כי לעולם חסדו (2 Ch. 7[3] *al.*).

The idea and form of expression : דכיר ת' (Sin. inscrip. Eut. 457[1]), 'Remembered be T.,' remind us of certain OT. phrases, *e.g.* אדני הגדול והנורא זכרו (Neh. 4[8 Heb.]). The verb דכר = 'make mention,' and is the Aram. equivalent for the Heb. זכר (*vide* Is. 12[4] Heb. and Targ.). Cf. the interesting Palm. דכירין [חברי]א אלן כלהון בטב, 'Remembered be all these [companions] for good' (Littmann, *Journal Assyr.* ii. 374–390, B ll. 10–11). I have suggested a new restoration [חברי]א =

colleagues (cf. N. Pun. 124, l. [4], Louvre); but Clermont-Ganneau restores שמא, and Lidzbarski אנשא or נבריא.

The phrase: מודן כל יום, 'giving thanks every day' (Vog. 93[1]), has quite a Jewish turn of thought, *e.g.* בכל־יום אברכך (Ps. 145[2] *al.*).   מודן is ptcp. pl. of ידא, *confess, give thanks.*

The poetical Greek expression: ἐν τῇ οἰκίᾳ τοῦ πατρός μου μοναὶ πολλαί εἰσιν (John 14[2]), may be compared suggestively with phrases in some Aram. inscriptions. The words בית אבי, 'my father's house' (Zenj. *Hadad*, l. 9; *Bar-rekub*, l. 12), בבית אבוה, 'in his father's house' (*Panammu*, l. 2); cf. the description of בית כלמו, 'house of fulness' (*Bar-rekub*, l. 12–20), probably refer to the royal palace rather than to the resting-place of the dead. But sometimes a king's palace became his mausoleum. From an early Phoen. inscrip. we learn that special 'houses' were built for special deities, אית בת אלם (*vide* CIS i. 3[15–18]). In the Palm. votive inscrip. the sun-god 'Shemesh' not only has his own central temple, but presides over the houses of his people, אלה בית אבוהן, 'God of their father's house' (*Oxoniensis*, 1, l. 7: Ashmolean Mus. Oxford).

The allusion in the Gospel is to the temple, בית אלה, in the precincts of which there were many apartments (cf. 1 K. 6[5], Ezra 8[29], Jer. 35[2. 4], 36[10]). So in the region beyond the grave there are degrees of existence suited to the different capacities and attainments of the departed. The Greek term for these mystic abodes is μοναί, and the Syr. version is ܐܣܢ. Now it is very interesting to find this word אונא in a Nab. inscrip. dating from the beginning of the Christian era (CIS ii. 202).

In the Syriac (Ephraem) this word is associated with the abode of the dead, and perhaps does not suggest anything much more advanced than the משכב את רפאם, 'resting-place among the Shades' (Phoen. *Tabnith*, l. 8, CIS i. 3[8]). Yet the use of the term in the Nab. inscrip. suggests something more than the resting-place of the dead: דנה כפרא ואונא, 'this is the tomb *and mansion,*' i.e. *lodging, habitation.* The idea is probably more elevated than בת עלמא, 'house of eternity' (CIS i. 124; Eccl. 12[5]; Diod. i. 51. 2; Vog. 36[a. b]; Clermont-Ganneau, *Études*, ii. 5), which usually means 'the grave.' It is to be presumed that the Aram. word behind μοναί was אוניא, and that our Lord's vernacular ran: סניאין אנון אוניא בית אבי.

Other phrases which have analogies in Scripture are: הראני בכל שנאי, 'he caused me to see (my desire) upon all my enemies' (Moab. St. l. 4, cf. l. 7); cf. יראני בשררי, 'let me see (my desire) upon my adversaries' (Ps. 59[11], 118[7]). כ שמע) קל), '(for she hears) my voice'; ושמע קל, 'and has heard my voice' (CIS i. ll. [3, 8]); cf. ישמע קולי (Ps. 116[1]). קדם אלהי קדם אנש, 'before gods and before men' (Zenj. *Panam.* l. 23, cf. CIS ii. 113[20]); cf. אלהים ואנשים (Judg. 9[9]). This phrase appears in the Gk. παρὰ Θεῷ καὶ ἀνθρώποις (Lk. 2[52]).

IV

COMMON TERMS 'HEIGHTENED' IN HEBREW

The general conclusion to be drawn from this study is that many terms and ideas, which at one time were regarded as exclusively Biblical, are found to belong to the common stock of Semitic and eastern language and conception.   If, on the one hand, it can be shown that a considerable number of Old Testament expressions had earlier existence in Babylonia or Phoenicia, on the other it must be remembered that many forms of speech and turns of thought, found in later Aramaic and other writings, owe their peculiar use to the sacred books of the Jews. A term or phrase is not necessarily of a religious origin because it is found in a sacred document, nor is it necessarily of a secular origin because it is found in a profane writing. Common language was employed to set forth divine things, and religious phraseology was used to express secular affairs. This representation will tend to make the religious cult and moral code of the Israelites more natural; not less real, but less mechanical. After all, apart from some verbal likenesses, there is a vast gulf between the spiritual conceptions of the Jews and their proud contemporaries.   In all the Babylonian, Phoenician, Aramaic and Greek inscriptions, there is no mention of Yahveh, or of any god comparable to Yahveh. Here is the secret and the mystery of the unique and abiding influence of the Israelite.

It will appear that many terms found in the inscriptions have become heightened in spiritual significance. Ancient religion was more objective, and states of consciousness were not differentiated. Neither Semites nor Greeks clearly separated the study of the soul from the study of the mind. Psychology is comparatively a new science, and modern thought is interpreting life from within, rather than from without. It must not be supposed that men in any age were devoid of psychical phenomena, because we do not find in their literature words to express these experiences. These facts have always lurked dim, though unexpressed, in the background of human nature. They simply required the proper impulse to bring them into clear vision. The following terms found in the Semitic inscriptions referred to in the foregoing pages will illustrate what is meant. צדק = right conduct to fellow-men ; טב = kindness or external pity ; קדש = sacred, devoted to service, revered by a subject ; תמנחא = assiduous in temple rites and offerings ; נפש = animal life, or simply being living or dead ; בריד = respect to the tomb of the deceased, the welfare of his posterity. Most of these terms were heightened in the vocabulary of the Hebrew prophets and the Jewish apocalyptists. They attain their full spiritual import in the religion of the Galilean, which is καρδίας ἐν πνεύματι, οὐ γράμματι.

V

DIVINE NAMES CONSTITUTE A RACIAL FACTOR

The factors which contributed most to an ἔθνος—a tribe, race, nation—were religion and language. There is a natural connexion between these factors ; religion needed language for its expression, and language required religion for its development. Of the two factors, religion probably has been the larger contributor to nationality. It can be shown historically that kindred languages have not been sufficient to hold tribes together, but oneness of religion has held together peoples of variant tongues. Both parts of this statement find striking confirmation in the history of the Jewish

nation.[1] It was their religion rather than their language
which separated the Hebrews from the surrounding tribes.
It was the distinctive worship of a specific Deity which
marked off the Jews from the other Semitic nations. Some
divine titles nearly all the Semites possessed in common.
These go back to a period before the segregation of the
Semites into different nations, and when they united in a
common theology and worship. The real origin of these
terms is very obscure, and is a fruitful field for conjecture.[2]

Another name common to many of the Semitic nations
is *Baal*, בעל, 'master,' 'owner,' 'lord.' The word is very
common in Phoen., and probably from this source it was
adopted by Philistines, Moabites (Moab. St. ll. 9, 30),
Hebrews and other Canaanite tribes. The name occurs in
Nab. (*e.g.* Euting, 327, 559), where it is associated with
Arabic in an interesting way : אלבעלו, '*the* Baal,' אושלבעלי,
'Aus-al-ba'ali'; here the אל or ל is the Arab. art. The term
came into Palm., though 'Baal' was not apparently reckoned

---

[1] Max Müller has given illustrations from the case of the aborigines of
N. America, from the Greek communities, as well as from the Semites.
Science of Religion, 144 ff.

[2] The name *El* is very ancient, and is found throughout the Semitic
group. In Assyr. ►─┐, *ilu*, 'strong' (cf. Schrader, *Zeitschrift der
Deutschen Morgenländischen Gesellschaft*, xxiii. p. 350), appears in the
word *Babil*, 'gate of God.' This perhaps means باب بل, 'gate of Bel
(or Belus)'; this would connect אל with בעל in the primitive worship of
Babylonian Semites. In Phoen. אל was worshipped as the son of heaven and
earth. In one inscrip. אל is associated with אשרת, but the latter probably
is not the female deity אשרה (cf. CIS ii. 113[16]), but a designation of the
locale of 'Ashtart.' The whole phrase לעשתרת באשרת אל חמן, lit. 'to Ashtart
in the Asherah, the god of Ḥammon,' is worth study (Phoen. inscrip.,
Louvre: Ma'ṣub, l. 4). The Arabic *Ilah*, الله, 'Allah,' is the same as the
Heb. אלה. Probably at first this *Ilah*, 'Eloah,' was an abstract substantive, *agitation*, *fear*, and then came to denote the object of fear.
Hence 'the אלהי Abraham, ופחד Isaac' [note the Onk. idiom : אלהא דאברהם
ודדחיליה יצחק, Gen. 31[42, 53]]. The Arabic feminine form, اللات, *Allât*, is
same as 'Αλιλάτ of Herod. iii. 8. The name *El* in some form probably found
its way beyond Semitic people, retaining the idea of 'power,' and inspiring
fear. The most dreaded god among the Kolymyans of Siberia is named *Ulu-
Tayon*, incarnated in the brown bear. Is the meaning of *Ulu* connected with
the root idea of the Heb. אול or the Arab. أول, 'formidable'? It is noteworthy that the Kolymyans, in supplicating this deity, regard it as sinful
to pronounce his name. Cf. Skhlovsky, *In far N.E. Siberia*, pp. 22–23.

among the national gods of Palmyra; בעל שמן (Euting, 4) = מרא עלמא (Vogüé, 73); cf. Gk. inscrip. from *et-Tayyibe*, near Palmyra: Δὺ μεγίστῳ κεραυνίῳ. It is probable that at first the feminine idea of Baal was not that of a separate deity, but an expression of activity, personification of an attribute. Hence in a Carthaginian inscrip. (CIS i. 181), Tanit (תנת) is described as the פן בעל, 'Face of Baal'; similarly in a Sidonian inscrip. (CIS i. 3), Astarte (עשתרת) is spoken of as שם בעל, 'Name of Baal.' In Heb., too, the Name of יהוה is used for His manifested presence (*e.g.* Ex. 23²⁰, Is. 18⁷ *et al.*).

The name *Bel*, בל, is the Babylonian deity, and not simply an abbreviated form of the Canaanite *Baal*, בעל. Bel was both a domestic and a chief god among the Babylonians, worshipped in the tower of Babel (cf. Is. 46¹, Jer. 50² 51⁴⁴, Dan. 14, LXX). Greek and Roman authors compare Bel with Jupiter (*vide* Diod. Sic. ii. 8, 9; Plin. xxxvii. 19; Cicero, *De Nat. Deorum*, iii. 16). It is not surprising that some Semitic people associated Bel with their solar deity. In a Palm. inscrip. (Vog. 3, l. 4) we find the word מלכבל, 'King Bel.' Malak-bel was the solar deity who stood at the head of the Palm. pantheon. The sun-god Bel was equivalent to שמש, so that מלכבל, שמש, and בל are in effect the same presiding deity with differing associations. For some Semites this deity was the author of good fortune, and from religious reverence was not named. A late (*circa* 125 A.D.) Palm. inscrip. begins thus: לבריך שמה לעלמא טבא ורחמנא, 'To him whose name is blessed for ever, the good and the compassionate' (Vog. 75). No doubt the unnamed god was בל, *i.e.* שמש=מלכבל. The introduction of Bel into Semitic proper names shows a Babylonian influence in the language and cult of Canaan.

Other divine names not peculiar to the Hebrew people may be briefly mentioned. *Shaddai*, שדי, was in Assyr. associated with Marduk and Bel, e.g. *Marduk-sadua, Bel-sadua, Bel-Harran-sadua* (*vide* Hommel, *Ancient Heb. Tradition*, 109 ff.). Compare the Babyl. *Samsu-satana, Ammi-satana*; the suffix *na* is apparently the first plural 'our' (*vide* Jensen, *Die Kosmologie der Babylonier*). The divine name *Ilu* seems associated with Babylonian royal names.

Samsu-iluna was the son of Hammurabi. Does *Samsu* = שמש,
' the sun ' ? Then the name might mean ' our god Shemesh.'
Just as Bel is used with *sadua*, ' high,' ' great,' ' strong,' in
Babyl.-Assyr., so in Heb. El is associated with *shaddai*.

Elyon, עליון, is perhaps from the Arabic, علوان, ' high.'
It is found as a proper name in Palm. עלינא, Gk. *'Αλαινῆ*
(Vog. 11). *Adonai*, אדני, may be either ' his lord ' (as in
Phoen., *CIS* i. 5, *et al.*, and in *Carthage*, CIS i. 269), or
' Lord ' (*pluralis excellentiae*, as in the Heb. Scriptures).
Melech, מלך, is found in most of the Semitic languages. It
appears as early as the Tell el-Amarna tablets in the name
Abd-milki (77. 37); this name is found in a Phoen. inscrip.,
עבדמלך (CIS i. 46). In another Phoen. inscrip. (CIS i. 123ᵃ),
the compound title מלכבעל shows that the idol-pillar, נצב, of
one deity could be dedicated to another. The chief idol of
the Ammonites was מֹלֶךְ, ' Moloch,' whom the Israelites sometimes worshipped (Lev. 18²¹ *et al.*, 1 K. 11⁷ *et al.*).

On the other hand, some deity-names seem peculiar to
separate Semitic peoples, or at least fixed as special titles of
local and national objects of worship. The origin of these
tribal deities is wrapped in great uncertainty. Doubtless
different causes operated in different localities. In some
instances natural features and climatic phenomena would
suggest a presiding deity. At times some great crisis—
disaster or triumph—in the history of a people might initiate
belief in an abstract genus, which grew into the recognized
tribal god. More frequently, it may be, some old superstitious idol-worship among the people conquered by the
Semites, gave to the latter a term which heightened into
the name of their deity.[1] The Semitic nations, though they
had usually one chief god, were not henotheistic, that is,
devotees of one deity utterly excluding all others. The
Israelites cannot be regarded as an exception, though

---

[1] The national god of the Moabites and Ammonites was ' Chemosh,'
כמוש, from an unused root כמש = כבש, ' subdue.' The Babyl. ' Nebo ' may
have received his name from the mount on which he dwelt, or the mount
may have been named from the god ; cf. Arab. نب = high. The compound
name, עשתר כמש, on the Moab. St. (l. 17), is rather remarkable. The mas.
form עשתר belongs exclusively to S. Arabia, hence most scholars think
that the fem. עשתרת should here be understood.

'Yahveh' was their God *par excellence*. It is certainly true that יהוה had a peculiar significance for the Hebrew people, and an altogether unique position in their thought and action. Yet even the roots of this word may run back into earlier Assyrian and Chaldaean associations.[1] It is not probable that the Hebrews would accept an entirely new god, with an entirely new and peculiar name. It is almost certain that the name in some form was already known in the Sinaitic peninsula when the Hebrews reached this region. The name was earlier than Moses, as the word יוכבד, 'Jo-chebed,' shows (Ex. 6[20]), and he may have heard it from the Kenites, who inhabited the peninsula when the Israelites came out of Egypt. How did the name get to Sinai ? The source of the term may best be sought in Semitism. Even if *Yahu* be found in Assyrian inscriptions, it is not necessarily an Assyrian word. It may have been borrowed from a Semitic source before Semitic became the popular language of Assyro-Babylonia. We should perhaps look to Arabia for the Semitic form of this name, just as we look to Arabia for the home of the Semites themselves. The desert of Mount Sinai was in Arabia Petraea. As this latter name suggests, it was a region of precipitous rocks, wild and void of herbage. Here was a fit home for a storm-god, whose voice was heard in the tempest. When the thunder shook the hills and the winds came rushing through the valleys, how natural to think of the *living, breathing* One shaking the mount to its very base (Ex. 19[18]). This was *Hayah*,[2] the existing, acting deity, who dwelt on Mount Sinai. The original meaning of the word, we may suppose, was quite simple and concrete.

[1] Οἱ Χαλδαῖοι τὸν θεὸν ΙΑΩ λέγουσι, ἀντὶ τοῦ φῶς νοητόν· τῇ Φοινίκων γλώσσῃ καὶ ΣΑΒΑΩΘ δὲ πολλαχοῦ λέγεται, οἷον ὁ ὑπὲρ τοὺς ἑπτὰ πόλους, τουτέστιν ὁ δημιουργός (Lydus, *De Mensibus*, iv. 38. 14). The Assyr. place-names from the list of Thotmes III. are much too uncertain (*vide* W. W. Müller, *Asien u. Europa nach altägyptischen Denkmälern*). So, too, is the reference to the Phoen. *I-zebel*=Jezebel, איזבל, *et al.* (cf. Hommel, *op. cit.* 115).

[2] In Arab. هَوَا, *hawâ*, lit. 'air,' then *to breathe, to blow*. Hence in Heb. הוה, היה and חוה, חיה, all of the same origin, *to be, to live*; cf. Arab. حَيَاة, *ha-yah*, life. As the name of deity this word was apparently not used by other Semitic people. Cf. Schrader (Eng. tr.), *The Cuneiform Inscrip. and the OT.*, Gen. 2[4b].

VII

SEMITIC SCRIPT:
EVOLUTION AND TRANSITION

I

HISTORICAL EVOLUTION OF SQUARE CHARACTER

THE learned controversy respecting the relation of the
Phoenician and Aramaic script resulted in very little definite
knowledge, until the positive data of inscriptions and papyri
came authoritatively into the field. It is now quite clear
that both types have been formed from one original. A
careful comparison of the alphabets of the various Phoenician
and Aramaic dialects from the eighth century B.C. to the
second century A.D. will abundantly prove this statement.[1]
The theory of a sudden change of script in the time of Ezra
is very old. It is definitely asserted in the apocryphal Ezra,
where the skilled scribes are said to write in a character
which they did not understand.[2] The reference is to the
transition from the Phoenician (= old Hebrew) script to the
so-called 'square writing' which is thus attributed to Ezra.
This old Jewish theory is utterly without foundation, and is
contradicted by all the available evidence. There never was
a distinct time when the character of the Semitic writing in
Palestine was deliberately changed. The script did change,
but the transition was very gradual, extending from the Exile
down to a period subsequent to the Christian era.

[1] *Vide* Hupfeld, *Ausführlich hebräisch Grammatik.*
[2] 4 Ezra 14⁴² : 'They (the five scribes) wrote by course the things that
were told them, *in characters which they knew not.*'

The evidence of inscriptions and coins points to the conclusion that immediately before the Exile the script of Phoenicians, Hebrews and Samaritans was one and the same. With the historical and ethnological changes which followed the Exile, changes developed in the character of Palestinian writing. The changes, however, as said, did not take place *per saltum*, any more than the changes of language. Two tendencies or principles led to the transformation of the ancient script into the later ' square' character : (1) Tachygraphy. By this term, in this instance, is meant *swift-hand*, rather than short-hand. Anciently the characters were formed by free and bold strokes of the stylus, and assumed the shape of a cursive hand. This was the result of an effort to write quickly, and would naturally follow from the attempt to write much in the shortest time. This running hand considerably altered the form of many letters as exhibited in Phoenician script. It was employed by Aramaic writers in earlier and later times, as the Aramaic monuments clearly testify.[1] That some scribes were distinguished for quickness of writing is plainly indicated. The Jewish authors regarded Ezra as an expert, and referred to him as ' the quick writer.'[2] (2) Calligraphy. By this is meant the attempt to produce an elegant and ornate script. More care was taken in the formation of the letters, and they inevitably assumed a more definite and symmetrical character.[3] The tendency in this direction grew as the interest in writing developed. This was particularly the case in the transcription of sacred records, and the production

[1] For earlier, *vide* Carpentras Stele (v–iv cent. B.C.), CIS ii. 141. The later Aram. cursive is found on many Pales. inscrip., *vide* Nöldeke, *Zeitschrift für Assyriologie* (1894), pp. 264–267.

[2] *Vide* Ezra 7[6] : והוא‎ספר מהיר בתורת . . . הוא עזרא. This was in the fifth cent. B.C., but probably earlier in the sixth cent. a similar hint is found, Ps. 45[2] : לשוני עט סופר מהיר. The script of this period (vi–v cent. B.C.) is represented in the inscriptions of Abydos (CIS ii. 108), Têma (*ib.* 113, 114), Memphis (*ib.* 123).

[3] The foll. sentence is copied from a Phoen. inscript. from Kition (Brit. Mus. Cyprus Room, No. 31), as a specimen of elegant script :

מ‎ך‎א‎ל‎, that is, מצבת אז אש ימנא ארש רב סרסרם לאבי לפרסי, ' This pillar which Arish, head of the brokers, set up to his father, Parsi.'

of important national decrees and State documents. The two types of writing, the cursive and the 'uncial,' existed contemporaneously, but with the institution of professional scribes the *scriptio rectissima* became the recognized and most general standard.

The introduction of the 'square' script cannot be definitely dated, but certainly prior to the fourth century A.D. Probably the 'square' character appeared shortly after the period of the Palmyrene inscriptions, indeed it seems to have arisen out of the Palmyrene script. The description of this writing as כְּתָב אַשּׁוּרִי by Talmudists is to be taken literally, *i.e.* geographically.[1] The word 'Assyria,' on the authority of the Hebrew Chronicler,[2] was readily used for Chaldaea or Babylonia, and the early writers may well have believed that the new type of writing did come into Palestine from this source. Since Origen and Jerome held this view we may conclude that it was the common opinion in their day. No doubt Aramaic was written in Babylonia before if was written in Canaan, and it was Aramaic influence which gradually changed the Phoenician cursive script into the uncial character.

II

AEGEAN INFLUENCE

The Phoenicians appear to rise to some considerable importance rather suddenly *circa* 1000 B.C. The Hebrews and Aramaeans may have borrowed their literary methods from the Phoenicians. But no satisfactory explanation has yet been given how the Phoenicians gained their knowledge of writing, and this as it seems very rapidly. A new solution may possibly be found along the following lines. The

---

[1] Principio data est lex Israelitis scriptura Hebraea et lingua sancta, iterum vero iis data est diebus Esrae scriptura Assyriaca . . . ; elegerunt autem sibi Israelitae scripturam Assyriacam et linguam sanctam et reliquerunt idiotis (*i.e.* Samaritanis), scripturam Hebraeam et linguam Aramaeam.—Licet non data sit lex per manum Esrae, mutata est per manum ejus scriptura, cum vocetur ejus nomen אשורית, quia ascendit cum iis ex Assyria (Gemara, *Sanhedr.*, fol. 21² 22¹).

[2] 2 K. 23²⁹.

suggestion of Herodotus may be taken as a starting-point. He suggested that the Phoenicians were forced to sea exploits by over-pressure of population on the one hand, and by the encroaching activity of the Aramaeans on the other. But these elements are not sufficient to account for the sudden development of Phoenician art and literature. Can we find these attainments among an earlier people in any adjacent regions ? The one feasible theory is that the civilization of the maritime colonies of Cyprus, Crete and the Aegean generally thrust forth a great migration about this time, which mightily influenced the Asiatic coast-lands, and readily accelerated art and writing. To a great Anatolian wave from the Aegean, Phoenicia was indebted in the early historical times for its rapid civilization and its developed script. By some sort of reaction Phoenician pirates and merchantmen visited the islands of the Mediterranean and the coast-lands, and marked their presence and their influence by numerous literary remains. It has been shown that among the earlier antiquities of Phoenicia and of south Syria there are many imported arts and ideas. The character of these importations points to Cyprus and other Aegean centres of civilization of the Minoan age. The Pulesti (Philistines), too, came into contact with this Aegean culture, and the Tikkarai and Washasha, who accompanied the Pulesti on their Egyptian raids, were probably of Cretan origin. The conclusion thus tentatively reached is ' that the historic Phoenician civilization, and especially the Phoenician script, owed their being in great measure to an immigration from those nearest oversea lands which had long possessed a fully developed art and a system of writing.' [1] It is suggestive and remarkable that other Semitic people in Syrian west Asia, very soon after this time, adopted writing in analogous script, but in their slightly differing dialects. This is seen in the literary remains of Moab, of north-west Syria, and of Samaria.

[1] *Vide* Evans, *Scripta Minoa*, vol. 1. Cf. Hall, *The Ancient History of the Near East* (1913) ; Garstang, *Land of the Hitties* (1910). On the Phoen. compared with other Canaanite languages, *vide* Stade, *Morgenländische Forschungen* (1874).

III

LINGUISTIC TRANSITION EPOCHS

It is possible from the available data to indicate the periods which marked the changes in the Semitic language and script. 1. To begin with the Phoenician, it may be granted that the Phoenician alphabet was derived from the Egyptian Hieroglyphics, through Hieratic and Demotic. The sacred literature of Egypt was written in Hieratic; Demotic was the language of social and commercial intercourse. The Phoenicians gained a knowledge of it through commerce, probably early in the ninth century B.C. Our study does not go behind the Phoenician inscriptions, so that Assyriology proper does not come within our period. The native language of Babylonia-Assyria did no doubt influence the language of Canaan, but chiefly through Phoenician script. One of the oldest specimens of Phoenician is the inscription on the Moabite Stone. The language is found to be practically identical with Old Testament Hebrew. This inscription is easily read by any Hebraist. This fact supports the conclusion that the languages of the Phoenicians, Syrians, Moabites, Ammonites, Arabs and Babylonian-Assyrians, were almost identical in grammatical structure, and closely related in vocabulary in the centuries ix–viii B.C. There were only local dialectical differences, which were probably mainly accentual. The Phoenician inscriptions of Cyprus and the oldest Zenjirli inscriptions are found in a similar script. All the Phoenician and Aramaic types of script may be traced back to this prototype on the Moabite Stone.[1] The earliest historical sources of the Old Testament were probably written in a similar script. The custom of writing data for future reference is clearly hinted in respect to the historical literature of the Old Testament. The phrase respecting the destruction of Amalek, כְּתֹב זֹאת זִכָּרוֹן בַּסֵּפֶר,[2] almost certainly

---

[1] As an example of the earliest Phoen. the following from the Moabite Stone (l. 14) is selected: 𐤋𐤊𐤔𐤌𐤔𐤅𐤀𐤌𐤓𐤉𐤋𐤊𐤋𐤊𐤀𐤇𐤆𐤀𐤕𐤍𐤁𐤄𐤏𐤋𐤉𐤔𐤓𐤀, 'And Kemosh said to me, Go take Nebo against Israel.'

[2] Ex. 17¹⁴.

proves the custom of writing for reference contemporary events.   Several sources are mentioned in the Old Testament,[1] but the most noteworthy are the official records of the Palestinian kings preserved in the royal archives.   Six titles are given to these records, the last of which suggests that they were gathered into one work.[2]   These literary memorials would naturally be written in the script of their respective ages.   They belong to the period of the Phoenician script, and therefore the type is illustrated by the Moabite Stone.

The script would depend to some extent on the character of the writing material, whether clay, wood, metal, stone, papyrus, parchment.   Probably the Israelites in Palestine never used any material for writing other than papyrus and parchment.   That the Israelites before they entered Canaan were acquainted with hieroglyphic and cuneiform writing is not unlikely.   That these types of script were known in Palestine before the Israelitish conquest is also probable. But when the Israelites in Canaan began their literary work the Phoenician script and parchment were in use.[3]   It is to be concluded that the earliest Hebrew scribes employed papyrus or parchment.   The Hebrew words for 'write,' however, do not afford any positive evidence.[4]

2. The Zenjirli inscriptions represent an intermediate period between Phoenician-Aramaic and Arabic-Aramaic. These north Syrian inscriptions, viii–vii centuries B.C., exhibit many likenesses to Phoenician, Moabite and other Canaanite dialects.   At the same time they show some of the outstand-

---

[1] *E.g.* 2 S. 1[18], 1 K. 11[41], 1 Ch. 29[29], 2 Ch. 9[29] 12[15] 13[22].

[2] The six titles are: ספר מלכי (2 Ch. 16[11]); ספר המלכים ליהודה וישראל (20[34]); ספר מלכי ישראל (27[7] *et al.*); ספר מלכי ישראל ויהודה (25[26] *et al.*); יהודה וישראל (33[18]); מדרש ספר המלכים (24[27]).   When the records were collected into one book, probably with editorial notes, the whole was appropriately referred to as a *Midrash (commentary) of the Book of the Kings.*

[3] Even the letter from the King of Assyria, which we should expect to be on a clay tablet, was evidently written on some flexible material ויפרשהו חזקיהו לפני יהוה (2 K. 19[14]=Is. 37[14]).

[4] In Job 19[20] the two verbs are used—כתב, *to write*; חקק, *to engrave.* The latter is found in Aram. inscrip. חתק עליה, 'Thou shalt inscribe concerning him' (Zenjirli: *Hadad*, l. 34).   This suggests Phoen. influence, and shows affinity to the older Canaanite language.

ing characteristics of Aramaic. This indicates that during
the period named, the script and language were passing
through a transition from the pre-exilic to the post-exilic
type. As a simple illustration the oldest Zenjirli inscription
gives אנך,[1] the Phoenician and Moabite form of the pronoun;
a later inscription gives אנה,[2] the form approximating the
later Aramaic. In general the inscriptions at Nêrab very
well represent the script of this period. They are rather less
archaic than Zenjirli, and rather more archaic than the Têma
inscriptions.[3]

About this period the great prophets of Judah and
Israel wrote their stirring messages. It is no part of this study
to discuss the composition of the books of the Old Testament.
Some portions are probably as early as the tenth century B.C.
It may be confidently affirmed that no part of the Old
Testament was written in the cuneiform character. The
evidence of the Tell el-Amarna tablets does not weaken this
conclusion. Some points should be clearly kept in mind:
(1) A knowledge of the language of the Tell el-Amarna
tablets was probably very restricted even in Babylonia. The
mass of people while speaking this language could hardly have
been able to read or write it. It is true that Canaanite officials
conducted correspondence with Egypt in the Babylonian script,
but that the Canaanites generally understood the cuneiform is
quite improbable. (2) Even if the Tell el-Amarna tablets
(1400 B.C.) represented the language of Canaan at any time
in any degree, they are far too early to represent the language
in which the most ancient portions of the Old Testament
could have been written. Probably the oldest fragments,
which were later worked up into the Jewish records, were not
earlier than the tenth century B.C. The Moabite Stone, as
stated already, goes back to the middle of the ninth century

---

[1] *Hadad*, early viii century B.C.

[2] *Bar-rekub*, *circa* 735 B.C. The form אנכי (Zenjirli: *Panammu*, l. 19,
745–727 B.C.) is really foreign to Aramaic, as also to Phoen.; it points to a
Hebrew source. In later Aram. Arabic and Ethiopic the form is אנא (Syr.
ܐܢܐ; B. Aram. Targ.).

[3] Two inscriptions were discovered at Nêrab near Aleppo in 1891. A
good text is given by Clermont-Ganneau in the *Journal officiel d. l. Repub.
franç*, March 1896.

B.C., and already shows some advancement in the Hebrew language, and in a script closely allied to Phoenician. (3) It is pretty clear that considerable portions of the Old Testament history and prophecy were produced about the time of Hezekiah. Now it appears that we have a specimen of the script dating from this period. We know that Hezekiah brought water to Jerusalem by a channel through a rock from the only natural source outside the city. The reservoir within the walls was probably the 'pool of Siloam.' This was *circa* 700 B.C., and the inscription cut in the rock of the tunnel belongs to this period. The language is Hebrew, and the character is similar to the Moabite, and therefore of the Phoenician type. In a script not unlike this we may believe Isaiah wrote his autobiography on parchment [1] in the form of a roll, which method is of ancient date.[2]

In the absence of a bit of autograph we can never know the exact appearance of an Old Testament original writing. The world would treasure a stele, or brick, or skin, on which were scratched a few lines by Isaiah. A passage (*e.g.* Is. 40[1-2]), in general appearance, would possibly look something like the following, which imitates, in the main, the Siloam script:

These lines are intended to illustrate the type of script, and not the system of orthography that would be employed in the age of the great prophets of Israel. Apart from the peculiar form of some letters,[3] the Siloam inscription indicates certain

---

[1] We have the authority of Herodotus that the skins of animals were the most ancient materials for writing books in western Asia, that this method, with writing itself, came to the Greeks from the Phoenicians. He says : καὶ τὰς βύβλους διφθέρας καλέουσι ἀπὸ τοῦ παλαιοῦ οἱ Ἴωνες, ὅτι κοτὲ ἐν σπάνι βύβλων ἐχρέωντο διφθέρῃσι αἰγέῃσί τε καὶ οἰέῃσι· ἔτι δὲ καὶ τὸ κατ᾽ ἐμὲ πολλοὶ τῶν βαρβάρων ἐς τοιαύτας διφθέρας γράφουσι (v. 58).

[2] This is inferred from מְגִלַּת סֵפֶר, Ps. 40[8], Jer. 36[14f.], Zech. 5[1-4], Ezek. 2[9-10]. The use of ink is suggested in Num. 5[23], and named in Jer. 36[18]; cf. 3 John [13].

[3] The letter ם is not found on the Siloam inscr., but is supplied in the passage above from the Moabite Stone.

idiomatic features,[1] which it would be necessary to observe in any attempt to reproduce a facsimile of the prophetic writings.

One or two other inscriptions of Canaanite origin may be mentioned. The so-called ' Calendar ' inscription from Tel ej-Jezer, the site of ancient Gezer, is written in old Hebrew, a type of Moabite, and resembles the script of the Moabite Stone, and the Phoenician inscriptions. The ' Calendar ' cannot be exactly dated, but may be placed between the viii–vi cent. B.C.[2] Another interesting inscription is found on a seal, which was discovered at Tell el-Mutesellīm, the ancient Megiddo. It is written in old Hebrew, and indicates clearly the script commonly employed in the viii cent. B.C. The ' Jeroboam ' mentioned on this seal was probably Jeroboam II., king of Israel, *circa* 783–743 B.C.[3]

A thorough examination of the inscriptions on seals and pottery would throw some light on the linguistic problem. At present, however, this phase of the subject is very incomplete and uncertain. The Hebrew inscriptions on jug-handles, *e.g.*, give no definite knowledge beyond the mere form of certain letters. The terms Ḥebron, Ziph, Socoh, Mamsheth, are perhaps geographical and not personal names. The script is early Phoenician.[4] The jar-handles found at Jericho are

[1] Among these may be noted : (*a*) the vowel-letters were not written *within* the word ; (*b*) the final vowels were represented by consonants ; (*c*) the suffix of the 3 mas. sing. was ו, instead of the older ה ; (*d*) the *cholem* when representing a diphthong was written in full, otherwise it was written defectively ; (*e*) the words were separated by dots (so Moab. St. ; CIS i. 11 ; some Zenjirli inscrip.) ; it is doubtful if these would appear in a hand-written document.

[2] The stone measures 4·25 × 2·75 inches ; the inscrip. occupies 8 lines. Cf. Macalister, *The Excav. of Gezer*, ii.

[3] This representation of the seal is reproduced from Handcock, *The Archæology of the Holy Land*, by kind permission of Messrs. T. Fisher Unwin Ltd.

The words are : ﬡﬡﬡﬡﬡﬡﬡﬡﬡﬡﬡﬡﬡﬡﬡ=לשמע עבר ירבעם, ' To Shama, servant of Jeroboam.' *Vide* Steuernager and Schumacher, *Tell el-Mutesellim*, pp. 99–100.

[4] *Vide* Macalister, *Gezer*, ii. 210 ; *Pales. Expl. Fund Q. S.*, 1905, pp. 243, 328 ; Driver, *Schweich Lectures*, 1908, p. 77.

frequently stamped with Hebrew or Aramaic characters.[1] Some
of the earliest are written in ligature and probably belong to
the vii cent. B.C.   The later specimens with Aramaic characters
are suggestive in several ways : (a) They probably date from the
v cent. B.C., and indicate a type of script then in common
use.   (b) The script resembles that found on the Elephantine
papyri, and suggests some connexion between Palestine and the
Jewish colony at Yeb.   (c) Some of these jar-handles or seals
have the name Yah, and others Yahu ; these are, of course,
abbreviations of Yahveh.   Perhaps יהו was the true form.[2]

3. The script of the middle period, v–iv centuries B.C.,
shows clearly the transition towards the later type of Aramaic
in the forms of several letters.   A comparison of the Nêrab
inscriptions with the Egyptian papyri will at once reveal the
change of several letter-forms.[3]   The script of this period
was very widely used in north Syria, Arabia and Egypt.   It
must be presumed that the Jewish literature, such as Ezra,
Nehemiah, Esther, Chronicles, Ecclesiastes, was written in the
common script of the time.   It is possible to distinguish an
earlier and a later middle Aramaic, the former is seen in the
Têma inscriptions, north Arabia,[4] and the latter in the papyri
of upper Egypt.[5]   This seems to show that both Aramaeans
and Hebrews employed the same language, i.e., the Aramaean
colony in N. Arabia and the Jewish colony in S. Egypt.

An inscription of Sidon, which has been regarded ' as an
example of the style, as regards character and general appearance, in which the autographs of the Old Testament must

---

[1] Vide Sellin-Watzinger, Jericho, p. 149.

[2] The form in pap. is יהו, B 4, 6, 11, J 6 ; once יהה, E 14 ; this may indic.
some variation and uncert. in the pronun. of the Name.

[3] The letter-forms on the Carpentras stele (CIS ii. 141) are similar to
those found in the Egyptian papyri.

[4] For Têma script vide CIS ii. 113, 114 ; cf. Euting, Nab. Inschriften,
35. תּימָא in the OT. is a descendant of Ishmael (Gen. 25[15]=1 Ch. 1[30] ;
cf. Is. 21[14], Jer. 25[23]).   Anciently Têma (the modern Teyma in El-Hejaz,
N. Arabia) was a noted halting-place on the caravan route to Assyria, on
the one hand, and to Egypt on the other (cf. Job 6[19]).   Probably there was
a tribe of Temanites, to which there may be reference in the Nabataean
תימנא (CIS ii. 199 ; cf. Euting, loc. cit. 4).

[5] Vide Plates accompanying Assuan Papyri, ed. by Sayce and
Cowley.

have been written,'[1] does come near in place and time to the
production of some of the sacred Books. The inscription is
in Phoenician, as might be expected from the place of its
discovery; it must be assigned to *circa* 300 B.C. It is the
famous sarcophagus of 'Tabnith, priest of Ashtart,' which
bears two inscriptions, one hieroglyphic and the other alphabetic, the former Egyptian and the latter Phoenician. The
hieroglyphic inscription, which has no connexion with the
Phoenician, suggests that the אָרָן (coffin = mummy-case) was
originally for use in Egypt (for Penptaḥ, an officer), but was
surreptitiously taken from an Egyptian tomb to receive the
body of a Phoenician priest.[2] This inscription is certainly a
good illustration of what may be called the Palestinian script
at the beginning of the iv cent. B.C. We must not, however,
make this inscription a type of the script of the earliest or of
the latest autographs of the Old Testament writings. It
is at best a good specimen of iv cent. Sidonian engraved
writing.

But whether we take illustrations from the Phoenician or
from the Aramaic inscriptions, the general character of the
script is much the same, the latter perhaps showing a somewhat greater adaptability.[3]

The authors of the Old Testament, for the greater part,
wrote in the Hebrew language, but in what script? The
Jewish colonists in Egypt, v–iv cent. B.C., used Aramaic, and
this was probably the case with nearly all Jewish settlements.
Except in Phoenician centres it is probable that the script of
western Asia generally about this period was Aramaic. Later
attempts to write in old Hebrew were sporadic and exceptional.
It can hardly be asserted that the few Hebrew inscriptions
that have been discovered were all written in Phoenician
script. If some distinction is to be made, it may be said
in a general way that the Hebrew inscriptions before 500–

---

[1] Driver, *Notes on Heb. Text of Bks. of Samuel*, p. xxiii.

[2] Cf. ll. 1, 2, 3 : אנך תבנת כהן עשתרת . . . שכב בארן ז.

[3] The following is a specimen of Sidonian : ᚱᚱ ⁴⁰ ᚻᚱ ᚱᚱ ⁴ᚷ
ᚷᚱ �⁹ᚤᚢᚱ ᚱᚱᚱᚹᚩ ᚱ⁹ᚩᚻᛦ ᚧᚱᚱᚱ ⁴ᚷᛦ, 'Do not open
my over-lid, and do not disturb me, for that thing is an abomination to
Ashtart' (*Tabnith*, 5, 6).

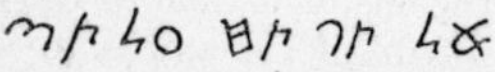

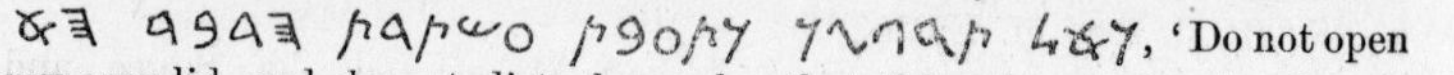

400 B.C. were written in a script more akin to the Phoenician, and the Hebrew inscriptions after that period were written in a script more akin to the Aramaic. Among the earlier type we have the Moabite Stone and the Siloam inscription. These are Phoenician, not to be distinguished from old Hebrew.[1] The Hebrew inscription, the *Gezer Calendar*, is in the same script. It dates *circa* 600 B.C., and is considered the most ancient *Hebrew* inscription yet available for comparison.[2] The letters of this inscription, as a whole, belong to the archaic type. The later Hebrew inscriptions, such as the *Arak el Emir*, from the old province of the Ammonites, *circa* ii cent. B.C., and the *Bĕnē Ḥēzir*, on the Mount of Olives, *circa* i cent. B.C., belong to the Aramaic transition type of alphabet. The former of these consists of one word, some letters of which are similar to Egyptian Aramaic, and some are continued in Palmyrene.[3] The latter shows more advancement towards the final square type.

4. The intermediate period between the close of the third and the beginning of the first century B.C. provides considerable material in the Phoenician dialect. The inscriptions of this period include those of Piraeus, the Punic and the Neo-Punic. These inscriptions do not afford any light on the development of the letter-forms; they are often archaic, and sometimes suggest a reversion to type. This is easily explained by the isolated nature of the places where these inscriptions have been discovered. Colonies so far from the centre of Phoenician life as Malta and Tunis, might well perpetuate a rude and unprogressive alphabet. The inscriptions found at Malta represent the earlier Punic, and those found at Sardinia the Neo-Punic character. The inscriptions from Constantine (Cirta in Algeria) may be taken to represent the passage between the Punic and the Neo-Punic

---

[1] The former is usually described as ‘ Moabite,’ the latter as ‘Hebrew,’ but the script of both belongs to the series which we term ‘ Phoenician.’

[2] Some Ostraka, discovered 1910 near ancient Samaria, may be older, but the present writer is not aware of any published facsimiles. But probably the script will be found to be of the Samaritan type (cf. *Quarterly State. Pales. Expl. Fund*, 1911, p. 79 ff.

[3] The word is רזעיבוט = טוביה ; on the whole, the letters are more allied to the Aram. than to the Phoen. series.

writing.[1] In the Neo-Punic the same letter has often different forms, and the script is altogether uncertain and uncouth.

In the script of this period (300–10 B.C.) several Jewish books were written, some in the Aramaic language and others in Hebrew. The *Book of Tobit* (iii cent. B.C.) was almost certainly written in Aramaic. It is not clear whether *1 Maccabees* and *1 Esdras* (both ii cent. B.C.) were originally written in Aramaic or Hebrew. The *Book of Sirach* (ii cent. B.C.) was written in Hebrew as the Greek translator tells us. The *Book of Judith* (ii cent.) was perhaps composed in Hebrew. But it is most natural and most probable to conclude that the script in each case was allied to the Aramaic. The *Book of Daniel* (ii cent. B.C.) may have been written originally in Aramaic,[2] and afterwards partly translated into Hebrew to meet the tastes and satisfy the prejudices of the Jewish Apocalyptists. That the script was Aramaic need not be doubted. There is here a clue to the solution of the question raised. Books of a sacred character among the Jews were commonly written in the sacred language. Both Hebrew and Aramaic were familiar to the Jewish ecclesiastical and civil leaders. Books composed in the language of the former would be intelligible to the average reader by being written in the script of the latter.

5. The script of the MSS from which the LXX was made can only be conjectured from the character of the translation. Judging from this point of view it would appear that the script used by the translators was characterized by (*a*) a similarity of some letter-forms, which led to confusion in the translation ; (*b*) the *scriptio defectiva*, which resulted in

---

[1] *E.g.* of Malta script (CIS i. 132³): 𐤊𐤒 𐤊𐤔𐤅 𐤊𐤒 𐤔𐤀𐤒𐤔, 'The sanctuary of the house of Ashtart.'

Constantine (Costa, 8⁴): 𐤗𐤍𐤉𐤒𐤒 𐤗𐤋𐤐 𐤏𐤔𐤔 𐤉, 'Because he heard his voice (and) blessed him (?).'

Sardinia: Sulci (CIS i. 149³): ᛌ𐤕𐤒𐤒𐤊𐤋·𐤕𐤍·𐤍𐤒𐤉𐤗𐤊𐤔𐤕·𐤕𐤗𐤉𐤒𐤋 𐤋𐤗𐤊𐤋, 'To build this sanctuary to the ruling goddess.' Most scholars read this differently : 'To build . . . to the lady Elath.'

[2] The dialect of the *Bk. of Daniel* was west Aram., distinguished from east Aram., *inter alia*, by the form of the rel. and dem. pron., *i.e.* ד for ז.

variant numbers and tenses, and consequently led to wrong interpretations.   It is not likely that all LXX 'various readings' came into the first copies of the translation.   Doubtless new confusions were introduced and old ones corrected in the process of transcription.   No one script can be named which adequately accounts for all the peculiarities of the LXX, especially when it is remembered that the translation extended over a considerable period.   Driver suggests 'a type not greatly differing from that of Kefr-Bir'im.'   But he rather weakens this statement in a footnote, which reminds us that 'the Kefr-Bir'im alphabet is considerably later than the LXX.' [1]   In other words, the Kefr-Bir'im inscription is 500 years too late.   We should look for a type a little earlier than the LXX rather than later.   Perhaps we must think of some intermediate alphabet, some type of script transitional between the Egyptian Aramaic (*circa* iv cent. B.C.) and the Hebrew inscriptions of Palestine (*circa* end i cent. B.C.).   Generally the type required would be best described as a form of Phoenician, of which the *Bĕnē Ḥēzir* inscription is a later Hebrew imitation.   The Samaritan script had doubtless many likenesses to the common writing of the Jews in the centuries immediately preceding the Christian era.   But the general tendency was towards a more Aramaic type.   If a script may be named as possibly on the whole supplying the best specimen of the pre-LXX MSS, we venture to suggest the inscription of *Eshmun-'azar*, of Sidon, *circa* 275 B.C.[2]

No argument can be based on the form of the tetra-grammaton found in the fragments of Aquila's recension of

---

[1] *Notes on Heb. Text of Samuel* [2], p. lxiv.

[2] The following is an illustration of this script; it is scarcely to be distinguished from the script of the *Tabnith* inscription of the same place of a rather earlier date (*circa* 290 B.C.):

נגולת בל עתי בן מסך ימם אזרם יתם = , 'I have been despoiled before my time, the son of perplexed days, a premature orphan, the son of a widow, and I repose in this sarcophagus and in this tomb, in the burial-place which I built' (CIS i. 3[2-4]. The present writer is responsible for the above translation).

the LXX.[1] This form preserves a type of the old Hebrew alphabet long after that type had ceased to be used. It is not, however, to be concluded that the Hebrew MSS from which Aquila worked were written in the old Hebrew alphabet throughout. It is rather to be supposed that the Divine Name alone was transcribed in its ancient form, while the MSS generally were written in the modernized square character. One of the earliest inscriptions in the square character is that over the tomb of the Bĕnē Ḥēzir, already mentioned. It is interesting to point out, especially in view of the section on 'Nabataean,' that the script of this inscription closely resembles the Nabataean. In the Bĕnē Ḥēzir the lines are more direct and the ligatures less frequent. This suggests that the script of Judaea was rather more advanced than that of Arabia Petraea. Early in the ii cent. A.D. the square character, כְּתָב מְרֻבָּע, was common.

It might be thought that the Hebrew inscriptions on coins would afford some reliable information respecting the script of Palestine. But the peculiar circumstances of the origin of these coins render them of little use as an index to the general type of writing employed by city and rural populations. Coins with Hebrew inscriptions appear at two or three periods, when special efforts were made to reinstate the Jewish cult and the Hebrew language. The first period dates from the time of Simon Maccabaeus (141–135 B.C.), the second was the First Great Revolt against Rome (65–68 A.D.), and a third period was the Second Revolt under Simon Bar-Cochba (132–135 A.D.). The patriotic and religious sentiments of the Jews find some expression on these coins. The character of the writing varies so little during this time (more than a century and a half) that it gives no certain guidance in the matter of date. The fact that the old type of script was employed on these coins shows that it was still known and could be read in Palestine down to a late period. On the other hand, it is quite conceivable that people who were familiar with a few archaic forms on current coins,

---

[1] *Vide* ed. F. C. Burkitt, Cambridge, 1897. Aquila retains the form 𐤉𐤄𐤅𐤄, which is a corrupt imitation of old Heb. In Phoen. the *vav* and *yod* are usually 𐤅 and 𐤉.

would have no acquaintance with this type of script generally. That the older script was really superseded in Palestine and that the newer was in use and generally understood, is certainly to be inferred from the reference to the ἰῶτα (= יוד) in the Gospel (Mt. 5[18]).

6. The latest epoch in the history of the script, which comes within our period, is represented by the Nabataean and Palmyrene inscriptions, dating shortly before the Christian era, and go down as late as the third century A.D. The character of the writing shows that Nabataean was homogeneous from El-Ḥejra, north Arabia, the most southern point of the Nabataean kingdom, to the Sinaitic peninsula.[1] The Sinaitic inscriptions, though later than the north Arabian, are less cultivated. This is probably explained by the cosmopolitan character of the writers—chiefly merchantmen trading with India, Arabia, Syria and Egypt. That a few of these inscriptions are in Arabic, Greek and Latin, suggests the mixed character of the travellers, and the late date of some of them. Within this period a few Palestinian inscriptions are found in a dialect which is best described as Hebrew. Some of the letters nearly attain their final form, some keep to the Nabataean type, and one or two are peculiar. Ligatures are occasionally employed similar to those found in Palmyrene, and the *matres lectionis* are more consistently inserted.[2]

The Palmyrene inscriptions are generally too late for our period, but they are very valuable as indicating the script at the beginning of the Christian era. The writing shows some advancement on the earlier Nabataean, and is the most marked step towards the later ' square ' character. It is not surprising that in these Syrian inscriptions the diacritic point should first make its appearance to distinguish *Dālath* from *Rēsh*.[3] Perhaps the script of the Palmyrene *Tariff* inscription (137 A.D.) may be accepted as, on the whole, the best

[1] An examination of the original writing would reveal some differences of script between the Ḥejra and Sinaitic inscriptions in certain letter-forms. For the former *vide* CIS ii. 197 ff. ; for an account of the latter, *vide* Euting, *Sinaïtische Inschriften*, 1891.

[2] Illustrations of this script may be seen in Driver, *Samuel*[2], xx–xxiii.

[3] Strictly *Rēsh* is distinguished from *Dālath* (*i.e.* ܪ from ܕ), the latter not having the point. Distinction omitted Oxon. 1 (= Vog. 123[a]).

specimen of Aramaic writing during the period of the New
Testament compilation. If this *Tariff* at Palmyra was drawn
up by Roman officials who understood Greek, and the Greek
text of the *Tariff* supports this view,[1] and if for example,
the second Gospel was compiled in Greek at Rome by one who
understood Aramaic, we have a very interesting problem of the
relation of the two languages. The Aramaic known at Rome was
probably of the Palmyrene type, and if the second Gospel had
been written in Aramaic it would have been in a similar script.

7. To complete the illustrations and comparisons, a
reference to three inscriptions may here be made. (1) The
Běnē Ḥēzir, i cent. B.C., is written over the entrance to the
tomb of St. James on the Mount of Olives. The script is
Hebrew, but of a type considerably advanced towards the
square character.[2] This shows that at the very centre of
Palestinian Judaism the pressure of the newer Aramaic script
could not be resisted. (2) The *El-Ḥejra*, *circa* i cent. B.C.–250
A.D., is the name of a number of inscriptions found at El-Ḥejra,
north Arabia, and forming the most southern extremity of the
Nabataean kingdom. The dialect is Nabataean and the script
Aramaic.[3] This type of writing must have had wide use on
the great trade routes between Arabia and Egypt, passing
through a portion of Palestine and Syria. (3) The *Kefr-
Birʿim*, *circa* 300 A.D., is inscribed over the door of an old
synagogue at Kefr-Birʿim, a village in Galilee. The script is
more firm and finished than anything of an earlier date. It
may be said that the transition to the 'square' character is
practically attained in this inscription.[4]

---

[1] The very first phrase is a mixture of Greek and Aram. רגמא די בולא,
'Decree of the Council' ; Gk. δόγμα βουλῆς.

[2] Illus.: ‎וחקכן וחת אבגד.ל.ב.אער... כר (some letters in the
original are indistinct, but are here restored)=בני ... זה קבר והמשכב לאלעזר,
'This is the tomb and reclining place of Eleazar . . . sons of.' Notice
the ligatures towards the end ; this common in Palm.

[3] Illus. : ‎ = דנה
‎קברא די עבר כהלן אסיא בר ואלן לנפשה, 'This is the tomb which Kahlân the
physician, son of Va'lan, made for himself' (CIS ii. 206¹).

[4] Illus. : ‎=יהי שלום במקום ‎וחו
‎הזה ובכל מקומות ישראל, 'Let peace be in this place, and in all the places of
Israel' (cf. Chwolson, *Corp. Inscr. Heb.* 17).

One outstanding fact made clear by these illustrations and comparisons is the gradual process by which alphabetic writing in Palestine and adjoining provinces attained its final form.   The old idea, having its origin in Jewish sentiment, that the change of script was introduced at a certain period and by one man—Ezra—is quite inconsistent with the testimony of inscriptions and papyri.   Both Aramaic and Greek were earlier modified towards their final forms than Phoenician and Hebrew.   The old script was retained, without substantial change, much longer in Hebrew than in Aramaic, a fact due largely to the conservative spirit of Judaism.   The transformation, however, overtook Hebrew at last, which was forced to surrender to the growing influence of the Aramaic in Palestine and the Jewish settlements everywhere.

8. It is pretty certain that many Semitic inscriptions were written in Palestine about the Christian era.   The majority have disappeared, a few have been discovered, and others will yet come to light.   New discoveries will probably confirm the conclusion that these writings were in the dialect of the province in which they were made.   In the dark Jewish days immediately before and after the dawn of Christianity, the services of the synagogue were difficult to continue, and funds were not easily procured for the maintenance of the priests and the charities.   Appeals were made for gifts to the Holy Places.   These would be in the Aramaic dialect of the locality.   The mosaics, for example, of the Galilaean synagogues at Kefr Kenna (Cana) and Sefuriye (Sephoris), are in Galilaean Aramaic.[1]   It would be surprising if no similar inscriptions were found in Judaean.   It is interesting to add that quite recently a mosaic has been found at Ain Duk, near Jericho, written in characters of the square-cursive type and in the Judaean Aramaic.[2]   In this inscription the synagogue is called the 'Holy Place.'   This reminds us of Philo's statement that the Essenes called the synagogues

---

[1] For details, *vide* Lidzbarski, *Ephemeris für Semitische Epigraphik*, i.

[2] This mosaic was unearthed by a chance Turkish shell during the war. It was photographed and sent to the French *Academie des Inscriptions et Belles-Lettres*. It was examined and its inscription translated by the veteran Orientalist Clermont-Ganneau.

'Holy Places.'[1] Now, from other sources, we know that the Essenes dwelt in these regions round the Jordan and the Dead Sea. This sect does not appear to have exercised much influence after the Christian era. This, however, is not a very safe clue to the date of the mosaic. Even if the term 'Holy Place' can be traced to an Essene source, it may have survived through other Judaeo-Christian societies, such as the Nazarenes or Gibeonites. The date may be tentatively given as about the same as that of the *Kefr-Bir'im* inscription, that is, *circa* ii–iii cent. A.D.

[1] Cf. Philo, *Quod omnis probus liber sit*, § 12 (of the Essenes) : εἰς ἱεροὺς ἀφικνούμενοι τόπους οἳ καλοῦνται συναγωγαί.

VIII

ARAMAIC:

ALPHABET—PRONUNCIATION— VOCABULARY—ABBREVIATION

GENERAL STATEMENT

The subjects introduced in this section are very obscure, and nothing like certainty can be attained. The points emphasized have been carefully selected, and lines of investigation have been opened along, which better results may yet be found. To trace the evolution of the Semitic ALPHABET, and the production of varying scripts, has not only an antiquarian interest, but is of value in the attempt to exhibit the language of a people at a specific period. The suggested symbolic use of certain signs in early inscriptions is novel and tentative. The subject of the PRONUNCIATION of the Semitic dialects is usually regarded as hopeless, but a few clues exist and these are considered and illustrated in their proper place. The question of vocalization comes up again when the Targums are under discussion. The extent of the Semitic VOCABULARY cannot be fully ascertained, owing to the paucity of suitable data. But the discovery of inscriptions and papyri has greatly aided this research. A few pages are devoted to the subject of Semitic ABBREVIATIONS. That there was some system of shorthand writing is probable. But it is often difficult to decide whether the shortening of a word is due to deliberate abbreviation, or to a native and normal *scriptio defectiva.*

A.—ALPHABET

I

ITS ORIGIN

The Aramaic alphabet was not derived from Babylonia. Inscriptions in Semitic character on some Babylonian and Assyrian weights and contract tablets show that the alphabet was known in Babylonia. But as these inscriptions are in the Aramaic language, it is probable that the Semitic character was introduced into Babylonia by the Aramaeans. It can be shown with tolerable certainty that the inventors of the alphabet spoke a Semitic language, but whether Phoenician, Aramaic, or some other, cannot at present be settled.[1] The evidence available, however, points to the Aramaeans as the authors of the Semitic alphabet which rapidly took possession of the East, and of Egypt after the age of hieroglyphs. The age when the Aramaic script became general can be shown approximately from the inscriptions.

The two inscriptions—the Moabite Stone and that of Panammu, king of Yadi—are suggestive in this connexion. (1) Both can be dated with certainty; the former belongs to the early half of the ninth century B.C., and the latter to the beginning of the eighth century B.C. The style of the Moabite inscription suggests the existence of something like a historical literature, hence, by implication, the script was not at this period quite new. (2) They are in different dialects, or different forms of the same language. The Moabite inscription may be described as Hebrew, and the Yadi inscription as Aramaic, though of a peculiar type.[2] It may be added that the Siloam inscription (*circa* time of Isaiah), the oldest type of Israelitish writing, is in a character similar to the Moabite Stone.[3] The alphabet type in each case is that commonly known as 'old Phoenician.' The

---

[1] *Vide* Lidzbarski, *Handbuch der nordsemitischen Epigraphik.*
[2] *Vide* Müller, *Die altsemitischen Inschriften von Sendschirli.*
[3] *Vide* Driver, *Notes on the Heb. Text of the Bks. of Samuel.*

language of the Moabite Stone has features which are peculiar to Hebrew, and the vocabulary is almost identical. There are a few forms which point to Aramaic, and suggest that Aramaeans began to press on the Israelites in the region of Dibon and around the Arnon in Moab.[1] (3) They are widely separated geographically—the former is in Moab, on the site of the ancient Dibon, east of the Dead Sea, and the latter is in the extreme north of Syria. A similar language therefore was known over a wide area. It is reasonable to conclude that the regions lying between these points, including the whole of modern Palestine and Syria, were familiar with this common tongue. (4) The letter-forms in these inscriptions are practically identical, and for the present may be called 'Phoenician.' This identity of letter-shapes strongly suggests that the alphabet was comparatively new. Had the type of writing been ancient, it is almost certain that the characters locally would have diverged far more widely. There are several facts which point to the original likeness of Canaanitish and Aramaic : (a) These languages have the same modification of the Arabic alphabet. (b) The most ancient type of Aramaic is that which approaches the Canaanitish most nearly. (c) An Aramaic term occurs in one of the oldest Canaanite inscriptions (ראשת, CIS i. 5 ; the script of this inscr. resembles that of the Zenj. Aram.). (d) Aramaisms appear in some of the oldest Canaanite writings (יתנו, Judg. 5[11] ; תחלימני, Is. 38[16]). The data suggest that the two communities migrated at the same time, that they had a common linguistic stock, that they developed different types of script—Phoenician and Aramaic—and that afterwards they borrowed certain words from each other.

Reference has been made to the Phoenician and the Aramaic series of scripts. It is possible to mark a difference, but no series is quite consistent. If Samaritan be taken as preserving the main features of old Hebrew it will be found

---

[1] The Aramaeans were in early contact with different dialects, and this tended to add foreign elements to their language. In one direction were the Hittites, and in another the Mitanni, both powerful kingdoms with native and peculiar dialects. The Assyrians called the tribes East of the Euphrates *Amurru*, and those West *Aramu*, etc. Cf. Winckler, *Geschichte Israels*, 51–54.

that in some letters the Phoenician series agrees, and in some
letters the Aramaic series agrees. On the whole the Phoenician series was more archaic, and the Aramaic more inclined
to the cursive. The Phoenician series, from the Moabite Stone
(ix cent. B.C.) to the *Tabnith* sarcophagus (iii cent. B.C.),
reveals no essential transformations. The Aramaic series, from
the *Zenjirli-Hadad* (viii cent. B.C.) to the Palmyrene (i cent.
B.C., *sq.*), reveals a slight yet growing tendency to modification.
The final 'square' character was developed from the Aramaic
series.[1]

II

THE TYPE

Originally Hebrew was similar in letter-forms to Samaritan, and both resembled Phoenician. Thus it was the
Hebrews, and not the Samaritans, who changed their alphabetic
characters. The Samaritans retained the older Semitic forms,
while the Hebrews adopted the so-called 'Babylonian' type.
This change of handwriting began during the Exile, and was
encouraged after the return, perhaps by Ezra. That the
letters and general character of the Aramaic language entered
upon a period of change from the time of Ezra is proved by
all the literary remains. In the fifth century B.C., as shown
by the Egyptian Papyri, the writing had advanced from the
rectangular form on the stone inscriptions towards the later
square character. The tendency of the writing was decidedly
towards a more cursive or freehand, rather than the rigid
lapidary type. Curved lines already appear in these papyri,
which are absent from the older monuments. Distinctive

---

[1] The following selection of letters will illustrate :

Phoen.	Aram.	Mod. Square.
△	ד	ד
Ϥ	ז	ו
日	H	ח
Θ	y	y
ϯ	ת	ת

final letters had not yet found permanency.[1] The *matres
lectionis* are sometimes omitted in the papyri, as in the later
Targums. The insertion of the *matres lectionis* appears to
have been a matter of some indifference all through the history
of Aramaic literature. These papyri show that the distinction between ו and י was already clearly marked, and we cannot suppose that the distinction was afterwards obliterated.[2]

There is no reference to the form of the letters in any of
the ancient data. The passage in Ezekiel respecting the *Tav*
or *mark* does not help us to understand the form of this
letter, even if a letter be meant.[3] The verb תוה means *to
mark, write, sign,* and does not appear in inscriptions or
papyri. The phrase concerning David is doubtful: -ויתו על
דלתות, 'and he made marks on the doors.' The common
translation is 'scrabbled,' which is probably most appropriate
if the verb be retained.[4] The word is found as a noun in
Job, תוי, and means 'my (written) mark,' that is, 'my

---

[1] These seem first to become distinct in the Nabataean inscriptions,
1–100 A.D. Cf. Euting's *Table of Characters*, col. 5, at end of Nöldeke,
Syriac Grammar.

[2] Dalman (*Worte*, pp. 5–6) says that *vav* and *yod* were both represented
by a long perpendicular stroke, and that *yod* with its hook was really
longer than *vav*. This statement is disproved by the Tables of Euting
(*loc. cit.*). There is an interesting, though perplexing, reference to *yod* in
the Assuan Papyri (K. 4, 5. *Vide* Ed. note, p. 48). The text appears to
read: יוד שנית על ידה בימן שניתח מקרא ארמית, 'a *yod* I have tattooed on his
right hand, the writing being tattooed in Aramaic.' It is to be noticed:
(*a*) The Jewish writing in Egypt was alphabetic, not hieroglyphic; (*b*) it
was called 'Aramaic,' not לשן יהורית; (*c*) one letter was called 'yod.' We
may infer that at this early period the Aramaic alphabet already attained
the general characteristics with which we become acquainted later. That
yod was not always the smallest letter in the Aramaic dialects, nor always
the smallest in different scripts of the same dialect, is quite evident. Its
form in some of the Nabataean scripts (e.g. *El-Ḥejra*, CIS ii. 206) is written
in pleno and is unusual. It has two parts—its main down-stroke and its dis-
tinguishing head-stroke. The apex or crescent-like line formed two horns,
and (by the gradual crumpling up of the tail) finally became the characteristic expression of the letter (cf. illus. p. 236). Is there any connexion between the proverbial reference to the יוד and the קרן, and the original of this
one letter? Did the two κέρατα become the one ἰῶτα? Is this why Luke
(16[17]) mentions the κεραία only, and Matthew (5[18]) the ἰῶτα only (possibly)?
In the latter Gospel ἢ μία κεραία may be a later editor's harmonizing gloss.

[3] Ezek. 9[4]: והתוית תו על-מצחות האנשים, 'and thou shalt mark a mark (? cross)
upon the foreheads of the men.'

[4] 1 S. 21[14]: Many scholars prefer ויתף, 'and he drummed,' 'slammed.'

signature,' 'my attestation.'[1]   Jerome, referring to the passage
in Ezekiel, could scarcely have had any evidence for the
remark that the form of the *Tav* or *mark* was that of a cross.
Still it is interesting to note that the script presupposed in
Ezekiel's time was Phoenician (*ib.* old Hebrew), and that the
form of *Tav* was a cross.[2]

III

LETTERS AS SYMBOLS

The making of a X as a substitute for a name dates from
very early times.   At the Council of Chalcedon some of the
bishops, unable to write their names, put the sign of the Cross
on the decretal documents.   In the apocalyptic literature a
mark appears to represent a name, either on the hand or the
forehead.[3]   According to the Targum of Jonathan ben Uzziel,
the 'mark' given to Cain was from the great and sacred name,
probably one of the letters of the word יהוה.[4]   Some
Talmudists say that the sign was the letter *Tav* (old
Hebrew = X) marked on his forehead.   This is quite unlikely,
inasmuch as the original text should be rendered : 'The Lord
appointed to Cain a token.'   That is, Cain had some assurance
that he should not die by the hand of another.[5]   The use of
letters for names and numbers need not be considered here,
but would require discussion in any attempt to explain the
cryptic reference in the Apocalypse to τὸ ὄνομα του θηρίου ἢ
τὸν ἀριθμὸν τοῦ ὀνόματος αὐτοῦ.[6]

The symbolic and mystical use of letters is possibly

[1] Job 31[35] : הֶן־תָּוִי, 'Lo, I pledge myself,' or 'Behold, here is my bond.'

[2] The following variations are found : X (Moab. St., Siloam inscrip.) ;
† (CIS i. 5) ; ⳾ (CIS i. 166, *et al.*) ; Ͳ Τ (CIL viii. 793 ; CIS i. 149). In
some Aram. inscrip. the form is X (Zenjirli : *Nêrab*) ; this, too, is the form
on some Hasmonaean coins.

[3] Apoc. 13[16. 17] 20[4], cf. 14[1] 22[4].

[4] Gen. 4[15] : in early Heb. the characters would be ‎. That
initial *yod* could be written for the sacred name is probable. Is this the
explanation of the reference to *yod* in the *Assuan pap.* (K 4, 5) ?

[5] The Heb. is : וַיָּשֶׂם יְהוָה לְקַיִן אוֹת. So LXX : Καὶ ἔθετο . . . σημεῖον τῷ Κάϊν.

[6] Apoc. 13[17].   The use of letters to denote dates is found on some of the
earliest Phoen. inscrip. Various signs are used for numbers.

found in some inscriptions in Aramaic dating from the earliest Christian times. Attention has been called to the presence of a X at the beginning and end of a line of a Palmyrene votive inscription *circa* 135 A.D.[1] This is quite unique, and some scholars have seen in the use of the X a veiled symbol of the Christian community, by one who though still heathen was turning towards the new religion. It is suggestive that anciently the faithful were marked with a *Tau* (*i.e.* X, *vide supra*); with a deeper meaning the same sign became the mark of Christians. If there is here a hint of Him who is 'the Last,' it would not be surprising if there were also a hint of Him who is ' the First.' Is there such a hint?

In some Palmyrene inscriptions there is found a curious sign ☌, which seems to have no connexion with the text. It has generally been regarded as a punctuation mark, often as a full-stop. It is, however, sometimes found where we should not expect a full-stop.[2] It is found most frequently at the end of the line which gives the date of the inscription.[3] In some instances it is found at the end of lines referring to number and time.[4] But most suggestive of all it is found both at the beginning and end of a line, precisely as X is found in the inscription mentioned above.[5] Now just as X is the sign of *Tau* in old Hebrew, so ☌ is the sign of *Aleph* in some Aramaic-Nabataean inscriptions.[6] Is it possible to see in this sign in the Palmyrene inscriptions a veiled suggestion of one who heard of Him who is both *Aleph* and *Tau*, τὸ *A* καὶ τὸ *Ω* of the Apocalypse?

[1] Vog. 76[3]. This inscription is a curious mixture: it sounds Jewish; it is on a Palmyrene altar, and the cross suggests some Christian influence. The X, of course, may be mere ornamentation. Cf. **+ ΧΡΙΣ + ΤΟΣ ΝΙΚΑ +** , from the Hauran (Wadd. 2253).

[2] *E.g.* ☌ ק ה עמורין שתא ושריתהון
ותפלילהן
' Six pillars and their beams ☌ and their coverings ' (Vog. 8[4. 5]).

[3] *Vide* Vog. 3[6] 7[5] 17[6] 22[6] 73[5]; cf. Nöldeke, *Zeitschrift für Assyriologie*, 1894, pp. 264–267.

[4] *E.g.* Vog. 8[4] 93[4].

[5] Vog. 17[6]. The line is: ☌ /Ɣ⅃ƷƷƷ —⊃ Ɣ ☌, '566.' Here again the sign may be merely a bit of literary embellishment.

[6] This is the form of Aleph found on some of the *El-Ḥejra*, *Petra*, *Ḥauran* and *Sinaitic* inscriptions.

IV

NABATAEAN 'CURSIVE' STYLE

The type of writing found in the earliest Hebrew and Targum MSS can aid us but little in our research. In the first century A.D. the Scriptures existed for the Jews in a character which they call 'Assyrian' or 'square' writing.[1] We have no sufficient data for proving definitely what this 'Assyrian' writing was like at the end of the first century B.C. The Aramaic square character seems to have come into use somewhat later. It was apparently employed about the beginning of the second century A.D. in MSS of the Old Testament. The old Hebrew character was used as late as the Hasmonaean dynasty, as the inscriptions on coins prove.[2] An Aramaic panel found in Egypt, with the old type of writing, dates from the second century A.D.[3] The literature which covers the period we are considering is the Aramaic of the Nabataean inscriptions (down to 100 A.D.), the Palmyrene inscriptions (down to 300 A.D.), and the Sinaitic inscriptions (first and second centuries A.D.). Probably the best general type of writing to represent the Aramaic of 100 B.C.–100 A.D. is that which Euting calls 'nabatäisch,' compared with the kindred 'palmÿren.'[4] In support of this statement we have the chronological, historical and geographical positions and relations of the Nabataeans, and the further important fact that Nabataean and Palmyrene agree in most essential features with the Aramaic of Ezra and Daniel. A careful examination of the Tables of the Syriac written characters by Euting leads to the conclusion that the Aramaic alphabet at the beginning of the first century A.D. was passing through a transition period. That is, the type was slightly changing from the old Hebrew to the later Palmyrene.[5] Hence several

---

[1] כְּתָב מְרֻבָּע or כְּתָב אַשּׁוּרִי. 'Assyrian' probably simply means that this type was used by the N.E. Syrians.

[2] On coins struck as late as 66–70 and 132–135 A.D.

[3] This panel is in the collection of Theodor Graf, Vienna. There are only six letters on it.

[4] For an account of Nabataean inscriptions and coins, *vide* Euting, *Nab. Inschr. aus Arabien*; Nöldeke, *Sem. Sprachen*; De Luynes, *Rev. Numism.*

[5] Cf. Euting in Chwolson's *Corpus Inscr. Heb.*

letters were written in somewhat different ways. The
Nabataean appears on the whole the most 'cursive' style,
and this may suggest the type employed in ordinary
correspondence.[1]

B.—PRONUNCIATION

I

INITIAL DIFFICULTY

There is no certainty respecting the pronunciation of the
alphabet. This is true of both the consonant and vowel
sounds. The pronunciation of Aramaic letters preserved in
Greek translations does not always represent the vocalization
in Palestine in the first century A.D. There is a rather
remarkable passage in the *Gospel of Thomas* about Jesus
entering the school of Zacchaeus: καθίσαντος δὲ αὐτὸς τοῦ
διδάξαι γράμματα τῷ Ἰησοῦ, ἤρξατο τὸ πρῶτος στοιχεῖον τὸ
Ἀλεθ· ὁ δὲ Ἰησοῦς λέγει τὸ δεύτερον στοιχεῖον, μπεθ, γκιμελ.
καὶ εἶπεν αὐτῷ πάντα τὰ στοιχεῖα ἕως τέλους.[2] The forms
μπέθ and γκίμελ represent בית and גימל. It would thus appear
that Jesus gave a pronunciation different from that which was
commonly taught in the later schools. The Greek forms
suggest that the pronunciation of ב partook of the sound of
two of its interchangeable labials, מ and פ, and that ג combined the sound of one of its interchangeable letters, ח.[3] The
permutation of letters was much commoner among Orientals
than Westerns.

Unfortunately the shorter (and apparently imperfect)
Syriac version of the *Gospel of Thomas* does not help us. It
gives a corresponding passage, but the orthography of the

---

[1] Some of the Nabataean letters might easily develop into the now
common Heb. square character, or into the Nestorian Syriac. *E.g.* ٦ = ר
or ٦ ; ١ = ו or ١ ; ٧ = ט or ٤ ; ٦ = ל or ٨ ; ٥ = פ or ٤ ; ٦ = ר or ٠ ;
٦ = ח or ٨ .

[2] *Codex Apocryphus, Novi Testamenti*, collectus, etc. A. Fabricio,
Hamburgi, 1719-1743. *Evang. Infantiae*, vi.

[3] For example cf. בריא and מריא (Judg. 3[17] and Ezek. 39[18]); ברול and פרול
(Gen. 4[22], Heb. and Targ.). Also גבל and חבל (Ex. 28[22] and Dan. 6[23]).

letters named is that which became usual.[1] A comparison of
the vocalized Syriac alphabet and the Hebrew Massoretic
alphabet, will suggest certain modifications of the vowel
sounds.[2] It is to be presumed that the Aramaic of Palestine
was nearer in sound to the early Syriac than to the pointed
Hebrew. It is probable that the Arabic preserves the sound
of some letters better than either Hebrew or Syriac. The
original pronunciation of ה is hopelessly lost; it probably
represents a sound which we have no means of expressing.
No wonder it became otiose in some words which required it
etymologically. Anciently this letter had variant pronunciations, as is evident from the Arabic use of two forms.[3] At
first it was the harshest of the gutturals, but gradually
assumed a softer sound, until it was little more than a
'breathing,' and finally negligible in pronunciation.[4] The
letter ף had two sounds in Hebrew, and apparently in Syriac,
corresponding to π and φ, but in Arabic ف consistently
represents f (= φ). The Aramaic was perhaps similar to the
Arabic.[5]

[1] The passage is as follows: ܗ‍ܘܳܐ ... , 'And the Scribe said to Him, Say Aleph, and Jesus
said it; and again the Scribe desired that He should say Beth; but Jesus
said to him, Tell Me first what is Aleph, and then I will tell thee about
Beth.'

[2] *Vide* Nöldeke, *Syr. Gram.*, pp. 3–4. It may be remarked here that
the Syriac vowel *Zekofo* represents *omicron*, but is usually transliterated by
alpha, *e.g.* ܐܳܕܳܡ, 'Αδάμ; ܡܳܪܬܳܐ, Μάρθα; ܡܳܡܘܢܳܐ, Μαμωνᾶς; ܡܳܪܰܢ,
Μαρὰν ἀθά. This suggests that the better pronunciation of ܦܫܺܝܛܬܳܐ
is *Peshitta* (not *Peshitto*), as by the E. Syrians; cf. Nestle, *Syr. Gram.*,
pp. 9–10.

[3] Thus : ܚ =hh, and ܟ̇ =kh.

[4] The transliteration of חקלדמא, 'Ακελδαμά (Acts 1[19]), is suggestive, the
Aram. ה is represented by the *spiritus asper*; cf. חזקיה, 'Εζεχίας, ה is represented by the *spiritus lenis*.

[5] The word 'Εφφαθά (Mk. 7[34]) will illustrate. The regular Aram. form
would be אֶתְפְּתַח (Ithpa. imper.). The ת becomes absorbed in ף, hence אֶפְּתַח,
but ף is sounded by φ, and ה is otiose. Moreover, movable *sheva* has the
sound of *a*, as in גַּבְּתָא, Γαβαθᾶ or Γαββαθᾶ; שְׁבַקְתַּנִי, Σαβαχθανί. Hence 'Εφφαθά
seems to be the correct pronunciation of אֶ(ת)פְּתַ(ח).

II

COMPARISON WITH OTHER LANGUAGES

Words whose pronunciation is suggested by their form in other languages. For illustration a selection of words from the Nabataean and Palmyrene inscriptions will be interesting. The Greek form of many of the proper names is known. Here allowance must be made for the characteristic Greek terminations.[1] The Syriac form of other words is known, the only difference often being the frequent addition of the Syriac *Alef status emphaticus*.[2] Arabic sometimes lends its aid by supplying vocalized equivalent terms.[3]

The inscriptions are particularly interesting in this connexion, inasmuch as many of the Palmyrene are bilingual, that is, the Palmyrene inscriptions are often followed by a Greek version. The Greek does not always represent the exact pronunciation of the transliterated words, but affords a clue to the original vocalization. These bilingual writings show that the vowel-letters had slightly different sounds in different positions and in different words, and no consistent rule can be adequately fixed.[4]

---

[1] For instance, א=as, ης, ος, and sometimes ιος, ις ; ו=ος ; ן=ην, etc. Thus: בגרת, N 8[1], cf. βάγρατος ; בסמא, N 4[1], cf. βάσις ; גריא, P 32[6], cf. γαδιας ; דוקנרא, P 24[2], cf. δουκη-νάριος ; ימלכו, P 36[a2], cf. ιαμλιχος ; מלכיון, N 5[1], cf. μαλχίων ; נקטיס, N 66, cf. Νικητής ; שלימת, N 12[4], cf. σελεμαθη ; שעירו, N 12[1], cf. σοαιδος.

[2] For example : אורשלם, CIS 320 B, cf. ܐܘܪܫܠܡ ; בעלשמן, P 16[6], cf. ܒܥܠܫܡܝܢ ; הינמונא, P 15[4], cf. ܗܓܡܘܢܐ ; סלוקוס, P 17[2], cf. ܣܠܘܩܘܣ ; צפרא, P 11[2], cf. ܨܦܪܐ ; קנטרינא, N 20[1], cf. ܩܢܛܪܝܢܐ.

[3] Thus : גלהמו, N 7[3], cf. جلهمة ; חקטין, N 59, cf. حقطان ; בהילן, N 9[1], cf. ; תימאלהי, N 7[1], cf. فخذ ; פחד, P 32[3], cf. ; עבד חרתת, פחד ; عبد حارثة ; עברחרתת, N 5[5], cf. ; تيمالله.

[4] Final א and ו in Palm. are differently represented in Gk., but probably were both pronounced as η : בולא=בּוּלֵא, βουλή (Vogüé, *Syr. Centr.* 1), cf. ירחבולא='Ιαριβωλή (Vog. *ib.* 2) ; קמרי=קטרי (Constantine : Afr. 1), cf. the two forms וברא (Vog. *ib.* 28, 29) and ובדי (Euting, *Sin. Inschr.* 4) ; מראא

III

ARAMAIC FORMS IN THE GREEK GOSPELS

The Greek Gospels supply a number of words and phrases which suggest the pronunciation of their Aramaic originals. The Syriac will aid us in this study. At the beginning of the Christian era Syriac had passed far through a transition in the matter of its final vowels. It had become usual to omit in pronunciation the final vowel in very common words. This was largely the result of the slurring over of words and their consequent abbreviation by the mass of people in ordinary conversation. The tendency in this direction was never so pronounced in Arabic.[1] It is not correct to speak of Aramaic as a corruption of Hebrew, but it is correct to say that Aramaic pronunciation degenerated from the first century B.C., a fact particularly apparent in the vulgarizing of vowel-sounds. These sounds, however, were retained to a later period in the more refined speech. The Kershuni, whose language was a mixture of Syriac and Arabic, and who retained the Syriac books in their religious services, were known to sound these vowels in their more solemn and deliberate utterances.[2] It is not always observed that ו and י

(Chăgigā, 77[d]) and מרחי (Palm. Vog., *ib.* 13; Nab. CIS ii. 158); שבא (Vog. *ib.* 3) and שבי (CIS ii. 215). Probably the *a*-sound was retained in the *st. emp.*, *e.g.* מלכא (CIS ii. 199). Final ו is usually pronounced as *u*; מלכו (CIS ii. 218), *Mâliku*, cf. the form Μαλίχας (Müller, *Geogr. Gr. Min.* i. 272); cf. עבידו (CIS ii. 221), Ὀβαιδος, and חביבו (*ib.*), Ἀβειβος. The letter ע is generally silent, *i.e.* absorbed in the previous vowel. In עתרעתה, the medial ע = γ, Ἀτεργάτις (Vog. *ib.* 3), but this is quite exceptional.

[1] The final *yud* and *vav* in verbs were often not sounded in Syriac, *e.g.* ܐܡܿܪ = *emar*; ܐܡܿܪܘ = *emar*. No doubt the original pronunciation was *emari* and *emaru*. The final vowel sounds are more consistently retained in Arabic, as اِبنَتِي = *ibnati*; دَلوُ = *dalwo*. So, too, the letters which became marked with the *linea occultans* were originally sounded, thus ܐܢܫ = *nosh* (orig. אֱנָשׁ); ܐܢܬ = *at* (orig. אַנְתְּ); ܒܬ = *bath* (orig. ܒܬ, the fem. of ܒ; cf. Heb. בַּת, originally the form בִּנְתְּ, the fem. of בֵּן).

[2] 'Only when they were posting through, then, I confess, for celerity sake, they leave out many letters' (Christianus Ravius, *Orient. Gram.*, p.

should retain their vowel-sound, especially at the end of syllables, and not be pronounced as *v* or *f*, as the former often is. In Syriac ܓܰܠܝܰܐ is *galliu* (not *galliv*); ܣܰܘܕܝ is *saudi* (not *savdi*). So in Hebrew אָבִיוּ is properly *abiu* (not *abiv*); מַלְכִּיוּ, *malkiu* (not *malkiv*).[1] Aramaic was originally the same, שָׁרִיוּ, *shariu* (not *shariv*), זִיוּ; *ziu* (not *ziv*).[2]

Among the transliterated Aramaic terms in the Greek Testament, bearing on the original pronunciation, the following may be mentioned:

Ταλιθά, κούμ (or κούμι). The correct grammatical form is κούμι (*i.e.* קוּמִי, imper. 2 sing. fem.). But, as stated above, the final vowel in such cases had become otiose, and the vernacular pronunciation would be κούμ (קוּם, in form imper. 2 sing. mas.). That the original written form was טליתא קומי is supported by the Syriac ܛܠܝܬܐ ܩܘܡܝ, which vocalizing suggests that the final *yud* was not sounded. The Greek variants may have arisen in the following way. The reading κούμ was based on MSS which preserved the native pronunciation, and the reading κούμι was based on MSS which followed the Aramaic spelling.[3] In the case of Ῥαββί and Ῥαββουνί the Greek MSS perhaps preserve both the Aramaic spelling and pronunciation, inasmuch as terms of personal address were not so likely to lose their final vowels in pronunciation.[4]

Ἀββᾶ is another term to be noted in this connexion. This form exactly represents the Aramaic אבא, and the Syriac

134). The language of these people, which is really Arabic in Syriac characters, is still called in Arabic كرشوني, 'Karshuni' (cf. Duval, *Traité de Gram. Syr.* 13).

[1] *Vide* Nöldeke, *Syr. Gram.*, p. 27.

[2] Cf. רעו (Gen. 11[19], Heb. and Onk.) with Gk. form Ῥαγαῦ; אביהוא (Ex. 6[23], Heb. and Onk.), אביהור (1 Ch. 8[3]) with Gk. form Ἀβιούδ. Probably simple words like גו and רו (Dan. 2[21] 3[25]) were originally pronounced *gau* and *reu*.

[3] The authorities are: for κούμ א BCLMN Σ, *et al.*; for κούμι, ΑΔΔΠΦ, *et al.*

[4] It is not certain whether *yod* in this word is simply paragogic or the personal suffix. The Greek equivalent διδάσκαλε would suggest the former; usage, the latter; cf. מרי (John 20[28]).

וְכֹל, and no doubt retains the original pronunciation. The usual absolute form of the word in Aramaic literature was the *status emphaticus*. This appears from the inscriptions and the Targums, but no instance of the absolute form of the word is found in Biblical Aramaic or in Aramaic papyri.[1] From other Jewish writings we learn that אבא was some-times used in the sense of אבי. This probably arose from the indistinct vocalization of the final vowels. There seems to have been considerable laxity in the use of the true suffixes of this term.[2] The real distinctions were made plain enough by the circumstances, or by the gesture of the speaker. It is probable that אבא and אבי were pronounced very much alike.[3]

Βοανηργές is perhaps a form which preserves the ver-nacular pronunciation. This word was supposed to mean υἱοὶ βροντῆς. The latter part of the word might stand for רֹגֶז (cf. Targ. Mic. 5[15]); but this term almost invariably (Job 37[2], a possible exception) signifies *agitation, raging*, in the sense of anger. The word might even arise from רֶשֶׁף, which is a Jewish-Aramaic word meaning *flame, lightning*, and so become associated with thunder; but this cannot be pressed.[4]

---

[1] *Vide* P 12[3]; the constr. is אב regularly, N 27[6]; Onk. Gen. 17[4]; *saepe*. In Bibl. Aram. אב is only found with suffixes. In Aram. papyri are found אבוה, J 7; אבוכם, H 6.

[2] We find אבא for אבי, Gen. 19[34] Onk., *Kethuboth*, ii. 6, *Nedarim*, ii. 1 (cf. אחא for אחי, Jer. Targ. Gen. 38[26]); אבא for אבונא, *Baba bathra*, ix. 3; *Shebuoth*, vii. 7.

[3] Probably Ἀββᾶ, ὁ πατήρ (Mk. 14[36]) represents אבא אבי (cf. Syr. ܘܟܠ ܐܒܐ), but the distinction was lost in pronunciation.

[4] In Job 5[7] בְּנֵי רֶשֶׁף is rendered 'sparks' (RV. marg. 'sons of flame'). That a word meaning 'lightning' can come to be used in the sense of 'thunder' is indicated by the word בָּרָק, Syr. ܒܪܩܐ, 'lightning' (Dan. 10[6]). We find the compound בְּנֵי־בָרָק (Jos. 19[45]), lit. 'sons of lightning,' but perhaps = 'sons of thunder,' *i.e.* of the storm-god Rimmon (cf. Assyr. *Ramman-birḳu*), Barak, called 'thunderbolt' (Cic. *Pro Balbo*, xv.; cf. Nepos, *Hamilcar*, i. 1). The Arabic رجس is the same in meaning as the Syr. رج, *to sound aloud*, hence *to thunder*. This word is well known in the Talmud, both as verb רְנַשׁ, *to shout tumultuously*, and as substantive רִגְשָׁא, *Geräusch, noise, storm*. Cf. CIS i. 10[4]; Zenj. *Hadad*, l. 2.

It is tempting to look with Jerome to רֶעַם, but it is not easy to obtain *reges* or *erges* from this term. On the whole, it is best to turn to רָעַשׁ, the root idea of which is *to make a vehement noise* (cf. Ps. 2[1]), though found with a somewhat different meaning in *Aphel* (Dan. 6[7]).

The former part of the word is still more difficult to explain. The quasi-diphthong *oa* constitutes the problem. Dalman says: 'If Mark really wrote *oa*, his unfamiliarity with Aramaic was the cause.' The suggestion here made is that if Mark really wrote *oa*, vernacular pronunciation was the cause. It is probable that the short vowel sound, *sheva*, in many words was sounded not as *o* or *a*, but as an inexact blending or slurring of the two letters. The sound consequently could best be represented by the juxtaposition of the two vowels. For the variants in the *sheva* sound, compare רְחֹבֹת, LXX = ʻΡοωβώθ, i.e. *sheva* = *o* (Gen. 10[11]) ; רְחַבְיָה, LXX = ʻΡαβία, i.e. *sheva* = *a* (1 Ch. 23[17]). That *sheva* in בְּנֵי had a broad *a*-sound is suggested by the LXX transliteration, בְּנֵי־בְרַק, Βαναιβακάτ ; cf. בְּנֵי־יַעֲקֹן, Βαναία. For the two sounds of final *yod*, *oui* and *i* or *ai*, in בני, compare Βανουί (Ezra 2[10]), Βανί (Neh. 3[17]), Βαναίας (Neh. 8[7]).[1]

IV

WORDS IN CONTEMPORARY AUTHORS

Many Semitic words are Graecized in the contemporary authors, especially in the works of Josephus. A study of these would indicate in many instances the pronunciation of the original term, at least the Greek forms would suggest the vocalization of the Hebrew or Aramaic. The words in the list below, selected to show the changes in the Greek to represent the same vowel sounds in the original, are for the greater part found in the Greek New Testament and in

---

[1] For other confusions in Gk. due to the uncertain sounds of the Semitic vowels, *vide* תֶּלֶם, found in LXX as Θελαμί (Num. 13[22]), Θολαμί (Jos. 15[14]), Θολμί (Judg. 1[10]), Θολμαί (1 Ch. 3[2]). Josephus has Θολομαῖος (*Ant.* xx. i. 1). The Codices AB have the additional forms Θαλμαί, Θολαμαί, Θολμεί, and most suggestive for our purpose Θοαλμεί. Cf. the rather strange LXX transliteration of רְחַבְעָם, ʻΡοβοάμ.

Josephus.[1] The forms in the two authorities sometimes differ, but on the whole the original pronunciation suggested is the same. Allowance must always be made for the characteristic Greek terminations.

V

GENERAL INFERENCES

The foregoing illustrations will reveal a tendency in the history of language, a tendency due to common usage, by which the stronger and harsher sounds become softened in pronunciation. This is particularly the case in the Semitic languages in the vocalization of the gutturals ה and ע, which in Aramaic and later Hebrew are frequently supplanted by א.[2] Even the א ceased to have any distinct sound in the later pronunciation of the language, and several Hebrew words beginning with א were written in Aramaic without this letter. But what by aphaeresis was thus lost at the beginning of a word, was sometimes by euphony added at the end.[3] On the other hand, in some cases a prefixed א is found in words beginning with two consonants, separated only by vocal sheva.[4] This prosthetic א is for the purpose of making the pronunciation easier.

[1] בת צידא, Βηθσαϊδά ; cf. Joseph. *Ant.* 18. 2. 1 ; *B.J.* 2. 9. 1.
מתושלח, Μαθουσάλα, LXX. *ib.*
שמרין, Σαμάρεια ; cf. Joseph. *Ant.* 8. 12. 5, 13. 2. 3.
גרגשי, Γεργεσηνός ; cf. Joseph. *Ant.* 1. 6. 2 ; Origen, *Opp.* iv. p. 140.
קדרין, Κεδρών ; cf. Joseph. *Ant.* 8. 1. 5, Κεδρῶν ; *B.J.* 5. 4. 2.
פסחא, Πάσχα ; cf. Joseph. *Ant.* 5. 1. 4, Φάσκα ; *B.J.* 2. 1. 3.
צדיק, צדיקא, צדוקא, Σαδδουκαῖος ; cf. Joseph. *Ant.* 13. 5. 9 ; *Erubin,* 18ᶜ.
מן הוא, Μάννα (מָנָא, Targ. Eccl. 12¹¹) ; cf. Joseph. *Ant.* 5. 1. 4, ἡ μάννα.
שבתא, Σάββατα ; cf. Joseph. *Ant.* 12. 6. 2 ; *B.J.* 2. 17. 10 ; *de Vit.* 32 ;
1 Mac. 2³⁴.
יעקב, Ἰακώβ ; cf. Joseph. *Ant.* 1. 18. 1, Ἰάκωβος.
סודרא, Σουδάριον ; cf. Lat. *sudrium* ; *vide* Pollux, *On.* 7. 71.
[2] Cf. Heb. Hithpael : התקטל, and Aram. Ittaphal : אתקטל.
[3] *E.g.* Heb. אחר ; Aram. חר or חרא.
[4] Thus : Heb. סְנֶה, *bush,* Aram. אַסְנָא (Onk. Ex. 3². ³, Dt. 33¹⁶) ; Heb. זְרוֹעַ, and later אֶזְרוֹעַ (cf. *e.g.* Ex. 6⁶ and Job 31²²). Cf. אַרְפּוּבָא (Dan. 5⁶), and בְּרַךְ (by transposition, Dan. 6¹¹). In Targ. the two forms are found רְכוּבָא and אַרְכּוּבְתָא (Targ. Jerus.). The latter is the same as Syr. (Ch. Pales.) ܪܟܘܒܬܐ (*vide* Schwally, *Idioticon d. Chris. Pales.,* p. 89).

In general it must be concluded that the accentuation of the Palestinian Aramaic was the same as the Biblical Aramaic, the Nabataean, the Syriac, and as understood by the first Targumists. The same has been assumed for the Talmudic Aramaic. There is no necessity whatever for seeking any other accentuation for the Palestinian Aramaic. There is a strong presumption that it was essentially the same as the Aramaic of Babylonia, whence it was in some sense derived.[1] At any rate, there are no possible data available for introducing and establishing a new set of accentual principles. No doubt with the progress of the language westward there was a shifting of the accent, which however, did not materially change the vocalization.

C.—VOCABULARY

I

GENERAL SCOPE

In the absence of a full literature dating from the period under discussion it is impossible to fix the extent of the vocabulary. There may have been provincialisms which have left no trace in literature, but which constituted a considerable element in the vernacular of the people, especially of the peasantry. The question of dialect enters into the problem, inasmuch as the Aramaic of northern Palestine differed in several respects from the speech of Judaea. Moreover, some words and phrases which were common in the language in the first century A.D. may have become obsolete, either by the natural transformation of speech or by contact with other tongues, especially Greek. It may be said at once that the Aramaic vocabulary was as wide as that of Hebrew.

---

[1] It will be shown in the section on 'Targums' that the Babylonian text underwent considerable revision. The more literal and better accentuated text was cultivated at Nehardea. This type of text was also preserved at Yemen, and the Yemen MSS of Onkelos constitute one of the best guides to the vocalization of this Targum. Since the Onk. Targ. embodies the tradition of the language at the beginning of the Christian era, it is to some extent a guide to the vocalization of the literary speech during the period i cent. B.C.–i cent. A.D.

Compared with Greek, for instance, Aramaic grammatical constructions are included in fewer syntactical principles, and consequently the expression of ideas is limited to a smaller vocabulary. The LXX unnecessarily introduced many words to represent the same Hebrew term. In the Hebrew Psalter there are 2527 verses, but all the different words employed are contained in 564 verses. Though the Aramaic vocabulary was limited, yet it readily expressed. all the ideas of the age and people.

The wealth of a people's vocabulary must be judged by its ability to express any idea that came into the field of thought and action of that people in their own age and locality. Judged by this standard the Semitic language as a whole was adequate and in many respects abundant. It is manifestly unfair to estimate the character of the Palestinian language by the requirements of modern advancement. The number of its words and the form of its constructions, on the one hand, and the lack of particles and abstract nominal types, on the other, are safe criteria of its vocabulary and wealth only when considered in relation to its time and place. The real extent of a language is to be calculated 'by its capacity for calling into existence words and forms sufficiently numerous for the intuitions, representations, ideas and conceptions within which the minds of the people moved and acted.' The Jewish language of Palestine was not in one sense copious, but it was capable of wonderful manipulation, and could readily be made to express the purest prose and the loftiest poetry. Often there is a plethora of terms for the same idea, which gives picturesqueness to the language.[1]

II

CHARACTER OF SOURCES

The sources of the vocabulary are in several respects limited. The Biblical Aramaic is the fullest, considered

---

[1] *E.g.* Heb. has 24 words for *breaking a law*; 20 for *uttering sounds*; 18 for *breaking in pieces*; 14 for *seeking*; 9 for *trusting in Yahveh*; 9 for *dying*; 8 for *darkness*.

as general literature.   But this writing is special in its
subject-matter, and does not represent the ordinary life and
habits of the people.   Moreover, the scene is for the greater
part laid in Babylonia, and not in Palestine.   Yet the
Biblical Aramaic must be regarded as the best single source
for recovering the general vocabulary.   The Aramaic papyri
constitute an important asset, but they are restricted in range ;
in point of time and place they are not a sufficient guide to
the vocabulary of Palestine in the first century A.D.   They
deal too exclusively for our purpose with legal and domestic
contracts ; it is difficult to distinguish the technical from the
vernacular in such documents.   Yet these papyri make their
contribution to our study.   The Aramaic inscriptions, especially those dating from 100 B.C. to 100 A.D., ought to afford
material aid.   Unfortunately, however, they consist largely of
proper names.   About one half of the total words given in
Cook's *Glossary of Aramaic Inscriptions* are proper names.[1]
It is impossible to discover whether many of the terms, which
are found only in these inscriptions, were common in the
ordinary speech of the people.

III

LINE OF DISCOVERY

The vocabulary must be sought in the available sources,
and the method of research must proceed along certain lines.

1. A word common to the Semitic languages has considerable claim to be admitted.[2]   A word, for example, found
frequently in Hebrew, in Arabic, in Aramaic and Syria, also
in Jewish apocalyptic literature and the Targums, may with

---

[1] In the Appendix out of a total of 59 words, 43 are proper names.

[2] The following are examples of common words in Semitic :

Heb.	Arab.	Aram.	Syr.
בעל	بعل	בעל	ܒܥܠ
מים	ما	מיא	ܡܝܐ
נפש	نفس	נפש	ܢܦܫܐ
קול	قال	קלא	ܩܠܐ

much confidence be accepted.[1] A word common to the
Egyptian Aramaic and the Nabataean and Palmyrene inscriptions may be regarded as part of the general vocabulary. It
is, of course, always possible that a word found in one source
only, may have been common in the speech of the time.
Indeed, we may well believe that many terms were employed
in the language of the age which found no permanent record.

2. A phrase or idiom common to the Semitic languages
was probably part of the Palestinian speech. The pictorial
character of eastern languages is well known. So much was
expressed by figure, epigram and gesture. All languages
have their stock of proverbs, which, however, do not materially affect the character of the national speech. Some phrases
appear to have been common in the Semitic dialects.[2] The
question of idiom belongs rather to syntax than to vocabulary, but in its measure does affect the form of words. In
the use of idioms certain particles are employed which give
a general colour to the speech. Sometimes they are so per-
sistent that they appear in translation.

3. A word of frequent occurrence in the pre-Christian
and also in the post-Christian Aramaic, almost certainly
obtained all through the intervening period. This is an
important principle, inasmuch as we have very little literature
dating specifically from the first century A.D. But we have
the earlier Aramaic inscriptions from Têma, the Egyptian
Aramaic papyri, and the Biblical Aramaic. On the other

---

[1] The word חרם, *e.g.*, is Heb., Arab. خَرم, Aram. and Syr. It is found
in En. 6, in Nab. inscript. and in Targ. This, we may conclude, is the
Aram. equivalent to the Gk. ἀνάθημα (Lk. 21[5]), ἀνάθεμα (1 Cor. 12[13],
Acts 23[14] *et al.*).

[2] The following will illustrate the type of phrases referred to :

Heb.	Arab.	Aram.	Syr.
טוב לב	طب لب	טב לב(א)	ܠܒ ܛܒܐ
לך לשלום	مع السلامة	יהך בשלם	ܐܙܠ ܚܫܠܡܐ

Cf. Mk. 5[34], Lk. 7[50] 8[48], where perhaps ὑπάγω is best represented by אזל,
and πορεύω by הלך. The following Arab proverb : واجور من قاضي سدوم،
'more unjust than a judge of Sodom,' was probably familiar to Jesus of
Galilee (cf. Mt. 11[23, 24], Lk. 18[6]).

15

hand, we have the later Nabataean and Palmyrene inscriptions, and the Babylonian, Arabian and Palestinian Targums. Words common to all these, or to most of them, may with much confidence be accepted as elements of the language we seek to discover.[1]

4. Transliterated words in other languages, mainly Greek, indicate as far as they go the Aramaic of the age. Proper names of Semitic origin are frequent in Greek inscriptions and papyri; they are also found in Greek and Latin classical and other authors. These, however, do not affect the general vocabulary of a language. The knowledge derived from transliterated words must necessarily be very limited. Greek authors writing outside of Palestine and for Greek-speaking communities, when quoting or employing Aramaic terms and idioms, would naturally turn them as far as possible into Greek forms. It is only where the author transliterates, or in other ways imitates the original that we gain any information.[2]

5. Words in earlier and later Aramaic. Many terms found in the Egyptian Papyri, in Biblical Aramaic and in the Targums and Talmud, remained unchanged.[3] Some words underwent certain changes in orthography, but persisted essentially the same. A careful study of these minute changes would throw interesting light on the character of the

---

[1] For example, the word דין, as noun 'judge,' or as verb 'to judge,' is found in all the Aram. sources—Bibl. Aram. (Dan. 4³⁴, Ezra 7²⁵); Ass. Pap. (B 6, G 31, K 8); Aram. inscript. (Sinaitic 138 A ³); Targ. (Gen. 18²⁵, Dt. 17⁹); Samarit. (Gen. 49¹⁶); Syr. (Lk. 12¹⁴ 18⁶). Multitudes of words are similarly attested, such as יהב, חזה, כהן, מרא, נפק, עלל, תרע, צדק. Many others, though not found in all the sources, are sufficiently supported: טליא, 'youth'; קריא, 'villages'; רחמנא, 'merciful'; רגז, 'wrath'; זמן, 'time'; גברה, 'might'; תורא, 'bullock.' Rarer words must be used with caution, such as בילומא, 'senator'; פלותא, 'miracle'; שרתא, 'feast'; היכלא, 'temple.'

[2] The following will illustrate the transliteration of Aram. words: ἀββᾶ=אבא, Mk. 14³⁶, Rom. 8¹⁵; cf. Schlatter, *Heimat. u. Sprache des 4 Evang.* 54. ῥαββί=רבי, ῥαββωνεί=רבוני (perh. Gal.); cf. Böttcher, *Lehrb.* sect. 64. σάββατα=שבתא; cf. Joseph. *Ant.* i. 1. 1; Hor. *Sat.* i. 1. 69. πάσχα =פסחא; cf. Joseph. *Ant.* v. 1. 4; *Bell.* ii. 1. 3. μαμωνᾶς=ממונא; cf. *Pirke Aboth*, ii. 12; Jerome, *Ep.* xxii. 31. ἀσαρθᾶ=עצרתא; cf. Joseph. *Ant.* iii. 10. 6. ἀδώμα=ארומא, Joseph. *Ant.* ii. 1. 1. κορβᾶν=קרבן; cf. Joseph. *Ant.* iv. 4. 4; *Apion.* i. 22; *Bell.* ii. 9. 4. χαγίρας=חגיר, Joseph. *Bell.* v. 11. 5.

[3] Such words as בירה, *fortress* (cf. CIS ii. 164³); דין, *judge*; זרע, *seed*; צדק, *rightness*; קטל, *kill*.

language as fashioned by a time process.[1]   Other terms found
in the Egyptian Papyri, and in a somewhat altered form in
the Targums, have substitutes in Biblical Aramaic.[2]   This
shows how cautiously non-Palestinian Aramaic must be
employed to represent the vernacular of Galilee and Judaea.

D.—ABBREVIATION

I

COMMON FORMS

Generally the abbreviations are restricted to well-known
terms and phrases.   No instance whatever is found in
Biblical Aramaic, and the form חד for אחד (Ezek. 33[30]) is of
no importance, perhaps to be deleted in harmony with LXX.[3]
The abbreviations in the Talmud are for the greater part
too late, though some of the tractates may preserve very
early forms, such as או for אומר, and גמ' ל for גמליאל.   In the
Apocryphal literature certain common words and frequent
phrases are often abbreviated,[4] and numerals are frequently
expressed by letters.[5]   In the Assuan Papyri there are a few
abbreviations, chiefly denoting well-known coins.[6]   Just as

---

[1] Changes like ברה, *daughter*, אחה, *sister*, in Eg. pap. became ברת and
אחת in Targ. דלעין, *gourds*, became דלעין in Tal. מחוי, *mirror*, became מהויתא
in Targ. עד וי, *until*, became עד די. קמר, *wool* (Eg. pap. H 5), and עמר (G 7.
10), show that ק was yielding to the softer ע.

[2] *E.g.* שו, *couch* (Eg. pap. G 15), appears in Targ. as שויא, and Syr.
ܡܫܟܒܐ.   The Bib. Aram. term is משכב, which is also common in Targ.

[3] Cf. Cornill, *Das Buch des Propheten Ezechiel*, *loc. cit.*

[4] The following are common examples : אמ for אמר, *Tobit*, Prologue ;
ii. 2, v. 10. כת for כתוב, *Tobit*, iv. 16, 17 ; Epilogue. הקרוש ברוך הוא for הקב'ה,
Tobit, Epilogue ; *Bel and the Dragon*, beginning ; cf. שהק'בה, הב'ה, הק'בה
(who is Holy, etc.), *Midrash Thanhumâ*, § האוינו. ההו for הוה הדבר, *Bel and
the Dragon*, beginning ; cf. הה'ר, *Bereshith Rabbah*, § 68.   In the Aram.
text of *Tobit* '' is the sign for יהוה, as in the Tagums generally.   In the
same Bk. אנש=נש or אנשא (ch. 8. 12).

[5] *E.g.* ע=70 (*Tobit*, Prologue).   This method, however, was not
employed in the earliest times in Heb.   The common method was prob.
that found in the Phoen. and Aram. inscrip.

[6] *E.g.* ר=דרכמן, *drachma* (B 15, C 15, D 14, 21) ; ח=חלר, *Kallur*, a small
Assyr. coin (G 15[a]) ; ש=שקל, *shekel* (L 2, 3).   More interesting are the

the Hebrew and Aramaic text of the Old Testament is practically free from abbreviations, so the Egyptian-Aramaic Papyri shows but little tendency in this direction. This type of *defectiva* writing came into more general use later, and in the Talmud became abundant. There are many instances of defective writing in the Semitic inscriptions. It is difficult to state in every case whether the defective form should be regarded as an abbreviation, or as the normal form at the time of writing. An examination of the Nabataean in connexion with the Palmyrene inscriptions, would reveal considerable uncertainty in this matter. The shorter Palmyrene forms are not necessarily abbreviations, though generally so regarded. With the extension of Aramaic there was a tendency to drop letters, a tendency due perhaps to more rapid pronunciation. Both vowels and consonants were dropped in this way.[1] The Palmyrene shows some real abbreviations.[2] The earlier Phoenician and Aramaic inscriptions reveal these various characteristics.[3]

II

SOURCE OF DIFFERENCES BETWEEN LXX AND HEBREW TEXT OF OLD TESTAMENT

Some differences between the LXX and the MT. have been attributed to abbreviations in the MSS used by the

forms : יון=יונה (D 6, J 17) ; מחסה=מחסיה (A 9, 12, 20, D 35, 36). The full forms are also found : יונה (G 38), מחסיה (C 18, 20, D 29, 31, H 3, P 4). These variations suggest a transition period, and perhaps some scruple in the use of the termination. The יה, whether separate or joined to another word, would stand for, or at least indicate, the sacred name. It is possible, therefore, that in the early papyri the יה termination of proper names was sometimes omitted in deference to religious sentiment.

[1] Thus : נחיא (CIS ii. 213⁵) ; Palm. גומחא (Cl.-Gan. *Études*, i. 121). מרח (CIS ii. 213⁶), probably for מרנה. ביח (*ib.* l. 8) is probably for בירח. בתי מקברין (*ib.* 350¹) ; Palm. בת מקברתא (Vog. 64¹). פצאל (*ib.* 354³) ; Palm. פציאל (Euting, *Epigr. Misc.* 131).

[2] *E.g.* אמרשא (Vog. 2²) for אמר שמשא. ירחי (*ib.* l. 16) for ירחבולא. נשא (Eut. 102¹), probably for נשאל. מתוא (Littmann, 1⁴), probably for מתנבול ; cf. מתבול (=מתן בול) (Eut. 102²). עסתורנא (Müller, 46¹³), possibly for עשתור גרם.

[3] *Vide* ברא (CIS i. 10³), possibly for בר-ראשמן. בעת ר (*ib.* 132⁴), where רב=ר or רבן. תמא (Neo-Punic : *Shershel*, 2⁵) is perhaps for אתמא (CIS i. 151³). מחזה (*Nêrab*, 2⁵), מה=מ.

translators : *e.g.* את בית יהוה, LXX εἰς τὸν οἶκόν μου = אל ביתי
(Judg. 19[18]); עבדי אנכי, LXX Δοῦλος κυρίον εἰμὶ ἐγώ = עבר
יהוה אנכי (Jonah 1[9]). Several others might be cited.[1]
Abbreviation is a possible explanation, but not the most
natural or likely. It cannot be shown that such abbreviations
characterized the MSS from which the LXX version was
made. It seems much more probable that the translators
had before them MSS which in many details differed from
those which came down to the Massoretes. Another point,
which has escaped scholars generally, may be appropriately
mentioned here. We refer to the *scriptio defectiva* which were
frequent in Phoenician and old Hebrew. The plural ending
in י is an easy illustration : כלאי (Moab. St. 1. 23), אסרי (*ib.* 1. 25),
עבדי (Phoen. *Mu'sub*, 1. 3), קרני (CIS i. 165[5]) ; so in early
Aramaic, פחי (*Zenj. Panammu*, 1. 12). The final letter of verbal
forms was also sometimes omitted. This, however, was not
so much the result of intentional abbreviation as the result of
carelessness and defective orthography. The abbreviations on
Hebrew coins probably arose from limitation of space, and
from these data alone we cannot conclude that such
abbreviations were at all common in Hebrew writing. The
presence of real and deliberate abbreviations in the MSS used
by the LXX authors is possible, and would readily explain
some variant readings. But the differences referred to
between the LXX and the MT. are more frequently to be
attributed to defective writing, to ignorance on the part of
the writers, to textual corruption, and even to laxity on the
part of the translators.[2]

---

[1] *Vide* Driver, *Notes on Heb. Text of Samuel*, pp. lxviii f.

[2] The fragments of the Hebrew text of Ecclesiasticus appear to belong to
two different MSS. It is interesting to find in these MSS, dating perhaps
circa x–xi cent., the abbreviation of the divine name by three marks.
These marks are arranged in two ways, which suggest that they belong to
two different MSS : (1) Triangular ; (2) Horizontal . It is
impossible to say whether these forms were known in pre-Christian times.
The probability is that they were introduced later, possibly to suggest
some sort of trinity in the Godhead. (Cf. Schechter, *Ben Sira.*) In the
MSS of Onkelos the Tetragrammaton is variously written : (1) ,
editio Bomberg ; (2) , MS A ; (3) , MSS BCD. In the text
published by Monasch (Breslau, 1860), is the invariable form.

IX

NABATAEAN:

A CHARACTERISTIC TYPE OF ARAMAIC

I

GEOGRAPHICAL AREA

IT will now be necessary to state more fully the chief reasons in favour of the opinion that the Nabataean on the whole best represents the Aramaic dialect of the first century A.D. It must be understood that the literary dialect is here meant. There is no method of showing the language actually spoken by the mixed people in the Nabataean kingdom. It is quite possible that while the literary language was Aramaic of the Nabataean type, the common speech was different. In the same way in the same regions there are Greek inscriptions, but Greek could not have been the vernacular.[1] The reasons in favour of the Nabataean as the chief Aramaic dialect of the period may be stated as follows:

GEOGRAPHICAL AREA.—The centre of the Nabataean kingdom was at Petra,[2] perhaps the Hebrew Sela, an early fortress of the Edomites. The kingdom extended as far north as Damascus, and as far south as the north-east shore of the Red Sea. Within these limits came the Sinaitic Peninsula, Coele-Syria, Palestine and north Arabia. The great trade route from Yemen to Palestine and Syria passed through the

---

[1] A small number in Greek; a few in Arabic and Latin.

[2] Hence ἡ κατὰ Πέτραν Ἀραβία, or Ἀραβία ἡ πρὸς τῇ Πέτρᾳ, *i.e.* 'Arabia Petraea.' Perhaps סלע (Judg. 1³⁶, 2 K. 14⁷, Is. 16¹) = 'the rock.'

Nabataean kingdom, thus the influence of these people was carried both northward and southward. There is evidence that the Nabataeans even touched Europe. Traders from this kingdom established themselves and their religion at Puteoli, on the shores of Italy.[1] It is possible that some of the tribes inhabiting Mesopotamia were of the same race as the Nabataeans. Arab writers use the term 'Nabat'[2] not of Arabians, but of Babylonians. From these writers some scholars have concluded that Nabataeans occupied Mesopotamia between the Euphrates and the Tigris. These Mesopotamian Nabataeans were said to be agriculturists and scientists, while those of Petra were pastoral and commercial.[3] If a branch of the Nabataeans did dwell in Mesopotamia, this would help to explain the Syro-Chaldaean elements in their language. Pliny connects the *Nabataei* and *Cedrei* in the same way as Isaiah.[4]

Within the boundaries of the Nabataean kingdom there was a considerable Aramaic population, and Aramaic was regarded as a highly cultivated language. For this reason partly the Arab settlers in Nabataea made use of Aramaic in correspondence with distant provinces. It became the recognized language of commerce, the *lingua franca* of eastern diplomacy. It is quite possible, and even probable, that the early Nabataeans spoke an Arabic dialect for some time after Aramaic became their official and literary language. In the same way the peasantry of Palestine continued to speak Aramaic after Greek and Latin became the language of literature and government. It is clear that the Nabataean dialect extended over a wide area in the period immediately preceding the Christian era. The Nabataeans gave their name to the whole country between Syria and Arabia, from

---

[1] The Puteoli inscriptions (=CIS ii. 157, 158) are proof. It is said (CIS ii. 158) that Ṣaidu (צידו) dedicated some object for the life of the Nab. royal family, and deposited it in the restored sanctuary (יהבו בנו מחרמתא דא). Cf. Acts 28[11, 13].

[2] Arabic نَبَطِي, 'in which ט has sprung from ת servile of the Hebrew.'

[3] The Nab. were possibly thus divided into two sections, yet in origin they were the same people—probably Arabs. Cf. Joseph. *Ant.* i. 12. 4.

[4] Pliny, *Hist. Nat.* v. 11, 65 ; Is. 60[7].

the Euphrates to the Red Sea. Within these boundaries the kindred dialects—Palmyrene and Nabataean—were paramount. The aristocratic and leading classes were mainly of Arabian origin. They encouraged the use of Aramaic, and this fact gave an impetus to the dialect of the Nabataeans, who constituted the ruling element in these provinces. Perhaps the evident Arabic colouring of some of the Nabataean inscriptions, slightly reduces their value as specimens of the pure Aramaic of the age and locality. But the student will know how to discount this southern element.

II

DATE OF OCCUPATION

The time of the origin of the Nabataeans is quite uncertain. They are mentioned on inscriptions as *Nabaaiti* as early as the sixth century B.C.[1] Probably in the fifth century they migrated from their southern wilderness home, and made incursions into the provinces north-west and north-east. When Babylon subjugated the Jews, the Edomites began to oppress Judaea. About the same time the Nabataeans occupied the country of the Edomites, and firmly established themselves. They came into greater prominence about 312 B.C., when Athenaeus, a general of Antigonus, and Demetrius attempted in vain to subjugate them.[2] In the time of 1 Maccabees the Nabataeans were clearly distinguished from other Arab tribes, but in 2 Maccabees are simply termed Ἄραβες, as in some other Greek and Latin authors.[3] The Nabataeans held possession of their kingdom and their freedom till 105 A.D., when Trajan ended their independence and they became subject to Rome.[4] Thus the Nabataean influence was dominant throughout the period under discussion.

[1] Rassam Cylinder of Asurbanipal, vide *Keilinschriftliche Bibliothek*, ii. 216–222.

[2] *Vide* Diodorus Siculus, x. 95, 96, 100.

[3] 2 Mac. 5⁸; Joseph. *Ant.* i. 12. 4.

[4] Cf. Πάλμας τῆς Συρίας ἄρχων τὴν Ἀραβίαν τὴν πρὸς τῇ Πέτρᾳ ἐχειρώσατο, καὶ Ῥωμαίων ὑπήκοον ἐποιήσατο, Dio Cassius, lxviii. 14.

III

CONNEXION WITH JEWS AND PALESTINE

With the decline of Greek power in Syria and Egypt, the Nabataeans grew in influence. Towards the end of the second century B.C. they became a menacing power under King Erotimus.[1] They were closely associated with the Maccabaean family and exploits during the successful revolt of Judaism against Hellenism.[2] It is not quite clear what part the Nabataeans played in the struggle of the Maccabees against Antiochus Epiphanes for the independence of Judah. A series of 'kings' under the title of Aretas[3] came into close contact with the fortunes of Palestine. The first Aretas was hostile to Jason the high priest, who represented the Hellenizing section of the Jews, and opposed an alliance with Rome.[4] Another Aretas has possession of Damascus *circa* 85 B.C.,[5] but according to inscriptional evidence the Damascenes had autonomy in 70–69. They were again under Nabataean rule, 34–65 A.D.[6]

The most interesting of these kings was Aretas IV. (9 B.C.–40 A.D.), mentioned in Nabataean inscriptions.[7] He managed to keep terms with Augustus, and was recognized as king.[8] His daughter became the wife of Herod Antipas,[9] but she was set aside in favour of Herodias. This led to strife between the Nabataean kingdom and the Herodian government, and to an agreement with Rome. It has been conjectured that Caligula gave back Damascus to Aretas *circa* 38 A.D. in order to secure his favour and co-operation.[10] This agrees

[1] Joseph. *Ant.* xiii. 13. 3, 5, 15. 1, 2; *Wars*, i. 4. 4, 8; cf. Justinus, xxxix. 5.

[2] *Vide* 2 Mac. vi. 10–31, vii. ; Joseph. *Ant.* xii. xiii.

[3] Cf. title חרתת מלך נבטו, 'Aretas (Harethath),' king of the Nabataeans, CIS ii. 332, cf. CIS ii. 158[3-4].

[4] For contact with Maccabees, *vide* 1 Mac. 5[25] 9[35] etc., 2 Mac. 5[8].

[5] This was Aretas III. who intervened in the Hyrcanus-Aristobulus struggles.

[6] Damascene coins of Tiberius are not found later than 33–34 A.D.

[7] *Vide* CIS ii. 214 f., 332; cf. Joseph. *Ant.* xviii. 5. 1.

[8] Joseph. *Ant.* xvi. 10. 9.

[9] *Ib.* xviii. 5. 1.

[10] *Vide* Euting, *Nab. Inschr.* 85; cf. Schürer, *Gesch. Jud. Volk.*[3] i. 737.

with the time of the persecution of Paul by Aretas in Damascus (2 Cor. 11[32]).   The influence of the Nabataeans in Judaea is further indicated by the fact that they became the rivals of the Hasmonaean dynasty, though at first they were allied with the Jewish party against the Greeks. In 65–64 B.C. the Nabataeans formed a leading element in the disturbances in Palestine, which resulted in Roman intervention.[1]

IV

ADOPTED LANGUAGE

The Nabataeans were real Arabs, so that Semitic language and custom would not be foreign to them.   How early they left their primitive Arabian home we do not know.   But we find them overspreading Idumaea, the region east of the Jordan, the Syrian desert as far as the Hauran mountains.[2] These wanderings brought the Nabataeans into contact with Aramaic-speaking tribes, and with communities whose official language was Aramaic.   The type of Aramaic which the Nabataeans grew into became the language of interchange and commerce between Yemen and Damascus, the Red Sea and the Euphrates.   Many proper names on the Nabataean inscriptions are Arabic, a fact which points partly to their origin, and partly to association with Arab traders.[3]   Their prince, Emalchuel, was friendly with the Syrians, some of them joined the Syrian army as mercenaries, and this led the Maccabees to enter the field against them.[4]

---

[1] This was in the time of Aretas III. (*circa* 85–60 B.C.).   About this time the animosities between Pharisees and Sadducees sprang into prominence. Pompey and Scarus came into conflict with the Nabataeans *circa* 63 B.C. Joseph. *Ant.* xiv. 1. 4–2. 3, 5. 1 ; *Wars*, i. 8. 1.

[2] Cf. 1 Mac. 5[25] 9[35] ; Joseph. *Ant.* xiii. 15. 2.

[3] It is probable that travellers from Arabia to Syria passing the Sinaitic peninsula, scratched on the rocks their Arab names, adding some benedictory formula in Aram.   Thus : בריך ואלו, 'Blessed be Vailu' (Euting, *Sin. Inschr.* 463) ; דכיר תימאלהי, 'Remembered be Taimallâhi' (*ib.* 457); שלם אוישו (*ib.* 519).

[4] Cf. 1 Mac. 11[39] 5[39], 2 Mac. 12[10], 1 Mac. 12[31].

V

RELATION TO PALMYRENE

The position of Palmyra is clearly known. It was the noted city in the Syrian desert between Damascus and the Euphrates. Speaking generally, it stood in a central position between Syria, Babylonia and Mesopotamia. It was the ancient Tadmor of the inscriptions,[1] and the Πάλμυρα of the Greeks. The city became of some importance just before the Christian era. The Palmyrenes were of Arab race, and consequently connected ethnically with the Nabataeans. Several Arabic words are found in the Palmyrene inscriptions, and many of the proper names are Arabic.[2] The language in use at Palmyra was undoubtedly a dialect of western Aramaic, like the Egyptian Aramaic and the Nabataean. Familiar features of the language clearly show its kinship with the Palestinian Aramaic. The establishment of this fact is of considerable importance in support of the opinion here advanced.[3]

[1] In Palmyrene inscriptions תדמור, vide De Vogüé, La Syrie Centrale, 20, 22, 29; according to Joseph. the Syrians called it Θαδάμορα, Ant. viii. 6. 1. In Arabic تَدمُر.

[2] E.g. סנר, Arab. سجار (Vog. ib. 3); חרם, Arab. حرم (ib.); פהר, Arab. فخذ (Oxoniensis, 1, Ashmolean Mus. Oxford).

[3] Some of the likenesses of Palmyrene to Palestinian Aramaic may here be outlined:

(i.) The dem. pron. דה (Journal Asiatique, ii. 374 f.; Müller, 46). דנה (De Vogüé, La Syr. Centr. 4, 16, al.; Clermont-Ganneau, Études d'archéologie orientale, ii. 5). אלן (Vog. ib. 1, 2, 93; Jour. As., ib.).

(ii.) The rel. pron. די (Vog. ib. 16, 17, 22, al.; Euting, Sin. Inschr. 4. 102). This agrees with Bibl. Aram. and Onk. Targ. In Ps.-Jon. Targ. ד is more commonly joined to the following word; Samarit. ib.

(iii.) The conj. בדילי (Vog. ib. 1, 4 [בדיל], 6); frequent in Pales. Aram., but not in Syr. (vide Dalman, Gram. 187).

(iv.) The form ממלכות, 'on this account' (Vog. ib. 15), is unusual as a compound, but the separate words are found: מטל in Pales. Aram. (cf. Targ. Lev. 8¹⁵, Ps. 8⁴ 110⁷) and in Syr.; כות in inscriptions (CIS ii. 199), and in Pales. Aram. (cf. Targ. 2 Sam. 7²²).

(v.) The imperf. preformative י (and not as eastern dialects generally and Syr. נ or ל). Cf. יפתח, יקשט, ישבע (vide Cl.-Gann. Études, i. 121).

In turning from Nabataean to Palmyrene there would be little necessity to change the idiom. The script, too, is very similar, though some letters of the latter more nearly approach the final 'square' character. The following Gospel passage (Lk. 16[16]) is merely a transliteration into Nabataean script of a supposed Aramaic original. The type of script imitated was employed early in the i cent. A.D. : [1]

סירחתראיגס(ראנגדרע)ערגיכדרין
מן סכארבוהכלכאלסלגכלד ראצבא
כללמןוכחמשכסדיעחכ

The passage following (Mt. 11[27]), in the same way, is a transliteration into later Palmyrene, *circa* iii cent. A.D. : [2]

בלא דנ ככז ניליאכזנאריתדיראעלכזא
אלהן אוכא זוליתדיראעלעזיראכוכלא כאן
כיולאא ?זוכןגלליולילאיכדוא

Doubtless a writing on papyrus at this date would be different in many respects, and, *inter alia*, would show some

(vi.) The pl. termination אָ—, *e.g.* צלמיא (cf. Targ. Mic. 5[13]), אלהיא (cf. Bibl. Aram. Jer. 10[11]), אלהיא טביא (Vog. *ib.* 3, 8), אכסניא (Vog. *ib.* 16).

(vii.) The numeral תרויהן, תריהן (Vog. *ib.* 1, 2), same as Onk. and Ps.-Jon. (Gen. 2[25]). Cf. usual Nab. (fem.) תרתין (*e.g.* CIS 224, 186) with Palm. (fem.) תרתן (*e.g.* Vog. *ib.* 95). Pales. Aram. sometimes doubled the vowel-letters, תרוייהן, תרוויהן (*vide* Dalman, *Gram.* 98). Bibl. Aram. same as Nab. (cf. Dan. 6[1]). The simple Aram. (Nab.) form is תרין (cf. CIS 196, 212 ; constr. תרי, CIS 157). Sam. = Heb. √שנה.

(viii.) The distinction between ס and שׁ, as in the line : אתי לכא ית לגינא שניאן וזבן סגיאן והוא רב שוק וחסך רואן, 'he brought hither the legions many times, and he was chief of the market, and spent money in a most generous manner' (Vog. *ib.* 15). This distinction suggests some Heb. or more probably some Arabic influence. The Aram. letter is ס, as in Pales. Aram. (cf. Targ. Jos. 6[27], Mic. 4[2]), and the Yemen MSS of Onkelos.

This comparison might easily be extended to include Egyptian Aram., inasmuch as this dialect with Nabataean and Palmyrene were not only branches of western Aram., but were in all main features one language. The hint in Epiphanius should be noticed : Ἄλλοι δὲ δῆθεν τὴν βαθυτάτην τῶν Σύρων διάλεκτον σεμνύνονται, τήν τε [τὴν] κατὰ τὴν Παλμύραν διάλεκτον, αὐτήν τε καὶ τὰ αὐτῶν στοιχεῖα· εἰκοσιδύο δὲ ταῦτα ὑπάρχει (*Haer.* 66. 13).

[1] Cf. CIS ii. 206.   [2] *Vide* Vogüé, *La Syrie Centrale*, 15.

ligatures when certain letters came into juxtaposition.[1] Aramaic writing in the early Christian centuries would tend towards the so-called 'Syriac' character.[2]

VI

LIKENESS TO BIBLICAL ARAMAIC

It is evident that the two forms of Aramaic—Biblical and Nabataean—are practically identical. Biblical Aramaic has the advantage of being furnished with vowels and other signs which assist the orthography and pronunciation. Though these signs were added long after the composition of the Books, yet Aramaic was still a living language when this punctuation came into use. The general value of the Biblical pointing is attested by the kindred Syriac of which we have fairly definite knowledge. In the notes below proof is given of the substantial agreement of Biblical Aramaic with Nabataean, both in words and construction. The illustrative terms and phrases are selected from the whole field of Nabataean inscriptions, occasionally compared with Palmyrene and Syriac.

סלעין, *selas* = Gk. στατήρ (CIS ii. 198[9]); cf. סלעא, *shekel* = Heb. שֶׁקֶל (Targ. Onk. Ex. 30[13]). Cf. Syr. ܣܩܠܐ.

אנוש, *any one* (*ib.* 197[7]); cf. אנושא (Dan. 4[13] Keth.). In this sense (= Gk. τις) the word is used in Bib. Aram; Nab. and Palm. (cf. *Tariff*, i. 11); Targ. Onk. אנש (Lev. 13[2] *et al.*).

להן, *except* = לא הן (*ib.* 197[8]); cf. להן (Dan. 2[11] 3[28]).

עלא, *above* (*ib.*); עלא מנהון, *over them* (Dan. 6[3]); cf. *ib.* 196[2].

פתורא, *table*, here as proper name 'Pathora' (*ib.* 201[1]); cf. same word in Targ. Onk. (Ex. 25[23]).

גוא, *midst* (*ib.* 350[1]); cf. גוא (Dan. 3[6]); but elsewhere Nab. גו.

עבידתא, *work* (*ib.* 196[7]); cf. עבידת (Ezra 4[24]).

נקידו, *Neqidu* (*ib.* 161, Col. 2 [2]); cf. נקודא, 'Nekoda' (Ezra 2[48]).

איתיבל, *Aithi-bel* (*ib.* 196[3]); cf. איתי אלה, 'there is a God' (Dan. 2[28]); cf. איתיאל, 'Ithiel' (Neh. 11[7]); איתי, 'Ithai' (1 Ch. 11[31]).

---

[1] Particularly the letters א, ב, ד, ו, מ, נ, ר. For Palm. inscrip. with Nab. tone and colour, *vide* Littmann, *Journal Asiatique*, ii. 374 ff.

[2] *E.g.* the script named by Euting, 'edessenisches Estrangelo.'

אצדק באצדק, *each kinsman* (*ib.* 201³); cf. the distributive use of
ב in שנה בשנה, 'each year,' = Targ. Onk. שתא בשתא (Dt. 15²⁰);
חדש בחדש, 'each month' (1 Ch. 27¹).

חרתת מלכא, *King Ḥarethath* (*ib.* 198⁸); cf. same order in נבוכדנצר
מלכא, 'King Nebuchadnezzar' (Dan. 3¹, cf. 5¹).

עשר ותלת, *thirteenth* (*ib.* 199⁹), this appears to be the usual order
in Nab. with fem. nouns (cf. *ib.* 201⁴, 221⁶, 182³). Onk., however,
prefers the other order, תרתא עשרי (Gen. 14⁴); so in Syr. ܬܠܬܥܣܪ.

יתשנא, *it shall be changed* (*ib.* 350⁴); cf. יחשנא, 'shall alter'
(Ezra 6¹¹, cf. Dan. 6⁹·¹⁸). Nab. is peculiar in retaining the ת before
the sibilant. Another Ex. is יתזבן, 'be sold' (*ib.* 208⁴).

זמנין תרין, *two-times* (*ib.* 196⁶); cf. זמנין תלתה, 'three-times'
(Dan. 6¹¹); cf. Palm. זבן סגיאן, 'many times' (Vogüé, 155⁵).

אונא, *lodging* (*ib.* 202¹); cf. Syr. ܐܘܢܐ, 'mansion' (Pesh. John
14²).

קנס, *fine* (*ib.* 198⁸), is same as Targ. קנסא (Ps.-Jon. Ex. 21³⁰).

תנא, *contract* (*ib.* 350⁵), = Syr. ܬܢܒ, and Targ. תנאה.

VII

SYRIAC CORROBORATION

The native dialect of Edessa in west Mesopotamia had
been reduced to something like a system before the introduction of Christianity, as is proved by the fixity of its
orthography and grammar. The subjects of the Persian
Empire in this province adopted this dialect for ecclesiastical,
diplomatic and academic purposes. In one outstanding feature
this dialect differs from Biblical Aramaic and Nabataean, *e.g.*
the use of ܢ as the preformative of the third person singular
and plural imperfect. But the affinities far outnumber the
differences, as the following notes indicate :

(i.) Predominance of consonants in grammatical formations.

(ii.) Fewer vowels sounds in words, *e.g.* עשתרת (Sidon inscrip.
circa 300 B.C.), pronounced עְשְׁתֹּרֶת, *Ashtart.* Cf. LXX pron. of Heb.
עֲשְׁתֹּרֶת, ʼΑστάρτη (1 K. 11⁵·³³).

(iii.) Absence of prefixed article. As in Babylonian Aram. final
א ceased to express with any consistency the definite article.

(iv.) Genitive indicated by די.

(v.) Accusative indicated by ל; ית was perhaps more original than previously supposed. Cf. the Yemen MSS.

(vi.) Distinction of gender in the third person plural of verbs perfect, e.g. קטלו, קטלא=ܩܛܠܳܐ, ܩܛܰܠܰܝ.

(vii.) Prefix את of all passives.

(viii.) The plural termination ין of all masculine nouns. Final ן was sometimes omitted in inscrip., e.g. חמין=המי; שערין=שערי; אלהין=אלהי (Zenjirli: Hadad, ll. 4, 5, 6). The י is sometimes omitted, e.g. מלכן רברבן (Zenjirli: Bar-rekub, l. 10). In some cases the absence of ן is due to the construct state, e.g. צבתי כל, 'ornaments of all kinds' (Elephantina, CIS ii. 137 B[1]).

(ix.) The form of the Aphel, e.g. אקטל, ܐܰܩܛܶܠ.

(x.) The use of imperatives passive.

(xi.) The use of active and passive Participles in Peal and Pael, e.g. גבא=נְבָא, Peal Part. active; גבי=נְבִי, Peal Part. passive (Tariff, ii. a.[11,13]); Syr. ܢܳܒܶܐ, ܢܒܶܐ.

(xii.) Formation of separate tense by Participle with Pronoun, e.g. דָּאֵן אֲנָא, 'I will judge' (Targ. Gen. 15[14]); אֲנָה חָזֵה נְבְרִין, 'I see men' (Dan. 3[25]).

(xiii.) The Hebrew termination ה usually becomes א. In a few cases ה is possibly written for א emphatic, e.g. אחרה (Nêrab, 1[13]), 'being an early form of the usual אוחרנא, ܐ݇ܚܪܺܢܳܐ.'

(xiv.) Pleonastic suffixes before the Genitive, e.g. אֲנַחְנָא הִמּוֹ עַבְדּוֹהִי דִי אֱלָה, 'we are the servants of God' (Ezra 5[11]); ܫܶܡܥܶܗ ܕܝܶܫܘܿܥ, 'the fame of (Him who is) Jesus' (Pesh. Mt. 14[1]).

(xv.) The third person plural active used as a passive (vide יכתב, מסק, Tariff, i. [8]).

Syriac properly so called was never perhaps a dialect of any province in Palestine. It was, however, closely related to Babylonian Aramaic and to Samaritan, and like these forms of Aramaic had many likenesses to Hebrew. Many words and phrases in Nabataean and Palmyrene inscriptions have parallels in Syriac, and these prove the essential oneness of the language over a considerable area of Asia Minor at the time. The following list of words and phrases may be found in standard works on the inscriptions, but the list is here summarized for the first time, for clearness and comparison. The forms of the Aramaic terms are given according to the inscriptions quoted; for the Syriac equivalent the simple form—absolute or emphatic—is given:

שמדין, *curses* (CIS ii. 198[8]); Syr. ܚܡܪ.

דמי, *full* (*ib.* 199[8]); Syr. ܕܡܝܢ.

פסלא, *mason* (*ib.* 201[5]); Syr. ܦܣܠܐ.

אנתתה, *his wife* (*ib.* 204[3]); Syr. ܐܢܬܬܐ; Palm. אתת, איתא; Pales. Aram. איתא, איתה.

איר, *Iyar* (*ib.* 205[10]); Syr. ܐܝܪ.

הפרכא, *the Eparch* (*ib.* 207[2]); Syr. ܗܦܪܟܐ. The prefix ה is quite Syriac. In Sin. Aram. הפרכיה; Gk. Ἐπαρχία.

חביבו, *Ḥabibu* (*ib.* 221[3]); Syr. ܚܒܝܒ; Gk. Ἅβιβος.

כרכא, *wall* (*ib.* 350[2]); Syr. ܟܪܟܐ.

פקדון, *contents* (*ib.* 350[4]); Syr. ܦܩܕܘܢ.

תנא, *contract* (*ib.* 350[5]); Syr. ܬܢܐ.

משריתא, *camp* (*ib.* 196[4]); Syr. ܡܫܪܝܬܐ.

טעמא, *adoption* (*ib.* 161, col. ii. [2]); Syr. ܛܥܡܐ.

ארהומיא, *Romans* (*ib.* 161, col. iii. [2]); Syr. ܪܗܘܡܝܐ; cf. ܐܪܗܘܡܝܐ (Clement, *Thes. Syr.*, *s.v.*).

מדיתהון, *their city* (Vogüé, 1[3]; cf. *Tariff*, ii. b. [7]); Syr. ܡܕܝܢܬܐ; in Bibl. Aram. מְדִינָה, emph. מְדִינְתָּא = *province*.

אקים, *set up* (*ib.* 4[3]); Syr. ܐܩܝܡ, final vowel being quiescent.

תגרא, *merchants* (*ib.* 4[3]); Syr. ܬܓܪܐ.

שירתא, *caravans* (*ib.* 4[3]); Syr. ܫܝܪܬܐ.

כרך, *karak* (*ib.* 5[3]); Syr. ܟܪܟܐ, *citidal*.

תטלילהן, *coverings* (*ib.* 8⁵) ; Syr. ܠܠܝܠܬܐ.

למקמו, *to set up* (*ib.* 9⁴) ; Syr. ܡܩܡܘ.

תצביתהן, *their ornaments* (*ib.* 11⁴) ; Syr. ܨܒܬܐ (*vide* Pesh. Esth. 2³ *et al.*).

במיתויתא, *at the coming* (*ib.* 15²) ; Syr. ܡܐܬܝܬܐ (cf. Pesh. Mt. 24³).

תמן, *there* (*ib.* 15³) ; Syr. ܬܡܢ.

לכא, *hither* (*ib.* 15⁴) ; Syr. ܠܟܐ, this Pales. Syr.

חרשא, *Ḥarsha* (*ib.* 20³) ; Syr. ܚܪܫܐ.

תגמא, *order, guild* (*ib.* 23³) ; Syr. ܬܓܡܐ ; Gk. τάγμα.

קיומה, *patron* (*ib.* 26⁵) ; Syr. ܩܝܘܡܐ ; Gk. προστάτης.

מתקננא, *corrector* (*ib.* 28²) ; Syr. ܡܬܩܢܢܐ.

ארנבי, *Arnabi* (*ib.* 73³) ; Syr. ܐܪܢܒܐ, *a hare.*

דדא, *Dada* (*ib.* 93²) ; Syr. ܕܕܐ, *paternal uncle.*

כמרא, *Komara* (Euting, 102²) ; Syr. ܟܡܪܐ, *a priest.*

פרנס, *administrator* (*ib.* 102³) ; Syr. ܦܪܢܣ.

שקקן, *streets* (Müller, 46³) ; Syr. ܫܩܩܐ ; Targ. שְׁקָקָא.

אבגר, *Abgar* (*ib.* 46¹¹) ; Syr. ܐܒܓܪ, common name in Syr.

מראגרא, *Mar-agra* (Clermont-Ganneau, *Études*, i. 121²) ; Syr. ܡܪܐܓܪܐ.

יקשט, *prosperity* (*ib.* 121⁵) ; Syr. ܩܫܛܐ.

עלותא, *altars* (*Journal As.*, 1901, ii. 374–390, B¹) ; Syr. ܥܠܘܬܐ.

חירתא, *fort* (*ib.* B³) ; Syr. ܚܝܪܬܐ.

יקרור, *Yaqrur* (Nöldeke, *Zeitschrift für Assyriologie*, 1894, pp. 264–267, line 5) ; Syr. ܝܩܪܘܪ, *a toad.*

נמוסא, *established* (*Tariff*, i. ³) ; Syr. ܢܡܘܣܐ.

עלימיא, *youths* (*ib.* ii. a. ¹) ; Syr. ܥܠܝܡܐ.

16

אנוש כלה, *every one* (CIS 209[5]); Syr. idiomatic use of כל with suffix, *e.g.* ܟܠܗ ܣܒ̈ܐ (Nöld. *Syr. Gram.* § 218).

בר חרי, *freedman* (Vogüé, 75[3]); Syr. ܒܪ ܘܐܝ.

בת עלמא, *house of eternity* (Cl.-Gan. *Ét.* ii. § 5); Syr. ܣܒܕ ܟܝܟ̈ܐ; cf. Qoh. 12[5]; Vog. 36[a. b], CIS i. 124.

בזבן זבן, *at any time* (*Tariff*, i. [10]); Syr. ܙܒܢ ܘܙܒܢ (Pesh. John 5[4]).

משחא בשימא, *sweet oil* (*ib.* ii. a.[12]); Syr. cf. ܡܫܚܐ ܕܒܣ̈ܡܐ (Lk. 7[46]).

ודבר עמרה שכיתיח, *and he led his life peaceably* (Vog. 15[6]); cf. Syr. idiom : ܕܒܪ ܚ̈ܝܘܗܝ, *to lead a pure life*.

VIII

INCENTIVES TO NABATAEAN

Among the factors that contributed to the writing of the Nabataean Sinaitic inscriptions, perhaps the chief was the mining industry near Sârabît-al-Khâdim. This point seems overlooked by the editors of these inscriptions. Serabut el-Khadm was the site of an ancient Egyptian temple and colony, which arose in connexion with the turquoise mines of Wadi Maghârâ. The mines were worked as early as 4000 B.C., and now described as 'a warren of tunnellings, and burrows in the cliffs, where was some written trace of Pharaoh's luckless bondslaves, runes of antique hieroglyphics, cartouches and sculptures of the kings.' The inscriptions are scrawled on walls of reddish rock, the *Gebel el-Mukattib*, or 'Written Mountains,' and they are for the greater part the records of the mining adventurers, including nobles and serfs.[1] Some of them are remembrances to comrades left behind by the speculator as he

---

[1] The Prefetto of the Franciscans in Egypt, early in the 18th cent., called attention to these inscriptions: 'Though we had in our company persons who were acquainted with the Arabic, Greek, Hebrew, Syriac, Coptic, Latin, Armenian, Turkish, English, Illyrican, German, and Bohemian languages, yet none of them had any knowledge of these characters' (Rbt. Clayton, *apud* Thompson, *A Pilgrim's Scrip.* 175–176). That is, the rude cursive Nab. script was not then familiarized.

entered these regions seeking gain. Sometimes they are greetings to fellow-workers in the mines by the homeward-bound pilgrims, who, successful or unsuccessful, leave the Wadi Maghârâ behind. One inscription seems to embody both ideas : שלם אוישו בר פציו בטב, ' Welcome ! Oyashu, son of Patzyu : success ! ' [1] This looks like the greeting of an old acquaintance, and at the same time a parting expression of good-luck. The writer is perhaps returning from the mines ; he meets an old friend from Arabia,[2] who has come to seek a fortune in the turquoise quarries. They meet near the ' Written Mountains,' and the homeward-bound traveller incises his words of welcome and benediction in the bold red rock. Many of the Sinaitic inscriptions are undated, some of which probably belong to an earlier period than that usually assigned. Those dated are later ; some belong to the time of the Eparchy,[3] and others to the days of the ' three Caesars.' [4] No doubt some of these inscriptions owe their origin to traffickers on the great trade routes, who rested in the rocky passes of the peninsula, and spent their idle hours in inscribing greetings to fellow-travellers and to absent friends.[5]

IX

INTERMEDIATE ARAMAIC VERSION

To what extent the sacred language of the Jews· was written in Aramaic before the Christian era, is a question to which no certain answer can be given. It is probable that portions, select passages at least, of the Old Testament were transcribed in the Palestinian vernacular. This subject is worth a brief illustrative study. Some quotations from the Old Testament apparently owe their form in the New Testament to an intermediate Aramaic source. That is, between the Hebrew of the Old Testament and the Greek of the New Testament there stood an Aramaic written paraphrase. The so-called ' Logia ' of Matthew, or the indeterminate ' Q,'

---

[1] Euting, No. 519.   [2] The names appear to be Arabic.
[3] Beginning 106 A.D.   [4] הלחת קיסרין (Eut. 457)=210-211 A.D.
[5] Cf. Euting, *Sinaitische Inschriften*, 1891.

may have supplied some of the paraphrases and interpretations
which characterize the quotation and use of Old Testament
passages in the Gospels.   Along this line we may look for an
explanation, not only of the ' variants ' from the Hebrew text
and the LXX, but also the distinctly Messianic character of
these quotations in the Synoptists.   The following examples
will show the Targumic method of introducing terms—
Messianic, explanatory, exegetical—into the Aramaic renderings of the Hebrew text.   (1) Messianic : הָא עַבְדִּי מְשִׁיחָא,
' Behold, my servant, *the Messiah* ' (Is. 42¹, Targ. Jon. b. Uzz.) ;
הָא יִצְלַח עַבְדִּי מְשִׁיחָא, ' Behold, my servant, *the Messiah*, shall
prosper ' (Is. 52¹³ *ib.*).   (2) Explanatory : in the Hebrew
נַחֲמוּ נַחֲמוּ עַמִּי, the party immediately addressed is not named,
but the Targum supplies נְבִיאַיָּא, *prophets*, LXX ἱερεῖς, *priests*
(Is. 40¹).   (3) Exegetical : the reading of some authorities
(ADΠΦ *al.*), καὶ ἀφεθῇ αὐτοῖς τὰ ἁμαρτήματα (Mk. 4¹²), is
perhaps due to an intermediate Targum.   The form of the
Targum now extant, וְיִשְׁתְּבֵק (Jon. b. Uzz. Is. 6¹⁰), is suggestive.
Matthew (13¹⁵), Luke (Acts 28²⁷), John (12⁴⁰) borrow the
LXX reading καὶ ἰάσομαι αὐτούς, which in meaning is like
the Hebrew וְרָפָא לוֹ ; but Mark's ἀφεθῇ is clearly nearer to the
Targum יִשְׁתְּבַק.

It would appear from Paul's use of the Old Testament
(especially in Romans), that there was already a custom of
quoting passages to prove the calling of the Gentiles.   It is
probable that such passages, first quoted orally, were very
early collected together in writing.[1]   That collections of Old
Testament passages, supposed to be Messianic, were drawn
upon in the composition of the Gospels may be assumed.
Such collections would first appear in Aramaic, possibly in
pre-Christian times, and no doubt very early in Greek also,
perhaps compiled from the LXX.   Of the existence of these
' Testimonia ' or collections of Messianic proof texts in the
primitive Church, we have some evidence in the similar
' Testimonia ' edited by Cyprian, from which several Latin
writers quoted as from Scripture.   In these *catenae*, passages
of similar bearing were probably grouped under general
headings.   This would explain some discrepancies in the

---

[1] Cf. Hatch, *Essays in Bibl. Greek*, p. 103.

present Gospel text. Thus the words ἐν τῷ Ἡσαΐᾳ τῷ προφήτῃ (Mk. 1²) refer to language in Malachi as well as to words in Isaiah. The writer of the second Gospel probably had before him a *catena* of Old Testament excerpts in which Mal. 3¹ stood before Is. 40³, and the leaf was very likely headed ישעיה in Aramaic (or ⲏⲥⲁⲓⲁⲥ if in Greek).[1]

The quotation ὑποκάτω τῶν ποδῶν σου (Mk. 12³⁶ = Mt. 22⁴⁴) is against both the Hebrew הֲדֹם לְרַגְלֶיךָ and the LXX ὑποπόδιον τῶν ποδῶν σου (Ps. 110¹). Luke, however, follows the LXX exactly (20⁴³, Acts 2³⁵; the same form is quoted in Heb. 1¹³). The extant Targums give the same meaning as the Hebrew. Thus : כְּבִישׁ לְרִגְלָךְ, 'a footstool to thy feet.' It is best to suppose that the quotation came into Mark and Matthew from an Aramaic *catena* of Old Testament passages, in which the preposition תְּחוֹת (= ὑποκάτω) was used. The phrase 'beneath his feet' was quite familiar in Jewish thought and language. But the Targumists did not hesitate to vary the phrase; thus the Hebrew תַּחַת רַגְלָיו, 'under His feet,' becomes in Onkelos תְּחוֹת כֻּרְסֵי־יְקָרֵיהּ, 'under the throne of His glory' (Ex. 24¹⁰). We postulate, therefore, between the Hebrew of the Psalmist and the Greek of Mark and Matthew, an intermediate Aramaic document with a phrase such as תְּחוֹת רִיגְלָךְ.

The citation, καὶ ἔσονται οἱ δύο εἰς σάρκα μίαν (Mk. 10⁸ = Mt. 19⁵), corresponds verbally with the LXX (Gen. 2²⁴), but it is evident that the Gospel passage as a whole was not borrowed from that source. The reading is not according to the Hebrew, וְהָיוּ לְבָשָׂר אֶחָד, nor according to Onkelos, וִיהוֹן לְבִשְׂרָא חַד.[2] How then did δύο come into the Gospel text? We suggest an Aramaic paraphrase, as we actually find : והוו משניהן לבסר חדה (Ps.-Jon.), and וִיהוֹן תַּרְוֵיהוֹן לְבִישְׂרָא חָד (Samarit. Targ.). It is probable that these Targums preserve the common paraphrase of the Old Testament passage as quoted in the Synagogues, and perhaps written in the Aramaic *catenae*. The Synoptists simply followed the Aramaic paraphrase.

[1] A case like this is found in Irenaeus, where quotations from Mic. 7¹⁰ and Am. 1² are introduced by the formula : *Amos propheta ait* (*Adv. Haer.* iii. 20. 4).

[2] Note here, what is common in Aram., the idiom by which the direct object is denoted by לְ; cf. Dan. 2¹⁴.

Possibly the changes from the Hebrew and the LXX of Mic. 5¹ found in Mt. 2⁶, are due to some extent to the presence of an intermediate Aramaic. Originally אֶפְרָת was apparently very near Bethlehem, indeed connected with it (Gen. 48⁷). It was Bethlehem's suburb, Ephrath (hence אֶפְרָתָה, towards Ephrath, i.e. ה loc.), to which the Deliverer's royal ancestry was traced (1 S. 17¹²). But at the time of the Advent the distinction between Ephrath and Bethlehem was forgotten; hence the second place-name in the prophecy was not inserted in the Aramaic paraphrase. The phrase γῆ 'Ιούδα in Matthew may represent the בֵּית יְהוּדָה of the Targum, where 'house' might stand for a division of a province. The expression ἐν τοῖς ἡγεμόσιν 'Ιούδα is clearly not from the LXX, which reads ἐν χιλιάσιν 'Ιούδα, and so translates the present Massoretic text. Matthew's source appears to have read the Hebrew as if it were בְּאַלּוּפֵי, 'heads' or 'princes of' (tribes). The LXX in several places renders אַלּוּף by ἡγεμών (Gen. 36¹⁵, Ex. 15¹⁵, 1 Ch. 1⁵¹, Ps. 55¹⁴. Targ. has רַבָּא). The word in the intermediate Aramaic was probably רַבְרְבֵי, 'princes of' (cf. Gen. 36¹⁵ Onk., Mic. 5⁵ Jon. b. Uzz.). The words in Matthew, ὅστις ποιμανεῖ τὸν λαόν μου τὸν 'Ισραήλ, no doubt represent in some way the Hebrew מוֹשֵׁל בְּיִשְׂרָאֵל, which the Targum renders שׁוּלְטָן עַל־יִשְׂרָאֵל, 'ruler (Sultan) over Israel.' But the שׁוּלְטָן was not to be 'Ruler' merely. He was also to be 'Shepherd' (Zech. 13⁷), and this further Messianic idea was perhaps expressed in the Aramaic paraphrase. Just as the Targum on Micah 5¹ introduced the word מְשִׁיחָא, who was to be 'Servant-Prince' (עֲבִיד שׁוּלְטָן), so presumably the Aramaic paraphrast behind Matthew inserted the word רָעִי, 'Shepherd,' to characterize the work of the Messiah.

The quotation in Mt. 12¹⁸⁻¹⁹ from Is. 42²⁻³ may owe its form to an Aramaic rendering. The suggestion is based on the following words: (1) ἀπαγγελεῖ, 'shall declare.' This seems nearer to the Targum יְגַלֵּי, 'shall reveal,' than to the Hebrew יוֹצִיא, 'shall bring forth.' (2) ἐρίσει, 'shall strive.' This is nearer to a supposed Aramaic (Syr.) יְרִיב (ܢܪܝܒ), 'make a noise' (as in strife), than to the Hebrew

יִשָּׂא, 'shall lift up' (as the voice). (3) ἐκβάλῃ, 'send forth,' is really nearer to the Targum יַפֵּיק, 'cause to go forth,' than to the Hebrew יוֹצִיא, 'shall bring forth.' (4) εἰς νῖκος, 'unto victory.' This is, of course, nearer to a supposed Aramaic לִזְכוּת (Syr. ܠܙܳܟܘܽܬ), 'justice,' and (in Talmud) 'victory,' than to the Hebrew לָאֱמֶת, 'unto truth.' It should be added that εἰς νῖκος in the Gospel passage may be used Hellenistically for לָנֶצַח, 'for ever,' as LXX in 2 S. 2²⁶, Job 36⁷; cf. Hab. 1⁴. The idea of 'victory' was certainly associated with נצח in Hebrew in a few late passages, but this meaning of the word is more naturally Aramaic, in which language alone the relation of the Hebrew and other derivatives of the term become apparent.[1]

The foregoing illustrations are among the evidences which tend to confirm the conclusion that earlier than the Greek Gospel, and perhaps in pre-Christian times, there was a written Aramaic paraphrase of certain Old Testament passages, chiefly Messianic. To what extent, if any, the Logia of Jesus of Nazareth were written in Aramaic, is a problem that scarcely comes within this study. That Jesus habitually taught in Aramaic is now practically agreed; and that after fifteen or twenty years of oral transmission the Sayings were gradually put into writing, is also now generally admitted. The tradition preserved by Eusebius,[2] in all probability, perpetuates a fact. Papias says that Matthew, the Apostle, set-in-order-together[3] a compendium of Sayings of Jesus, τῇ Ἑβραΐδι διαλέκτῳ. It must be understood that Ἑβραΐδι

---

[1] The root idea of נצח is *to make brilliant*. The primary Heb. idea of the word is *to lead on, to complete*; the primary Aram. idea is *to surpass, to vanquish*; hence the later ideas of 'perpetuity' and 'victory.' The Gk. translators render נצח by ἰσχύσας, εἰς τέλος, εἰς νῖκος. The Syr. retains the original meaning *splenduit*, for example: ܟܳܠܳܢ ܙܳܟܳܐ ܢܘܽܣܝܢ, 'raiment fine, shining' (Apoc. 15⁶, Pesh.). In Phoen. נצח was employed in the sense of *to conquer* (*vide* נצחת, 'I conquered,' CIS i. 91²). In Heb. נצחת (Pt.)=*enduring* (*e.g.* Jer. 8¹), and is the opposite to משבה=*apostasy* (*e.g.* Jer. 3⁶). Cf. Driver, *Samuel*², pp. 128 f.

[2] *Hist. Eccl.* iii. 39. 16.

[3] συνετάξατο (or συνεγράψατο, cf. Lk. 1¹ ἀνατάξασθαι); LXX for יצא, cf. Arab. وصى, *tie together*.

here means Συριστί (LXX for ארמית), and that as early as 50 A.D. Palestinian Christians adopted writing 'as a means of collecting, circulating, and preserving the Memorabilia of Jesus.'[1]   That the Λόγια were written in Judaea for Judaeans and in the Judaean dialect, is further to be concluded.[2]

X

GOSPEL PASSAGE IN 'CURSIVE' ARAMAIC

It may be little more than an idle speculation to attempt a representation of a bit of Gospel papyrus of the early Christian era.   The hand-written script would naturally be more cursive and less exact than that of the engraved stone or metal.   Probably the Egyptian Aramaic will be the best guide.   Adapting this script, a Gospel passage, if written by Jesus of Nazareth, or by one of His disciples, would appear something like the following:[3]

---

[1] Vide Votaw, Hastings' DB., extra vol., pp. 5-6.

[2] The testimony of Jerome favours this view: Matthaeus, qui et Levi, ex publicano Apostolus, primus in Judaea propter eos qui ex circumcisione crediderant, Evangelium Christi Hebraicis literis verbisque composuit, quod quis postea in Graecum transtulerit, non satis certum est.   De Vir. Ill. 3.

[3] The passage is Mt. 11^28ff., and the dialect supposed is Judaean Aramaic.   The saying is probably coloured by Ecclus. 51, and is more Semitic in form and conception than the context.   The Greek, ταπεινὸς τῇ καρδίᾳ, is represented by שפל בלב.   Delitzsch has put it differently in Hebrew, שפל רוח, 'lowly of spirit'; this agrees with Prov. 16^19, but the idea is different in the Gospel passage.   The phrase ταῖς ψυχαῖς ὑμῶν represents לנפשתיכן, 'for (to) yourselves.'   Compare the Hebrew: ומצאו מרגוע לנפשכם, 'ye shall find quiet to yourselves' (Jer. 6^16; מרגוע is poetical and rare).   The Phoen. for 'rest' is נחת (CIS i. 46, l. 2, al.); Aram. נוח (Targ. Ps. 93^2 al.).   The form ניחח (Ezra 6^10, Dan. 2^46) is apparently a reversion to Hebrew.

X

THE TARGUMS:
EXHIBITING THE LATER ARAMAIC OF PALESTINE

I

JEWISH ACADEMIES

AFTER the Exile the knowledge of Hebrew was perpetuated by the Scribes in great central academies. The first and most important college was at Jerusalem. The origin of the scribal party is very obscure, and may go back to Babylonian times. For the early growth of this school of thought the most useful sources are the Old Testament Apocrypha, and the Psalter of Solomon among the Pseudepigrapha. Opposed to the high-priestly caste, the Scribes originated the Synagogue service, and developed into a pronounced political party.[1] After the destruction of Jerusalem, literary institutions sprung up at Caesarea and Tiberias in Palestine, and at Nehardea and Sura in Babylonia. This phase of the subject takes us into the post-Christian age, but it is worth a little study, inasmuch as it shows the kind of influence exerted by these schools of learning on the Aramaic text of religious literature.

The points to be clearly kept in mind in this section of

---

[1] The Scribes were drawn mainly from the 'school' of the Pharisees. But Wellhausen is not correct in affirming that the Pharisees were the party of the Scribes (*Pharisaer u. Sadducaer*, 11). Their attitude towards the Law of Moses on the one hand, and towards the Roman Government on the other, is well expressed by Josephus (*Ant.* xviii. 8. 3).

the subject are the following: (1) There were two main lines
of the traditional Targum-texts, one in Palestine (the western
section of the north Semitic branch), and the other in
Babylonia (the eastern section of the north Semitic branch).
(2) The Jewish schools in Palestine were earlier than those
in Babylonia, and the tradition went from Palestine to
Babylonia. (3) The text which grew up in Arabia was due
chiefly to Palestine; possibly the Palestinian tradition, in
some degree, reached Arabia *via* Babylonia. (4) In both the
western and eastern schools the language was Aramaic, with
dialectic differences; there were also artificial attempts to use
and perpetuate Hebrew. (5) Two types of text resulted from
these scribal academies, west and east—a more literal, and a
more rabbinic. The purpose of the following pages is to
show that the more literal text was preserved in Palestine,
that this text was differently treated in Babylonia at
Nehardea and Sura respectively, and that the Nehardean (*i.e.*
the more literal) type was preserved in some of the Yemen
MSS of the Targum of Onkelos. Therefore the Yemen form
of this Targum is a better guide to the Palestinian
Aramaic than the generally accepted European (*i.e.* Babylonian) type.[1]

II

INTER-RELATION OF THE TARGUMS

Inter-relation of the Targums. Besides Onkelos there
are two Targums on the Pentateuch—the so-called Pseudo-
Jonathan and the Jerushalmi. Pseudo-Jonathan is considered
later than the Jerushalmi or Fragment Targum, perhaps, as
late as the seventh century. The dialect of these Palestinian
Targums is substantially the same, though the differences are
sufficient to prove diversity of authorship. Their likenesses
are due to their relation to Onkelos. The author of the
Jerushalmi took the work of Onkelos as his foundation. His
object was to correct and improve it by inserting a selection

---

[1] *Vide* Barnstein, *The Targ. of Onk.* . . . *exhibited by Yemen MSS*
(1896).

of Haggadahs (homilies, etc.) which were current in Jewish circles. Pseudo-Jonathan undertook much the same office, to continue and complete the work of his predecessor. Thus the basis of Pseudo-Jonathan was Onkelos plus the Jerushalmi; the basis of the Jerushalmi was Onkelos alone. It follows that the oldest and therefore the most important portions of these Palestinian Targums are due to Onkelos.[1] Consequently among these authorities Onkelos must be the chief source and guide.

III

DATE OF ONKELOS

There is no reason for making the date of Onkelos as late as the time of the Talmudists, as some continental scholars have done.[2] There is really no evidence for placing the date in the second half of the second century. The grounds upon which this date is based are the following, which it will be seen are not conclusive. (1) The absence of anthropomorphisms. But the tendency to avoid anthropomorphism is seen as early as the LXX.[3] (2) The admission of Greek forms. But these are few, and do not change the colour of the Aramaic as a whole; they are found rather in the Babylonian (hence European) MSS than in the S. Arabian, and the western text was more subject to Greek influence than the eastern. Moreover, Greek words are found in Biblical Aramaic; it is not surprising, therefore, if some forms had become naturalized in the Aramaic at the end of the first century. (3) The presence of Rabbinic principles. To assert that the Halachic and Haggadic methods of Akiba are followed by Onkelos is simply to beg the question.[4] These

---

[1] We do not discuss the authorship (cf. Bab. *Meg.* iii. 1; Pal. *Meg.* i. 11). The name אנקלוס is confused with עקילס, Aquila.

[2] Cf. Geiger, *Urschrift u. die Übersetzungen der Bibel*, Breslau, 1857; Frankel, *Zu dem Targum der Propheten*, Breslau, 1872.

[3] Such a simple expression as 'the hand of the Lord' is changed, *e.g.* יד־יהוה becomes πληγέντες κυρίου (Ex. 16³). The Samaritan Targum also removes many anthropomorphisms of the Hebrew text.

[4] Cf. Zunz, *Die gottesdienstlichen Vorträge der Juden*, 1892.

principles were common to Jewish schools of learning in the first century, and it cannot be shown that Onkelos was specifically influenced by Akiba.   It is still more important to observe that the Halachic and Haggadic features of the Onkelos Targum belong to the Babylonian (hence European) MSS ; these principles scarcely appear in the Yemen (original Palestine) text.   (4) The date of contemporaries.   It is said that a grandson of the elder Gamaliel[1] was the master and friend of Aquila (Onkelos).   But as the name Gamaliel was common in Judaism, there may be some confusion here.   In any case a grandson of Gamaliel does not necessarily involve a date later than the beginning of the second century. Gamaliel's grandson may well have been living when the Acts of the Apostles were written.[2]   Thus the date of Onkelos is probably to be placed early in the second century.

IV

LOCALE OF ONKELOS TARGUM

It is probable that the Onkelos Targum had its origin in Palestine.   The argument adduced against this is the fact that after the political changes in Palestine consequent on the Roman occupation, considerable literary activity was transferred to Babylon.   This, however, does not prove that sacred and Targumic studies were neglected in Palestine.   That the Jews in Palestine continued to be the pioneers in Biblical study is certain.   Of this there are the outstanding proofs : (a) The Massora.   This was for the purpose of perpetuating the exact text of the Old Testament.   It consisted in a mass of elaborate rules and calculations to guard the integrity of the sacred text.   The work was undertaken in Palestine, and extended over a considerable period.   (b) The Midrashim. These were imaginative developments of Old Testament

---

[1] Gamaliel the Elder (זָקֵן) died 52 A.D. ; his grandson, Gamaliel the Younger (זְעֵירָא), died 115.   *Vide* Lightfoot, *Horae Heb. et Tal.*

[2] Cf. Schürer, *Geschichte des judischen Volkes im Zeitalter Jesu Christi,* ii. pp. 299 f.; Grätz, *Geschichte der Juden,* iii. pp. 349 f.; Ewald, *Geschichte des Volkes Israel,* vii. pp. 193 f.

themes, homiletic and didactic explanations. These commentaries had their origin in Palestine, and bear witness to the activity of the Rabbinical institutions down to a period as late as the tenth century.[1]

V

TYPES OF PALESTINIAN TARGUM

The foregoing statements not only show that sacred studies were not neglected in Palestine, but they also indicate a suggestive and important fact. Two types of study were pursued apparently side by side—the literal (the Massora) and the haggadic (the Midrashim). This would lead us to expect Targumic literature in Palestine corresponding to these two types of study. This is precisely what we do find. The literal Targum is represented by Onkelos, and the haggadic by the Jerushalmi. The latter Targum, irrespective of its type, is evidence that the study was carried on in Palestine. This Targum, because of its haggadic character, is not a safe guide to the actual text of the Old Testament. Its phraseology, however, may be valuable in giving a clue to the written speech of Palestine. It is true that many words are found in this Targum, as also in the Palestinian Talmud, which are not found elsewhere in extant Aramaic literature.[2] By the side of this paraphrastic Targum there would undoubtedly be a literal translation into Aramaic. There was always a school of Jews who consistently endeavoured to maintain and perpetuate the exact text of Scripture. This literal translation of the Pentateuch is commonly ascribed to Onkelos. These types of Targum, we may believe, had a parallel history in Palestine. The literal translation is evidently more valuable for deciding the Old Testament text. But both types are valuable in the study of the dialect and idiom, inasmuch as where the two texts agree the vocabulary

---

[1] On Midrash generally, *vide* Wolf, *Bibl. Hebraea*; Zunz, *Die gottesdienstlichen Vorträge*; Frankel, *Hodegetica in Mischnam*; Weiss, *Zur Geschichte der judischen Tradition*; Derenbourg, *Histoire de la Palestine*.

[2] Note the frequent use of 'nur in Jer. Targ.' in Levy's *Lexicons*.

and construction are much the same.[1]   The texts, orthography
and punctuation of the Targums still remain in an uncritical
state.[2]   Buxtorf was the first to introduce into the Targums
a complete system of consecutive vocalization, based on the
Massoretic texts of the Aramaic sections of Ezra and Daniel.[3]
But this, as we shall see, must be supplemented by a study of
the S. Arabian text of Onkelos.

VI

DISPERSION OF PALESTINIAN TEXT

The text of the Onkelos Targum usually quoted must be
regarded with suspicion.   It is pretty certain that the MSS
from which most editions of this Targum have been made
present many imperfections of form and vocalization.   The
MSS available do not preserve the Palestinian text directly,
and it is a problem for criticism to decide how far the
original text has been vitiated by its passage through other
regions and other hands.   It would seem that the Palestinian
text went out in two main directions—north-east to the Jews
in Chaldaea, and south-east to the Jews in S. Arabia ; thus :

The Onkelos text found in the great Polyglotts and in most
modern editions is the Babylonian.   But here two types must
be distinguished.   Great attention was given to the Targum
in Babylon, but changes in the text would inevitably tend to

---

[1] The difference between the two Targums is illustrated in the following
passage, Gen. 1²⁷ :

Onkelos : וּבְרָא יְיָ   Jerushalmi : וּבְרָא מֵימְרָא דַיְיָ יַת אָדָם
יָת אָדָם בְּצַלְמֵיה   בִּדְמוּתֵיה בִּדְמוּת מִן קֳדָם
בְּצַלְמָא דַיְיָ בְּרָא   יְיָ בְּרָא יָתֵיה דְכַר וְזוּגֵיה
יָתֵיה דְכַר וְנוּקְבָא   בְּרָא יַתְהוֹן
בְּרָא יַתְהוֹן

[2] On the MSS of Onkelos, *vide* Winer, *De Onkeloso ejusque paraphr.
Chald.*, Leipsic, 1820 ; Berliner, *Targum Onkelos*, Berlin, 1884.

[3] Vide *Biblia Heb. cum Paraphr. Chald. et Comm. Rabbin.*, 1618–1619.

multiply. The vernacular of the Jewish settlers would be influenced by the regions round about them ; words would be pronounced differently, this would involve alterations of spelling and vocalization. Very soon, too, there would be a tendency to explain ; glosses at first only oral or written on the margin of MSS would be later incorporated in the text. That these processes went on in Babylonia is clearly indicated by the two forms of the text—the Nehardean tradition and the Sura tradition ; thus :

Babylonian Targum

Nehardean recension   Sura recension

An examination of the MSS shows that the Nehardean school in Babylon endeavoured to preserve the Palestinian text without accretion, while the Sura school allowed greater haggadic liberty. It would perhaps be better to state this in another way. Soon after the arrival of the Palestine text in Babylon a tendency began to substitute haggadic explanations in place of the original readings. In course of time a reaction was inaugurated in favour of the original Palestinian rendering. This is the so-called Nehardean recension. Strictly there never has been a satisfactory Targum text. An examination of the MSS and the printed editions shows that no serious endeavour was made to ensure a critical and faithful text. The Targums did not attain a fixed form until printing stereotyped certain copies. At first little care was bestowed on the vocalization, and this is still very imperfect. It will be seen that the Yemen MSS of Onkelos, perhaps influenced by the Nehardean school, provide in all respects the best recension.

VII

CONNEXION WITH BABYLON

That the Jewish settlement in Yemen had considerable intercourse with the Jews of Babylonia is evident enough. It is safe to assert that the Targum in S. Arabia was in some way influenced by the Babylonian tradition. Neubauer connects the Jews in Yemen with Babylon. Speaking of the epitaphs which have been discovered in Yemen, he says, ' these epitaphs, dated according to the era of the contracts, point to an acquaintance with the Babylonian schools. . . . The Jews of Yemen continue up to the present day to date from the era of the contracts, using Aramaic formulae, which point more to Babylonia than to Palestine.' But Neubauer quite unwarrantably continues : ' The use of superlinear vowel-points (usually called Assyrian Punctuation) in the pointed Hebrew texts written in Yemen would argue their connexion with the eastern Massoretic Schools rather than with the Palestinian one at Tiberias.' [1] This conclusion is not convincing (vide infra), as Margoliouth has clearly shown.[2]

It is not easy to decide the kind of influence exerted by Babylon on the Targum in Yemen. The only evidence is derived from a careful examination of the MSS. It is at once apparent that the Yemen texts are less haggadic than those of Babylon, and this suggests a purer form. The Babylonian tradition which probably most influenced the Yemen Jewish School was the Nehardean. This more literal version would appeal to the Jewish colony in S. Arabia, whose tradition appears less paraphrastic than that from the further East. But this Babylonian influence was probably complementary rather than causal. We have seen that the Palestinian tradition went out in two directions—to Babylon and to S. Arabia. Therefore it is not at all necessary to suppose that the form of the Yemen MSS was decided by any connexion with Babylon. It is just as easy to assume, and more natural to conclude, that the Yemen type of text came directly from Palestine. It is now clearly proved that the Yemen MSS of Onkelos are of the Nehardean type, while those which have come to Europe (via Babylon) are more in harmony with the Sura type. The defect of nearly all western editions of

---

[1] Jewish Quarterly Review, iii. pp. 604-622.

[2] ' On the Superlinear Vocalization ' (Transactions of the 9th Congress of Orientalists, ii. 1893), pp. 46-56.

Onkelos is that they are based almost exclusively on the European MSS.[1]

VIII

CHARACTERISTICS OF YEMEN TEXT

The Yemen MSS reveal some differences among themselves. Only the features of text which seem to suggest originality need be considered here. The value of this study is not merely in ascertaining the more correct text of Onkelos, but in taking us some way towards the discovery of the Palestinian Aramaic. For this purpose it is important to state clearly the outstanding characteristics of the Yemen MSS of Onkelos.

The vocalization is superlinear. Since this is simpler than the sublinear, it may be assumed to be the older system. It is most suited to the Aramaic language, since vowel-signs peculiar to the Hebrew can the more easily be omitted. Probably the earliest vocalization of Syriac was superlinear, and some editors have regarded this as the more convenient and elegant system.[2] There is no direct evidence on the origin of this system, and scholars have too readily attributed it to Babylon. The place of origin is not itself important; it is far more important to emphasize the primitive character of this system. At the same time the simplicity of the vocalization, and its likeness to the earliest pointed Syriac, suggest Palestine rather than Babylon as the place of origin. Neubauer, as stated before, would connect this system with the East rather than with the West. Dalman's investigations led him to a similar conclusion.[3]

[1] Bomberg and Buxtorf, *Biblia Complutensis*, Venice, 1526; Walton, *Polyglott*; Luzzato, *Philoxenus sive de Onkelosi paraph. chald.*, 1830; Berliner, *Targum Onkelos*, Berlin, 1884, whose text is a reprint of the Sabionetta edition of 1554.

[2] Cf. the Syr. Pentateuch edited in this way by Kirsch, Hofa, 1787.

[3] *Grammatik jüdisch-palästinischen Aramäisch*, 1905, pp. 11 ff., 70 ff. Strack makes the uncertain statement: 'The so-called Babylonian or more accurately the superlinear punctuation, the vowel-signs of which are simplified forms of the matres lectionis א, ו, and ׳, and the detached accents of which usually have the shape of the letters with which their name

17

But no proofs have been given to show a Babylonian source, and the conclusion rests on pure assumption. It seems more natural to suppose that the superlinear vocalization was initiated in Palestine, and was taken to Babylon and Yemen with the written text of the Targum. The statement of Nöldeke is in harmony with this view, that 'the authoritative Targum although redacted in Babylon exhibits a dialect whose fundamental characteristics are Palestinian.'[1] The simpler and more primitive the punctuation, the more original it is likely to be. It is quite contrary to well-defined laws that a completely developed vocalization should regress to a primitive and more archaic form.

The vowel-signs.—There are six signs, placed above the consonants, which correspond to the Hebrew as follows: ᘯ = ָ; ᘰ = ֶ; ̈ = ֳ; ˙ = ֹ; ˙ = ִ; ᔿ = ֻ. Probably these signs do not represent the most primitive Aramaic pointing. They are, however, manifestly more suited to Aramaic than the more elaborate Hebrew system. The case of the Syriac punctuation confirms this statement. There is possibly some connexion between the vowel-signs revealed by the Yemen MSS and the earliest pointed Syriac MSS. But there is absolutely no evidence for the theory of Margoliouth that this system of vocalization represents a mixed Nestorian-Jacobite punctuation.[2] This becomes the more unlikely as we discover indications of a Palestinian origin. In the following passage the use of the six signs is illustrated from the Yemen MSS.[3] This is compared with the same passage as found in the European editions of Onkelos:

Yemen.	Babylonian.
וְקרָא יָתֵהּ שִׁבְעָה עַל כֵּן ·	וּקְרָא יָתֵהּ שִׁבְעָא עַל־כֵּן
שְׁמֵהּ דִּקַרְתָּא בְּאֵר שֶׁבַע	שְׁמָא־דְקַרְתָּא בְּאֵר־שֶׁבַע
עַד יוֹמָא הָדֵין	עַד־יוֹמָא הָדֵין

Omitted vowel-signs.—In the foregoing illustration the horizontal line appears to represent *sheva mobile*. In some of

begins, was in use among the non-Palestinian Jews of Asia.'—*Einleitung in das alte Testament*, 1888, p. 74.

[1] *Mandäische Gram.*, Introd. p. v.
[2] 'On the Superlinear Vocalization,' *loc. cit.*
[3] Gen. 26^33, from Codex Heb. Gaster No. 2.

the Yemen MSS, too, there is a sign which probably indicates the *Raphe*, and occasionally a point within a letter of the value of *Dagesh*. But in the best and most perfect of these MSS there are no signs for *Segol*, *Kibbuts*, *Dagesh*, *Raphe*, nor for *sheva compositum*.[1] These signs, which suit the Hebrew, and which in later Aramaic were imitated, are inappropriate to Aramaic, whose original vocalization was superlinear. They are also unknown in Syriac, whose vocalization is simpler and more original than the system which was adopted in Babylon in imitation of the Hebrew.[2] It is probable that the earliest MSS of Biblical Aramaic had no sign for *sheva compositum*. In any attempt to write the Aramaic of the first Christian century, we should omit *Dagesh*, as well as the other vowel-signs named. 'The oldest known MSS only use the *Dagesh* in the Hebrew, but not in the Targum, a fact which seems to show that the *Dagesh* is not a part of the superlinear system as such.'[3]

Matres lectionis.—Before the vowel-signs were adopted, the vowel-letters א, ו, י aided the pronunciation. It was natural that these letters would be dropped in many instances when the Massoretic pointing was introduced.[4] This we find to be the case in the Yemen MSS, but the Targums of Europe retained a redundancy of vowel-letters.[5] These letters should be retained in any attempt to represent the unpointed Aramaic script of the first Christian century. It is quite noteworthy that the *matres lectionis* are scarcely ever omitted in the Egyptian (Assuan) Papyri.[6] The doubled letters וו and יי are rare in the Yemen MSS, and are not found in Ezra and Daniel, but are frequent in our usual Targum editions.[7] This

---

[1] *E.g.* Codex Heb. Gaster No. 2.

[2] Nöldeke, '*Beiträge zur Kenntniss der aramäischen Dialecte*,' in *ZDMG* xxii.

[3] Margoliouth, 'On the Superlinear Vocalization,' *loc. cit.* p. 46.

[4] Berliner, *Targum Onkelos*, p. 133.

[5] Nöldeke, *Beiträge zur Kenntniss der aramäischen Dialecte*, p. 447.

[6] The following have been noted: בניהם for ביניהם, and שקא for שוקא (cf. E 14 and A 12, 14); עתק for עתוק (cf. E 12 and D 16).

[7] The first י is probably a later substitution for א, due to a phonetic cause. We find in Yemen MSS both כמחייך and כמאיך. The vocalization is כְּמִחֵ֖יְ, כמחֵ֖אְיְ (cf. our Targ. כְּמֵחָיִר, Gen. 19¹⁴). That the original א was

is quite explicable, inasmuch as the earlier writings were necessarily as simple as possible. It is doubtful whether the early Jews had any system of shorthand, but in writing the vowels were unexpressed. There were some apparently shortened forms in the earliest Hebrew, such as אש for איש, צר for צור, ימן for ימין, החצבם for החצבים; but this defective writing was really the full writing of the age. The absence of the vowel-letters is not to be regarded as abbreviation, but as characteristic of the primitive writings, which consisted often of brief formulae, particularly in burial and votive inscriptions. The use of ו and י in the middle of words, especially when doubled, was a later development, when the ancient pronunciation was in danger.[1] The pronunciation of Semitic was earlier advanced than the orthography.

Verbal forms.—In the extant Targum MSS there is considerable interchange in the conjugations. But doubtless in the pre-Massoretic period there was greater consistency in the expression of ideas by appropriate verbal forms. If data were available, it would probably be found that Aramaic originally used the *Ethpeel* in many instances where the *Peal* now stands. This finds some support in the characteristic employment of the *Ethpeel* in Syriac.[2] The best Yemen MSS point in the same direction, though there is some confusion in these MSS in the use of the conjugations.[3] There are instances in

pronounced as י is suggested by the Syriac, *e.g.* ܩܳܐܶܡ =*ka-yem*. Cf. the

Samaritan אד (אד=later יד), Ex. 16[3].

[1] Cf. Babyl.	Yemen.	Babyl.	Yemen.
תְּנֵין (Ps. Jon.)	תנֵּן (G. 1[8])	וְאַבְרִיכִנָּךְ (Onk.)	וֶאֱזְּבִנֵךְ (G. 26[3])
חייתא (Ps. Jon.)	חִיֵּא (G.1[20])	סוֹרְחָנִי (Onk.)	סֻרְחָנִי (G. 31[36])
חֵיוַת (Ps. Jon.)	חִיוֹת (G. 1[25])	וְרַעֲיָן (Onk.)	וּלְאֵנִי (G. 41[18])
הֵילְיֵהוֹן (Ps. Jon.)	הֵילֵיהוֹן (G. 2[1])	לְקַנִין (Onk.)	לְאֵנִי (G. 41[23])
פַּרְוֵיהוֹן (Ps. Jon.)	אֵלְדִיתוֹן (G. 2[25])	דְּיֵייְמַר (Onk.)	דִּיאָמַר (G. 41[55])
וַאֲקַיֵּם (Onk.)	דָּאֵיסִים (G. 26[3])	עַנְיִי (Bomberg ed.)	עֲנִי (G. 31[43])

In the oldest inscrip. a medial ו or י indicated a diphthong, *au* or *ai, e.g.* עוד *'aud*; דיבן, *Daibon* (*Siloam*, l. 1; Moab. St. ll. 21, 28).

[2] The preformative אִת is perhaps a fragment of the verb אֲתָא, *he came,* which was originally written in full. In course of time it was pronounced, and consequently written with the verb which it qualified (cf. Lee, *Heb. Gram.*).

[3] *E.g.* in some Yemen MSS we find ואסתלק (Gen. 26[23]) and דאיתילידו (Gen.

Biblical Aramaic in which the Ethpeel preformative has been dropped, probably to simplify the script, and in some cases to imitate the Hebrew. The terms מנא, תקל, פרס (Dan. 5[25. 28]), would more naturally express the ideas intended in the Ethpeel: אֶתְמְנִי, 'it is numbered'; אִתְּקֵל, 'it is weighed'; אֶתְפְּרֵס, 'it is divided.'[1] The following passage (Gen. 17[26-27]) in the Yemen MSS of Onkelos compared with the western (= Babylonian) text, will indicate how much more appropriate the Ethpeel of גזר is compared with the Peal:[2]

Yemen.	Babylonian.
בכרן יומא הדין אתגזר	בְּכְרַן יוֹמָא הָדֵין גְּזַר
אברהם … וכל אנשׁ	אַבְרָהָם . . . וְכָל אֱנָשֵׁי
בית־ה …אתגזרו עמ־ה	בֵיתֵיהּ . . . גְּזָרוּ עִמֵּיהּ

Other traits.—The absence of almost all punctuation signs in the S. Arabian Targum MSS shows that the Aramaic of these MSS is much nearer the Biblical Aramaic and the Syriac than the editions of Onkelos which are based on European MSS, which had their origin in Babylon. Even *Athnach* and *Soph-pasuk* are not found in the best Yemen MSS. This suggests an independence of Babylon, and indicates originality. The Absolute and Emphatic states are not strictly observed in these MSS. This was characteristic of primitive Aramaic, and also of the kindred Mandaean.[3] The confusion of genders in the S. Arabian texts points to a conclusion otherwise supported, that originally Aramaic had no distinct forms for

46[32]), but in others וסליק and דילית. The western text has וסלק and דאתילידו; the Samaritan Targ. has וסלק and דילדת; the Hebrew has ויעל (act.) and ילד (pass.).

Interchanges are found between Peal and Pael (Gen. 31[54]); Peal and Aphel (Gen. 4[3]); Peal and Ethpaal or Ethpeel (Gen. 3[19]); Pael and Aphel (Gen. 34[19]); Ethpeel and Ethpaal (Gen. 42[19]).

[1] Cf. Baer's edition of Philippi's *Libri Danielis, Ezrae et Nehemiae*, p. lix.

[2] The Heb. text from which this Targ. was made was almost identical with that of the Massoretes. It is rather curious that the Heb. word נמול (Niph.), corresponding to the Aram. גזר in the above passage, is vocalized as an Aram. form. The Heb. text is given for comparison; the Yemen recension best agrees with it: בְּעֶצֶם הַיּוֹם הַזֶּה נִמּוֹל אַבְרָהָם . . . וְכָל אֱנָשֵׁי בֵיתוֹ . . . נִמֹּלוּ אִתּוֹ

[3] Nöldeke, *Mandäische Grammatik*, p. 300.

masculine and feminine. The use of הוא in the Pentateuch
(Heb. *Kethib*) for both הוא and היא points in this direction, and
is possibly due to Aramaic influence.[1] The distinction, however, had come into Aramaic earlier than 500–400 B.C.[2] It
may be added that the letter שׂ does not belong to Aramaic at
all; it is found in the western editions of Onkelos as an
importation from Hebrew. The Aramaic letter is ס, and
should be consistently employed.

IX

INITIATION OF WRITTEN TARGUMS

It is probable that written Targums were in existence
earlier than the first direct reference to them. The chief
synagogues had a Targumist of their own; for instance, Rabbi
Chuzpith, early in the first century, was התורגמן[3] at the
important synagogue at Jamnia on the northern border of
Judah (*Berakhoth*, 27ᵇ). Rules regulating the practice and
duties of the 'Targumists' are given in the Mishna (*Meg.*
iv. 4). At first the use of written Targums was forbidden
for the interpretation of the Law on the Sabbath (Jerus. *Meg.*
iv. 1; Tal. Bab. *Sabb.* 115ᵃ). Not till the beginning of the
fourth century do we hear of the formal reading from a
written Targum: עאל לכנישתא חמא חד ספר מושט תרגומא מן גו סיפרא
(Jerus. *Meg.* 74ᵈ¹⁵). On the other hand, the preparation of
written Targums was allowed for private study and tutorial
work. It is to be presumed that the interpretations were
written and committed to memory before they were given
orally by the מתורגמנים in the synagogues. In this sense the
written Targums were initiated as early as the institution of
the guild of interpreters. Notice: (*a*) The Targum was
probably written a considerable time before it was read in the
synagogue. (*b*) The practice of learning these interpretations,
and their constant repetition, would tend to fixity of phrase-

---

[1] Cf. for use of common gender, Brit. Mus. MS. Orient. 2374.

[2] Both הו and הי are used in Egyptian (Assuan) Papyri.

[3] For the form and pronunciation of this word, *vide* Bacher, *Die älteste
Terminologie der jüdischen Schriftauslegung*, p. 206.

ology. (c) The Targumic form of some Old Testament passages, quoted in the New Testament, may be accounted for in this way (e.g. Mt. 27⁴⁶, cf. Ps. 22²; Mk. 10⁸, cf. Gen. 2²⁴; Eph. 4⁸, cf. Ps. 68¹⁹).

X

TARGUMS PERPETUATE SOME OLD FORMS

In concluding this section on the value and characteristics of the Targums, the position may be briefly restated. (1) The Onkelos Targum stands first, and presents the purest Aramaic, being most free from Hebraisms. Nöldeke[1] contends that Onkelos was considerably revised throughout, but he does not sufficiently differentiate between the Palestinian, Babylonian and Yemen recensions. (2) The Biblical Aramaic comes next in importance. It is similar to Onkelos in vocabulary, orthography and grammatical construction, but has a larger intermixture of Hebrew characteristics.[2] Its punctuation is in some respects more trustworthy than that of some versions of the Babylonian Onkelos. (3) The other Targums have many foreign words and abound in peculiar forms.[3] (3) The later vernacular of Galilee is perhaps best represented by the so-called Jerusalem Targums.

It is obvious that any study of the Targums for linguistic purposes has its limitations. The Targums, for instance, have little value for a critical discussion of the text of the Old Testament. The latter was practically fixed before the former were written. Yet a study of these recensions is an important factor in any attempt to recover the language of Palestine at

---

[1] *Encycl. Bibl. s.v.* ' Aram. Lang.,' sect. 6. Cf. Dalman, *Gram. d. jüd. pal. Aram.*

[2] *E.g.* Bibl. Aram. has ה for א ; pl. ending ים for ין and יא ; the Hophal conj. which is unknown in pure Aram.

[3] *E.g.* Aphel אוקים for אקים (fr. קום) ; מ preformative of the inf. Pael, Ithpeel and Ithpaal. Peculiarities of later Aram. arise from (a) Assimil. to Syr. and Rabbinic, thus : נ prefixed to 3rd pl. fut., instead of י ; the syll. נת prefixed to Passives, instead of את (cf. Targ. 1 S. 23⁷). (b) Contractions. *E.g.* in the case of the Numerals : חדסר for חד עסר (mas.) ; חדסרי for עסרי חדא (fem.). Onk. חַד עֲשַׂר, G. 37⁹ ; חֲדָא עֲשָׂרֵי, E. 26⁷; Syr. *ib.* ܚܕܥܣܪ.

the close of our period. The main facts are : (*a*) that the Targums were composed in Palestine, (*b*) that they were written in the Aramaic of Judaea, (*c*) that the Judaean Aramaic, though later, is essentially the same as that of Ezra and Daniel,[1] and (*d*) that this type of Aramaic is best exhibited in the Yemen MSS of Onkelos. The Targums which were edited in Babylonia inevitably owe something to the type of Aramaic spoken by the editors. On the other hand, it is true that the more literal editions of Palestine were to some small extent influenced by the Hebrew idiom. Though the Targums as we now know them are comparatively late,[2] they undoubtedly embody much that is older, and perpetuate forms and ideas of the pre-Christian age.

[1] Cf. Nöldeke, in *Gottingische Gelehrte Anzeigen*, 1872, 828 f.
[2] There was apparently a written Targum on Job in the i cent. A.D. (Bab. *Shab.* 115. 1).

EPILOGUE

I

UTILITARIAN VALUE OF STUDY

WE have reached the end of our study, but not the end of the subject. Each generation will have its discoveries, and these will make their contribution to the world's store of knowledge. Any attempt to inspire thought and incite the mind to activity may have a value in the illimitable cosmic process. Yet tested at the bar of utility the present study may seem void of any direct and useful purpose. Of what practical value can be the study of the archaic and the dead ? Even this study is a part of the history of humanity on this planet. History is the unveiling of cryptic purposes, the revealing of occult plans. There are inexorable forces at work, principles as inflexible as the granite hills. Some forces are constructive, others destructive ; some principles lead to triumph, others to disaster. If we understood more thoroughly these forces and principles which made ancient history, we should be able to predict with some degree of certainty the future course of the world. In other words, we should recognize a design in the scheme of things, and a divinity in the evolution of spoken and written thought. To plunge into the midst of the surging, babbling nomadic tribes in western Asia a thousand years B.C. is like visiting a gigantic Babel. But to follow the emerging of the great nations and the growing of the great languages, is to witness the manifestation of an intelligence extra-temporal and supra-human. The Yahveh of Israel is still the Lord of Hosts :

אֲנִי יְהֹוָה לֹא שָׁנִיתִי

II

SIDE-LIGHTS ON TEXTUAL CRITICISM OF THE OLD TESTAMENT

The line of investigation followed in this study should throw light on the textual criticism of the Old Testament. In the composition of the books of the Jewish Bible there is frequently a marked difference in the style and construction. The date can sometimes be fixed approximately by the literary character of the composition. It is well known the Semitic authors and editors freely incorporated documents of other times and provinces into their works. Differences in style in the composition of the same books are often to be explained on the hypothesis of such incorporations. These interpolations in some instances amount only to words and phrases, but in other cases to whole paragraphs and complete incidents. Thus we find late Aramaic elements in some early Hebrew writings, and sometimes archaic forms in late records.[1] It is hoped that this study has shown the type of language that prevailed at each successive stage in the millennium preceding the Christian era. In this case we shall be able to refer the interpolated passages in the Sacred Scriptures, as well as the original documents themselves, to their approximate chronological setting.

III

PRIMAL AND ULTIMATE UNITY OF LANGUAGE

The original unity of language is assumed in any theory of the original unity of the human race. The early separation of the primitive clans initiated certain deviations from the parent speech. With the migration of the growing tribes

---

[1] In much the same way Arabic (and other) words and constructions are found in the inscrip. (1) Moabite and Heb. : Moab. St. ll. 11, 19 ; Siloam, l. 1 ; (2) Phoen. : CIS i. 3, l. 3 (for loan from Assyr. *vide* CIS i. 95, l. 5 ; from Aram. vide *Larnax Lapethos*, 2, l. 13) ; (3) Aram. : Zenj. *Hadad*, ll. 3, 13, 16 ; *Bar-rekub*, l. 15 ; (4) Nabat. : CIS ii. 209, l. 2 ; (5) Palmyr. : Vog. 3, ll. 3, 4 ; *Oxoniensis*, 1, l. 6, and many prop. names.

into new regions, with new environment and occupation, dialectic differences increased and new languages were formed. As soon as one tribal settlement began to communicate with another for diplomatic and commercial purposes, it was found necessary to reduce in some way ideas and purposes to writing. The first attempts were pictorial, that is, ideographic, then phonetic, which was either syllabic or alphabetic or both. With the growth of the art of writing, many types of script were developed. An examination of these reveals manifold grammatical and syntactical devices for the expression of thought. Language is thought in projection, history is language in action. Language declares the expansion of human thought, history unfolds the scroll of a world-plan. As thought widens, language will correspondingly develop ; as men conceive new ideas, they will readjust their speech. Thought, language, history, all move in harmony with a great cosmic process, whose beginning we cannot unveil, and whose ending we cannot predict. As a result of this mighty and rhythmic march will all varieties of human speech ultimately return to one universal language ? It is not for us to fix the bounds of possibility in any direction, but such a consummation is scarcely to be contemplated during the mundane drama of the human race. But it may be in some other state, in some higher phase of the soul's evolution, there will be uniformity of language, because there will be unity of ideal.

Multae terricolis linguae, coelestibus una.

INDEXES

I

INDEX OF SUBJECTS

II

INDEX OF GREEK TERMS

III

INDEX OF HEBREW AND ARAMAIC

IV

INDEX OF TEXTS

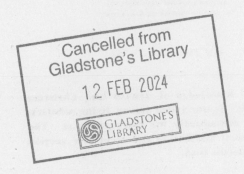
PRINTED BY MORRISON AND GIBB LIMITED, EDINBURGH

In Two Volumes (totaling 1076 pages). Price 20/- net per Volume

The International Critical Commentary

A CRITICAL AND EXEGETICAL COMMENTARY

ON

THE REVELATION OF ST. JOHN

WITH INTRODUCTION, NOTES, AND INDICES

ALSO

THE GREEK TEXT AND ENGLISH TRANSLATION

BY

R. H. CHARLES, D.Litt., D.D.

ARCHDEACON OF WESTMINSTER
FELLOW OF THE BRITISH ACADEMY

(IN TWO VOLUMES)

EDINBURGH : T. & T. CLARK, 38 GEORGE STREET
LONDON : SIMPKIN, MARSHALL, HAMILTON, KENT, & CO. LIMITED

1/7/20